Dream Catchers

Also by Philip Jenkins

The New Anti-Catholicism: The Last Acceptable Prejudice
Images of Terror: What We Can and Can't Know About Terrorism
The Next Christendom: The Coming of Global Christianity
Beyond Tolerance: Child Pornography on the Internet
Hidden Gospels: How the Search for Jesus Lost Its Way
Mystics and Messiahs: Cults and New Religions in American History
The Cold War at Home: The Red Scare in Pennsylvania 1945–1960
Synthetic Panics: The Politics of Designer Drugs
Moral Panic: Changing Concepts of the Child Molester
in Modern America
A History of the United States
Hoods and Shirts: The Extreme Right in Pennsylvania 1925–1950
Pedophiles and Priests: Anatomy of a Contemporary Crisis
Using Murder: The Social Construction of Serial Homicide
Intimate Enemies: Moral Panics in Contemporary Great Britain
A History of Modern Wales 1536–1990
Crime and Justice: Issues and Ideas
The Making of a Ruling Class: The Glamorgan Gentry 1640–1790

Dream Catchers

How Mainstream America
Discovered Native Spirituality

Philip Jenkins

OXFORD
UNIVERSITY PRESS

2004

OXFORD
UNIVERSITY PRESS

Oxford New York
Auckland Bangkok Buenos Aires Cape Town Chennai
Dar es Salaam Delhi Hong Kong Istanbul Karachi Kolkata
Kuala Lumpur Madrid Melbourne Mexico City Mumbai Nairobi
São Paulo Shanghai Taipei Tokyo Toronto

Copyright © 2004 by Philip Jenkins

Published by Oxford University Press, Inc.
198 Madison Avenue, New York, New York 10016

www.oup.com

Oxford is a registered trademark of Oxford University Press

Library of Congress Cataloging-in-Publication Data
Jenkins, Philip, 1952–
Dream catchers : how mainstream America discovered native spirituality /
Philip Jenkins.
p. cm. — Includes bibliographical references and index.
ISBN 0-19-516115-7
1. America—Religion.
2. Indians—Religion—Influence.
I. Title.
BL2500.J46 2004   299.7'93—dc22   2003026909

1 3 5 7 9 8 6 4 2

Printed in the United States of America
on acid-free paper

To Elliott Leyton

Contents

Preface

❦

This book describes a radical change in mainstream American cultural and religious attitudes over the past century or so, namely in popular views of Native American spirituality. Though the process of toleration and dialogue between any of the major religions has been slow, gradual, and often depressing, many Christians historically faced special difficulties in recognizing what American Indians were doing as authentically religious, let alone as something that could be permitted or accommodated. Yet attitudes did shift dramatically, until today, the vast majority of Americans respect and admire the Native tradition. Indeed, millions try, controversially, to copy it, to absorb Indian spirituality into their own lives. Americans today are prepared not just to grant that once-unfamiliar religions have virtues, but to admit that the whole concept of religion is much broader than they might once have imagined.

From the end of the nineteenth century, a growing number of white Americans came first to appreciate Native spiritual traditions and then to see in them something that was conspicuously lacking in the mainstream culture. Ideas that originated among a few intellectuals and artists reached a general public, until today they have become social orthodoxy. The extent and speed of that change suggest that an eager market existed for this more favorable view of Indians and Indian culture. Rightly or wrongly, mainstream America has seen Native spirituality as a means of fulfilling a hunger that could not be satisfied from its own cultural resources. This book describes how white America has deployed Native religious traditions for its own purposes.

My goal is to use the attitudes of mainstream, non-Native Americans as a means of tracing some critical themes in modern American religion: notions of religious diversity and pluralism; the legal position of religion and religious toleration; the cultural and religious impact of relativism; the shifting definition of "religious" actions or behavior; the growing recognition of women's spirituality; and a growing reverence for the primal and the primitive. In tracing the attitudes of the social and religious mainstream, we will also see the persistence of esoteric and mystical strands in American religion.

I should stress what the book does not attempt. It does not describe or analyze American Indian religions, or offer a history of their fate under U.S. rule. To take an obvious example, any worthwhile history of official religious repression in the late nineteenth and early twentieth centuries would have to make use of Native voices themselves; and many such are available, in the form of oral history records. I do not use these materials, because they are not germane to my purpose of describing the changing attitudes of the mainstream society.

Also, this is an *American* study, meaning the United States. I will be dealing with the changing ideas of white, non-Native, Americans, rather than of Europeans. European fascination with American Indians has been a powerful cultural theme, especially in Germany, but exploring or explaining that would really require a different book. Discussions of non-American attitudes will be confined to Europeans whose work had a major influence on American thought. In this category, we should certainly include such key figures as Aldous Huxley, Carl Jung, D. H. Lawrence, Ernest Thompson Seton, and Jaime De Angulo.

Especially when dealing with indigenous peoples, modern national boundaries make little sense. In the Native view, the Americas composed the continental landmass known as Turtle Island, and cultural interactions proceeded with little regard to what would some day become the political borders of the United States, Canada, and Mexico. Today, the homelands of some Native peoples sprawl over U.S. borders. For present purposes, though, I focus on the United States rather than Canada or Mexico, which represent quite different stories. And for similar reasons of what can feasibly be accomplished in a single book, I will not primarily be discussing how non-Natives imagined the civilizations of Central or South America. Again, that is a vast theme, albeit one that does overlap occasionally with the study of North America. At least for some New Agers, images of Central American pyramids and jaguars tend all too easily to get confounded with the world of North American Native spirituality.

Finally, the book describes changes in non-Native attitudes from the mid-nineteenth century onwards — roughly, from the time of the huge territorial expansion of the United States during the 1840s. I do not mean to understate the importance of white/Native interactions in earlier periods, which have been studied by many distinguished scholars. For the purposes of the present book, however, I will discuss earlier events only to the extent that they provided a foundation for concepts of Native spirituality in the late nineteenth and twentieth centuries.

Terminology

As concepts of race and ethnicity have changed over time, so has the associated language, posing real difficulties for modern writers. Just in the past fifty years, for instance, the respectful description for the people who are today termed African American has at various times been "Negro," "colored," and "black," though no serious author would today use "Negro" or "colored" except in an ironic sense. Similar, though less serious, problems exist for American Indians or Native Americans. "Indian" has fallen out of favor, because it represents a purely European perception of Native peoples, and moreover one based on a massive geographical error. Nevertheless, the word is nothing like as obsolete or offensive as "Negro," and the vast majority of "Indians" are comfortable describing themselves in this way. The U.S. Census Bureau, always responsive to ethnic sensitivities, still lists America's Native peoples as "American Indian, Eskimo, and Aleut." The radical American Indian Movement, AIM, retains the Indian name. With due awareness of the possible difficulties, I will therefore be using the term "Indian."

Other terms are more debatable. In recent years, writers on American Indian matters have tried to take account of Native pronunciation as well as cultural sensibilities, so that (for instance) "Navaho" is now commonly preferred to "Navajo," "katsina" and "katsinam" for "kachina" and "kachinas," and so on. Still, the older terms remain in use: members of the "Navajo Nation" read the *Navajo Times*. One loaded term is "Anasazi," which in recent years has given way to the archaeologically precise "Ancestral Puebloan." However, the word "Anasazi" also has a long and reputable pedigree, and is still widely used.

Acknowledgments

I am very grateful to Kathryn Hume for having read this manuscript. Thanks also to Gregg Roeber, and Cynthia Read, my editor at Oxford University Press, for their constant support and friendship. I also want to acknowledge the excellent research assistance provided by Laura Savino.

As always, my greatest debt is to my wife, Liz Jenkins.

Dream Catchers

1

𝔜

Haunting America

The American Indian will never again control the American continent,
but he will forever haunt it.

—D. H. Lawrence

Shape-Shifting

Across the United States, thousands of Native Americans practice their ancient religions, complex beliefs and rituals that can be traced back long before the arrival of European settlers. At the same time, many more
Americans with little or no Native heritage believe that they too are following the paths of Native spirituality. They engage in ritual drumming and
hold sweat lodges, they use Native-themed Tarot cards: they believe in all
sincerity that they are reviving shamanic traditions. Some travel as pilgrims
to places long sacred to Indian nations. Others incorporate Native ways into
their everyday lives, creating their own personal medicine bundles and domestic altars, which are grandly titled "Prayer Mesas." Roaming across the
endless plains of the Internet, pseudo-Native Americans tirelessly seek out
aspects of Native religious tradition that they can appropriate as their very
own. Spiritual consumers buy a great deal of bric-a-brac, including videos,
music, jewelry, dream-catchers, crystals, medicine bags, fetishes, and the
rest. A sizable industry caters to what is obviously a vast hunger for Native
American spirituality.

Throughout American history, non-Natives have invented the fantasy Indians they wanted and needed at any given time, and, as Philip Deloria has recorded, white Americans have often emulated Natives, "playing Indian."[1] This tradition goes back at least to the pseudo-Indians of the Boston Tea Party, and runs through the chiefs and sachems of Tammany Hall, and the intrepid warrior mascots of twentieth-century sports teams. Often, imagined Indian-ness is set against American realities, offering a model of resistance. Indian stereotypes are cultivated as a means of contesting "America." As American values change, so observers look to Indians to represent ideals that the mainstream Euro-American society is losing. By tracing the images that non-Natives construct of the first Americans, we learn about the changing needs of the mainstream society, the gaps that these invented Indians must fill.[2]

Attempts to understand the "white man's Indian" are far from new, as can be seen from the volume of contemporary writing on Westerns and popular culture.[3] Just as significant, though less noticed, are the reinventions of Native religious and spiritual traditions. As conceived by the non-Native public, Native spirituality has changed kaleidoscopically over time, mirroring the prevailing obsessions of the mainstream society. Originally, Indians were presented as benighted savages whose crying spiritual needs justified the colonial errand into the Wilderness. When white Americans wanted to believe that Indians were the lost tribes of Israel, they sought (and found) Old Testament parallels in their worship. When spiritualism was a national craze, Indians were exciting because of their ability to cross the worlds between living and dead. For other Victorians, Indians exemplified a pure, nature-oriented spirituality congenial to Transcendentalists and Unitarians. Later, Native pagans were thought to retain a sensual spirituality of the body that had been destroyed by the world-denying sterilities of Christianity.[4] This process of reimagining continued through the latter part of the twentieth century. If drugs were fashionable, then Indian religion was fascinating because of its integration of mind-altering substances. If white Americans were interested in gender issues, then the emphasis was on Native matriarchy. Indians today are models of ecological gender-sensitive religion, true sons and daughters of Mother Earth.[5]

But for all these changes, we can make one general observation. Over the past 150 years, the mainstream view of Native religions has more or less reversed itself, from a shocked contempt for primitive superstition verging on devil worship, to an envious awe for a holistic spirituality that might be the last best hope for the human race. Somewhere in the process, mainstream white Americans moved from despising and fearing Native religions to admiring and envying them. Colonial authors saw the hand of God in the wars and epidemics that wiped out their Indian neighbors; their modern descendants bemoan the destruction of utopian earth-sensitive Native societies by patriarchal sky-god worshipping Puritans. The new picture is just as religious as its predecessor, and equally apocalyptic, but the status of hero and villain has been neatly inverted.

The reversal is symbolized by changing images of the snake, a motif that often recurs in discussions of Native American religion. For early settlers, Indians served that old serpent, the devil. A diabolical linkage was confirmed in the nineteenth century when travelers reported seeing the Hopi Snake Dance, which to their eyes represented serpent worship of the most shocking kind. Through the first half of the twentieth century, the Snake Dance was perhaps the best-known symbol of American Indian religion, and it became a vastly important tourist attraction. By the end of the century, the growing mainstream interest in esoteric and New Age thought made the serpent image much more positive and attractive, and more comprehensibly religious. In the new perspective, the snake represented forces—sexual, ecstatic, chthonic, mystical, oracular—that traditional Christianity had neglected or lost. For early white Americans, the snake symbolized the depravity of American Indian worship and its distance from authentic religion; for their modern descendants, the snake represents the inspiring alternative traditions to be found in Native spirituality.

The reversal of attitude toward Indian practices was at least beginning even during the worst years of American maltreatment of its Native peoples, a pattern too well-known to be elaborated here. Broken treaties, racism both popular and official, and the disasters of the reservation system make for a grim story. Yet white opinions were far from consistent, and pro-Indian attitudes, even idealization, can be traced back much further than is popularly supposed. Alongside the Noble Savage myth, there has always existed the notion of the Natural Mystic. At least by the end of the nineteenth century, abundant materials were available about Native religious thought and practice, and a few white Americans praised these traditions, even exalting them above Christianity. Though the fashion for Native cultures is often seen as a phenomenon of the 1960s counterculture, a real movement of sympathy is obvious fifty years previously. White Americans before the 1960s did not simply dismiss Native religion as devil worship, only to achieve sudden enlightenment when books like *Black Elk Speaks* and the *Book of the Hopi* became popular. The New Age boom of the late twentieth century occurred when some long-familiar commodities found a new mass market.

The Tribe Called Wannabe

On occasion, too, recognition and respect has led to imitation or role-playing, as non-Natives adopted what they thought were the pristine beauties of Indian religion. Since the 1960s, this particular kind of "playing Indian" has moved far beyond play to become a major cultural phenomenon. Now, admiration does not necessarily lead to imitation. Much depends on what kind of Indian images dominated at a particular time, since some lend themselves much more feasibly to copying than others. Through the history of white/Native interactions, the mainstream society has encountered many different cultures and traditions, and at various times, particular Native groups have been taken as typical and representative. Today, the most powerful image is that of Plains nations such as the Lakota (Sioux), while in 1910 or 1920, the Pueblos of the Southwest utterly dominated the white consciousness. When Pueblo rituals were seen as the highest achievements of Indian art and culture, outsiders could try and copy them, but this activity required large-scale organization. Re-enactors always knew that even given the best settings and backgrounds, they could never catch the full flavor of performing a ritual in an evocative environment like a Hopi or Pueblo village, with its ancient kivas and dancing grounds. (Though this was not entirely impossible: as early as the 1930s, one long-enduring white "tribe" of Arizona re-enactors, the Smokis, actually did construct its own imitation ritual village, complete with kiva and pueblo).[6] Plains rituals, while no less complex in their significance, were designed for a mobile nomadic society, and offered themselves more easily to adaptation, at least in a bastardized form. The shift of interest to the Plains has contributed immensely to the growth of neo-Indian spirituality among Euro-Americans.

The shelves of chain bookstores now feature many works claiming to offer Native spiritual teachings. We find titles like *Mother Earth Spirituality: Native American Paths to Healing Ourselves and Our World*; *Secret Native American Pathways: A Guide to Inner Peace*; *Sacred Path Cards: The Discovery of Self Through Native Teachings*; or *Meditations with Native Americans: Lakota Spirituality*. These represent only a small fraction of a much larger publishing industry, which often finds its outlets in specialized New Age stores. In each case, the interest is meant to be applied rather than theoretical: these are books for would-be participants rather than mere observers. Besides books, the interest in Native American spirituality is manifested in countless workshops and programs offering activities such as sweat lodges and vision quests, shamanism and drumming, and "Indian" traditions in healing and divination.[7]

If there is a material symbol for popularized Native religion, an equivalent of the crucifix or the Magen David, it is the Medicine Wheel, originally a geometric arrangement of stones found in many locations across the northern Plains. Today, the image is stylized as a cross within a circle, a ragged and disjointed version of the universal symbol of the Sun Wheel, with the addition of a central cairn. According to recent books and workshops, the wheel contains within itself teachings of immense significance. One can learn to live the Medicine Wheel, to dance the Medicine Wheel, to pray it, to grow it.[8] From the wheel, and from the world of neo-Indian spirituality, many white Americans believe they can acquire a share of the mysterious wisdom that was traditionally the heritage of Native peoples, whose ancient practices unite the powers of earth and sky.

Of course, the appropriation of these Native ideas has been anything but straightforward, since these are fitted into a larger cultural pattern of esoteric and New Age thought. Ironically, since much of the appeal of Native religion is its supposedly ancient, timeless quality, many of the symbols and themes of the new synthesis are very new indeed, and their origins can be traced back no more than a few decades. This is obviously true of the UFO and space lore that now pervades pseudo-Native religion. Just as recent is the recovery and self-help therapy so often found in books purporting to unveil Native teachings, which use psychological concepts dating from the 1970s and 1980s. In the way the symbol is currently used, the Medicine Wheel itself dates only from the Nixon era.

Yet despite all these contradictions, neo- or pseudo-Indian spirituality has now achieved the status of an authentic new religious movement. The degree of interest or commitment varies enormously, from people who assume Native identities and wholeheartedly espouse Native spirituality as a religion, to those who just read avidly in the area. Perhaps millions graze the various materials on offer, sampling and adopting ideas that they find congenial. Many of the associated neo-Indian ideas have entered mainstream culture. Even a cartoon treatment like *Pocahontas* offers a tendentious crash course in Native spirituality. Critics speak disparagingly of the wave of would-be Native spiritual leaders, the Astroturf shamans and plastic medicine men (and, at least as often, women). Native activists assign them to what Rayna Green called The Tribe Called Wannabe, or Wanabi. But whatever the nature of that tribe's beliefs, they appeal to a substantial number of people, in the United States and beyond.[9]

Prisoners of Turtle Island

When white Americans construct their ideas of Indian spirituality, they face problems quite different from what occurs when they romanticize other alien cultures like Egypt or India. These other cultures are conveniently distant, so hard facts do not have to intrude too much on the picture. When Enlightenment thinkers wished to imagine a rational secular society far superior to their own clergy-ridden reality, they projected this vision onto a China that neither they nor their readers would ever visit, and they could speculate without fear of challenge. When later Westerners created their dream picture of Tibet, facts were scarce, and speculation easily turned this land into a Shangri-La. We might think that such a process could not work a similar miracle of transformation on American Indians, who are geographically very close. And Indian communities are extremely diverse, naturally enough, since they exist in physical environments ranging from the Amazonian jungle to the Arctic Circle. As Edward Curtis observed almost a century ago, "When we have before us a proud Sioux praying to the spirit of the buffalo, do not let us presume that the corn-growing Indian of Hopi land would know aught of the Sioux's prayer."[10] Since there is not and never has been such a thing as "Indian religion," it *should* be difficult to construct simple or uniform patterns.

But the popular image of Indians has rarely been too much troubled by inconvenient realities, and religious matters are no exception. The white portrait of Indians has changed over time with minimal reference to the lived realities of those societies. No later than the 1940s, white Americans were finding in Indian communities "our indigenous Shangri-La."[11] Time and again, mainstream observers produce accounts of Native societies that all too clearly reflect their own backgrounds, their own interests and obsessions, rather than those of the Natives they claim to be studying. One result is the creation of a generic Native spirituality so amorphous that it can be adapted to the interests and ideologies of the moment. Tribal and regional differences have been all but eliminated, so that modern New Agers borrow indiscriminately from Great Plains notions of the Vision Quest and the Medicine Wheel, and from radically different concepts taken from both the desert Southwest and the Pacific Northwest.

In most cases, we cannot describe this process as deliberately deceptive (though some outright frauds have occurred), but people find the usable Indians they are looking for. When a text becomes a major best seller—such as Frank Waters's *Book of the Hopi*, Carlos Castaneda's *Teachings of Don Juan*, or Lynn Andrews's *Medicine Woman*—it succeeds because the author is offering an interpretation that people want to hear at a particular time. Just as Western admirers of a fantasy Tibet of the mind have become what Donald Lopez has called the prisoners of Shangri-La, so millions of Americans intoxicated with Native spirituality have yielded to the temptation to become prisoners of Turtle Island. The story offers a striking tribute to the power of cultural imagination.

Most contemporary scholars have not been sympathetic to New Age adaptations of Native religion and spirituality, which they see as a glaring example of colonialist cultural intrusion and expropriation. Some writers portray the attempt to steal the Indians' religion as the latest callous phase of cultural genocide.[12] But even if the phenomenon were as simple as that, which is debatable, it still deserves closer examination. By seeing how non-Natives have understood Indian spirituality over the centuries, we are doing far more than exploring the obsessions of a fringe of emulators and enthusiasts. We are also mapping the changing contours of America's mainstream religions, and especially of Christianity.

The theme thus has a significance going far beyond the tragically small size of the Native population. In 1900, the U.S. government recognized an Indian and aboriginal population of only 250,000, around 0.3 percent of the national total; and even today, the corresponding figure is still below one percent. Though these figures obviously miss a great many individuals with part-Native ancestry, they are still tiny. (Canada's Native peoples—the First Nations—represent a much higher proportion of that country's population).[13] Even so, the story of how outsiders have viewed the religious practices of that tiny minority carries many implications for mainstream American religion past and present, and for the legal environment in which it has operated.

It was through interacting with Native religions that American Christians first confronted the critical issue of how to live alongside non-Christian faiths. Even after the growth of the Jewish presence during the nineteenth century, Natives were still better known as religious outsiders in many parts of the country. To appreciate just how remarkable this encounter with a living paganism was, we should recall how very few European countries faced anything like a comparable situation. By the late Middle Ages, organized paganism had ceased to exist in Europe, except in the furthest reaches of northern Scandinavia and the eastern limits of Russia. Elsewhere, pagan survivals continued only as Christianized folk customs. Even then, many such customs had nothing like the overt pagan ancestry that optimistic antiquarians liked to believe, especially in the Celtic lands. Interreligious dialogue in the European homelands involved competing Christian denominations, or rival branches of the Abrahamic faiths. Yet although European Christians were dealing with traditions that were closely akin to them spiritually, their encounters, more often than not, were disastrous. How would a Euro-American Christian society respond when confronted with the full-scale primal religions of the American Indians, with their animism and shamanism?[14]

Religious Toleration?

For much of the interaction between Natives and non-Natives, any thought of religious tolerance or diversity was simply not a question. This in itself affects our understanding of the U.S. Constitution, which famously forbids Congress from making "any law respecting an establishment of religion, or prohibiting the free exercise thereof." Well into the twentieth century, this noble clause had no effect whatever on the Indian policy of the federal government, which had as its explicit goal the spread of Christianity, preferably in Protestant forms.[15] From the 1880s through the 1930s, federal Indian policy sought to destroy most Indian religious practices, and that effort proceeded virtually unopposed. Only as late as the 1920s was there any serious suggestion that principles of religious liberty ought to apply to Indian issues. Between 1922 and 1924, an official attempt to suppress Native dances and other practices generated a national controversy over Indian religious rights, a debate that marks a critical turning point in the nation's religious and cultural history. The official principle of Indian religious freedom was established as late as 1934, and even then, the ideal was often violated in practice.[16]

The enduring intolerance of Native belief should not be seen as a rare exception to an otherwise-comprehensive tradition of religious tolerance. In the late nineteenth century, American courts were quite prepared to curb any religious conduct that was thought to be dangerous or antisocial. Mormons were imprisoned for polygamy, and in the First World War, the government paid scant respect to the conscientious objections of religious pacifists facing military service. Nevertheless, Indian religion was singled out, in the sense that it was targeted for utter elimination: the only good Indian religious practice was a dead one. Given this desire for cultural extermination, it is surprising how little Indian policy features in standard works on religious liberty. When the theme does appear, it is usually in the context of peyote use.[17]

Changing attitudes to Native religious rights arose from shifts in the self-confidence of American Christianity. Through the nineteenth century, most Protestants had no doubts about the truth and certainty of their faith, or about their right and duty to spread it to others less fortunate. Of course there were exceptions to this rule, people who believed that all religions contained a seed of truth, or much more than a seed. When the Transcendentalists of the 1840s popularized the Hindu scriptures, they saw them as worthy counterparts to the Judeo-Christian holy texts. But at least these were recognizably the scriptures of an organized religion with its buildings and hierarchies. This was quite different from acknowledging the seemingly primitive customs of America's own aboriginal peoples.

The idea of religious toleration grew by the end of the nineteenth century, partly in recognition of the growth of diversity, as both Catholic and Jewish populations swelled. Also significant was the rejection of even token Christian adherence among many of the social and intellectual elites. Protestant Christianity became more pluralist as liberals came to doubt Christianity's claims to a monopoly on religious truth.

Much of the change occurred between about 1890 and 1925, and reflected the growth of theological liberalism and critical Bible scholarship. The American war between modernists and fundamentalists is commonly taken to have begun in 1893, with the heresy trial of Presbyterian leader Charles A. Briggs. Applying the new critical scientific scholarship, Briggs declared that "in every department of Biblical study we come across error . . . reason is a fountain of divine authority no less savingly enlightening than the Bible and the Church." (Modern feminist Bible criticism dates from these same years). Over the next thirty years, debates over Biblical authority rent many seminaries and colleges, and ultimately provoked the notorious fiasco of the Scopes trial in 1925. In the era of debates between Modernists and Fundamentalists, religious claims to exclusive truth became suspect. Also, liberals growing accustomed to seeing the Christian scriptures as essentially mythical were less likely to look down on tribal peoples who lacked authoritative scriptures of their own. As anthropologist James Mooney argued in 1892, the patriarchal ancestors of the Biblical Hebrews "had reached about the plane of our own Navaho, but were below that of the Pueblo. Their mythologic and religious system was closely parallel." If much of the Bible was the record of the barbarous tribes of ancient Israel, how could it be presented as superior to the legends and tales of the Navajo or the Cherokee? Myths are myths.[18]

Meanwhile, globalization created a new awareness of other religions. At the World's Parliament of Religions held in Chicago in 1893, the great religions conversed on notionally equal terms, although within a framework devised by Protestants. At least among the social elites, Buddhist and Hindu teachers now acquired a cachet they would never entirely lose.[19] A new cultural relativism affected views of America's own Other religions. Within the first quarter of the twentieth century, views about Christian exclusivism that would once have been normal and customary were now denounced by hostile terms like bigoted, narrow, and fundamentalist. By the end of the century, the whole idea of missionary endeavor anywhere on the globe had become suspect in most of the mainline churches, and most liberal Protestants utterly rejected any idea of trying to convert monotheists such as Jews and Muslims.

The mainline churches also lost much of their power to influence secular public affairs. Though the United States did not undergo a straightforward pattern of secularization in the early twentieth century, older Protestant churches did suffer a decline of prestige. They faced new rivals, namely Roman Catholicism, and the new secular professions, which took over many social service functions that would once have been regarded as religious. The Prohibition experiment created sharp divisions between secular society and the once-dominant Protestant churches, and made religious interventions in politics more suspect. The liberation of Native American religions in the 1920s and 1930s is part of a broader social trend.[20]

New Ages

The toleration of Native religions did not arise solely from a principled belief in diversity, but also from a growing recognition that Indian beliefs and practices had much to offer the Euro-American majority. This was not just a matter of live and let live. For the Protestant and evangelical traditions that have so often dominated American culture, the thought that Indian religions might have anything to teach them would be ridiculous. At every point, Indian cultures contradicted such basic evangelical principles as the supremacy of written texts, the stress on literacy, and the rejection of intermediaries between God and humanity. But evangelical Protestantism has never been the only strand in American religion. From earliest times, esoteric and metaphysical themes have always been in evidence. Since the mid-nineteenth century, these alternative traditions have enjoyed wide influence, often by deploying innovative means of merchandising and spiritual consumerism. Often, these ideas have enjoyed such widespread influence that it is difficult to think of them as "fringe" rather than as another section of the mainstream. And the fringe has often found much to value in Indians.

Esoteric and mystical themes have repeatedly reached mass audiences: at the start of the twentieth century, between the two world wars, and again from the 1970s onwards, in the well-known form of the New Age movement. In each era, such movements became popular because they capitalized on powerful social and intellectual trends. At the start of the twentieth century, as at its end, women played a critical role in the new esoteric movements, as their religious aspirations reflected their growing social and political involvement. In 1900, women led and organized influential new groups, including Spiritualism, Christian Science, Theosophy and New Thought. The emerging sects taught a new multicultural sensitivity and a respect for non-Christian spiritual traditions. Their message also appealed to the contemporary faith in science, with the popular belief in evolution and progress now applied to spiritual matters. Just as scientific insights and methodologies fueled the modernist debate, with the importance of Biblical criticism and the rise of evolutionary theory, so the esoteric movements preached their distinctive versions of science and evolutionism. Instead of a Judeo-Christian universe some thousands of years old, with a final vision of heaven and hell, many esoteric movements offered a vision of multiple worlds millions of years old, in which individuals reincarnate through countless lives.[21]

Repeatedly, esoteric believers have cherished the Native religions, onto which they have projected their own beliefs and doctrines. If reincarnation was a cardinal belief of the alternative religious worldview, then someone would argue that this belief was central to Indian thought, and likewise for later ideas like Goddess worship, UFOs, or shamanism. Because Indians were viewed as mystical teachers of unparalleled authority, as guardians and guarantors of spiritual authenticity, their image was borrowed to validate claims not apparently central to Indian traditions. However misguided the readings of Native traditions, this cultural sympathy was politically valuable, especially when the government was seeking to repress or destroy Indian practices. Esoteric or New Age well-wishers gave Native faiths a substantial constituency prepared to support them on issues of religious and cultural freedom.

Toleration for Indian religious beliefs was achieved late, slowly, and grudgingly. Yet before modern Americans feel smug about our own toleration for diversity, in contrast to earlier benighted ages, we should remember that Native religious issues are still contentious. As recently as 1990, the Supreme Court ruled in the *Smith* decision that Native use of peyote was not protected under principles of religious freedom, a finding that alarmed mainstream religious bodies. The subsequent history of Constitutional law on religious freedom has been shaped by *Smith* and its aftermath.[22]

What Is a Religion?

The fact that Victorian Christians were less tolerant than their modern successors need surprise no one, but even so, the long-standing disregard for Native religions is still startling. It also contrasts sharply with Protestant attitudes to other traditions. While most Victorian Protestants had no love for Catholicism or Judaism, few thought of forcible mass conversion. What placed Native Americans beyond the bounds of toleration was the view that they were not in fact practicing anything worthy of the name of religion. What Jews and Catholics were doing might be objectionable to Protestant eyes, but at least it was incontestably religious. But what about Native Americans? No observer of Native communities could fail to see that these people held strong beliefs about the supernatural, and carried out rituals based on that worldview. But did they actually have *a religion*? Many thought not. Meeting the Guanahaní Indians in 1492, Columbus remarked that "I believe that they would become Christians very easily, for it seemed to me that they had no religion."

We are observing a fundamental theme in the history of religious attitudes: namely, how mainstream Americans over time have come to perceive what is and is not religious; and, a rather different issue, what is "a religion"? The seemingly simple word is quite complex. Modern Western usage acknowledges the existence of religions, in the sense of overarching and mutually exclusive belief structures. A Christian, Jew, or Muslim belongs to one particular religion and, by definition, is not a member of others. Such major religions are seen as important human institutions. Even so, the whole idea of "a religion" is a relatively recent development. In medieval England, someone "entered religion" only when they joined what would today be called a religious order. At this time too, the distinction was between the Faith, namely the Christian faith, and the various forms of error held by Muslims and others.

The notion of separate religions, each with valid claims to truth, is a modern construct. As Westerners explored the outside world during the nineteenth century, they reimagined the religious systems they encountered in terms they could comprehend, often imposing their own familiar concepts, such as core scriptures, prophetic leaders, and central orthodoxies. Under Western eyes, Hinduism was now reconstructed as a more uniform system than it had ever been historically, and texts like the *Bhagavad Gita* were now presented as pivotal scriptures analogous to the New Testament. In response to Western pressure, Asian religious traditions now presented themselves as coherent religious systems in a way that hitherto had not been thought necessary.

Linked to the idea of "a religion" is that of "religious" behavior. This is also defined in quite narrow ways that separate it from other seemingly related activities, such as superstition and philosophy, though it is not always easy to understand the differences. Is a belief in UFOs a religious doctrine? It has much in common with religious notions, given the concept of superior beings who live Up There and who deign to visit this globe, bearing messages of warning or enlightenment. Is the U.S. flag a religious symbol? It must be, if it can be "desecrated." American courts agonize whether particular symbols are religious, and so cannot be displayed on public property, or whether they are merely seasonal and civic. What about a crèche at Christmas or a menorah at Hanukah? What is religious, as opposed to "just" cultural?

The different words—religion, superstition, philosophy—carry powerful value judgments. A religion is more respectable and venerable than an unsystematic collection of beliefs and rituals. Similarly, religious behavior is taken as being more serious and worthwhile than mere superstition, and the critical distinction between *religio* and *superstitio* has its roots in Roman times. (Christianity was at first dismissed as an illicit *superstitio*.) In separating the different categories, modern scholars sometimes betray a rather Protestant suspicion of rituals and popular religious practices, which are treated condescendingly as mere folk religion, not quite the real thing. Once a cultural package has been labeled as religious, that designation shapes how observers see the particular society, which is interpreted according to the patterns familiar from the Great Religions. Outsiders are then more likely to describe the cherished tales of the society by respectful terms like myths or scriptures, rather than mere folklore.

These distinctions help explain the extreme official hostility toward Indian religions. When in the late nineteenth century, U.S. administrations prohibited Indian practices such as dances, the potlatch, and the activities of medicine men, they genuinely did not believe that they were attacking religion or religious practices. Indians were free to pursue their religion as it was perceived by white authorities, namely an ethical worship of the Great Spirit, which was only a variant form of Protestant Christianity. For bureaucrats or missionaries, this noble Indian creed could easily be isolated from the evil habits with which it had regrettably become associated, such as dancing. For a Pueblo or a Cheyenne, though, the dancing and related customs were not only inextricably linked with the religion, they *were* the religion, quite as much as the cerebral beliefs that enchanted white observers. Suppressing Indian practices was not seen as a violation of religious freedom precisely because these were aspects of superstition rather than true religion. As an alarming parallel, imagine a government informing a Jewish community that while it was welcome to retain its religion, it would have to abolish outdated and sinister customs like circumcision, the food laws, the Sabbath, and the cycle of high holy days. The religion was fine, but the superstitions would have to go.

During the nineteenth century, we see a gradual and rather grudging recognition that Native American cultural practices might deserve the label of religion, however much they were polluted by superstitious additions. Critical to this acknowledgment was the publication of what certainly looked like "scriptural" texts, of chants, hymns, and rituals. By the early twentieth century, observers could speak more confidently of Indian religion, and even to recognize the dances, shamanism, and rituals as a fundamental part of it. That change constituted a minor revolution in religious sensibility.

Doubts about the nature of Indian religions survived into recent times, when public attitudes toward Native cultures had become vastly more sympathetic. One instructive moment came in 1970, when Congress passed a major bill returning to the Taos Pueblo control of the Blue Lake that was sacred to them. On signing the measure, President Nixon spoke warmly of the Pueblo struggle for justice. Then he added, oddly, "This bill also involves respect for religion . . . long before any organized religion came to the United States, for seven hundred years, the Taos Pueblo Indians worshiped in this place." The sentiments are impeccable, but why did he contrast the Taos practices with "organized religion," here used as a synonym for Christianity? Were the Pueblos not practicing religion, or was it—all appearances to the contrary—not organized?[23]

These supercilious attitudes sound odd from a contemporary perspective, since much of the modern appeal of Native culture is that it does *not* constitute a religion in the accepted Western sense, with all the left-brained dogmas and constraints that term implies, all the Puritan inheritance. While nineteenth-century Americans despised Indians for having less than a true religion, their modern descendants extol Native peoples for their spirituality. This quality rises far above the tawdry claims of mere religion, and especially that much-maligned category, *organized* religion.

Pilgrims from Civilization

Writing about Indian cultures in 1867, Francis Parkman brusquely dismissed Native spiritual practices as a

> chaos of degrading, ridiculous, and incoherent superstitions. . . . Among the Hurons and Iroquois, and indeed all the stationary tribes, there was an incredible number of mystic ceremonies, extravagant, puerile, and often disgusting, designed for the cure of the sick or for the general weal of the community. . . . They consisted in an endless variety of dances, masqueradings, and nondescript orgies.

Indian religion taught little morality, and encouraged no scientific or philosophical questioning:

> It is obvious that the Indian mind has never seriously occupied itself with any of the higher themes of thought. . . . In the midst of Nature the Indian knew nothing of her laws. His perpetual reference of her phenomena to occult agencies forestalled inquiry and precluded inductive reasoning. . . . No race, perhaps, ever offered greater difficulties to those laboring for its improvement.[24]

Such a tirade is multiply offensive to modern readers, who expect a comprehensive tolerance for religious beliefs and practices, and who have learned an instinctive sympathy for the beauties of Indian ceremonies. The hostile accounts of Native rituals and ceremonials that were absolutely normal through the nineteenth century remind us that a remarkable shift has occurred in religious and cultural sensibility. At some point, describing customs as pagan and primitive became praise rather than condemnation.[25]

How and when, then, did mainstream Americans come to appreciate Native religions, not just as a tentative and inferior draft of Protestant Christianity, but as vibrant and inspiring traditions in their own right? Once again, the early years of the twentieth century mark a critical period of transition. Apart from purely religious developments, such as the liberalization of Protestantism and the growth of metaphysical thought, we can also see the impact of other social factors in the booming United States of the Gilded Age and the Progressive Era. One was the emergence of new academic traditions, and the appearance of scientific anthropology, ethnography, and archaeology. These disciplines were based in universities and museums, which were heavily funded either by the government or, more commonly, by private sponsors, tycoons prepared to distribute some of their largesse for the encouragement of science and learning. In consequence, far more people were enabled to research and write about Native religions, and in an objective and secular way.

Also, social changes vastly expanded the market for new findings about Native cultures, through the growth of national tourism. The expansion of transportation networks in the late nineteenth century allowed wider popular access to Indian sites and rituals, especially in the Southwest, supporting the creation of a full-scale industry of ethnic tourism. Here, white Americans could see Native cultures that were indisputably complex societies with elaborate ceremonials, a striking contrast to the demoralized and impoverished Indians so often seen elsewhere at this time. As the Cherokee John M. Oskison wrote in 1907, while "confined to a reservation and fed on rations," the " 'noble red man' became of no more interest than any other stall-fed creature. Admiration for the untamed savage gave way to contempt for the dirty beggar in the streets and under the car windows."[26] But that dehumanizing attitude changed dramatically when white travelers saw the ancient glories of Mesa Verde, the enduring mysteries of the Shalako ceremonial at Zuñi, or the Hopi Snake Dance. Indian cultures and religions were by the 1920s proving highly attractive products for marketing and merchandising, for presentation to a consumer audience with a new hunger for the primitive and authentic. The packaging of Native spirituality is certainly in evidence by this time, though it would receive a massive boost, from the 1960s onwards, with a new idealization of all things Indian.

But we must also understand the forces driving these successive generations of seekers. When Robinson Jeffers witnessed the tourists watching the dances at Taos Pueblo in the 1920s, he remarked on their quest for authentic religious experience that they could not find within their own worlds:

> Pilgrims from civilization, anxiously seeking beauty, religion, poetry;
> pilgrims from the vacuum.
> People from cities, anxious to be human again.[27]

We need not accept Jeffers's view that tourists saw their own world as a "vacuum." But after generations of exalting the glories of Western civilization, why did so many Americans feel that these glories were to be found elsewhere, in Taos or Zuñi? Why were they so ready to consume the images they were offered?

Partly, the response reflects declining confidence in the religious mainstream. As seen especially in the Southwest, Indian religious life offered several features that were not easily available in respectable mainline Protestantism: strong elements of mysticism, a very physical kind of communal worship, a highly ornate and theatrical ritual life, the manipulation of sense experiences to produce ecstatic encounters. Of course, all these elements existed in contemporary Christianity, in varieties of ethnic Catholicism and, to some extent, in Pentecostalism, but neither of these was a respectable option for educated Protestants, even for those wholly disenchanted with the mainline churches. Authoritarian Christian traditions were especially unacceptable to the liberated women of the early twentieth century, who rejected the explicitly patriarchal structures of both Catholics and fundamentalists. Mystical and ecstatic themes became acceptable, though, when presented as manifestations of a pristine paganism.

Political factors also played a role. As Philip Deloria points out, playing Indian is often a reaction to a lack of confidence in mainstream American civilization: "Whenever white Americans have confronted crises of identity, some of them have inevitably turned to Indians."[28] Such defections reach their height during periods of cultural or political crisis, like the 1910s, when America was riven by political, social, and ethnic conflict. A pervading sense of threat and pessimism was then reinforced by the catastrophe of the First World War. Through the early twentieth century, a growing admiration for the primitive can be traced in religion, as well as art and culture.

Even before the Great War, an interest in primitive and tribal cultures was found among the cultural avant-garde, but this became much more widespread during the 1920s.[29]

In the Native American context, these ideas were popularized by the celebrated group of writers and artists from the bohemian circles of Taos and Santa Fe, who saw Native Americans as the bearers of an ancient and priceless culture. Commenting on Pueblo ceremonials, artist Marsden Hartley complained that "in times of peace we go about the world seeking out every species of life foreign to ourselves for our own esthetic or intellectual diversion, yet we neglect on our very doorstep the perhaps most remarkable realization of beauty that can be found anywhere. It is a perfect piece with the great artistry of all time." This awed admiration extended fully to spiritual matters. Carl Jung, another visitor to Taos, remarked that the life of a Pueblo Indian was "cosmologically meaningful," in contrast to the psychic and social deprivation of a modern Euro-American. John Collier found among the Pueblos a Red Atlantis, still retaining ancient values that could literally redeem the world: "They had what the world has lost. They have it now. What the world has lost, the world must have again, lest it die."[30] Such figures would be decisive in publicizing Native religious grievances and in helping the Indians to victory during the religious freedom debates of the 1920s. Collier, that antimodern utopian mystic, became the overlord of federal Indian policy during the New Deal years.

Such romantic responses would surface again during periods of disaffection with Western and specifically American culture. During the Great Depression, which occasionally did look like the last days of Western civilization, we find an unprecedented effort to bolster and preserve Native culture and religion, and a new boom in cultural and religious tourism. Again, in the late 1940s, as fears of nuclear annihilation grew, the books of Frank Waters integrated the spiritual wonders of Native American religions into a broader New Age vision, creating in the process an immensely influential cultural synthesis.

With these precedents in mind, it is not surprising that a new era of starry-eyed neo-Indianism should mark the decade after 1965, the time of Vietnam and Watergate, of assassinations and urban rioting, of gasoline shortages and threatened ecological catastrophe. In somewhat altered form, the radical pro-Indianism of the counterculture years would be sustained by the renewed crises at the end of the 1970s, a time of apocalyptic war fears and renewed urban crises. These social and political stresses provide the essential context for understanding the emergence of the New Age movement in the decade after 1975, a far-reaching cultural and religious phenomenon in which Indians would once again be central. Though national morale would recover in later years, Indians have never ceased to provide the vehicles for social, cultural, and, above all, spiritual experimentation.

We can see this process as a growth of awareness, a greater sensitivity to the nature of Indian practices, and a praiseworthy willingness to see these cultures more in their own terms. But at every stage, non-Natives were using a good deal of imagination in creating their Indian stereotypes. Though the romanticized, environmentally sensitive Indians of *Dances with Wolves* or *Pocahontas* are much more attractive figures than the primitive savages of Victorian fantasy, their ideas and actions are still presented according to the tastes of the mainstream non-Native audience, and are not necessarily any closer to any objective reality. The newer image may constitute a socially positive stereotype, but it is still a stereotype, defined according to non-Native and specifically Euro-American interests. While it is a much more benevolent dream, it is, nonetheless, a dream, shaped by its consumers, the dream catchers.

2

❦

Heathen Darkness

Where paganism is supreme, there is sloth, and foul things unspeakable.
—*Marshall Owen Scott, 1900*

America's Indian dream began as phantasmagoric nightmare. Through most of Christian history, the most common view of other faiths has been that they are, knowingly or otherwise, serving the devil. During the Middle Ages and the early modern period, this was the standard interpretation of Islam and Judaism, and even rival branches of Christianity freely traded mutual charges of diabolism. If such abuse was so customary within the monotheistic fold, it is not surprising to find it directed against the pagans and animists whom the European colonists first encountered in the New World. The vast majority of European settlers had no sympathy for the religious activities of their new neighbors, while the clergy had little doubt that Natives were worshipping the devil.

Given the religious sensibilities of the time, European Christians really had little alternative to this grim view. As it was traditionally interpreted, monotheism allows few options for interpreting other religions. Essentially, two views are possible. One doctrine, the starker and more uncompromising, holds that the newfound pagans are simply and literally worshipping the devil and his minions. This view made good sense for a biblically oriented people like the Protestant English settlers of North America, since so much of the Old Testament concerns the war against idols, sacrifices to devils, and all the violence and sexual immorality associated with false gods. Another option was more benevolent in theory, though it still offered little hope for the Native faiths. In this view, pagans were struggling in darkness according to the limits of fallen human nature, though they occasionally received glimmers of divine truth. Paganism might include noble and even proto-Christian elements that would find their fulfillment in the truth of Christian revelation. Until that point, pagans were still in the bonds of sin and under diabolical authority, from which they needed to be liberated.[1]

Each of these views suggested an appropriate solution. The first interpretation, that of the pagan as child of the devil, justified the removal or destruction of the evildoers who carried out their atrocious religion and the suppression of their rituals and ceremonies. The second view was more open to compromise with older traditions. Conceivably, Natives already had some of the Gospel truth, which needed cultivating and making manifest. For Catholic missionaries, once the basic fact of conversion was achieved, many of the older rituals and ceremonies could be absorbed into the new faith, as some (though by no means all) of the old feasts were rechristened as festivals of the saints. Protestants, even those who believed that Native faiths might contain some core of truth, were less optimistic about traditional practices, and hoped to uproot vestiges of superstition.[2]

Of course, such explicitly religious attitudes were chiefly found among clergy and scholars, and did not influence every soldier or administrator who encountered Indians and their religions. Yet in this instance, clerical attitudes carried disproportionate weight, since through much of the nineteenth and early twentieth centuries, clergy and missionaries still dominated the implementation of U.S. policy toward Indians. Into the 1930s, Indian reservations still operated under a near-theocratic regime that was startlingly at odds with most assumptions about American government and society. Debates about the devil and his domain still mattered on the reservations, in a way that they had ceased to do in mainstream America a century before.

The rhetorical language of devils and diabolism also permeated secular accounts of Indian cultures and religions. As nineteenth century Americans moved toward secular ideas of progress, they asserted their modernity by distancing themselves from groups who symbolized primitivism and superstition, including "savages" like the Indians. Ironically, in expressing their revulsion at the religion of these supposedly primitive groups, these accounts still echoed the older contrasts between Christian light and heathen night. Whether writing in sacred or secular mode, Americans were slow to disentangle the image of the Indian from that of the devil.

Children of the Devil

From the earliest days of the European settlement, explicit statements linked the Indians to Satan. The first English explorers of Virginia in 1585 reported that the people "have commonly conjurers or jugglers which use strange gestures, and often contrary to nature in their enchantments: for they be very familiar with devils, of whom they enquire what their enemies do, or other such thing." In 1612, Captain John Smith reported of Virginia's Powhatans that "their chief God they worship is the devil. Him they call Oke and serve him more of fear than love." In contemporary Canada, Jesuit priest Joseph Jouvency wrote of the Indians, "There is among them no system of religion, or care for it . . . They call some divinity, who is the author of evil, Manitou, and fear him exceedingly." Even Roger Williams, perhaps the most tolerant of seventeenth-century Christians, followed his survey of Indian religious customs with a powerful disclaimer. He drew most of his account from the words of Natives themselves, "for after once being in their houses and beholding what their worship was, I durst never be an eye witness, spectator or looker on, lest I should have been partaker of Satan's invention."[3]

This diabolical connection raised expectations about Indian religion, based on the long Christian interaction with Jews and Muslims. The key idea was one of inversion. If Christians worshipped the Christ, Jews (for instance) must follow the Antichrist; if Christians practiced the Eucharist, Jews celebrated a vicious parody involving ritual child-sacrifice, while witches indulged in the Black Mass. These hostile groups were interrelated: Jews had their Sabbath, witches their Sabbat. For early Puritan writers, the Indians represented the dark shadow of the Christian mission into the wilderness.[4]

Indians, too, were in a blasphemous sense a chosen people, the special servants of hell. As Cotton Mather wrote in his *Magnalia Christi Americana* (1702), "Though we know not *when* or *how* these Indians first became inhabitants of this mighty continent, yet we may guess that probably the Devil decoyed those miserable salvages hither in hopes that the gospel of the Lord Jesus Christ would never come here to destroy or disturb his *absolute empire* over them." They were under "that old usurping *landlord* of America, who is by the *Wrath of God, the Prince of this world.*" The New England Puritans "have to their sorrow seen Azazel dwelling and raging there in very tragical instances." Mather's goal in writing was to "report the wonderful displays of [God's] infinite power, wisdom, goodness, and faithfulness, wherewith his divine providence hath irradiated an Indian wilderness." One demonstration of this "infinite Power" was the devastating epidemics by which much of New England was swept clean of its original inhabitants. Jonathan Edwards believed that before the Christian settlement, North America was "wholly the possession of Satan."[5]

For a people as deeply immersed in the Old Testament as the Protestant English, pagan horrors gave an added justification to policies of subjection and removal, on the analogy of the Children of Israel confronting the Canaanite adherents of Baal. In the biblical account of ancient Israel, which provided such a powerful intellectual template, chroniclers regularly denounced not just the heathens but also the supposedly godly rulers who failed to root out these heathen practices. Hebrew kings were condemned for tolerating the pagan sites, the high places, right up to the point at which God finally lost patience with his people and allowed their kingdom to fall. Woe to the devil worshippers, and woe to those misguided Christians who failed to eradicate them.

Indians and Witches

At every stage, Indian religion reflected its diabolical origins. Its priests, the sagamores or Powachs, directly served the devil, and Mather called them "horrid sorcerers and hellish conjurors and such as conversed with demons." A *Powaw* was "a priest, who has more familiarity with Satan than his neighbors"; they were "sorcerers and seducers."[6] Consistently, Indian religions are painted in the colors used for contemporary European witchcraft. In 1613, Virginia's Alexander Whitaker described "the miserable condition of these naked slaves of the devil. . . . They serve the devil for fear, sacrificing sometimes . . . their own children to him. Their priests (whom they call *Quiokosoughs*) are no other but such as our English witches are."[7] Generally, the English literature on witchcraft differed from the Continental European in placing less emphasis on organized satanic worship. English courts rarely heard tales of the witches' Sabbat, the pact with the devil, or satanic priests like the notorious "Black Man." English witches were seen as isolated practitioners, rather than adherents of a vast alternative underground religion. In America, though, confronting the organized pagan worship of the Indian nations and their powerful priests and medicine men, British colonists increasingly looked to European witchcraft theories, to the grotesque mythology of organized satanic worship offered by the notorious witch hunters' text, the *Malleus Maleficarum*.[8]

Based on these ideas, Indian medicine men were believed to receive gifts comparable to those that Satan granted his witch followers in Europe. And at least as they appear in European writings, accounts of Indian contacts with the supernatural have many parallels to European stories of the appearances of the devil. When the Tewa medicine man Popé received a vision commanding him to launch the great Pueblo revolt against the Spaniards in 1680, European observers would immediately have understood the figure who bore that message as a demonic manifestation. His god appeared as a tall black man with yellow eyes; to a European, the classic Black Man of the Sabbat. Just as the devil appeared personally at European Sabbats, so Popé's gods appeared on another occasion as "three devils in the form of Indians, most horrifying in appearance, shooting flames of fire from all the senses and extremities of their bodies." Not surprisingly, Popé was "said to have communication with the devil."[9]

While Indian religion was false and, literally, of the Pit, its followers still commanded real power, parallel to the notorious sorcerers recorded in biblical and patristic texts. In the biblical book of Revelation, so familiar to colonial readers, the Antichrist is reported to do "great wonders, so that he maketh fire come down from heaven on the earth in the sight of men, And deceiveth them that dwell on the earth by the means of those miracles."[10] Medicine men might perform successful healings or miracles, though God would cause these powers to fail before a determined challenge from the godly. Narratives of early Christian preachers and missionaries regularly depict struggles with Indian spiritual leaders as demonic powers are confronted and overthrown.[11] These accounts draw on a long tradition of Christian literature, dating back to Roman times, and ultimately to the struggles with demons found in the Gospels.

From the Bible, too, the colonists knew that the followers of evil would inevitably try to subvert the kingdom of God. This perception became acute during the various crises that threatened to overwhelm New England in the last quarter of the seventeenth century, and may have contributed to the great witchcraft scare at Salem. Though interpretations of this event will always remain controversial, historian Mary Beth Norton has argued convincingly that colonists felt deeply threatened by a supernatural challenge mobilized through the devil's Indian servants. Some of the leading activists in the Salem affair were refugees from disastrous wars against the Wabanaki Indians in what is now Maine, and the reputed leader of the witches, the Reverend George Burroughs, had supposedly bewitched English soldiers fighting in this war. (Like his contemporary Popé, Burroughs was reputedly under the direct control of the Black Man.) The slave woman Tituba, whose magical practices directly provoked the crisis, was herself a Caribbean Indian.[12] Colonial Americans connected witches and Indians just as naturally as Continental Europeans linked witches to Jews.

The Survival of Satan

Not all colonists were as uncompromising as Mather and the Salem ministers, but the concept of Indian devil worship remained a powerful force among Christian clergy, whose role as missionaries usually made them the primary interpreters of Native ways to ordinary Americans. For every nineteenth-century American who read a sensitive and sophisticated anthropological account of Native ways, probably a hundred others derived their interpretations from the pamphlets and lectures of clergy and missionaries.

Also, the hostility of these accounts remained remarkably constant over time, as the nation's geographical expansion provided repeated new infusions of pagan peoples. By the mid-nineteenth century, evangelism had made great progress among surviving Indian communities east of the Mississippi, many of which had absorbed into their own culture significant elements of Christianity. Though they did not necessarily convert as fully or explicitly as Protestant clergy might have wished, they drew from Christianity those elements they found relevant and inspiring, and the resulting amalgams were often impressive. Looking at the revivalist religion of Handsome Lake among the Seneca, even the narrowest cleric would have been pressed to interpret this as devil worship. From his enlightened perspective, Thomas Jefferson could describe the prophet as "favored by the Divine Spirit," a religious figure quite comparable to those of the Old or New Testaments.[13] Yet through the second half of the nineteenth century, Americans found themselves in contact with societies far less exposed to their own values and still retaining their religions in fairly pure forms. Much of the mountain West and Southwest fell under U.S. jurisdiction only in the decade after 1844, and the even more alien land of Alaska was acquired in 1867. Even after annexation, warfare and political chaos meant that it would be decades before white observers would have full access to the new lands. Well into the twentieth century, missionary writers were still responding to the overt paganism of America's new-caught sullen peoples, whom they saw precisely as half devil and half child.

Into the twentieth century, too, these missionaries were still writing in terms of the works of the devil. Magazines like *Missionary Review of the World* kept this view alive, and influenced new generations of clergy. Writing of the Canadian Algonquins in 1917, the *Review* remarked that "their pagan religion is practically devil worship. . . . His whole aim in religion is to propitiate the bad spirits in order that they might not do him harm. In common with all other devil worshipers, their religion consists of fetishism and incantations accompanied by the use of drums and rattles . . . the pagan life of these people is pitiable in the extreme."[14] Indian ways were simply part of a parcel of evil customs to be eradicated. Writing in *Missionary Review* in 1917, one Presbyterian pastor argued that "while the Navajo is religious, there is nothing in his religion that leads a soul closer to God, and nothing that will help him in his fight against evil. On the other hand there is much that will lead him deeper into sin."[15]

Against this background, any notion of religious liberty would be simply absurd, and the faster the Native religions were suppressed, the better. Reporting on conditions in Alaska in 1884, the *New York Times* reported that, "Within a few years Presbyterian missionaries have been exhorting [the Natives] to give up their practices of slave-holding, plural marriages, witchcraft, shamanism, and cremation of the dead."[16] Though "shamanism" in this context implies nothing less than the central structure of the religious system, it is here listed among other evil practices that retarded the assimilation of Native peoples to the modern world, in North America as much as in Africa and Asia. Christianity equated with progress, and tribal religions and cultures with primitivism and obscurantism.

In this instance, the *Times* was uncritically reporting the remarks of a Protestant missionary, who had a strong partisan motive for painting the Natives in the worst possible colors. This genre of hostile or mocking reporting endured long after anthropologists had taught educated Americans the complexities of Native spirituality. As late as 1927, the same newspaper was again basing a story about Alaska entirely on the words of veteran missionary S. Hall Young, who boasted how the territory was "developed from a land of savagery, witchcraft and corruption, peopled by rough miners who knew no law, and ignorant Indians who practiced polygamy, slavery and immorality." More recently, though, "the medicine men with their unholy incantations have disappeared."[17] The newspaper would have known better than to quote a Protestant pastor delivering a polemic against the supposedly primitive doctrines of Catholicism or Judaism. Of course, these other groups had organized voices with which to protest such coverage, which Native peoples lacked.

Hearts of Darkness

Long after the concepts of hell and the devil had lost their central position in mainstream American religion, a very similar rhetoric was applied against Native religions. During the nineteenth century, accounts by quite liberal and secular observers still applied the familiar language of primitive darkness and savagery, although they were now basing these views on racial and evolutionary theories rather than explicitly religious concepts.

The more they condemned Native primitivism, the more "advanced" observers paralleled the traditional language of light and darkness. Such perceptions were only confirmed by seeing the products of Native craftsmanship. Though by the end of the nineteenth century primitive art would attract worldwide admiration, earlier generations generally saw it as crude and meaningless, and words like "weird" and "hideous" abounded. In 1876, the Centennial Exhibition in Philadelphia included a vast haul of Indian ethnographic treasures, including the first of what would soon become a flood of objects from America's new Alaskan territories. The crafts and carvings of Northwest Coast peoples attracted special notice, little of it good. House fronts had been "rudely carved into a series of hideous monsters one on top of another, painted in crude colors." William Dean Howells saw one Indian figure as "a hideous demon, whose malign traits can hardly inspire any emotion other than abhorrence."[18] Diabolical peoples produced diabolical art.

One condemnation of Indian religions—proof, perhaps, of its diabolical origins—was the ritual use of snakes found among southwestern peoples. For a Christian, the serpent had obvious connections with Satan and the powers of darkness: the Christian Bible begins with a diabolical serpent and ends with the fall of "that old serpent, which is the devil, and Satan." Finding snakes used in Native rituals, Christian observers had only to debate whether this amounted to full-scale ophiolatry (serpent worship) or whether there might be some less sinister explanation. Seeing a Pueblo ritual involving a snake in the 1580s, a Spanish traveler said, "We thought this snake might be the devil, who has them enslaved."[19]

Nineteenth-century Americans were equally disturbed to find snake rituals on what was now their soil. In *The Snake-Dance of the Moquis of Arizona*, Cavalry officer John G. Bourke created a sensation with his account of the "revolting religious rite" of the Hopi. The book was widely reviewed and summarized. Could such "heathen" rituals be perpetrated so close to the outposts of civilization? "This was the snake dance of the Moquis, a tribe of people living within our own boundaries, less than seventy miles from the Atlantic and Pacific Railroad, in the year of our Lord 1881." Just as serpent rituals provided the ultimate condemnation of Afro-Caribbean religions such as Voodoo, so they marked Native American practices as primordial and sinister. At least one Heart of Darkness was firmly located on the North American continent.[20]

Human Sacrifice

Whatever the theological dangers of devil worship, critics believed that Native religions included a great many practical, this-worldly dangers. Even readers grown skeptical of the real existence of a devil or demons were prepared to accept that genuine horrors could be wrought in the name of devil worship. Familiar to the common Victorian critique of pagan religions was the element of violence, of what elsewhere would be termed "jungle" savagery, which manifested itself in sacrificial rituals and cannibalism.

Human sacrifice was incontestably known among some Native peoples. Of course, some cultures lacked the practice entirely: in the 1540s, Cabeza de Vaca wrote that in all his travels, "nowhere did we meet either sacrifices or idolatry." But in some places at particular times, the practice may have been widespread. Early Spanish visitors to the southeastern states were appalled by the scale of the seasonal offerings of human victims burned at the stake, commonly drawn from slaves and war captives. Human sacrifice continued long after the period of first contact. The anthropological literature would often repeat the story of a young woman sacrificed by the Pawnees to the morning star in 1838, in what is now Nebraska. The story had a long afterlife, due to its inclusion in Sir James Frazer's *Golden Bough* (1890). For most Native peoples, such killings were by this point extremely rare, but one would never realize that from the spate of news stories at the end of the nineteenth century.[21]

The popularity of human sacrifice tales owed something to the exaggerated impression that southwestern cultures bore a close resemblance to the Aztecs, who were credited with many of the great stone structures in the region. U.S. maps still feature names like Aztec and Montezuma's Castle. Nineteenth-century Americans knew the Aztecs well, or thought they did, through Prescott's much-read *Conquest of Mexico* (1843). Prescott discussed human sacrifice at length, in a section littered with words such as "loathsome," "degrading," "appalling," and "blind fanaticism." "Without attempting a precise calculation . . . it is safe to conclude that thousands were yearly offered up, in the different cities of Anahuac, on the bloody altars of the Mexican divinities." Even worse, sacrificial victims were sometimes cannibalized. "Surely, never were refinement and the extreme of barbarism brought so closely in contact with each other!"[22] If a society like the Aztecs had ruled the southwest, then something like their sacrificial cults would have operated, and this idea shaped interpretations of archaeological sites at which people had died violently. When the Anasazi site of Lowry Ruin (Colorado) was excavated in 1929, with bodies showing possible evidence of ritualized violence, even the nonsensational *New York Times* featured the headline "FIND TRIBAL MURDER FARM." An Indian site in Nebraska appeared to show evidence of a highly developed urban community; but the newspaper report had to mention that "on this spot stood torture racks where human sacrifices were made to the morning star" (more shades of the *Golden Bough*).[23]

The supposition that Indians were involved in sacrifice or ritual murder shaped media reporting of violent acts, and stories proliferated at the end of the nineteenth century. This boom in Indian horror stories owed much to developments in the media industry and the new sensationalism of the Hearst and Pulitzer newspaper chains. The most successful newspapers had a strong taste for stories of exotic violence, especially when connected with cults and bizarre religions, and even the most respectable media outlets followed this lead. Usually, any story featuring the words "medicine man" could be relied on to include themes of bloodshed, criminality, or fanaticism. In 1902, the *New York Times* presented the story "BIG MEDICINE MAN TORTURED," telling how the Yuma people of Arizona had responded to a smallpox epidemic. Reportedly, a shaman was chosen to expiate the sins of the tribe. Despite his efforts to flee, he was tortured to death because "their customs required them to make a heavy sacrifice." We often hear tales of the murder of medicine men, though it is never clear whether these acts were truly sacrificial in nature, or whether, more prosaically, these leaders were killed as punishment for repeated failures to heal. In 1903, the *Times* offered a long article on the murder of shamans by the Yakima people of Washington.[24]

Tales of blood and sacrifice were supported by the unquestioned realities of the Sun Dance. In this ritual, young men practiced a kind of self-torture, tying themselves to a pole by skewers passed under their skin and dancing until they fell into ecstatic states. White observers were appalled. As one journalist wrote in 1871, "The blood streams from the torn and lacerated flesh, while the devotees with demoniac yells plunge around in a perfect frenzy." Reportedly, a Sun Dance was performed as part of the Canadian anthropological displays at the World's Columbian Exhibition in Chicago in 1893, to the horror of spectators. The incident, which generated a minor international incident, seemed to prove that Indians did practice forms of self-mutilation and blood sacrifice.[25]

Horror stories proliferated in the still-mysterious lands of the Southwest. When Frank Cushing published his celebrated and generally sympathetic account of his stay at Zuñi in 1882–1883, he included some harrowing tales. In one incident, a dog ritually identified as a Navajo man was disemboweled in a scene "too disgusting for description. It finds parallel only in some of the war ceremonials of the Aztecs, or in the animal sacrifices of the savages of the far northwest." The killers belonged to a "secret order" pledged to carry out such a "horrible ceremonial." Cushing describes other horrible "ordeals" among the secret orders and brotherhoods, "excruciating rites" of self-torture.[26] Consciously or not, such accounts of blood rituals and secret societies closely recall the older stories of witches and Sabbats, and they would have resonated with Cotton Mather and his contemporaries.

Reportedly, even human sacrifice could still be found in these mysterious new territories. In 1905, journalist Gilson Willets alleged that human sacrifice was a regular feature of the religion of the Pueblo Indians of southern New Mexico. "Each year, at Christmas time, up to five years ago, [they] held a barbarous dance publicly in the churchyard of the town, and there publicly compelled a little girl to dance herself to death, beating her with whips to keep her spinning till she dropped dead."[27] In 1913, anthropologist Matilda Coxe Stevenson reported a bizarre tale about the continued practice of human sacrifice in two villages, involving infants in one case, of women in the other: "after certain weird performances, starved rattlesnakes were turned loose from pottery vases and allowed to feast until not an atom of flesh remained." The more such stories circulated, the more they shaped the questions that journalists asked about Indian cultures, and the more they conditioned the answers that imaginative Native informants were prepared to supply.[28] Anthropologists noted how easy it was to get southwestern Indians to tell human sacrifice tales to gullible whites. Tales about bloodthirsty Indian rituals remained commonplace until the 1920s, when media interest shifted to almost-identical stories of human sacrifice, snake worship, and witchcraft in Haiti.

Witches and Wendigos

Sacrificial stories merged with periodic accounts of other religiously motivated violence, notably the killing of Indian witches. Long after white Americans were condemning Indians for actually being witches, they were denouncing them just as fervently for still believing in witches, and thus demonstrating their primitive savagery. The two themes intersected neatly in 1882 when a group of Zuñi emissaries visited Salem, where they congratulated the citizens for their ancestors' determined response to the witchcraft problem. Through the 1890s, U.S. authorities were struggling to suppress Zuñi persecutions of witches in conflicts that nearly led to war.[29] In 1897, the *New York Times* reported on federal efforts to suppress the killing of suspected witches among the Zuñi people at the behest of their "medicine men" and their allied "fanatics." Shortly afterwards, an Indian girl in California "was poisoned recently by the medicine man of the tribe because, he declared, she had bewitched her sister."[30]

Paganism supposedly inspired bloodshed, whether of the organized kind found in sacrifice or witch-hunting, or through individual brutality. Through the late nineteenth and early twentieth centuries, news accounts of Native religion featured sensational tales of extreme violence linked to Indian religious worship and shamanism. One recurrent tale involved the Cree legend of the Wendigo, an evil spirit that stalked through the northern woods, possessing Indians and making them run amok with "an insane desire to kill and eat the flesh of their victims." Fears of possession probably did lead some Natives to restrain or exorcise their neighbors, and violence and death resulted. Through horror writers like Algernon Blackwood, the

Wendigo became familiar to white readers as a demon figure, a deadly ghost (as it survives today in role-playing games).[31]

Particularly in the early twentieth century, news stories about the crimes and follies of medicine men became a staple of sensationalized news reporting. Apart from hunting witches, medicine men gave advice that caused the death of patients or led their followers to destruction through what were seen as their superstitious delusions. In 1886, in a story headlined "SUPERSTITIOUS NEGLECT," the *New York Times* reported how interference by an Alaskan medicine man had resulted in the deaths of three poisoned Natives. Some years later, the same paper told how a family of Alaska natives was wiped out when a "sorcerer" failed in his boasts that he could quell a storm, so that the boat in which the group was traveling was lost. When a Colorado Ute was accused of burying his baby alive, he cited the instructions of his medicine man, who claimed that the burial would resurrect the man's dead wife.[32] When the media reported cases of medicine men being punished or killed for failing to live up to their claims, the context was again sinister and alarmingly primitive.

Only slightly less pernicious, for white readers, were cases in which medicine men defrauded or deceived their peoples for their own personal advantage. In 1873, a medicine man reportedly taught the Modoc people of California a special dance that would result in the extinction of whites and the resurrection of the Native dead. Obviously, the tribe soon found that neither event would come to pass. For the press, this was a simple and mildly amusing story of a "false prophet," a religious confidence trickster, though the ritual described sounds like an early manifestation of the famous Ghost Dance.[33] When Lowry Ruin was excavated, archaeologists found secret passages in kivas, which allowed figures to make seemingly supernatural entrances during rituals. The archaeologist concerned was quoted as saying that "the shamans (medicine men) had to make a living and to do that they had to fool the people."[34] The media would never have offered such cynical fare about Christian or Jewish clergy, whose misdeeds and scandals were kept strictly confidential until quite recent times.

The cumulative effect of such reporting was to associate Native religious practices and practitioners with crude violence and fraud. Even when they were not overt exposés, media treatment of Indian rituals into the 1920s emphasized the bizarre, the frightening, and the sinister. These labels would all apply to the coverage of the pagan funeral of an Onondaga medicine man in 1929. According to the *New York Times*, "Attired in grotesque costumes and hideous masks, the Indians began a weird dance around the house."[35]

Satan's Own Brood: Indians and Catholics

Encountering Indian religion, white Protestant observers reacted with a mixture of disgust and contempt. When in 1840 naturalist John Audubon actually met an Indian spiritual leader, he was appalled by the ludicrous trappings that the religion seemed to demand.

> We had entered this curiosity shop by pushing aside a wet elk skin stretched on four sticks. Looking around I saw a number of calabashes, eight or ten otter skins, two very large buffalo skulls with horns on, evidently of great age, and some sticks and other magical implements with which none but a "Great Medicine Man" is acquainted. During my survey there sat, crouched down on his haunches, an Indian wrapped in a dirty blanket with only his filthy head peeping out.

Yet for all the squalor and gross superstition (as Audubon saw it), Indians treated such mountebanks with awe and devotion. These accounts of cynical priests and fanatical superstition recall another potent kind of religious polemic that flourished in America at this time, namely anti-Catholicism. Anti-Catholic rhetoric and political activism flourished especially in the 1840s and 1850s, during the 1890s, and again in the Ku Klux Klan years of the 1920s. In each period, anti-Catholic assumptions shaped views of Indian religion. Many of the reasons why Native religions offended and irritated American Protestants—ritualism, fanaticism, clericalism, a veneration for sacred objects and places—have to be understood in the context of contemporary anti-Catholicism.[36]

Protestant prejudice is evident in descriptions of the superstitious awe accorded to American Indian shamans or medicine men, which was analogous to the Catholic subservience to priests. Indians, too, had "conjurers" and "priests," the latter if anything being an even more suspicious word. English Protestant tradition had long dismissed priests as "conjurers" because of their outrageous claims to be able to transform bread and wine into the body and blood of Christ. Reinforcing the Catholic analogy, Indian holy men inflicted severe bodily penances on the faithful, recalling the despised Catholic penitential system. And in the eyes of nineteenth-century historians, fanatical priests had led the European witch hunts, which merged into images of the Inquisition. Modern Indian witch hunters were only following this disreputable precedent.[37]

This was an ancient bias. Already in 1613, Alexander Whitaker was using Catholic analogies to describe Virginia's medicine men. The people "stand in great awe of their *Quiokosoughs*, or Priests, which are a generation of vipers, even of Satan's own brood. The manner of their life is much like to the popish Hermits of our age." In the same region in 1720, Robert Beverly described an Indian idol that:

> must needs make a strange representation, which those poor people are taught to worship with a devout ignorance. . . . In this state of nature, one would think they should be as pure from superstition, and overdoing matters in religion, as they are in other things; but I find it is quite the contrary; for this simplicity gives the cunning priest a greater advantage over them, according to the Romish maxim, "Ignorance is the mother of devotion."

This view of "priestcraft" as primitive superstition would supply a common matrix for Anglo-American encounters with many other cultures. Tibet's religion was dismissed as "Lamaism," supposedly a degenerate and inferior form of true Buddhism, and likewise characterized by superstition, corruption, idolatry, and clericalism.[38]

Nineteenth-century critics also depicted American Indians as childishly superstitious, wasting large proportions of their time and wealth on religious rituals. Again, this recalled the stereotypical Papists of American cities. Protestant missionaries repeatedly complained about Catholic tolerance of traditional Indian ceremonies, and their failure to suppress festivals that had clear pagan origins. For Protestants, these conflicts clearly suggested the broad affinity that existed between the primitive paganism of the Indians and the more sophisticated variant proffered by Rome. The analogies are often drawn explicitly. Prescott's *Conquest of Mexico* describes Aztec tortures that "doubtless, were often inflicted with the same compunctious visitings which a devout familiar of the Holy Office [the Inquisition] might at times experience in executing its stern decrees."[39]

Ghost Dancers

At least until the end of the nineteenth century, Indian religions were feared because they could inspire anti-white military and political movements. The century's Indian conflicts roughly began with the movement inspired by the Shawnee Prophet, and ended with the Ghost Dance movement, which culminated with the Wounded Knee massacre of 1890. Americans were also familiar with religious movements that challenged contemporary European empires, like the Thuggee of India, or the radical Islam represented by the Mahdi in the Sudan, who was repeatedly in the news between 1885 and 1898. And contemporaries did draw analogies between Islam and American Indian cultures. When James Mooney analyzed the Ghost Dance, he included a substantial discussion of Sufi ecstatic practice and trance states. If the Mahdi or the Thugs could challenge British rule, might not an American Indian prophetic movement bring warfare and massacre to the U.S. frontier?[40] Potentially, Indian religion could yet produce a rival ideology to challenge and even derail Manifest Destiny.

At least until the collapse of Native American armed resistance in 1890, rumors of new Indian ceremonies or dances were of interest not just as ethnographic study, but also as possible auguries of warfare. A "new pagan mystery dance" in Wisconsin seemed intended to restore the land to the Indians, and to drive the whites back across the Atlantic. Official attempts to interfere with the rites were opposed by a "turbulent and threatening" "cabal" of religious leaders. White fears found a focus in the Ghost Dance, which was described in terms of new Indian messiahs. It was the "Messiah dance," the "Messiah agitation and the Ghost Dance."[41]

Such fears did not cease entirely after Wounded Knee, and again, anti-Catholic imagery helped sustain fears of religious warfare. In the mid-1890s, the American Protective Association became a national political force by spreading scare stories that Catholic priests were about to lead the faithful in an armed crusade against Protestant America. This precedent reinforced Protestant suspicions about the medicine men, who were equally prone to manipulate popular superstitions for their own ends. In 1898, the newspapers were reporting a possible uprising by the Cheyenne in Oklahoma. Reportedly, the Indians were "holding a ghost dance and making medicine," and were "being worked into a frenzy by the medicine men, who are holding strange rites and ceremonies." As late as 1900, a Canadian observer wrote that "the painted red men of the prairies and forests we still have with us. In the Sun Dance, the potlatch and other pagan practices—the war-whoop is heard, and the tomahawk and scalping knife flash in the light."[42]

Not of the Devil?

Not all the criticisms of Native religions were so extreme or lurid, and after the 1890s, the idea of a serious Indian political threat was ludicrous. The many mainstream Americans who dealt with Native peoples knew quite well that the charges of bloodthirsty rituals were largely media sensationalism, though initiation rites might well include demanding ordeals. Also, there was from earliest times at least a fringe tradition of admiration for Native cultures, reflected by the numbers of white people who voluntarily moved to Indian communities and adopted their culture and customs. In that limited sense, religious conversion was a two-way street. As Russell Bourne shows in his account of religious interaction in colonial America, some white Americans were prepared to concede that, in some sense, God spoke to and through the Indians. De Crevecoeur wrote that "the Supreme Being does not reside in peculiar churches or communities; he is equally the great Manitou of the woods and the plains." Such tolerant ideas appear in speeches credited to Native leaders, though it is uncertain whether they authentically reflected the views of the speakers or if they were embellished by Euro-Americans. White authors have long used Indians as vehicles for politically attractive sentiments, which are then presented as the authentic voices of pristine Nature. In 1805, the Seneca chief Red Jacket reportedly protested against the idea that "there is but one way to worship and serve the Great Spirit. . . . We also have a religion which was given to our forefathers and has been handed down to us, their children. . . . We do not wish to destroy your religion or take it from you. We only want to enjoy our own." Whatever the origins of these words, the fact that they were published (and often quoted in later years) alerted white readers that Native religion might have its own validity.[43]

Such universalist beliefs offered a fundamental challenge to the missionary endeavor. If Indians already knew God, why did they need to be taught the message anew, and through coercive means? This liberal idea became all the easier to accept as enlightened Americans themselves questioned the existence of hell and the devil, and scorned the intolerance of their ancestors. In the early nineteenth century, the rise of fiery evangelical revivalism gave a new urgency to calls for religious toleration. In 1809, Washington Irving's *History of New York* satirized the assumption of Christian superiority to Indian faiths by imagining the earth being subjected to an alien invasion, directed by the Man in the Moon. Noting the differences from the Lunatic creed, the invaders conclude that earthlings have scarcely a gleam of true philosophy among them, but are, in fact, utter heretics, ignoramuses, and barbarians. . . . We have insisted upon their renouncing the contemptible shackles of religion and common sense. . . . But such was the unparalleled obstinacy of these wretched savages, that they persisted in cleaving to their wives, and adhering to their religion, and absolutely set at naught the sublime doctrines of the moon.

The appalled emperor of the moon orders that "the colonists who are now about to depart to the aforesaid planet are authorized and commanded to use every means to convert these infidel savages from the darkness of Christianity, and make them thorough and absolute lunatics." Irving's satire foreshadows much of the anti-imperialist critique of the late nineteenth century, not least in attacking the religious justifications for conquest—especially by "lunatic" evangelicals.[44]

Yet while some acknowledged the existence of Native spirituality and disliked missionary arrogance, this feeling rarely translated into defense of the practice of Native religions themselves. Much of the problem involved how white people saw and defined religion in their own terms. Viewed through a liberal lens, Native religions had much that was good precisely because they echoed or prefigured Christianity. These religions were a foreshadowing of Christian truth, a *preparatio evangelica*. Even the staunch Red Jacket is made to sound like a liberal Protestant with Deist leanings ("We worship that way. It teacheth us to be thankful for all the favors we receive; to love each other, and to be united. We never quarrel about religion."). Obviously he was not preaching an animist worldview.

From this perspective, Indians did indeed have a religious outlook, even a noble or exalted one. But this pristine faith had become contaminated with pagan practices, ranging from the lethal—witch-hunting or human sacrifice—to the merely embarrassing, such as shamanism and ceremonial dances. Indian religion therefore had its friends, but in practice, they supported policies that were quite as devastating to Native cultures as those of the most intolerant missionaries.

Indians as Proto-Christians

The idea of the ignorant Native possessing a simple kernel of divine truth is epitomized by oft-quoted lines from Alexander Pope: "Lo, the poor Indian, whose untutor'd mind / Sees God in clouds, or hears him in the wind." The phrase "Poor Lo" became a standard newspaper term for Indians, while the idea of the "untutor'd mind" had a long afterlife. As the Indian Peace Commission noted in 1868, "They have not the Bible, but their religion, which we call superstition, teaches them that the Great Spirit made us all." Scholar Arthur Caswell Parker believed that "the Indian thirsted for a knowledge of God, though at times he but faintly apprehended the true God."[45]

As nineteenth-century Americans moved toward liberal and less dogmatic theologies, they were more prepared to find common cause with other faiths that extolled the basic principles of monotheism and human brotherhood. By the time his supposed words were published to a mass audience about 1840, Red Jacket had come to sound like an American prophet. In Longfellow's *Song of Hiawatha,* too, Indian religion is presented in a way that would be quite palatable to a New England Unitarian or Transcendentalist. There is a Great Spirit and, of course, a messianic expectation:

> I will send a Prophet to you,
> A Deliverer of the nations,
> Who shall guide you and shall teach you,
> Who shall toil and suffer with you.
> If you listen to his counsels,
> You will multiply and prosper;
> If his warnings pass unheeded,
> You will fade away and perish![46]

For present purposes, it does not matter whether Longfellow was accurately portraying the religion of the Iroquois or of Indians more generally. But at least some Americans saw Native peoples as already holding congenial beliefs, and resemblances were strengthened when words like "God," "Prophet," and "Messiah" were capitalized.[47]

This hopeful attitude shaped some early accounts of Native religions, in which clerical writers especially maximized anything they could plausibly read as a foreshadowing of Christianity. Describing Indian communities of the southeastern United States, William Bartram commented that "so far from idolatry are they that they have no images among them, nor any religious rite or ceremony that I could perceive; but adore the Great Spirit, the giver and taker away of the breath of life, with the most profound and respectful homage." The alleged refusal of Native peoples to worship idols was cited by those enthusiastic Christians who wanted to claim Indians as the lost children of Israel holding fast to their ancient Jewish roots. Even George Catlin, who had seen many Indian peoples at first hand, was prepared to consider theories of their Jewish origin: "The North American Indians are nowhere *idolaters*—they appeal at once to the Great Spirit, and know of no mediator, either personal or symbolical."[48]

Most often, this approach meant stressing evidence of Indian monotheism, and the idea that Native peoples exalted a Great Spirit, like the Lakota concept of Wakan Tanka. Arguing in 1922 for "the educational or moral value for boys and girls in reading the books about the American Indian," an educational theorist noted that "the Iroquois had one god, who was omnipotent, beneficent, and permeated the universe, and most of the tribes of North America held a belief in immortality and a heaven which they designated as the Happy Hunting Grounds. Also the mythology of various tribes contains legends of a Messiah." Indians offered good object lessons for white Protestant youngsters. In 1923, evangelical activist G. E. E. Lindquist claimed that:

> The religious instinct is of the very fiber of the race. The crude messianic beliefs prevalent among many Indian tribes responded readily to the teachings of the early missionaries, and the Indian of today continues to respond by outward and visible signs to the inward and spiritual grace bestowed upon him through increasing knowledge of the word of the "Great Spirit."

The Hopi "are sometimes called 'Natural Christians' from the fact that they are kind and hospitable and 'not soon angry.' "[49]

Once white Americans had helpfully identified what they felt was the real core of Indian religion, they were happy to weed out the childish and dangerous superstitions that had grown around the healthy plant. As Charles Burke, head of the Bureau of Indian Affairs, wrote in 1923, "The Indian's spirituality is nourished by traditions as ancient as his racial infancy. Many of these are as beautiful and as worthy of historic preservation as the finest fancies of classic mythology. Many may be retained and cherished in the Indian's cultural progress, but many are benighted and sometimes degrading." The noble goal was "to lead the Indian away from debasing conceptions which the loom of time has interwoven with the sacredest aspirations."[50] Once again, we can see parallels with anti-Catholic thought. Good Protestants held that the Catholic religion had at its core the same doctrine that they held, though distorted and polluted through the tolerance of superstitions and the cynical wiles of priests. Properly re-educated, Catholics might be persuaded to abolish their childish superstitions and accept full Christianity; and so might Indians.

The spiritual content of Native cultures was evaluated by the extent to which they stressed religion, defined in Protestant terms, as against ritualistic behavior, or superstition.[51] The pages of the *Missionary Review of the World* commonly describe Indian peoples who "have held constantly to their pagan rites and myths" or, at best, pursue "an esoteric system of religion." The seemingly liberal division between religion and superstition emerges repeatedly in clerical writings, such as the report of the American Indian Survey launched by missionary bodies in 1919. Among the Mescalero Apache, "Superstition and the old Indian religion still have a strong hold," while missionary efforts among the Papagos meant that "the old Indian religion and superstition consequently present no problem." Among the Hopis, "the outstanding form in which superstition expresses itself is of course in the dances, of which the most famous is the 'Snake Dance.' "[52]

Sometimes, the failure to see the religious content of Native cultures approaches the absurd. In 1888, the *New York Times* published a sympathetic account of the Navajos, whose lives, then and now, are profoundly shaped by religious beliefs. As far as the journalist could see, though, "They have little religious belief. Its exercise is the worship of a Great Spirit, whom they consider typified in the sun and the moon, and the performance of a few secret ceremonies that have been derived from the Zuñi Indians." As for the dances, ceremonies, and chants that dominate Navajo life, these were merely superstitious.[53]

Against Progress

While Indian rituals and ceremonies did no good, the harm they caused was evident. By far the commonest complaint was not that Native religion caused violence or immorality, but rather that it was an obstacle to social progress. Though U.S. Indian policy has gone through many changes of direction, the dominant belief in the late nineteenth and early twentieth centuries was that Native peoples needed to be assimilated quickly into the American nation, eliminating vestiges of the old tribal societies. Though modern observers have little sympathy for the assimilation policies, these were implemented because they seemed to be the only plausible way of preventing Indians from dying out as a race, or surviving in terminal squalor. Cultural genocide looked like the only alternative to literal extermination. From this perspective, Indian refusal to abandon their evil religions was a form of racial suicide.

Few whites doubted that Christianization was necessary and desirable, or regretted the loss of the old religions. In 1868, Indian Commissioner Nathaniel Taylor boasted that "certain tribes of our Indians have already emerged from a state of pagan barbarism, and are today . . . sitting under the vine and fig tree of an intelligent scriptural Christianity. . . . Medicine lodges and their orgies, and heathen offerings are mingling with the dust of a forgotten idolatry." From the 1860s, moreover, federal Indian policy entered a radical new phase. As Indians were being concentrated on reservations, the government moved toward much greater intervention in their cultural and religious life. President Grant sought to end the persistent warfare by a negotiated peace with the Western tribes, a solution that would also include increased conversion efforts. As the president hoped, "If you can make Quakers out of the Indians it will take the fight out of them. Let us have peace."[54]

Under Grant's Peace Policy, control of reservations was transferred from military officials to religious and missionary groups. Some of these, particularly the Quakers, worked hard on behalf of their charges, but missionary activism now intensified, inspired by a widespread national mood of evangelical enthusiasm. The destruction of Native religion and culture increasingly came to the forefront of federal policy. As Indian Commissioner Hiram Price argued in 1882, "If we expect to stop Sun Dances, snake worship, and other debasing forms of superstition and idolatry among Indians, we must teach them some better way."[55]

The key components of the "better way" were the new Indian schools, which took young people away from their tribal settings and taught them American ways and the English language—and Christianity. The Indian Industrial School at Carlisle, Pennsylvania, was founded in 1879, and within a decade, 150 more schools were modeled after this pattern. Religious conformity was a mainstay of this scheme, and the Protestant Home Mission Society used the boarding schools to promote their vision of Christianity. Likewise, communalism was to be replaced by American competitive individualism. This was the underlying principle of the Dawes Act of 1887, which broke up reservations and allocated the land to individuals and families. Indians were to become hardworking, self-sufficient farmers and artisans, and taught the appropriate work ethic. The policy would ultimately lead to economic catastrophe, and within a few decades, Indian nations would lose two-thirds of the lands they had held in 1887. At the time, though, the measure was heralded as the best opportunity for Indians to flourish in the modern world.[56]

Indian religions fitted into this worldview as the principal obstacles to assimilation, and thus to modernity, education, and progress. If Indians were to become farmers and mechanics, they simply could not afford to take lengthy periods of time away from their work for dances and pilgrimages. In addition, the ceremonies were powerful symbols of the old tribal order, which presented a powerful counterattraction for the young. The American Indian Survey of 1919 heard time and again about the social pressures exercised on modernized Indians, who were ostracized from their tribes if they refused to join the dances. The ceremonial life was the largest single force persuading Americanized Indians to "go back on the blanket."

Indian Offenses

Officially enforced religious uniformity now became a cornerstone of assimilation policy. As it did so, the rhetoric aimed at the old religions escalated, drawing freely on ancient charges of diabolism and immorality. In 1882, Interior Secretary Henry Moore Teller created Courts for Indian Offenses, which would suppress Native "savagery," including ceremonials and "old heathenish dances." Teller expressed outrage that "a few non-progressive degraded Indians are allowed to exhibit before the young and susceptible children all the debauchery, diabolism and savagery of the worst state of the Indian race." He wished to end "the demoralizing influence of heathenish rites," from which he singled out "the Sun-Dance, scalp dance, etc." These events were neither religious nor even social in nature, but were solely intended to excite aggression and "warlike passions." Native spiritual leaders, the medicine men, were denounced as the inevitable opponents of progress and education. But they were also attacked for their religious crimes as "impostors," "conjurers," who "[used] their conjurers' arts to prevent the people from abandoning their heathenish rites and customs."[57] Also stigmatized was the destruction of goods at funerals. In the same years, Canada likewise began a harsher repression of Native traditions, and in 1884 an anti-potlatch law tried to suppress a fundamental institution of the peoples of the western coast.[58]

We look in vain for significant public complaints against the repressive policies launched in the 1880s, for voices demanding Indian religious freedom. And public silence does not simply reflect callousness to Indian conditions, since pro-Indian activism already had a long and distinguished record. In the 1830s, Emerson had led protests against the forced removal of the civilized tribes, and another wave of activism coincided precisely with the new definition of "Indian Offenses" in the 1880s. It was in these very years that Helen Hunt Jackson's campaigns for Indian rights made her a national celebrity. The title of her 1881 book *A Century of Dishonor* epitomizes her condemnation of U.S. Indian policy, the treaty violations, the trail of broken promises over land rights, and the persistent official corruption. Her 1885 novel *Ramona,* a work often compared in its emotional impact to *Uncle Tom's Cabin,* denounced the maltreatment of California's Mission Indians. But like the earlier campaigns, Jackson focused on economic issues and, above all, land rights. Cultural issues rarely surfaced; religious rights never. Jackson never made a case for the defense of Indian rituals or religious practices. In *Ramona,* her Mission Indians are unquestionably Catholic, and the fact that they are more humbly Christian than their oppressors adds to the indictment of white society.[59]

One reason for the public silence was that the federal government was not issuing a religious code, but was merely suppressing "customs." And though it is no defense of the policy, Indians were not entirely being singled out in this policy. As construed at this time, religious liberty implied an unfettered right to believe, but not a right to act according to that belief. Jefferson himself had said that "the legislative powers of the government *reach actions only,* and not opinions." When, in 1878, the Supreme Court's decision in the *Reynolds* case prohibited Mormon polygamy, the justices ruled that "Congress was deprived of all legislative power over mere opinion, but was left free to reach actions which were in violation of social duties or subversive of good order."[60]

Hostility to Indian faiths was aggravated by the Ghost Dance affair. In 1892, new rules for the Courts of Indian Offenses prohibited participation in the "Sun Dance, scalp dance, war dance, or any other similar feast, so-called." Violators were to be punished by the withholding of rations, or imprisonment. Penalties were specified for the "practices of medicine men," namely "any who shall use any arts of a conjurer to prevent Indians from abandoning their barbarous rites and customs." Also banned were plural marriages or polygamy, and by the end of the century, reservation authorities were organizing

bonfires of sacred objects, of sacred pipes and spirit bundles. Even some ceremonies that were still permitted lost most of their traditional features. By 1903,
George Grinnell found that the Blackfoot medicine lodge ceremony had been
tamed to the point where it was "only a Fourth of July celebration."[61]

The Bureau of Indian Affairs (BIA) placed strict limitations on religious
practices, and not just potentially seditious outbreaks like the Ghost Dance. In
1902, Commissioner William Jones identified "a few customs among the Indians which . . . should be modified," among which he listed long hair, body
paint, native dress, dances, and feasts. Dress and hair were not "objectionable
in themselves," but constituted "a badge of servitude to savage ways and traditions which are effectual barriers to the uplifting of the race." But the festivals
and dances, which could spread over weeks, were anathema to BIA leaders.
The Court of Indian Offenses placed growing restrictions on Indian dances,
and they met remarkably little resistance. A few activists did protest. Sioux
writer Zitkala-Sa complained that "I would not like to say any graceful movement of the human figure in rhythm to music was ever barbaric," and that
banning Indian dances made sense only if all dancing were banned throughout the world. But the idea of suppressing the relics of paganism was echoed
by some "civilized" Indians themselves, the Christian and Americanized leaders who represented a growing faction on most reservations. In 1921, Christian
Lakota prohibited traditional dances at their Powwow.[62]

Still, complete suppression was difficult. As John Collier said, "To track
down the Navajo 'sings' in remote deserts, the Pueblo vigils and the rituals in
the inviolable kivas, and Seminole rituals in the deep Everglades, the solitary
keepers of visions on the Mojave desert, was a task beyond the government's
resources." The long-term solution to paganism was "to immolate the Indian children in boarding schools and there compel them to join Christian
churches." But the long-term prospects for cultural survival seemed grim. In
1910, an Assistant Commissioner of the BIA wrote of the Pueblos that:

> Regarding their ancient laws and customs, although in some respects ad-
> mirable, those which do not coincide with the national laws must in-
> evitably give way. To the older Indians, who cling to these customs, this
> may seem a hardship, at times bringing them into more or less conflict
> with the representatives of the Government. But these matters are being
> gradually adjusted with as much tact and diplomacy as is consistent with a
> positive attitude toward the situation. Thus the Office is confronted with
> conditions not altogether of its own making, and however desirable from

an aesthetic point of view it might be to maintain this quaint, old, semi-civilization in our midst, it is not altogether practicable.

As Charles F. Saunders remarked, reasonably enough, "This may be considered official notice that the death-warrant of Pueblo life has been signed." From the point of view of bureaucratic America, Indians were worse than dangerous; they were untidy.[63]

One devastating blow against Indian religions was unintentional, or at least incidental. Like most primal religions, Indian spirituality is generally rooted in a particular landscape, focused on *this* particular river, on *that* mountain. The more white America encroached on Indian lands, the more Indians were separated from their holy places, and in the second half of the century, an ever-larger share of the Native population was concentrated on reservations far removed from original homelands. Though the policy was designed for economic and military ends, it could not fail to have religious consequences. Once Indians were confined to reservations, U.S. officials did not want their Native charges to travel to traditional sacred places, since such wandering disrupted the hard-won social and political order. At the start of the century, Utes were forbidden to travel to their sacred site in Colorado, the Garden of the Gods, and when in 1912 the BIA relaxed its policy, it did so through consideration of white rather than Native interests. Permitting a tribal ceremony

> is intended to allay a great deal of dissatisfaction that exists among the Utes because of the opening of their reservation to settlement. The affair is promoted primarily for the purpose of drawing tourist travel to the Garden of the Gods in the interest of the Colorado boomers, but the Indians have no such idea. It is a very serious matter with them.[64]

By the 1920s, the assimilation policy reached new heights with serious proposals to eliminate most of the dances and ceremonials on which Indian religions were founded, which would have been a terminal blow to Native cultures as a whole. This proposal can be seen as a logical outcome of the sensationalism and misinterpretation that had long been the basis for official policies toward Indian spirituality. Given recent history, the move should have succeeded. Though the attack on Native dress and customs in 1902–1903 attracted some public criticism, mainly for its petty vindictiveness, the BIA had never encountered serious resistance in attacks on Native religion.

What is remarkable, though, is that in the 1920s, the government's scheme generated a ferocious public debate and the prohibition was defeated, permitting the dances to survive. By this point, powerful public constituencies were prepared not just to assert Indian religious freedom, but to defend those aspects of Indian culture that many would have dismissed as superstitious trappings. By this point, the authentically religious character of the rituals was taken for granted, while even the policy of Christianization was openly challenged. Together, these changes suggest a shift of attitudes toward Indian religion that was little short of revolutionary.

3

Discovering Native Religion
1860—1920

White people do not understand your songs nor know what your dances mean. . . . When they do, they will no longer try to destroy them, but will themselves want to see, and hear, and learn.

—Natalie Curtis

Before mainstream Americans could even think of Indian religious freedom, they had first to accept that what Indians were doing did in fact constitute a religion, and that was a slow process. At least since colonial days, we can find accurate and perceptive reports of Native cultures by observers who had no difficulty in applying the straightforward label of "religion." These accounts coexisted, though, with a large body of romanticized legend that failed to see Native ways as worthy of that name. Indian rituals became a kind of children's play, their myths and stories no more than fairy tales. Could the noble label of "religion" be assigned to activities that so violated morality and common sense as defined by Euro-Americans? If Indians did have religions, did these really include the despised superstitions that so irritated U.S. authorities? However naïve these questions seem in hindsight, they ignited real debate at the time.

During the late nineteenth century, Western attitudes to primal cultures were transformed. Based on firsthand observation, a new generation of anthropologists and ethnographers began to appreciate the complexities and the cultural wealth of Native cultures, and to make their religious life much better known to mainstream America. In doing so, they also eroded the traditional

distinctions between "high" cultures and religions, like Western Christianity, and the ways of Native peoples, presenting both as adaptations to particular environments. At a time when American elites were beginning to
ask troubling questions about the values of their own civilization and the
unique truths of orthodox Christianity, the new study of the continent's
own "primitives" made available alternative worldviews that were intriguing, even attractive.

Children's Tales

Even in the nineteenth century, not all white observers were obsessed with
visions of tomahawks and sacrificial altars, but even those sympathetic to
Native religion interpreted Indian stories and beliefs strictly according to
their own cultural perceptions. Natives might not actually have a religion
worthy of the name, but they did have charming myths and fairy stories that
deserved to be explored according to the values of European Romanticism.
And while they might be amusing, even moving, these simple tales clearly
did not belong in the same category as the noble narratives of the Bible.
Western scholars had an uncompromising belief in the superiority of literate
over oral cultures, and the fact that Indian "tales" were not written texts condemned them to the intellectual nursery.

This approach meshed well with contemporary scientific theories, which
similarly consigned primitive peoples to a kind of racial childhood. Several
anthropological schools competed during the nineteenth century, divided
partly by how they explained the world's primitive and "savage" races. One
view, that of polygenesis, suggested that different human groups in fact had
separate origins, so that primitive peoples were only loosely related to the
higher races. Indians might thus be, literally, animalistic. Others accepted a
common human origin, but believed that different races stood at different
developmental stages, corresponding roughly to phases of human growth.
This was the view of Lewis Henry Morgan, the "father of American anthropology," whose book *Ancient Society* (1877) told the story of "Human
Progress from Savagery through Barbarism to Civilization." Higher races
were adult and mature; lesser breeds were children. The difference of approach had far-reaching policy consequences, since the developmental view
implied that Indians could and should progress toward civilization. Those
who held the separate origin theory rejected this prospect.[1]

But in either case, whether Indians were children or quasi-animals, they stood at a much lower stage of human development, with an appropriate taste for myths, folktales and fairy stories. E. B. Tylor's influential *Primitive Culture* (1871) saw myths corresponding to lower stages of intellectual development, so that mythic animism was the preserve of primitive and doomed races. As Spencer Trotter wrote in 1910, "The gift of the mythopoeic faculty belongs to childhood—individual and racial." Religion was for grown-ups; folktales and fairy stories were for children. "So as we love Aesop and Uncle Remus, the Odyssey and the Celtic tales, so we love these folk stories of aboriginal America." Writing a survey of missionary accomplishments in 1914, Thomas Moffett remarked that the "impressive characteristic" of the Indian "is his childishness—in his simplicity, his vanity, his sensitiveness to ridicule, and his instinct for the supernatural. . . . The Indian is like a child in his mirthfulness."[2]

Indian customs had analogies to European religion and culture, but only to the lowest levels of that tradition: to magic rather than true religion. Already in the eighteenth century, German settlers appropriated the Algonquin word "pow-wow," which originally signified a medicine man, to describe their own traditional forms of folk magic, that is, of "low" religion. Pennsylvania Dutch pow-wowing survives to this day. Timothy Dwight scorned the "infidel" so absurd and relativistic that he would dare place Christian worship on a par with "the Indian's pow-wows." Indian spiritual leaders were described by names suggesting magical skills, like conjurers or jugglers.[3]

The best-known Victorian interpreter of Indian cultures was Henry Rowe Schoolcraft, who published heavily sentimentalized versions of Native tales, including the legend of Hiawatha. Titles such as *The Enchanted Moccasins* reflect the romantic and fairy-tale quality of his work, and that of his many imitators. Still, Schoolcraft was widely read, and his work shaped local white folklore around the nation. By the 1920s, folklorist Stith Thompson complained that through Schoolcraft's baneful influence, "all sections of the country have acquired legends of 'lovers' leaps.' "[4] Schoolcraft's followers included Henry Shoemaker, Pennsylvania's official State Folklorist, who generated reams of spurious folktales of Indian princesses, haunted stones, evil medicine men, and proud chieftains. As a sample of the havoc he wrought on Indian legend, we might take Pennsylvania's Mount Nittany, today the unofficial shrine of Pennsylvania State University, and of its football tradition. According to Shoemaker, the name commemorates the Lenni-Lenape princess Nita-Nee, who carried on a love affair with a Huguenot traveler.

Ultimately, the princess's seven brothers drowned the white interloper, though at the site of the murder, one can still hear the wind whisper "Nita-Nee!" That is one version of the source of the mountain's name, but the whole story was apparently a pure invention of Shoemaker's, part of his voluminous "fakelore." In fact, the word Nittany probably means "lone mountain."[5]

Harmless as these invented tales seem in their own right, they had a damaging effect on the reception of actual Native myths. Readers preferred the stories that most resembled children's tales, so that stories like those of Coyote were treated as "folklore myths" as opposed to genuine expressions of religion. The word most commonly used to describe such tales is "charming," the benevolent version of the "weird" usually applied to Indian ceremonies.[6] This supercilious attitude affected the serious academic studies that were appearing in such numbers from the 1880s: the *Journal of American Folklore* was founded in 1888. Though the new ethnographic studies were often of the highest quality, the folklore label was not flattering. Detailed descriptions of Indian beliefs and rituals were placed alongside accounts of low or folk religion, like the healing customs or witch beliefs of the Pennsylvania Dutch, rather than in the context of literate high religion. Even at that time, this discourtesy would not have been extended to (say) Buddhist rituals, which were seen as authentically religious. After all, they were written down at great length, and in archaic languages.

When John Wesley Powell wrote the laudatory introduction to Frank Cushing's *Zuñi Folk Tales* (1901), the condescending language he used suggested that folklore material had few claims on the attention of any serious scholar. "The folk-tales collected by Mr. Cushing constitute a charming exhibit of the wisdom of the Zuñis as they believe, though it may be but a charming exhibit of the follies of the Zuñis as we believe." The whole genre of folklore seemed suspect: "Mythology is the term used to designate the superstitions of the ancients. Folk-lore is the term used to designate the superstitions of the ignorant of today. . . . Folk-lore is a discredited mythology— a mythology once held as a philosophy."[7]

Even the great anthropologists of the day were cautious about applying the label of religion to what they were witnessing. When Jesse Fewkes, one of the founders of southwestern archaeology, described the Hopi Kachina dances, he wrote, "It is commonly agreed that these performances are religious—giving to the adjective 'religious' a meaning which would include primitive expressions of a religious sentiment."[8] The word "performance," though strictly accurate, is mildly dismissive in its suggestion of theatricality.

However strong their dramatic content, one does not usually speak of a Christian Eucharist or a Jewish Seder as a "performance."

Travelers

Throughout American history, we find white travelers who encountered Indians, in some cases knew them well, and who were sufficiently unfamiliar with scholarly quibbles to speak freely of Indian "religion." What changed during the nineteenth century is that, increasingly, such direct encounters became the basis for a large and widely read scientific literature. Ethnography made respectable the idea of Indian religion.

While many writers applied their own prejudices toward Native religions, some white Americans tried, as far as possible, to understand these faiths on their own terms. In the earliest days of the English encounter with the New World, John Smith wrote in 1612 of Virginia's Indians and "Of their Religion." He believed that "there is yet in Virginia no place discovered to be so savage in which the savages have not a religion, deer, and bow and arrows." Other observers were at least prepared to grant that Indians had a religious system, however contemptible they considered it. Describing Virginia in 1720, Robert Beverley denied having explored "all the mysteries of the Indian religion," but at least he recognized it as religion. He had visited "their *quioccosan* (which is their house of religious worship)." Lewis and Clark would describe "the religion of the Mandans," among other nations.[9]

Some travelers and historians wrote accurate accounts, based on personal observation, which counterbalanced the Schoolcraft approach to Native cultures. They offered serious, if unsentimental, portraits of Indian religious life. In the 1830s George Catlin met and described many Plains Indian peoples in rich ethnographic accounts that in some cases proved to be the epitaphs of tribes that would soon become extinct. Naturally, he was fascinated by the rituals he witnessed among peoples such as the Mandans, and like Beverley, he was prepared to apply the term "religion" to these ceremonies. He expresses revulsion at many Native rituals, especially those involving self-torture or mutilation. The most disturbing was an alarming variant of the Sun Dance, in which young men pierced their flesh with skewers, and were then suspended by ropes. These were "ignorant and barbarous and disgusting customs . . . truly shocking to behold," and "the cruelties of these scenes are frightful and abhorrent in the extreme."[10] The account (richly illustrated) is so disturbing that it probably could not have appeared in a book published much later in the century, when sensibilities had become stricter.

But a religion it was. Despite all these "horrid and sickening cruelties," Catlin believed that "all of the Indian tribes . . . are religious—are worship-ful—and many of them go to incredible lengths . . . in worshipping the Great Spirit; denying and humbling themselves before Him for the same purpose, and in the same hope as we do, perhaps in a more rational and ac-ceptable way. . . . They worship with great sincerity, and all according to one creed." In a Mandan village he saw an open space, set apart for their "annual religious ceremonies": "In the middle of this circle stands an object of great religious veneration, as I am told, on account of the importance it has in the conduction of those annual religious rites." Nearby stands a medicine lodge, in which "these wonderful ceremonies" take place.[11]

Another widely read author was Francis Parkman, whose 1867 study, *The Jesuits of North America in the Seventeenth Century*, presented one of the first systematic descriptions of Indian religions free of the popular misreadings of the day. Though by later standards his accounts are contemptuous of Indian cultures, they matter because he was trying to describe an objective truth rather than a Romantic ideal. Parkman was writing as a skilled historian, thoroughly versed in the documents and familiar with the critical standards of the day. He had an intimate grasp of the accounts of Iroquois and Algo-nquin religion compiled over the previous two centuries, and also had the benefit of direct encounters with Indian societies, both in New England and the West. His writings, together with Catlin's, represent a fair picture of what mainstream America actually knew about Indian spiritual life before the great expansion of anthropological fieldwork from the 1870s onwards.

After all the popular interpretations of his time, Parkman's myth-busting is refreshing. Schoolcraft's work he described as "a singularly crude and illit-erate production, stuffed with blunders and contradictions, . . . taxing to the utmost the patience of those who would extract what is valuable in it from its oceans of pedantic verbiage." He dismissed the idea of the Noble Savage and scoffed at the idea of the Indian as a natural Christian merely awaiting a New England missionary to perfect his faith. "Romance, Poetry, and Rhetoric point, on the one hand, to the august conception of one all-ruling Deity, a Great Spirit, omniscient and omnipresent; and we are called to ad-mire the untutored intellect which could conceive a thought too vast for Socrates and Plato." This, he believed, was grossly exaggerated. "The primi-tive Indian, yielding his untutored homage to One All-pervading and Om-

nipotent Spirit, is a dream of poets, rhetoricians, and sentimentalists."
White observers who produced this optimistic image were basing their impressions "upon savages who had been for generations in contact, immediate
or otherwise, with the doctrines of Christianity. Many observers have interpreted the religious ideas of the Indians after preconceived ideas of their
own; and it may safely be affirmed that an Indian will respond with a grunt
of acquiescence to any question whatever touching his spiritual state."[12]

Yet for all his tirades against Native ceremonial life, Parkman wrote
knowledgeably of the major principles common to Native traditions. He explained the idea of animism, and the thin boundaries separating the human
and natural worlds:

> To the Indian, the material world is sentient and intelligent. Birds, beasts,
> and reptiles have ears for human prayers, and are endowed with an infl-
> uence on human destiny. . . . Through all the works of Nature or of man,
> nothing exists, however seemingly trivial, that may not be endowed with a
> secret power for blessing or for bane. Men and animals are closely akin.

The supernatural world easily broke through into ordinary human affairs:
"dreams were to the Indian a universal oracle." Parkman knew the hierarchy
of spiritual professionals, the "sorcerers, medicine-men, and diviners," with
which an Indian village "swarmed."

He also described the various levels of spiritual beings, from the exalted
creator gods that had excited such interest among Christian writers, to the
ordinary guardian spirits whose power could be accessed through the Vision
Quest:

> Each primitive Indian has his guardian manitou, to whom he looks for
> counsel, guidance, and protection. . . . At the age of fourteen or fifteen,
> the Indian boy blackens his face, retires to some solitary place, and re-
> mains for days without food. Superstitious expectancy and the exhaustion
> of abstinence rarely fail of their results. His sleep is haunted by visions,
> and the form which first or most often appears is that of his guardian
> manitou—a beast, a bird, a fish, a serpent, or some other object, animate
> or inanimate.[13]

For all its scorn of the primitive, Parkman's account was a magnificent
survey of the literature then available about Indian religion. Admittedly, it

was not the sort of account that would drive people to imitate that religion. Reading his account of the Vision Quest or the guardian manitou, thousands of young white Bostonians would not be seeking guides or gurus who could give them a comparable experience. But at least reading Parkman, the mainstream audience knew that Indian religion was a religious system, however alien, with its own distinctive values and beliefs, not rooted in European soil.

Ethnographers

Shortly after the appearance of Parkman's book, the amount and quality of information available increased enormously, as a new wave of observers and seekers ventured into Indian societies, collecting materials about what most believed to be cultures on the verge of extinction. The last quarter of the nineteenth century was a golden age for ethnographic observation and writing by some of the great founders of American anthropology, who observed and collected stories, rituals, and myths. The new anthropology aspired to scientific rigor, demanding firsthand ethnographic observation that was both objective and thoroughly recorded. This was the age of distinguished academics like Jesse Fewkes and Franz Boas, but also skilled amateur observers, such as army officers Washington Matthews, who described the Navajo, and John G. Bourke, who wrote extensively about the Apache. There were also intrepid travelers like Frank Cushing, Alice Fletcher and Walter McClintock.[14] The sheer volume of available material about American Indians ballooned. The ethnological collection of the Smithsonian Institution grew from 550 items in 1860 to over 13,000 by 1873, and activity accelerated during the 1870s and 1880s. By 1877, Smithsonian Secretary Joseph Henry remarked that "anthropology is at present the most popular branch of science."[15]

The new anthropology had a strong institutional foundation. Anthropological research was supported by several universities and museums, including the Smithsonian (founded 1846), the Peabody Museum at Harvard (1866), New York's American Museum of Natural History (1869), the University of Pennsylvania Museum (1887), and the Field Museum in Chicago (1893). Also critical were private organizations like the American Ethnological Society and the American Folklore Society. By the 1880s, the research universities established graduate programs in anthropology, with students eagerly seeking out innovative projects.[16]

One outlet for the new research was the annual reports of the Bureau of American Ethnology, under the leadership of John Wesley Powell. In 1879, the bureau commissioned a daring expedition to Zuñi, "the first federally funded experiment in professional anthropology."[17] From 1881, the Bureau's reports offered space to researchers, both amateur and professional, who often reported on religious and spiritual matters. In the first decade or so, annual reports included such classic pieces as Powell's study on the mythology of the North American Indians; Frank Cushing's work on Zuñi fetishes and creation myths; Washington Matthews's translation of the Navajo Mountain Chant ritual; James Mooney's "Sacred Formulas of the Cherokees" and his monumental study of the Ghost Dance movement; John G. Bourke's "The Medicine-Men of the Apache"; and Jesse Fewkes's account of the Tusayan snake ceremonies. That was in addition to the early writings of Franz Boas on the culture and religion of the Inuit/Eskimo. Often, too, these writings would appear in more popular form in magazines or books. Cushing's "My Adventures in Zuñi" was serialized in the magazine *Century*.[18]

Apart from collecting and spreading information, the existence of an anthropological profession created an organized constituency with a vested interest in the preservation of Native cultures. Particular individuals may not have sympathized with Native peoples, and on occasion wrote derogatory words about their subjects, while other observers were far more sensitive and considerate. But in general the anthropologists, with their institutional roots in museums and universities, made up a powerful and articulate voice that counterbalanced the clergy and missionaries. Some individuals—James Mooney, Frederick W. Hodge, Edgar L. Hewett—worked heroically to defend Native religions and rituals against official attack.

Learning Religion

Anyone interested in the realities of Native religion and spirituality now had access to an enormous wealth of first-rate scholarship describing Native cultures from all parts of North America. Also, this material was now richly illustrated, due to advances in photography and the cinema. Between 1907 and 1930, the twenty magnificent volumes of Edward Curtis's *The North American Indian* appeared. In 1914 his documentary film *In the Land of the War Canoes* featured stunningly evocative footage of the shamanism of the Kwakiutl of the Northwest Coast.[19]

Much of the popular anthropological interest was unabashedly sensational: *In the Land of the War Canoes* was originally titled *In the Land of the Headhunters*. But whatever its origins, the new scholarship revolutionized attitudes toward Indian religions. John Wesley Powell wrote that "The primitive religion of every Amerindian tribe is an organized system of inducing the ancients to take part in the affairs of men, and the worship of the gods is a system designed to please the gods, that they may be induced to act for men, particularly the tribe of men who are the worshipers." Scholars still argued about the definition of "religion," given all the possible variants of belief and practice, but Powell's attempt was convincing.[20]

The religious quality of dances and related activities now became commonplace. In 1900, Walter McClintock's "Four Days in a Medicine Lodge," described the Sun Dance, with its self-torture and mutilation. Though McClintock had no difficulty with the principle of suppressing this "barbarous and revolting custom," he still knew he was describing a religious event:

> It is not, as commonly supposed, a mere festal dance, it is the most important of all religious ceremonies, the occasion when the tribe assembles—some to fulfill their vows to the sun, some to fast and pray, and some to find the diversions and social enjoyments which, the world over, are associated with large gatherings of people.

The much-abused term "medicine," so common in Native cultures, was clearly religious, referring as it did to "that which is mysterious or supernatural."[21]

Along with "medicine," medicine men were now treated more seriously. From the mid-nineteenth century, observers described these individuals by the Siberian term "shaman," and the two types were seen as synonymous. This identification was misleading, in that the common term ignored regional and tribal differences between religious leaders across North America, while North American "shamans" differed from the precise pattern well known from Siberia. Modern-day Native activists object to using the all-purpose term "shamanism" in the North American context. But in the nineteenth century, speaking of shamans marked real progress from the older analogy of the medicine man as deceptive Catholic priest. It established Native religion in a global context, appropriate to a particular stage of human development.[22]

The concept of shamanism forced ethnographers to explore more accurately what medicine men actually did, and in the process they found that these practitioners commanded impressive skills. In 1894, Washington Matthews wrote that "the accomplished Navajo shaman must be a man of superior memory and of great intellectual industry." John G. Bourke agreed. The medicine man was:

> not the fraud and charlatan many people affect to consider him; he is indeed the repository of all the lore of the savage, the possessor of knowledge, not of the present world alone, but of the world to come as well. At any moment he can commune with the spirits of the departed; he can turn himself into any animal at will; all diseases are subject to his incantations; to him the enemy must yield on the warpath; without the potent aid of his drum and rattle and song no hunt is undertaken; from the cradle to the grave the destinies of the tribe are subject to his whim.

Bourke knew that the medicine men were critical to tribal religion. They were so central, in fact, that they must be discredited, if necessary by deploying white professional conjurers and stage magicians, who could out-perform their spectacular tricks. However dubiously medicine men were regarded, they were now more closely studied and their religious system much better understood. In 1904, a startling exhibition at the American Museum of Natural History collected shamanistic materials from Asia as well as North and South America, in order to portray Shamanism (capitalized) as an archaic global faith. Reporting the exhibition, the *New York Times*'s headline read "ANCIENT RELIGION OF SHAMANISM FLOURISHING TODAY," the article remarking that the tradition was much older than Judaism. "It is perhaps the only remaining and enduring type of culture extending from the remotest, probably from Paleolithic, times, to date."[23]

Another commonplace of the new anthropology was the recognition that Indian peoples did not observe the Western dichotomy between secular and religious. For them, religious concepts and behavior were pervasive. In 1907, photographer Frederick Monsen reported, typically, that "every act of the daily life of these primitive desert people has some religious significance." In 1917, even a writer in *Missionary Review* wrote simply that "the Hopi Indians are very religious. . . . In connection with almost everything they do, whether work or play, there is something of religious significance."[24]

Relativism

For many modern historians, the anthropologists of this era have a suspect reputation, with their attempts to direct a superior Western gaze toward "lesser breeds." The whole enterprise has worrying colonialist connotations. Yet despite this, the cornucopia of new information demanded new theoretical models, which challenged older assumptions of automatic Western cultural superiority. And in sensitizing the American public to Native religious practices, the ethnographers quite plausibly did save those practices from destruction.

By the end of the century, Franz Boas was the main advocate of new models of cultural relativism, arguing that cultures took the shape they did because they were adapted to a particular environment, a particular social and geographical setting. This idea challenged the earlier Victorian view that different cultures represented evolutionary stages through which each society had to pass. In the new framework, Indian cultures were viewed as organic, deserving intensive study in their own right. They were much more than curious fossils of the supposed childhood of the race. Relativistic ideas affected the academic study of religions, which were seen as cultural and psychological artifacts, so that Christianity and other Western religions were not treated as uniquely privileged divine revelations.[25]

Like other cultural patterns, religions emerged and evolved, and what Indian peoples were practicing today might correspond with stages of the "higher" religions. One advanced use of this approach came in James Mooney's analysis of the Ghost Dance movement, which was undertaken at the very same time that Charles Briggs was applying historical and critical method to the Christian scriptures. Mooney similarly drew parallels between Native ways and the Judeo-Christian tradition. For an audience accustomed to thinking of Indian rituals as primitive or fanatical, Mooney placed the recent movement in a surprising anthropological context. The Ghost Dance was "the inspiration of a dream. Its ritual is the dance, the ecstasy and the trance. Its priests are hypnotics and cataleptics." Therefore, it differed little from "every great religious development of which we have knowledge from the beginning of history."[26]

Mooney consistently compared Indian religions to the Judeo-Christian tradition as it had existed at comparable stages of social development. After recounting the story of Abraham and the sacrifice of Isaac, he comments, "So Black Coyote is commanded to sacrifice himself for the sake of his children."

If Indian shamans and prophets were led by dreams, visions, and trances, so were the apostles described in the New Testament. Seeking parallels to Wovoka, the Ghost Dance Messiah, Mooney invokes direct comparisons with Jesus:

> In the Transfiguration on the mountain when "his face did shine as the sun" and in the agony of Gethsemane, with its mental anguish and bloody sweat, we see the same phenomena that appear in the lives of religious enthusiasts from Mohammed and Joan of Arc down to George Fox and the prophets of the Ghost Dance.[27]

If the Ghost Dancers appeared fanatical, so did modern European movements such as Methodists, Shakers, and Adventists. In the new anthropological perspective, European cultures were not unique, and neither were their religions. Nor were they necessarily superior.

While anthropologists were presenting pagan religions as "higher," more complex and more authentically religious, scholars like Mooney saw Christianity as less distinctive, even more "tribal." Mooney's application of psychological methods across cultural and religious traditions foreshadows the better-known work of William James in his *Varieties of Religious Experience*, which appeared in 1902. For both scholars, religious behavior reflected psychological impulses, which manifested in different ways according to cultural opportunities and limitations.

Scriptures

Other scholarly work in these years tended to lower the walls that had once divided higher and lower religions. Particularly important was the new awareness of Native American religious texts. In that era, the existence of significant scriptures was commonly taken as one of the characteristics of a major religion, evidence of sophisticated thought. However Europeans might despise Hindu rituals or shy away from India's erotic temple sculptures, they could not deny the existence of awe-inspiring texts such as the *Vedas* and *Upanishads*. Mesoamerican cultures also produced evidence of "high" textual religion. Through the 1880s, Daniel G. Brinton was publishing his multivolume "Library of Aboriginal American Literature." In fact, the literature included both ancient written texts and more recent collections of legends and poetry. Works in the series included *The Maya Chronicles, The Iroquois Book of Rites, A Migration Legend of the Creek Indians*, and *Ancient Nahuatl Poetry*. In 1890 a translation of "Sacred Songs of the Ancient Mexicans" appeared under the title *Rig Veda Americanus*, "after the similar cyclus of sacred hymns, which are the most venerable product of the Aryan mind." For a late Victorian author, this was the supreme praise: classical Mesoamerican civilization was indisputably advanced, socially and spiritually. In 1908, Lewis Spence published an English translation of the *Popol Vuh*, commonly termed the Mayan Bible.[28]

Initially, studies of North American Indians did not produce formal scriptures. The best early candidate for Native scriptures was the *Book of Mormon*, reputedly discovered in the 1820s, but whatever its claims to spiritual truth, few scholars were convinced by its authenticity as sober history. Also available was the *Walam Olum*, an equally controversial collection of supposedly ancient migration legends, which Brinton presented under the title *The Lenâpé and Their Legends*.[29] The new ethnographers could not unearth troves of ancient Indian ritual texts, since none existed in written form, but they did record and translate substantial bodies of oral material, which had a real impact. Matthews's translation of the Navajo Mountain Chant was a substantial work, and it revealed an aesthetic sense that deeply impressed contemporary Americans:

> Make beautiful all that is before me
> Make beautiful all that is behind me
> Make beautiful my words
> It is done in beauty
> It is done in beauty.[30]

Also widely cited was Alice Fletcher's account of ceremonies and chants of the Plains Indians. Through Fletcher's writings, mainstream readers now had access to detailed translations of ceremonies like the White Buffalo Festival of the Uncpapas, the Elk Mystery or Ghost Lodge of the Oglalas, or the Ceremony of the Four Winds of the Santee Sioux.[31]

By the early twentieth century, collections of Native and Native-inspired poetry were appearing, far truer to the original than those of Schoolcraft and his peers. In 1900 Andrew Lang wrote that "it would not be a profitable, but it would be a pleasant task for some American man or woman of letters to give us an anthology of Red Indian poetry and prose." In fact, the venture turned out to be quite profitable. Among the most read books in the genre was George Cronyn's anthology of Indian poems and chants, *The Path on the Rainbow* (1918), which popularized translations by Matthews, Mooney, Boas, and others. In 1920 Amy Lowell published a collection of Pueblo songs in *The Dial*, the modernist literary journal. Mary Austin's *American Rhythm* (1923) included both Native songs, and poems inspired by them.[32]

This literature was critical in terms of contemporary cultural and racial theory. Before the 1870s, Americans were prone to dismiss Indians as low in the evolutionary scale, since they lacked most aspects of civilization. Over the next half-century, though, it was easy to combat suggestions that Native peoples lacked cultural achievements. If Indians were not producing great written literature, they were on a par with venerated epic civilizations of the European past. As Mary Austin claimed, "From the Zuñi Creation Myth with its sustained narrative style to the Homeric Epic is but one poetic bound." The Zuñi myth was "the most superior literary form attained by any living primitive group, ranking second only to Homer, and superior to the Book of Genesis." In 1923 Alfred Riggs argued that "some of the finest examples of aboriginal literature extant are these ceremonial prayers of the red man. . . . One has only to read prayers of the Iroquois, of the Pawnee or of the Navajo to discover the real depth of the Indian's religious life." Ethnologist John Peabody Harrington boasted that "there is no purer literature in the world than that of Taos; there is no literature in the world that is more poetic than that of Taos."[33] That view represents a giant leap from enchanted moccasins.

The more Indians were allowed to speak in their own words, the more impressive their rituals appeared. "With this knowledge the dances and rites of these people no longer appear heathen and idolatrous but rather poetic and symbolical." Armed with these texts, a new wave of scholars and activists asserted that Native beliefs were not only clearly religious, but that they contained great truths. As Alice Fletcher wrote in 1920, "At last he stands forth in his manhood as one who has reverently thought and has formulated concepts which appear to be basic to his religious life."[34]

The new scholars did not consider themselves gullible enough to credit the old dream that Indians had foreshadowed the truths of Christianity. But, ever optimistic about finding universal truths among primitive peoples, some did assert that Indians had received a glimmer, or more than a glimmer, of the progressive truths expounded by leading thinkers of contemporary America, and even of German philosophy. Writing of the idea of

Wakonda, the Great Spirit of the Osage people, composer Arthur Farwell wrote in 1904, "It is more than worthy of note—it is of the deepest interest—to recognize the coincidence of this fundamental cosmic power of the Indian with the homogeneous Will in Nature pointed out by Schopenhauer, the *Ding an Sich* of Kant."[35] This romantic optimism exactly parallels the old idea of Indians as proto-Christians.

Lost Cities

New discoveries made Indian societies look far more complex than they ever had in the past, more aesthetically accomplished, and more a civilization in their own right. Indian spiritual practices looked less like the childish graspings of the primitive and more like a complex system—even, arguably, the vestiges of a great lost society of ancient cities and temples.

Evidence that Native peoples had achieved a high civilization was familiar from the great cities of Mexico. Prescott's books, which popularized ideas of human sacrifice, also reminded nineteenth-century Americans that these practices had occurred within the context of a great classic civilization. Just as influential was contemporary travel literature, such as John Lloyd Stephens's sumptuously illustrated *Incidents of Travel in Central America* (1841). Accounts of Maya and Aztec cities aroused expectations about the archaeological treasures that might exist on U.S. soil. Americans had long been used to finding ancient remains on their territory, at least since the discoveries of the mound complexes of Ohio and the Mississippi Valley, but these were long regarded as unworthy of preservation. The horrendous decades-long assault on Ohio's ancient Native landscape—through plowing and development—was only slowed in the 1880s, when a successful public campaign saved the great Serpent Mound. This event symbolized an awakening recognition of Native cultural accomplishments.[36]

The new awareness received a massive boost when the imposing sites of the Southwest reached public attention. In the mid-1870s, the *New York Tribune* published the sensational reports of Ernest Ingersoll, who accompanied the expedition that explored Anasazi ruins like Mancos Canyon. In addition to their scholarly potential, such sites offered enormous romantic appeal. Ingersoll's stories singled out the more spectacular ruins "particularly accessible to the ordinary tourist." With the tale of its accidental discovery by ranchers, the finding of the Cliff Palace at Mesa Verde (1888) combined the romance of lost ancient cities with the contemporary mythology of the Wild West. Over the next quarter century, the reports of the Bureau of Ethnology reflect the dramatic wave of archaeological findings from sites such as Canyon de Chelly and Mesa Verde. Keet Seel was discovered in 1895. In 1896, excavations began at Chaco Canyon.[37]

Southwestern archaeology soon came of age as a distinct discipline with professional scholars and scientific techniques, which were applied to subjects no less important than the great societies of the Middle East. In 1906, the Preservation of American Antiquities Act defended archaeological treasures from looting, and Mesa Verde became a National Park. The following year, a School of American Archaeology was founded through the efforts of Alice Fletcher and Edgar Lee Hewett.[38] Public interest in these ancient landscapes was reflected in news stories and fictional accounts, from novels like Adolph Bandelier's *The Delight Makers* through Zane Grey's best-selling *Riders of the Purple Sage* and Willa Cather's *The Professor's House.* Already by 1893, the fascination with romantic remains was familiar enough to be parodied in Henry Blake Fuller's *The Cliff-Dwellers*, in which modern-day Chicago streets and tenements serve as the "cliffs."[39]

The awe-inspiring archaeological finds gave a new dimension to the observations of contemporary Native societies and religions, suggesting that these represented deep-rooted civilizations. Though there were doubts about the exact connections between modern Natives and the ancient inhabitants, the evidence of continuity was strong, and is explicitly stated in *The Delight Makers.* By 1896, Charles F. Lummis could write, overconfidently, "that the Cliff- or Cave Dwellers were Pueblos and not some lost race is so absolutely established in science now that only the unread continue the old ignorance."[40] The mainstream public was now prepared to accept evidence of past Indian civilizations in a way it had not been in the time when the great mound communities of the Midwest were attributed to Hebrew and other foreign explorers. (Even as far north as Wisconsin, wandering Aztecs were invoked to explain the mound complex that was baptized "Aztalan"). By the 1920s, the media reported the finding of an alleged ancient city in Nebraska that might at its height have had a million inhabitants. The population estimate was grossly exaggerated, but the fact that it was given credence suggests how far views of America's own Indians had come in a few decades. Awe at Native civilizations was reinforced by continuing discoveries of great Maya cities in Central America, which made headlines through the 1930s.[41]

But the lost cities of the southwest offered a very different appeal from the great monuments of Mexico and Guatemala, with their temples and pyramids. For writers such as Grey and Cather, modern Westerners visiting sites like Mesa Verde were seeing the remains of true cities with domestic hearths and family homes. The ancients left pottery and weaving, not mausoleums and citadels. *The Delight Makers* tried to recreate the proto-Pueblo society of a thousand years ago, with sympathetic and recognizable characters, including some strikingly independent women. The lost city of *Riders of the Purple Sage* is Edenic, a place where the hero and heroine take refuge from the barbarities and violence of American civilization. "They," the cliff-dwellers, were just like us, civilized families living in stable settlements, not semi-human primitives.

Logically enough, then, Native religious belief and practice should have been comprehensible in modern terms. These discoveries inspired a new respect for the religious practices of modern Indians, especially the descendants of the Anasazi. Describing Taos in 1903, travel writer James LeRoy wrote of their "old feasts, dances and rites that were hoary with custom's firm sanction when our kind still was living in feudalism's bond."[42] This was a positive and helpful message in the years immediately following the Ghost Dance movement and the Wounded Knee massacre, when white hostility to Native culture reached unprecedented heights (*The Delight Makers* appeared in the dreadful year of 1890). Romantic stories from the "mysterious Southwest" helped counter-balance the negative news items so prevalent in the media of these years, the tales of witch-killing and blood sacrifice.

Exploring the ruins of these lost cities, reading the texts of the rituals, it now seemed obvious that Indian societies had authentic religions, and that these might be great spiritual systems in their own right, however unfamiliar their assumptions. Perhaps they were not inferior to modern creeds like Hinduism or Buddhism, or even Christianity itself. At a time of growing interest in Asian religions, and of the surging enthusiasm for America's own occult and esoteric movements, this was an exciting prospect. Amazing as it might have seemed in the aftermath of Wounded Knee, Indian matters and, specifically, Indian spirituality, were about to become popular and even fashionable.

4

Pilgrims from the Vacuum
1890–1920

To know the spirit of the Indians of the United States is to know another world. It is to pass beyond the Cartesian age, beyond the Christian age, beyond the Aristotelian age, beyond all the dichotomies we know, and into the age of wonder, the age of the dawn man.

—John Collier

Americans read about the exotic Indian cultures of the West and Southwest, and they could see photographs, but critically, from the end of the nineteenth century, they were also likely to travel to these regions themselves. Tourism and travel fostered an enthusiastic interest in Indian life, and focused on religious, ritual, and ceremonial aspects of those cultures. Since travelers were most likely to encounter the elaborate cultures of the Southwest, those glamorous rituals came to symbolize Indian religion for the white audience. Seeing southwestern religion as a microcosm of the Native experience as a whole was multiply misleading, but the long-term political effects were beneficial. The more white travelers knew and enjoyed their contacts with Pueblos or Navajos, the less willing they would be to see those customs and rituals suppressed.

By the era of the First World War, Indian religion was attracting attention that went beyond mere sympathy for the downtrodden. Significant numbers of influential Americans were prepared to defend Indian spirituality, and even, on occasion, to assert its superiority to white ways. By 1900, Indian religions had become familiar; by 1920, they were presented as national treasures, part of America's cultural patrimony. That shift could not fail to affect

65

attitudes to the orthodox policies of Americanizing and Christianizing Indian peoples.

Tourism

By the end of the nineteenth century, the Southwest was experiencing the beginnings of what would become a dramatic tourist boom. This was partly a result of greater political tranquility. The Indian wars effectively ended with the capture of the Apache leader Geronimo in 1886, the Wounded Knee massacre of 1890, and the collapse of the Ghost Dance movement. Once Indians were defeated, they could safely be seen as quaint and romantic.

Thereafter, the southwestern states in particular used whatever tourist resources they had to promote growth, and the railroads played a key role in this. The rail link from Chicago to Los Angeles was completed in 1880, and 1884 marked the completion of both the Southern Pacific and the Atlantic & Pacific Railroads. Thereafter, the railroads sponsored the building of new hotels and resorts across the Southwest, advertised by booklets and brochures.[1] These highlighted Indian and archaeological treasures, with a heavy emphasis on the exotic and the spiritual. The Denver & Rio Grande Railroad played up the romantic attractions of Mesa Verde, "America's sublime antiquity," which "has the lure of a mystery greater than the ruined cities of the old world." The railroad advertised a Mesa Verde trip at the heart of "the mystical Southwest." A 1915 book touted "our unknown Southwest: the wonderland of the United States—little known and unappreciated—the home of the cliff dweller and the Hopi, the forest ranger and the Navajo—the lure of the Painted Desert."[2]

Western travel became fashionable with the mushroom growth of Los Angeles in the early years of the new century, and the Western movement was assisted by the completion of the Panama Canal. California and the West were both advertised heavily, especially through the twin expositions of 1915, the Panama-Pacific in San Francisco, and the Panama-California in San Diego. Western boosters benefited when other popular tourist venues were effectively closed by war and revolution: Mexico after 1910, and most of Europe during the First World War. By the 1920s, D. H. Lawrence described the Southwest as "the great playground of the white American."[3]

Also promoting Western tourism was a radical change of sensibility toward Nature, and what later generations would call the environment.

Through writers like John Muir, cultured Americans came to share a much greater appreciation of wilderness and desert lands, which some viewed with sacramental awe. The desert Southwest was popularized by authors like Charles Fletcher Lummis, who claimed to have coined the slogan "SEE AMERICA FIRST." In 1903, Mary Austin published her classic *Land of Little Rain* about the Californian desert. Austin was among the first of a dazzlingly creative generation of women writers, artists, and activists who made the Southwest their home, and who were fascinated by the landscapes and cultures they found there. Alongside Austin, we find intrepid women such as Natalie Curtis, Alice Corbin Henderson, Elsie Clews Parsons, Mabel Dodge, and Georgia O'Keeffe.[4]

The new sensibility encouraged mainstream Americans to visit what might once have been regarded as a howling wilderness, which now appeared far more attractive than the supposed blessings of civilization. Disenchantment with civilization was all the greater during the urban crises and political conflicts of the Progressive era. Moreover, the new appreciation helped visitors see Native peoples in their home setting, to understand how superbly adapted Indian cultures were to inhospitable environments. Native struggles to defend these cultures seemed less a willful primitive resistance to progress and more a rational defense of something worth treasuring.

The discovery of wilderness achieved the status of national orthodoxy under the presidency of Theodore Roosevelt, with the establishment of the national parks system. By 1907, Mesa Verde was designated a national park, and Chaco Canyon a national monument. Having said this, one of the grim ironies of the new "scenic nationalism" was that the very efforts to defend wilderness often had the effect of displacing live Native populations. Equally contemptuous of Native tradition was the affair of New Mexico's Blue Lake, sacred to the Taos Pueblos. When, in 1906, a new national forest was created in northern New Mexico, the boundaries included the lake, which was thus removed from Native use. As so often in American history, the romantic image of the Indian counted far more than the living, breathing individual.[5]

The Snake Dance

Indians, and particularly Indian religion, represented a major element of the new Western tourist package. Already by the 1890s, white visitors were becoming a noticeable presence at Native dances and ceremonials. Southwestern

ceremonials were so enticing for the very reasons that had made them so suspect to some observers, and especially Christian missionaries, in previous
decades. The Southwest was attractive precisely because it seemed exotic,
bizarre, primitive, and pagan, with tenebrous suggestions of dark rituals. As
Gilson Willets complained in 1905, this was "the most un-American part of
the United States." Willets intended his writings as an argument that state-
hood should be delayed until Americanization had taken full effect, but un-
intentionally, he gave the area's tourist economy an added boost.[6]

The region's prime tourist attraction was the Hopi Snake Dance, which
had been described by Eastern newspapers in such shocked terms in the
1880s. Jesse Fewkes noted that "fully seventy white persons witnessed the 1895
Snake Dance at Walpi," a number that grew to two hundred by 1897. And
while a few local whites had often attended "that unparalleled dramatic pagan
ceremony," visitors now included "journalists, artists, public lecturers, and
ethnologists from distant cities." "Some of the newspapers of New York and
Chicago sent reporters to describe for their readers the details of the dance,
and several professional photographers were likewise present." Fearing that
the pueblo would soon be overwhelmed, some entrepreneurial younger Hopi
suggested that the dance should be moved to Albuquerque, though tradition-
alists overruled them. In 1912 Charles F. Saunders recorded that:

> the Snake Dance has been so industriously written up and talked over that
> it has become a magnet which, every August, draws more or less of a
> crowd of tourists and holiday-makers across the desert sands to witness
> this most entrancing and most dramatic half-hour entertainment that
> America has to offer.

Travelers who recorded their impressions of the event included Theodore
Roosevelt and D. H. Lawrence.[7]

With good reason, missionary writers were alarmed that this new ceremonial tourism would stall assimilation efforts. In 1914, Frederick Moffett complained that both businesspeople and anthropologists had a powerful vested
interest in defending the picturesque: they "make it worth the red man's
while to preserve and to practice his superstitious rites and ceremonies." Indicating the extent of white interest in Native rituals and ceremonies was the
growing number of imitators. From the end of the nineteenth century, re-
formers and activists had tried to create pseudo-Indian tribes or societies as
educational tools for the young, using the forest or wilderness as a means of

teaching manly values to adolescent boys. In 1901 Ernest Thompson Seton formed his Woodcraft Indians, a precursor of the Boy Scouts of America; while the Camp Fire program used Indian names and dress to help girls acquire proper womanly skills. From around 1910, though, re-enactments of Indian ritual attracted adults as well as children, and the rituals chosen were much more authentic than the Camp Fire versions. Imitation escalated in both seriousness and plausibility.[8]

Naturally, given its notoriety, the Snake Dance was one of the earliest models chosen. In 1914, fifty young society people presented their interpretation of the dance at New York's Astor Hotel, at a benefit for the blind. Choreography for the dance, which used papier mâché snakes, was prepared using films taken of the actual ritual. In 1921 the "Smoki Indian" tribe was created in Prescott, Arizona. This was a group of non-Indians—mainly Rotarians— pledged to preserve and imitate Native dances, including the Snake Dance. (The name is a parody of Moki, or Moqui, the contemporary term for the Hopi). These were imitations, theatrics or play-acting, rather than the serious kind of neo-Indian spirituality that would be found in the modern New Age; but the potential for more active involvement was present.[9]

Sacred and Profane

Already by the start of the century, a busy tourist economy had come into being, and jaded observers protested the commercialization of the dances and ceremonies. Across the West, every visitor wanted to pick up some tacky Indian souvenir, and manufacturers were happy to oblige: "The spears are machine-made, the shields are wrinkled sheets of calf-skin daubed over with scene painters' colors." Southwestern rituals were treated just as cynically. As early as 1903, James LeRoy was thinking of his experiences at Taos when he wrote:

Going to one or another of the old Indian festivals of the Southwest with an expectation of being greatly awed or impressed is nowadays to invite disappointment. Railroads bring tourists, the settlers for miles around make the occasion a holiday, and the Mexicans of our arid territories will supply any failure of Americans to present a crowd of spectators. . . . Mysterious ceremonies, desecrated by the stranger's eyes, are now the means of attracting a gawking crowd of the jostling profane, who find the Indian huckster offering beadwork, baskets, pottery or blankets. The camera, at first offensive, if not the object of superstitious dread, may now spread before the civilized world religious rites once rich with meaning; may even for a few dollars engage the celebrants to pose.

By the 1920s, such complaints were proliferating:

The dances held each day at the Grand Canyon have suffered through the call of commercialism and persons seeing them are expected to pay, much as they would at the circus. As a result of this, the dances have reached the point where they hold little interest except to the large-eyed and easily impressed Easterner who is thrilled to his city heart by anything sporting an eagle feather and so-called "war paint."[10]

The interaction between tourists and Natives soon demonstrated the familiar paradox of cultural and ethnic tourism, namely, that increased commercialization and exposure to wealthy outsiders inevitably destroys the primitive simplicity that visitors are seeking. While outsiders are attracted by the lure of the primal and unspoiled, the fact of their presence cannot fail to affect the culture they are observing. Meanwhile, poor Natives are only too happy to give them what they are seeking and what they are prepared to pay for. By seeking the unspoiled, we spoil it. In 1911 Charles Eastman was complaining about the bogus nature of the commercialized religion encountered by tourists: "Give a reservation Indian a present, and he will possibly provide you with sacred songs, a mythology, and folk-lore to order!"[11] Deceiving inquisitive outsiders was a positive virtue for cultures secretive about their beliefs, like the Pueblos.

But in complaining about commercialization and "desecration," such jeremiads suggest the religious interests of the audience for Native ceremonies. Visitors were not just there for the purpose of being appalled by obscene devil worship. Native religion was appealing because it was impressive, moving, awe-inspiring. It was also clearly religious: in order to be "desecrated," something first has to be sacred. These were "religious rites once rich with meaning." Charles F. Saunders in 1912 wrote of the fine "entertainment" of the Snake Dance, but quickly added, "I use the word 'entertainment' hesitatingly, knowing that is all it is to the average white onlooker; but it should be borne in mind that, to the Indian, it is a solemn and religious rite—the public *dénouement* of a nine-days' secretly-conducted intercession for the divine favor."[12] As Eastman suggests, tourists were especially in search of *sacred* songs and tales.

Native rituals attracted a preselected white audience already interested in religion, and often people willing to explore nonconventional spirituality. The settlers and visitors likely to be found in the West at the start of the twentieth century represented a distinctive set of interests and concerns. In these years, many eastern migrants traveled to the Southwest for medical reasons, hoping that the hot, dry climate would help solve health problems that had proved intractable back home. Again, this promise owed much to advertising by the railroads, which from the 1880s created the earliest spas and health resorts in the region. Sanitariums proliferated across Arizona and New Mexico. The more invalids migrated to the Southwest, the more this created a mass public for alternative medical treatments, often with a strong occult or metaphysical element. The existence of that market helps explain the occult boom that was already so marked in the Western states. At least from the 1890s, California and the Southwest states had become the natural home for religious communes, for occult and Theosophical settlements, and Los Angeles became proverbial for cults and cultists. An audience already sympathetic to spiritualism and the occult would seek out Native rituals and spiritual leaders, though it would generally impose its own interpretations on those practices.[13]

Against the Modern

Among the new arrivals in the Southwest were the bohemians, the writers and artists who flocked there in increasing numbers from the 1890s onwards. Some exiles, such as Alice Corbin Henderson, were seeking health in the sun and the dry climate, while artists were attracted by the spectacular colors and light effects. Taos traces its reputation as an art colony to the end of the nineteenth century, and the Taos Society of Artists was founded in 1914. This trend accelerated with the legendary circle associated with Mabel Dodge, who took up residence in 1917. Many of the new arrivals in the Southwest worked at least tangentially on Native themes, but for some, the encounter with Indian art, ritual, and religion was transforming. These intellectuals are important for our story not only because many were so profoundly impressed by Native cultures, but because they were able to disseminate their views in the media. Indian cultures and religions came to be appreciated for their aesthetic achievements, which were seen as equal to, or even greater than, the canonical triumphs of Western art.

The idea of the Indian aesthetic achievement predates the Taos circle. Critical here was the Arts and Crafts movement that, between about 1890 and 1910, transformed American ideas about architecture and design. The movement originated in England with William Morris, who idealized a past in which beautiful, well-made objects were accessible to ordinary people, and art and craftsmanship were accepted parts of daily life. Such a society had supposedly existed in the Middle Ages, but it was devastated by the Protestant Reformation, and later destroyed by urbanism and industrialism. Moderns lived in "the Age of Shoddy." In order to recover from their alienation, individuals should create and possess objects of simple beauty. Morris's creed was "Have nothing in your houses which you do not know to be useful, or believe to be beautiful."

In its American manifestation, dominated by Gustav Stickley, the Arts and Crafts movement admired Indians for their integration of craftsmanship and aesthetic values in everyday life, an idea confirmed by rituals like the Navajo Mountain Chant. In papers such as *The Craftsman*, Stickley opposed modern industrial society in the name of an idealized communitarianism, which found its models both in the European Middle Ages and in contemporary Native societies. Some leaders of the California branch of Arts and Crafts, the Arroyo Culture, were among the best-known advocates of Indian causes, including Charles F. Lummis, George Wharton James, and Mary Austin. On religious matters, the Arts and Crafts movement was ambiguous. Its leaders were politically to the left, and disliked contemporary Catholicism, but they idealized the medieval world in which faith and art had been indissolubly linked. This romanticism made Stickley and others sensitive about threats to uproot Native religion and culture: one Reformation had been too many. Directly or otherwise, Morris's views would have a great influence on perceptions of Indian culture, especially through his admirer, John Collier.

Arts and Crafts products were much in evidence at the World's Columbian Exhibition of 1893, held in Chicago. Also prominently displayed were Indian works, which were presented as belonging to a kindred tradition, to societies that did not acknowledge any artificial demarcations between art and life, secular and spiritual. Native displays included some of the finest products of the Northwest Coast cultures, including model Haida and Kwakiutl villages. Indian crafts had a special appeal for women's groups, since these represented a distinctly feminine achievement. Over the next decade, Indian arts and basketry were promoted by women's organizations like the General Federation of Women's Clubs, and were well advertised in women-oriented newspapers and magazines.[14]

"Primitive" crafts also appealed to the Modernist movements that would ultimately displace the Arts and Crafts sensibility. At the beginning of the century, American bohemian circles had a predilection for non-traditional religions, including Asian faiths, and for New Age and metaphysical beliefs. Primitivist trends became immensely stronger when Americans encountered new European artistic theories that glorified the tribal. Picasso's *Les Démoiselles d'Avignon*, with its faces drawn from African masks, dates from 1907; Stravinsky's *Rite of Spring*, based on tribal images of a lost pagan Russia, debuted in 1913. In 1915, Wallace Stevens' Modernist poem "Sunday Morning" rejected any religion based on the cold abstractions of Christianity, and imagined instead pagan rituals founded in blood and ecstasy:

Supple and turbulent, a ring of men
Shall chant in orgy on a summer morn
Their boisterous devotion to the sun . . .
Their chant shall be a chant of paradise,
Out of their blood, returning to the sky.

Gradually, Americans realized that such a pagan dream-world still existed very close to home: they had a comparable "Africa," a living pagan society, on their own territory.[15]

This was also the great era of the discovery of European cave paintings, which dated back tens of thousands of years yet indicated a thought-world not too different from those of contemporary Indian societies. In 1914 the Pyrenean cave of Les Trois Frères produced an evocative painting of a masked human figure with animal horns, which was known as "the Sorcerer." As this shamanistic image was widely reproduced in coming years, it suggested the truly ancient roots of American Indian art and religiosity.

Savage Beauty

American writings on the "Red Indian imagination" date from the 1890s, when Indian culture was seen as the potential source for a distinctively

American cultural efflorescence, independent of tired European models. As Mary Austin wrote in 1930, the mystery was just why it had taken Americans so long to recognize the treasures they possessed in Native culture. "Perhaps the American sense was dulled to the impact of beauty and strangeness, perhaps American intelligence was enslaved by the European tradition."[16]

Writers were alarmed that the ancient Indian peoples would literally become extinct before they could exercise their full cultural influence on the American mainstream, and that this might come to pass within a few decades. In 1896, Julian Ralph described Indians as "a dead but unburied race." Seeing the smoldering ruins of a medicine lodge, Walter McClintock concluded that "in a few years, the ancient customs and ceremonies of the Indians will have disappeared as completely." This view seemed all the more plausible with the well-publicized discovery in 1911 of Ishi, apparently the last survivor of California's Yahi tribe. He was the "last aborigine," "last of his tribe," who was emblematic of pristine Indian culture, so that his death in 1916 marked a symbolic end of ancient America. (Appropriately enough, Ishi spent his last years living in an anthropology museum.) The twilight vision of the "weird and waning race" was commemorated in *The End of the Trail*, James Earle Fraser's famous sculpture of the weary, defeated Indian warrior, a piece exhibited at the Panama-Pacific exhibition of 1915.[17]

The threat of cultural extinction aroused creative artists working in music and in dance, who saw Native peoples as a source of cultural inspiration. Americans now acknowledged the aesthetic glories of authentic folk music, and collectors shared the love of vernacular art that inspired European composers such as Dvořák. In 1900, folklorist Andrew Lang praised the splendid artistic qualities of Indian rituals like the Ghost Dance: "its rites were accompanied by an esthetic kind of dance, accompanied by hypnotic phenomena." One enthusiastic advocate of the musical potential of Indian culture was Arthur Farwell, who in 1904 praised "The Artistic Possibilities of Indian Myth." These possibilities were all the more accessible given the explosion of new texts such as "Alice C. Fletcher's discovery and eventual recording of the great rituals of the Omaha and Pawnee tribes." If European composers had so often been inspired by Christian rites, why should Americans not draw on these "great rituals"? The suggestion is that Christians and Natives both had religions, each with its own cultural achievements, and that artists could and should draw freely on both. In 1905, Farwell presented his *Impressions of the Wa-wan ceremony of the Omahas,* and his Wa-Wan Press became a primary publishing outlet for contemporary and experimental composers. Besides Farwell, others from the new Indianist school included Carlos Troyer, who interpreted *Traditional Zuñi Songs*.[18]

Others, too, were inspired by the imperiled musical heritage of Native peoples. One enthusiast was the prolific Frances Densmore, author of many books on various tribal traditions. Kenneth Rexroth would later comment that "there does not exist any comparable collection of primitive lyric and music made by one person. . . . Over and above its musical interest, Miss Densmore's work is also possibly the largest body of primitive lyric poetry in the original language and in translation in existence."[19]

In the same era, Natalie Curtis founded the American tradition of ethnomusicology. Though she had planned a conventional musical career in Europe, a visit to Arizona in 1900 alerted her to the vast cultural treasures to be found at home. Basing herself on the Hopi reservation, she began collecting traditional songs but soon ran up against the federal authorities, which were trying to suppress all aspects of the older culture. In 1902–1903, Curtis joined a campaign by Charles Lummis, Hamlin Garland, and others against coercive assimilation, against petty-minded attempts to force Indians to cut their long hair and abandon their traditional clothing. She published Native songs and chants in her *Songs of Ancient America* (1905). Her greatest achievement was, however, *The Indians' Book* (1907), a glorious collection of songs, music, drawings, portraits, and legends, endorsed by an introduction from President Theodore Roosevelt, who praised "the charm of a vanished elder world." Every detail of this superb book was carefully designed in accordance with authentic tribal styles, to the extent that the title page for each chapter is written in lettering appropriate to the tribe in question, drawing faithfully from their motifs. Everything follows to perfection the principles of the Arts and Crafts movement. The songs, drawn from across North America, inspired contemporary composers, including Percy Grainger. As the title suggests, Curtis tried to avoid the impression of appropriating Native traditions as her own, since each tribe's accomplishments were duly credited to Native authorities themselves: "The Indians are the authors of this volume." It was "an offering by the American Indians of Indian lore, musical and narrative, to form a record of the songs and legends of their race."[20]

Natalie Curtis remained a strong advocate of Indian culture. In *The Indians' Book*, she declared that "here among us, down-trodden and by us debauched, is a people of real creative artistic genius—the first Americans, and possibly the oldest race on Earth." Appreciating the culture of these quintessential Americans meant paying due attention to the dances and ceremonies that others regarded as superstitious. "We who look to Europe for art inspiration might well turn our eyes to our own Far West with the cry 'America First.'" She complained of American neglect of its domestic treasures:

> Why it is that America, who welcomes dancers from Russia and from India, Irish and Japanese players and folk music from all over the world, should remain deaf and blind to the drama and song of prehistoric America lying right at our door? . . . Will a widespread appreciation of what the Indian has to offer to the art, letters and music of America dawn only after the red man's sun is set?[21]

This appreciation of primitive culture extended beyond the musical. In poetry, George Cronyn's 1918 anthology *The Path on the Rainbow* noted the modernity, if not the Modernism, of Native poetry. As Mary Austin's introduction pointed out, the reader "will be struck at once with the extraordinary likeness between much of this native product and the recent work of the Imagists, vers librists, and other literary fashionables," who in fact were beginning "just about where the last medicine man left off." In the visual arts, too, several of the painters who found their way to the Southwest were excited by the potential they found among Indian themes and subjects. In 1923 Maynard Dixon wrote of his visit to the Hopis that "many people . . . might see only that these Indians are poor and dirty . . . that the kids go naked. . . . But when you see one of their ceremonies—there for an hour something fine flashes out clear; there is savage beauty in them. . . . They have dignity and form."[22] In 1920 Santa Fe opened a museum dedicated to the growing genre of contemporary southwestern art. Suggesting the intimate link between the aesthetic and the spiritual, the dedication ceremony included the Eagle Dance from the pueblo of San Ildefonso.

Already by the end of the nineteenth century, a few of the "aesthetic" travelers were finding among the Indians an authentic spiritual experience on which they could draw personally. Mary Austin records how a Paiute medicine man in the 1890s taught her techniques of prayer and meditation that revolutionized her spiritual life. Native practices offered her insights that she felt she could never have found within Protestant Christianity, or in white religion generally. She is perhaps the first white writer to describe the discovery and personal application of a whole technique of Native spirituality:

> Prayer, to the Medicine-Man, had nothing to do with emotion; it was an act; an outgoing act of the inner soul toward something, not a god,

toward a responsive act in the world around you, designated as The-Friend-Of-The-Soul-Of-Man, Wakonda, to use a term adopted by ethnologists—the effective principle of the created universe. This inner act was to be outwardly expressed in bodily acts, in words, in music, rhythm, color, whatever medium served the immediate purpose, or all of them. Prayer so understood and instigated acted with the sureness of a chemical combination.

So transformed was she by applying these insights that she thought she might be in the process of repossession by "an uncorrupted strain of ancestral primitivism," perhaps through her distant Indian forebears; and her interpretation was supported by no less an authority than William James. She concluded, "What I got out of William James and the medicine-man was a continuing experience of wholeness, a power to expand the least premonitory shiver along the edge of primitive apprehension to the full diapason of spiritual sophistication, which I have never lost." The phrase "William James and the medicine-man" is intriguing. Already, an influential writer was seeing Native spirituality as a counterpart to sophisticated psychological techniques, a juxtaposition that would become commonplace later in the twentieth century. Cultural explorations had potentially far-reaching religious consequences.[23]

Indian Voices

The defense of Indian cultures and religions was entering a new phase. Since the beginning of the century, a number of disparate activists had been campaigning for greater rights for Native peoples. These movements won the sympathy of President Theodore Roosevelt, who had personal or family connections with many of the key activists, including Charles Lummis, Natalie Curtis, George Grinnell, Hamlin Garland, and Edward Curtis.[24] Though it may seem a trivial symbol of social change, the portrayal of Indians on U.S. coins indicates a shift of attitude toward Native peoples, and perhaps to their cultural self-awareness. The original "Indian Head" penny of 1859 is clearly a white man's head, bearing a Native headdress; and so, in a more sophisticated form, is Saint-Gaudens's ten-dollar coin of 1907. Only in 1913 does an indisputably Indian face, modeled on actual Indian chiefs, appear on the head of James Earle Fraser's buffalo nickel. Indians were acquiring public faces.

Indian intellectuals themselves helped bring Native culture and religion
to the attention of a national public. These were members of a new Americanized elite, usually graduates of the Indian schools. They became active
in American public life through movements like the Society of American
Indians (founded in 1911). Just as this was the era of the New Negro, so the
New Indian now came to prominence. Politically their demands were self-
contradictory, since they presented themselves as enlightened and Americanized, and therefore worthy of full citizenship rights, free of the
demeaning servitude to the BIA; yet at the same time, they stressed the cultural elements that made them distinctive. They were seeking to be recognized as fully assimilated yet radically different. This paradox was much in
evidence at the end of World War I, when Indian activists demanded rights
of self-determination akin to those being offered the small nations of Europe.
Much like African Americans, Native intellectuals were deeply divided over
issues of assimilation and self-determination, and more radical leaders like
the Yavapai, Carlos Montezuma, sporadically criticized the Society for its
willingness to deal with BIA officials. (The BIA reciprocated by describing
Montezuma and his allies as *Bolsheviki*).[25]

In these years too, Native writers and thinkers articulated profound
doubts about white cultural supremacy, including in the realm of religion.
Native acts of protest and resistance never entirely ceased, though most received scant attention from the white public. One well-publicized voice was
Simon Pokagon, who in 1893 addressed the World's Columbian Exposition
in Chicago, an event designed to celebrate four centuries of achievement
since the arrival of Columbus. Pokagon, naturally, had very different views
about the so-called discovery of his land, and his *Red Man's Greeting* stated
many themes about Native culture that have since become familiar. One was
that of the "ecological Indian," living in harmony with nature. Early America had teemed with game and fish: "All were provided by the Great Spirit
for our use: we destroyed none except for food and dress, had plenty and
were contented and happy."[26]

In the early twentieth century, the best-known Indian intellectuals were
Zitkala-Sa and Charles Eastman.[27] Like the contemporary artistic community, such Indian activists were offering a much more assertive statement of
the intrinsic merits of traditional religion. These writers were not claiming
that Native religion was worthwhile because it already possessed many of the
truths of Christianity, but rather that it was good in itself. Having said this,
Native writers were in many ways less ambitious in their claims than their

white counterparts, or at least than white intellectuals would become after the cultural watershed of 1918. The religion defended by Native intellectuals had little to do with the lived experience of Indian peoples themselves. They offered no defense of ceremonies such as the Sun Dance or the Snake Dance, still less the apocalyptic Ghost Dance, and their views are heavily influenced by Euro-American Romanticism and Transcendentalism, with a heavy dose of contemporary mysticism. Yet the fact that Indians themselves were prepared to speak in defense of their religion, however conceived, was a new departure.

One influential statement of the old values was a 1902 article by Zitkala-Sa in the visible outlet of the *Atlantic Monthly*, bearing the title of "Why I Am a Pagan." Affecting paganism was not in itself shocking, since this had been the stance of English writers from Shelley to Swinburne. She preached a similar kind of pantheism: "I fain would trace a subtle knowledge of the native folk which enabled them to recognize a kinship to any and all parts of this vast universe. By the leading of an ancient trail I move toward the Indian village." Responding to Christian preaching, she declared that she preferred to their dogma "my excursions into the natural gardens where the voice of the Great Spirit is heard in the twittering of birds, the rippling of mighty waters, and the sweet breathing of flowers." What made Zitkala-Sa distinctive was that she was asserting the virtues of a living tradition rather than an intellectualized revival of the beliefs of Classical antiquity. Unlike in Swinburne's England, America in 1902 really did have living pagans and animists, whose practices were being strictly regulated by the government of the day. The essay infuriated assimilationists.[28]

Similar doctrines emerge from Charles Eastman's *The Soul of the Indian* (1911), a proud assertion of Native spiritual accomplishments. Like Zitkala-Sa, though, Eastman was anything but a Native traditionalist, and he had a dazzling ability to explain away any aspect of native thought that he did not like as an intrusion from white society. (Eastman's writings may have been shaped by his New England wife, Elaine Goodale Eastman, to whom his book was dedicated.)[29] White influences were certainly to blame for troublesome militancy, and not just in the time of the Ghost Dance:

The only religious leaders of any note who have arisen among the native tribes since the advent of the white man, the Shawnee Prophet in 1762 [sic], and the half-breed prophet of the Ghost Dance in 1890, both founded their claims or prophecies upon the Gospel story. Thus in each case an Indian religious revival or craze, though more or less threatening to the invader, was of distinctively alien origin.[30]

Contact with white civilization had corrupted many beliefs and rituals. In some ways, Eastman was presenting something close to the common view of Indians as proto-Christians, whose pure beliefs coexisted with crude superstition: "In this manner the 'Sun Dance' of the Plains Indians, the most important of their public ceremonials, was abused and perverted until it became a horrible exhibition of barbarism, and was eventually prohibited by the Government."

Underlying these superficial corruptions, though, Eastman claimed to discover pristine Native thought, basically a noble Transcendentalism that would have been instantly attractive to middle-class white Progressives:

There were no temples or shrines among us save those of nature. Being a natural man, the Indian was intensely poetical. He would deem it sacrilege to build a house for Him who may be met face to face in the mysterious, shadowy aisles of the primeval forest, or on the sunlit bosom of virgin prairies, upon dizzy spires and pinnacles of naked rock, and yonder in the jeweled vault of the night sky!

(A passage like this sounds so much like the aesthetic commonplaces of Victorian New England that Elaine Goodale may very well have had a hand in it.) True Indianism was also true Christianity, though a more spiritual creed than the contemporary version preached in white churches. Charles Eastman attributes these words to a tribal elder: "This Jesus was an Indian. He was opposed to material acquirements and to great possessions. He was inclined to peace. . . . These are not the principles on which the white man has founded his civilization."[31]

Against Conversion

By 1915, scholars, activists and intellectuals had developed a much greater respect for Native religions. This new attitude raised serious issues about the conventional response to the "Indian Problem," which involved assimilation and evangelization. Far from being unquestioned orthodoxy, the idea of converting the Indians became controversial. Assimilation was doubly questionable given the new upsurge of critical attitudes toward Western civilization, and to Christianity in particular.

One early critic was Charles F. Lummis, who in his writing on Indian schools attacked the whole notion of assimilation. As early as 1890, Lummis was using exactly the critique of cultural imperialism H. G. Wells would make famous a few years later in *The War of the Worlds*, namely, to ask Euro-Americans how they would like it if some superior race tried to impose its standards upon them. (The idea harks back to Washington Irving's *History of New York*). For Lummis, "The fundamental objection [to Indian education] is the very same one that we or any other decent people would have if a superior race (self-asserted) were to come from Mars, overrun the land and force us to send our children away from home to be rid of our silly superstitions, religion and customs, and instructed in the better ways of the people of Mars."[32] Absent from his statement is any suggestion that the ways of the people of Mars (or of white Americans) were at all superior to those of the lower races.

The antiassimilation approach raised fundamental questions about the whole idea of missionaries, those people sent to bear the message of light and civilization to those supposedly lost in darkness. But who defined what was light and what darkness? At the turn of the century an antimissionary critique was rising from progressives, from secularists, and from pro-Indian activists. One of the most effective was Hamlin Garland, whose articles appeared in papers like *Harper's Weekly*. His story "The Iron Khiva" presented in harrowing terms the plight of a Pueblo family whose children are to be torn away to attend a missionary school in the East. After the family has suffered death and ruin, a U.S. military commander promises to help the Indians against the missionaries. (The khiva represents the forbidding structure of the white schoolhouse). In 1902, Garland wrote that, while most Christian missionaries were personally decent men and women, "I would not care to live where they had power to define what recreations were proper and what were not. Their view of 'profane' songs and pleasures is absurdly narrow and (to put it mildly) inelastic." Garland was using an argument that would carry particular weight with contemporary scholars and intellectuals, namely, that the clergy practiced a hidebound intolerance that was equally inappropriate whether inflicted upon Indians or on white elites. He scoffed at the hypocrisy of white Christianity. Just what good would it do to "convert the man of the stone age into a 'Christian citizen'?" The convert would then be told: "In order that you may know how sweet it is to live the life of the white farmer, you may go to church on Sunday and hear a man talk in words which you do not understand and sing songs like the white people sing when they have nothing better to do." Garland's hostility owed something to his own religious heterodoxy: his deep involvement in occult and psychic speculations made him sympathetic to the Indians' right to pursue their own spiritual paths, free from clerical meddling.[33]

The new generation of Native writers themselves was just as critical of missionary efforts. In 1907 John M. Oskison's story "The Problem of Old Harjo" explored the dilemma of a well-intentioned Christian missionary who believes she can convert an elderly Native. The difficulty is that Old Harjo is happily married to two wives, and forcing him to renounce either one would be "cruel and useless." Though Harjo fervently seeks church membership, the missionary is sensible enough to doubt that demanding a separation "would in the least advance morality amongst the tribe, but I'm certain that it would make three gentle people unhappy for the rest of their lives." In this instance at least, when Indian custom and missionary certainty come into conflict, the missionary must back down.[34]

Charles Eastman portrayed the conflict of values in less subtle terms:

> The first missionaries, good men imbued with the narrowness of their age, branded us as pagans and devil-worshipers, and demanded of us that we abjure our false gods before bowing the knee at their sacred altar. They even told us that we were eternally lost, unless we adopted a tangible symbol and professed a particular form of their hydra-headed faith.

Eastman's argument about the equally absolute claims of many different sects of Christians resonated among both liberal Christians and skeptics, painfully aware of the diversity of denominations. Equally powerful was Eastman's rejection of the absolute claims of the Christian missionaries, who so confidently denounced the falsehoods of Indian belief. "Who may condemn his superstition? Surely not the devout Catholic or Protestant missionary, who teaches Bible miracles as literal fact! The logical man must either deny all miracles or none, and our American Indian myths and hero stories are perhaps, in themselves, quite as credible as those of the Hebrews of old."[35]

Eastman was writing at the time of the publication of *The Fundamentals*, the tracts that solidified the division between modernists and the newly named fundamentalists. In an age when doubts about the Bible and creeds had become so widespread among social elites, these were effective argu-

ments. The more commentators criticized Christian failings, the less justified it seemed to convert pagans. Denouncing the materialism of the
churches, even an Episcopal missionary of Native heritage proclaimed that
"I would rather have the religion of the Arapahoes, of my fathers, and sit in
that sacred tent, than a religion auctioned off in that way." Gustav Stickley
asked in 1912, "Whoever heard of an Indian offering to convert a missionary?" This would have been "astounding impertinence. . . . All that [Indians]
asked of us was the privilege of retaining their own ideals, of living their
own healthy life on their own lands." Instead of forcing Western ways upon
them, the West should learn from Indian spirituality: whites should pray as
Indians do, "mind open, soul free, heart thirsting, without words, ready
silently to receive."[36]

The Higher Civilization?

The tone of writing about Native cultures shifts dramatically around
1917–1918. Before that point, some authors speak admiringly of Native cultures and the religious practices that lay at their core; but very shortly afterwards, we find frequent suggestions that Indian civilization might actually
be superior to its Western counterpart. Far from being a troublesome road-
block on the route to progress and civilization, Indian religions were an essential safeguard against those very curses.

One reason for this change was the presence of the booming bohemian
colony at Taos.[37] After the arrival of Mabel Dodge, the ensuing pattern of
chain migration meant that a direct highway now ran from Greenwich Village to Taos. She was followed by artists such as Georgia O'Keeffe, Maynard
Dixon, John Marin, Ansel Adams, and Marsden Hartley; novelists like
Willa Cather, Aldous Huxley, and D. H. Lawrence, poets like Robinson
Jeffers; and activists like John Collier. Culturally, Taos Pueblo itself became
one of the most powerful symbols of the newly discovered Indian civiliza-
tion. New Mexico also became a fashionable literary theme. Alice Corbin
Henderson produced collections such as *Red Earth* (1920) and *The Turquoise
Trail* (1928), and went on to write her celebrated book on the Penitentes,
The Brothers of Light.[38]

The other epochal change around this time was, of course, the Great War.
Many of the new intellectual arrivals came from liberal circles opposed to
American involvement in the war, which they saw as a cultural disaster.

More immediately, the patriotic reaction in 1917 made urban life unconge-
nial for radicals, socialists, and feminists. It was the war that drove Elsie
Clews Parsons to the Southwest, to seek refuge in her research among the
Pueblos. But the long-term effects were also obvious. In the aftermath of
Verdun and the Somme, claims about the natural superiority of European
civilization sounded brittle, if not ludicrous. Perhaps European civilization
had maimed itself once and for all. Scott Fitzgerald believed that educated
Americans returned from the war "to find all gods dead, all wars fought, all
faith in man shaken." In 1920, Natalie Curtis argued that "the war, with its
hideous revelation of barbarism may at last teach us of the white race that
we are not so far ahead of the darker races as we thought." And the war had
other implications, given the Wilsonian rhetoric of self-determination. If
the United States was fighting for the rights of small nations abroad, Americans should fight at home for "the right of the American Indian to *be himself*; to express his own ideals of beauty and fitness in his religion, his
customs, his dress and his art." America's own prospects seemed bleak given
the political conditions of 1919–1920, those red years of riots, strikes, race
wars, and terrorism.[39]

Through the 1920s, Native peoples were extolled for resisting the forces of
modernity, urbanism, industrialism, and mass society, the evils of bourgeois
civilization of which the Southwest seemed so blessedly free. Once again, Indians symbolized those features that the West was losing or betraying.
Against a Christianity that worshipped the bourgeois ethic and despised sexuality, the bohemians sought a romanticized pure culture still in touch with
nature and with the body, free of the curse of civilization. The rejection of
Christianity was accelerated by the churches' embarrassingly vocal support
for nationalism and imperialism in the war years, followed in the 1920s by
the excesses of fundamentalism and neo-Puritan moral campaigns. Reinforcing their disaffection from traditional organized religion, the new arrivals lived in a subculture sympathetic to sexual experimentation and
unorthodox relationships. Marsden Hartley was gay, while Ruth Benedict,
Willa Cather, and Georgia O'Keeffe were lesbian or bisexual. Amy Lowell,
another popularizer of Indian poetry, was lesbian. When Harry Sylvester's
novel *Dayspring* presented a hostile picture of Taos's bohemian world in the
1930s, he held in special contempt the easy tolerance for promiscuity, both
hetero- and homosexual.

After 1917–1918, some writers on Indian culture adopted a tone that
would become familiar during the 1970s and 1980s, listing ways in which "we

whites" could learn from the Indians. In this view, Western material wealth concealed spiritual poverty. Mabel Dodge experienced a kind of conversion experience hearing Indian music for the first time, in December 1917:

> For the first time in my life, then, I heard the voice of the One coming from the Many. . . . The singular raging lust for individuality and separateness had been imperiling me all my years as it did everyone else on earth—when all of a sudden I was brought up against the Tribe, where a different instinct ruled . . . where virtue lay in wholeness rather than in dismemberment.[40]

In 1918, Natalie Curtis was arguing explicitly for the superiority of Indian religion on grounds that would become mainstream later in the century: "Surely not the least of the lessons that we may learn from the red man is *reverence* for the earth-mother, giver of life; for no Indian would dream of calling a mountain reaching skyward 'Old Baldy' or 'Pikes Peak,' nor would he slaughter game, sacred to the needs of man, for sport only."[41] It was while watching "the Indians dancing to help the young corn at Taos Pueblo" that Robinson Jeffers recalled "that civilization is a transient sickness."[42]

In 1920, Marsden Hartley published an ambitious statement of Indian cultural superiority in "An American Plea for American Esthetics," an essay that offered powerful ammunition against current attempts to suppress Indian rituals. Hartley saw "the red man [as] the one truly indigenous religionist and esthete of America. He knows every form of animal and vegetable life adhering to our earth, and has made for himself a series of striking pageantries in the form of stirring dances to celebrate them, and his relation to them." Throughout the dances of the southwestern Pueblos, "the same unified sense of beauty prevails, and in some of the dances to a most remarkable degree." At Tesuque, "You find a species of rhythm so perfected in its relation to racial interpretation, as hardly to admit of witnessing ever again the copied varieties of dancing such as we whites of the present hour are familiar with. It is nothing short of captivating artistry of the first excellence." The religious quality of the rituals was beyond question, however much "we whites" might fail to appreciate it: "The redman is essentially a thankful and a religious being."[43]

Anglo-Saxon Christian civilization was not necessarily the peak of human achievement, a subversive message in the early 1920s, the years of peak success for the Ku Klux Klan. We now find clear statements of multiculturalism, the necessity of treating diverse cultures respectfully as necessary components of a civilization. This was a pressing need in an America at the center of the greatest migration movement in human history. If the new America was to absorb Slavs, Italians, Jews, and other peoples, then it also had to take account of its oldest cultures. In 1926, archaeologist Edgar Hewett complained that white people despised other races as inferior, "forgetting that it takes several factors to constitute a fully developed civilized people, and that in some respects the peoples whom we have called primitive or savage or uncivilized have been far in advance of ourselves"[44]

Influential European visitors agreed that Indians retained what Western society had lost or destroyed. Visiting the Pueblos in the 1930s, Carl Jung discovered that the imperturbable dignity of an Indian

> springs from his being a son of the Sun; his life is cosmologically meaningful, for he helps the father and preserver of all life in his daily rise and descent. If we set this against this our own self-justifications, the meaning of our own lives as it is formulated by our reason, we cannot help but see our poverty. . . . Knowledge does not enrich us; it removes us more and more from the mythic world in which we were once at home by right of birth.

Jung's argument echoes the familiar Romantic notion that the process of maturing can mean losing valuable childlike qualities and perceptions, and that this process of loss applies equally to societies and races as to individuals. As in the work of the folklorists, Indians are again depicted as closer to racial childhood, but in a positive rather than a demeaning sense. Others of the Taos circle reflect this exalted idea of "Indian childhood," the foolishness that is wiser than the wisdom of Western civilization.[45]

Another European convert was D. H. Lawrence, who said that New Mexico "certainly changed me forever. . . . [I]t was New Mexico that liberated me from the present era of civilization, the great era of material and mechanical development. . . . It is curious that it should be in America, of all places, that a European should really experience religion." He saw the Pueblo society as the living incarnation of a paganism rooted in the body and the elements. Lawrence found among the Pueblos "a vast old religion, greater than anything we know; more starkly and nakedly religious. There is no god. No conceptions of a god. All is god. . . . It is the religion which precedes the god-concept, and is therefore greater and deeper than any god-religion." Their spiritual superiority meant that Native peoples might well endure long after the flawed European world had gone down to ruin, after the transient sickness had passed. "The skyscraper will scatter on the winds like thistledown, and the genuine America, the America of New Mexico, will start on its course again. This is an interregnum."[46]

In 1925, *The Dial* published Lawrence's story "The Woman Who Rode Away," about a white woman who transfers her loyalties to the Indians of the Mexican mountains, although she knows that the decision will cost her life. (The character recalls Mabel Dodge.) She is to become a human sacrifice, and in the closing passage of the book, she is lying nude on a stone altar as the Natives await the setting of the sun. Her fair skin and blonde hair contrast with their dark features. She looks into the black eyes of the old priest:

> And in their black empty concentration there was power, power intensely abstract and remote, but deep, deep into the heart of the earth, and the heart of the sun. . . . Then the old man would strike, and strike home, accomplish the sacrifice and achieve power. The mastery that man must hold, and that passes from race to race.

In *The Plumed Serpent* (1926), Lawrence envisioned Mexico in the throes of an Aztec pagan revival, with the return of the serpent god Quetzalcoatl, and the mass rejection of Christianity.[47]

I Knew That the Old World Was Finished

Lawrence, Jung, Jeffers, and the rest would all influence vast audiences through their literary works, but in terms of his direct ability to shape practical policies toward the Indians, the most important of the new arrivals was John Collier, a social worker and community activist. At Christmas 1920, Mabel Dodge took him to witness the Red Deer Dance at Taos Pueblo. He was astonished at what he saw, at the ceremony that was

> religious (as we white people know it) and cosmical (as we white people do not know). . . . The tribe's soul appeared to wing into the mountain, even to the Source of Things. . . . Here was a reaching to the fire-fountain

of life through a deliberate social action employing a complexity of many arts. . . . These men were at one with their gods."

He was not entirely new to Indian themes, partly due to his friendship with the Gulicks, the founders of the Camp Fire movement, but this was something different. For Collier, the experience was life-changing, literally a moment of religious conversion: "I was rocked; it was like a hallucination or earthquake; a sudden dread-fear; the time-horizon pushed back in a moment and enormously. . . . That solitary experience of 'cosmic consciousness' had been mine, that forever *solitary* translation."[48] The dances "entered into myself and each one of my family as a new direction of life—a new, even wildly new, hope for the Race of Man."[49]

Because he will be so central to this story, Collier's background needs explaining in some depth. Born in 1884, Collier from his teens was deeply imbued with mystical ideas about nature and the spirit, which were inextricably bound up with human communities and folk life. Collier was certainly exposed to esoteric thought, and he derived the concept of cosmic consciousness from Richard Bucke's influential book of that name, published in 1901. (Bucke was one of the major sources used by William James in his discussion of mysticism). Probably, Collier had known the book from the time of its publication. He compared his Taos conversion experience to the revelation he felt in 1901 when he first discovered Bucke's mentor and confidant Walt Whitman.[50]

Collier had mystical ideas about Race (a word he generally capitalized) and he portrayed the race-soul as a sentient being. He was alarmed that modern civilization was destroying natural linkages to blood and soil through ills such as capitalism, urbanism, the free market, private property, and individualism. "Man was sundering himself from the life-web . . . which is the home of Spirit of the Universe," while social change was uprooting natural communities, "his grouphoods embosomed within the life-web, which was being trampled down."[51]

Collier exemplified the antimodernism that was so widespread in turn-of-the-century America, but, unlike the antimodernist figures discussed by Jackson Lears, he was not content to return merely to a rose-window-tinted vision of the High Middle Ages. In seeking a historical model of a society that successfully integrated the material and spiritual, he looked, rather, to the lost pagan worlds of the druids, and to Norse and Germanic barbarism. He loved William Morris's heroic *Sigurd the Volsung*, and felt that Morris's romantic epic *The House of the Wolfings* (1889) best matched "the achieve-ment of the Indian."[52] Morris's once-popular *Wolfings* recalls to a modern reader Tolkien's *The Lord of the Rings*, that other nostalgic manifesto of anti-modernism. Like *Lord of the Rings*, the *House of the Wolfings* combines pseu-dosaga narrative prose with snatches of songs and lyrics. The parallels are not surprising, since Tolkien, too, was heavily influenced by the *Wolfings*, which he discovered in 1914: among other things, he took from Morris the name Mirkwood. (Another key influence on Tolkien was Andrew Lang, whom we have already encountered as an admirer of Indian folklore and mysticism.) Collier's explicit reference to Morris's fantasy says much about the historical and mythological framework with which he would view the Indians. To pursue the Tolkien analogy, Collier felt an instinctive need to de-fend Middle Earth in its hour of crisis.

When Collier encountered the Pueblos, then, his response was condi-tioned by the intellectual baggage that he was carrying, all the mystical ideas of *Volk*, race, organic community, Teutonism, blood and soil, and extreme antimodernism. These notions clearly had much in common with the thought of the European Far Right, and especially with contemporary Ger-man traditions: he was an early reader of Nietzsche. Collier's own ideas translate painfully well into German. But he was also influenced by anar-chist and socialist writers, who bolstered his principle of community. From Prince Kropotkin he learned that the best social arrangement was one of vol-untary cooperation, of what the master's book termed "mutual aid." William Morris taught him that art and human creativity would flourish best under libertarian socialism. But whatever the political label he es-poused, Collier was primarily motivated by a total rejection of modernity.[53]

Like many Americans, Collier was suffering badly from the fading of the hopes of social improvement that had flourished during the Progressive era, and he was devastated by the World War and its aftermath. In his autobiog-raphy he wrote, "The year 1919 saw the fading away of practically all that I, we, all of us, had put all our being into. My own disillusionment toward the occidental ethos and genius as being the hope of the world was complete. . . . I knew that the old world was finished."[54] Desperately in search of a new world, he saw it at Taos or, rather, he convinced himself that the Pueblo dancers fulfilled his dreams. The power to live "is the ancient lost reverence and passion for human personality, joined with the ancient lost reverence and passion for the earth and its web of life." And this is "what the Ameri-can Indians almost universally had; and representative groups of them have it still."[55] Instead of glorifying noble Nordic roots, as many reactionaries did in these years, Collier transferred his Teutonic dreams to living Indian societies.[56]

Collier famously declared that, in the Pueblo communities, he had found a Red Atlantis, a term that was even more evocative in the context of the time than it would be today. It implied more than just a romantic dream. In the early twentieth century, the idea that Atlantis had been a genuine lost civilization was widespread, and not just among esoteric true believers. To assert any kind of connection between modern Pueblos and Atlantis was to locate their rituals in remote antiquity. But whether he believed in a literal Atlantis, Collier knew that Indian religions were truly ancient, far older than the Judeo-Christian faiths, and on these grounds alone deserved respectful sympathy. "These 'pagan' religions have sustained a whole branch of the human race across ages in comparison to which the epoch of Christianity dwindles to a brief time." Describing a Pueblo ritual, Collier saw "a religious institution where the passions of inner mysticism are blended with social joy—where human nature is at once disciplined, fed and seductively led into the temple of animistic and pantheistic vision."[57]

Among the Pueblos, he could see his political and cultural values put into practice: social, political, mystical, and aesthetic actions were as perfectly integrated as any disciple of Morris could ever have wished. Here he saw a tradition that "realizes man as a co-partner in a living universe—man and nature intimately co-operant and mutually dependent." Indians symbolized the mystical relationship between human communities and the land, which in many ways foreshadows later environmentalism. "What we mean mystically by the Universe, the ancient Indian meant by the Land. From it, the Source, no single member of the tribe must be shut away. Beneficial use of resources was the measure of ownership. The profoundest of tribal ceremonialism was inspired by the will to help the land do its work and to renew the soul out of the land."[58]

With his Nature worship and his rejection of industrial civilization, the Collier of 1920 would obviously have found himself completely at home in the counterculture of the late 1960s. Collier was one of the first writers to publicize the speech attributed to Smohalla, a Native prophet from the Columbia River country, who in the 1880s refused to sell his land to white settlers. The historicity of the speech is controversial since, like many such texts, it was written down by white interpreters, who probably inserted much of their own thought and rhetoric. (The same problem would emerge with the comparable speech of Chief Seattle.) As recorded, though, Smohalla reportedly declared his loyalty to the land as his holy mother: "You ask me to plow the ground! Shall I take a knife and tear my mother's bosom? . . . You ask me to dig for stone! Shall I dig under her skin for her bones? . . . You ask me to cut grass and make hay and sell it, and be rich like white men! But how dare I cut off my mother's hair?" For Collier too, dividing the land "was like cutting to pieces the living body of the Mother."[59]

Obviously, Collier did not represent a mass movement in his revulsion from Euro-American cultures in these years, or in his profound sympathy for things Native, but nor was he unique. Just how influential such views had become was evident from the religious freedom controversies of the early 1920s.

For all the growing doubts about religious assimilation, Indians still remained under the authority of the federal government, and the Bureau of Indian Affairs exercised extraordinary control over Indian fortunes. It therefore posed a real danger when, in the decade after 1915, the authorities began a campaign that could permanently have ended the exercise of Native religion.

But in cultural terms, the new policy could not have been worse timed. By the early 1920s, the idea that Indian religions had much to teach the white world was commonplace in artistic and intellectual circles. This offered the potential for a serious opposition to attempts to suppress or limit Indian religious rights. The resulting controversy provoked one of America's great debates over religious liberty.

5

Crisis in Red Atlantis
1914–1925

All Indian "dances" are ceremonies of a religious nature, and cannot be described without reference to the life and beliefs of the Indian. Even the medicine men, less frequent today than formerly, are deeply religious in significance.

—Alida Sims Markus

The ancient ways were now endangered by social and political trends that were pushing toward forcible assimilation. The First World War, which discredited Western civilization in the eyes of some intellectuals, also promoted the growth of the federal government, and encouraged intervention—even regimentation—in moral matters. In the second decade of the century, too, Americans were debating new concepts of racial and national identity. Mass immigration provoked demands for homogenization, for Americanization, while the wartime rhetoric of national unity reduced toleration for dissent and dissenters. Between 1919 and 1925, a series of Supreme Court decisions on free speech and political dissent placed severe limits on the First Amendment right to free expression. Repeatedly, too, religious minorities ran afoul of new laws intended to promote conformity. Pacifist sects suffered for draft resistance during the war years, and during the early 1920s, the Amish were persecuted and jailed for refusing to send their children to public schools. In the name of assimilation, some states tried to force all children into the state schools, including Roman Catholics. Not until 1925 did the Supreme Court temper these efforts, reaffirming that "the child is not the mere creature of the state." Generally, though, minority rights did not fare well in these years. Pressures to Americanize augured very ill for those regions that attracted visitors precisely because they were so far removed from the dominant civilization.

In these same years, Americans became deeply concerned about moral threats, and again, sweeping new laws regulated private conduct. In 1914, the U.S. Congress enacted the antidrug Harrison Act, a forerunner for the 1919 prohibition of alcohol. The nation experienced a wave of panic over sexual violence and exploitation, as serial killers, sex offenders, and child molesters became national demon figures, alongside "drug fiends." Concern over sex crime, like that over substance abuse, allowed the mushroom growth of novel federal criminal justice agencies, most famously the FBI. And there was intense concern over fanatical fringe religions, then as now known as "cults." Throughout these emerging social issues, we can trace a rhetoric of racial danger and the threat of degeneracy, which related closely to contemporary debates over Americanization and immigration. In the alarmist view, the white race was endangered by drink and drugs as much as by the sexual diseases spread by "sex perverts," while cults symbolized a descent into racial primitivism. Suppressing these threats—which were eugenic as much as moral—was essential for the preservation of a strong, pure America.[1]

In all these areas, Native cultures were a source of special concern. The Indian "peyote cult," united the menaces of dangerous drugs and seductive cults. Meanwhile, traditional rituals were under assault for their alleged sexual immoralities, a charge that was relatively new in the antipagan polemic. There was every reason to believe that a frontal federal assault against Native religion would be successful. If neither Catholics nor respectable sects like the Amish were immune from state interference, Indian faiths could expect no better treatment. Reviewing a book on Cheyenne religion in 1924, a writer complained about the over-lengthy accounts of religious rituals, "but it should be remembered that these ceremonies are rapidly dying out, and that it will not be many years before they cease to be practiced. From a scientific point of view, it is highly important that we have an accurate picture of them."[2]

Given the forces ranged against them, it is all the more remarkable that Native religions survived and even flourished. In part, this victory reflected the growth of influential pro-Native interest groups over the previous two decades, but resistance could not have succeeded if America was not experiencing a significant change of religious attitudes, a much greater openness to non-Christian religions.

Peyote

In the early twentieth century, the most visible and scandalous aspect of Native spirituality was the rise of the new peyote religion. Troubling in itself to white observers, the peyote movement threatened to discredit all aspects of Native religiosity by association. Exposés of peyote highlighted all the traditional accusations against Indian cultures, and in the frightening context of a very modern antidrug panic. Since peyote was a symbol of resistance to assimilation, moves to suppress this practice threatened to spill over into attacks on all Native religions.[3]

Peyote had a long history in Mexico, where it had been denounced by Spanish authorities since the early seventeenth century. The fact that the drug was used for divination proved "the suggestion and intervention of the devil, the real author of this vice, who . . . avails himself of the natural credulity of the Indians and their tendency to idolatry."[4] Confessors' manuals placed the practice on a moral par with cannibalism. From the 1890s onwards, ceremonial peyote use spread across Indian lands from Mexico into Canada, and the practice received a massive boost from the collapse of the Ghost Dance movement. In an age of despair and social dissolution, Indians were attracted by the peyote movement's doctrine of responsibility and social integration. The emerging peyote church taught faithful marriage, personal discipline, and the avoidance of alcohol. The movement spread through missionary tactics borrowed from the Mormons, as pairs of young men wandered the country, converting Indians to the new message. Ironically, what whites saw as a grim reversion to mystical savagery had largely been made possible by their own technological advances, namely the spread of the railroads. The movement won the support of James Mooney, who first saw the rituals in Oklahoma in 1891, and who believed they could benefit the Indian nations. Mooney advised the peyote leaders that they should incorporate legally as a church, in order to secure greater protection and legal status. Peyote practice was formalized by the establishment of the Native American Church of North America, incorporated in Oklahoma in 1918.[5]

Mainstream white reaction to the new movement was overwhelmingly hostile, as concern over peyote popularized the word "cult" as a description of Native religion. This term originally had no negative connotations. Scholars continue to speak of a kind of worship or veneration as a "cult," like the "cult of saints," and archaeologists might decide that an ancient religious site was "cultic" in nature. But at the end of the nineteenth century, the word "cult" entered American speech with very much its modern meaning, as a malevolent fringe religion associated with fanaticism and exploitation, with megalomaniacal leaders and gullible adherents.[6]

In the Indian context, the word usually maintains its objective meaning, so that observers of Hopi religion speak respectfully of the thriving kachina cult. Fewkes had written of this "intricate cultus," while John Wesley Powell described the "cult societies" of the Zuñi. In the early twentieth century, though, the modern derogatory sense of "cult" is much more in evidence. In 1915, a writer in the *Missionary Review* reported on the gallant souls "fighting to save the American Indians from the degrading cult of peyote worship . . . the pernicious mescal cult." By 1923, missionaries denounced "the new and insidious cult of peyote (the Indian's cocaine)." This was "the greatest and most insidious evil. . . . The use of peyote or mescal has become one of the most serious menaces in the progress of the Indian race in the United States." Accounts of these "cult gatherings" or "peyote séances" sound familiar from any modern exposé of sinister cult movements. Participants were involved in a "weird ceremony," a "peyote debauche," with trappings suggesting ancient paganism and primitive savagery. In 1923, the *New York Times* headlined, "PEYOTE USED AS DRUG IN INDIANS' 'CULT OF DEATH.'" The peyote movement integrated "ancient beliefs and practices dating back to the Aztecs, among whom the use of the drug in connection with religious rites is supposed to have originated." Citing the Aztecs raised grim shades of human sacrifice and bloodletting, and although actual violence was not cited, peyote caused "imbecility, insanity and suicide."[7]

The terminology had legal consequences, since a "cult" did not deserve religious protections. In 1917, a *Denver Post* story told how "to get a better hold on the victims, the peyote peddlers have lent a religious tone to the ceremony of eating the drug, so that the peyote is worshipped in a semi-barbaric festival before the orgy is held." Reporting the peyote "craze," the *Times* spoke of a "new 'religious' movement." The quotes suggest incredulity about the authentically religious nature of this, or perhaps any, distinctively Native movement. Peyotism was at best "a new semi-religious movement." The challenge to Christianity was explicit: missionaries were alarmed by "a system of worship inimical to Christianity." The *Times* asked: "How long will the Christian citizenship of this country now giving its money to maintain schools and churches, to emancipate and Christianize the Indian, permit this menace to continue?"[8]

Peyote use attracted the hostility of advocates who were normally sympathetic to Indian cultures and traditions. Even Zitkala-Sa complained in 1916 that "the human system, disabled with dope, is no receptacle for the jewels of education and civilization. The Indian is no exception." The drug alienated key white allies. Since the end of the nineteenth century, peyote had attracted the curiosity of celebrities who experimented with it out of scientific curiosity, including William James, James Mooney, and Havelock Ellis. As often happens with such substances, serious experimentation gave way to recreational or amateur use, and peyote appeared in exotic parties in New York. The drug had some presence in the bohemian and decadent countercultures of the day, and the occult milieu around Aleister Crowley used both peyote and mescaline.[9]

One such Greenwich Village soiree in 1914 would be important in shaping white responses to the drug. The event was organized by anthropologist Raymond Harrington, with guests including Mabel Dodge, Max Eastman, and Andrew Dasburg. The group intended to reproduce an authentic Indian religious ritual, complete with "a green arrow, some eagle feathers, a fire, the Mountain of the Moon, and the Peyote Path. . . . For a fire he laid a lighted electric bulb on the floor with my Chinese red shawl over it. . . . But the Peyote Path was a white sheet folded into a narrow strip, running toward the east along the floor." This is one of the first examples of a white attempt to reproduce an authentic Native ceremony in its entirety, and the event made suggestive connections to other cultures: several of the participants reported powerful Aztec themes in their dreams and visions over the coming weeks. But the experiment proved disastrous, as one participant suffered what a later generation would call a bad trip, leading to a nervous breakdown. The outcome so horrified Mabel Dodge that she campaigned against peyote for decades afterwards, trying to exclude it from what she regarded as her private fief at Taos Pueblo.[10]

Predictably, the BIA tried to suppress the practice, lobbying for the drug's proscription in individual states. In 1914, when a U.S. District Court failed to prohibit consumption of peyote under antialcohol statutes, the bureau tried to circumvent the courts by defining it as a narcotic, placing it in the same category as heroin and cocaine. But enforcement was patchy, and peyote rituals spread during the interwar years. Legal brushfire wars ensued through these decades, and not until the 1960s did courts generally recognize the right of Indians (and Indians alone) to use the substance ritually.

Pagan Dances

The fact that concern about peyote was at its height in the early 1920s could not fail to shape public attitudes to other Indian religious issues. Native religion, it seemed, promoted systematic vice and immorality. The new conflict originated with the traditional foes of Indian paganism, the Christian missionaries.[11] In 1919, the Interchurch World Movement sponsored an "American Indian Survey" with a view to promoting the spread of Protestant Christianity among the Natives. The report was published in 1923 as *The Red Man in the United States*, edited by G. E. E. Lindquist, and it had much that was positive to report about missionary efforts. In some instances, though, the report saw grave drawbacks to religious and civil progress. The new peyote religion was heartily condemned. Also, some Protestant activists denounced the traditional Indian for keeping alive old religious ways, for wasting valuable work time, and—and this was a new emphasis—for promoting sexual immorality. Though originally ceremonial and recreational, "under modern conditions, these dances have developed into some of the strongest influences for race demoralization and degeneracy." Though the writers work from the missionary standpoint, the language borrows from racial and eugenic theory.[12]

Missionary complaints found a sympathetic ear in the BIA, which, during the new Harding administration, was in the hands of politicians interested in the West, and unsympathetic to Indian causes. The new Secretary of the Interior, the ultimate overlord of Indian affairs, was Albert B. Fall, who was then intervening in a long-running land dispute in his home state of New Mexico. White and Latino squatters claimed ownership of extensive Pueblo lands, and Secretary Fall fulfilled their expectations by drafting a sweeping bill introduced by New Mexico Senator Holm Bursum. The Bursum Bill would have massively reduced Pueblo landholdings. Even worse for the tribes, the bill would transfer jurisdiction over their cases to state courts, which would be empowered to investigate tribal structures and religious practices, all of which the Pueblos treated with the utmost secrecy. In effect, the Bursum Bill threatened to dissolve Pueblo society. Meanwhile, the new BIA Commissioner was former South Dakota Congressman Charles H. Burke, who had contributed a laudatory introduction to *The Red Man in the United States*. To Indian eyes, the cast of characters in Washington could hardly have seemed more threatening.[13]

To the astonishment of BIA officials, though, the Bursum Bill faced a mobilization organized by well-connected members of the American elites, which marked an entirely new stage of organization on behalf of Indian rights. One key activist was Stella Atwood, a leader of the General Federation of Women's Clubs, which claimed a membership of two million. Atwood was already working with Zitkala-Sa, and she now mobilized other allies, including John Collier. The intellectuals of Taos and Santa Fe organized a public campaign under the slogan "LET'S SAVE THE PUEBLOS," which became a leading liberal cause. A "Protest of Artists and Writers" included the familiar Indian loyalists such as Mary Austin, Elsie Clews Parsons, Alice Corbin Henderson, and Zane Grey, as well as such leading lights as Carl Sandburg, D. H. Lawrence, Vachel Lindsay, Edgar Lee Masters, and William Allen White. (Natalie Curtis's absence from the campaign was explained by her tragically premature death in 1921.) Catholic organizations were also involved, and as Collier remarks, "from this time on, the Catholic Church never deserted the Indian cause." Indians themselves also organized. In 1922, the council of the combined New Mexico Pueblos met for the first time since the great revolt that in 1680 briefly expelled the region's Spanish occupiers—an auspicious precedent. Mabel Dodge was thrilled by the swelling of public support: "The country almost has seemed to *go Indian.* There hasn't been a single denial or refusal. *Universal* response. Is it possible that the little drop of Indian in every one awakened and answered the call?" She hoped that this could be channeled into a longer-term program, at once political and aesthetic. "We want interest and appreciation of the Indian life and culture to become a part of our *conscious* racial mind."[14]

The protest cause was helped by the coincidental revelations during 1923 of the Teapot Dome scandal, in which Albert Fall and the Department of the Interior played a pivotal role. It looked implausible for the Interior Department to try and teach Christian morality to anyone, let alone to an ancient civilization like the Pueblos. (Fall would be imprisoned for perjury.) The public mobilization ensured that Pueblo society never suffered the devastation threatened by the Bursum measure.

Under the Fall-Burke regime, traditional Indian practices could expect little mercy. In 1921, BIA Circular 1665 declared that "the Sun Dance and all other similar dances and so-called religious ceremonies are considered 'Indian Offenses' under existing regulations and corrective penalties are provided." But the prohibition effort now extended far beyond such controversial rituals, and threatened to attack all ceremonies. The following year, a conference of missionary groups active among the Lakota recommended stringent limitations on dances, and demanded "that a careful propaganda be undertaken to educate public opinion against the dance and to provide a healthy substitute." Shortly afterward, Commissioner Burke urged Indians to restrict tribal dances: "I do not want you to torture your bodies or to handle poisonous snakes in your ceremonies. All such extreme things are wrong and should be put aside and forgotten." There was an implied threat that tougher sanctions would follow: "if the reports show that you reject this plea, then some other course will have to be taken." An official circular urged superintendents to act in the spirit of the missionaries' recommendations, though avoiding compulsion as far as possible.

By 1923, official policy toward the dances was further spelled out on exactly the lines recommended by the missionaries. Ceremonies were "to be limited to one each month in the daylight hours of one day in the midweek, and at one center in each circuit; the months of March and April, June, July and August be excepted; that none take part in the dances or be present who are under fifty years of age." Burke offered some possible concessions—for instance, those under fifty might attend "if the occasion were properly controlled and unattended by immoral or degrading influence." But overall, it was critical to suppress "ancient and barbarous customs."[15] (According to Collier, the attack on pagan dances was a direct consequence of the Bursum agitation, to divert attention from land issues, but the policy had been gestating at least since 1921.)

The Sexual Menace

The new policy was not explicitly religious in intent, being chiefly concerned with suppressing "idleness, waste of time at frequent gatherings of whatever nature." Throughout, the new assault deployed sexual themes, stressing the prevention of immorality, and the defense of pure womanhood. Paganism condemned women to early marriage and childbearing, while the dances themselves were thin disguises for orgiastic behavior. The shift in the rhetoric denouncing Indian religion makes sense in terms of the national audience for claims about social problems, since women were now more likely to be involved as activists and social reformers. Especially in the aftermath of the Eighteenth and Nineteenth Amendments to the Constitution, framing an issue in gender terms could be politically effective. In the event, the pro-Indian cause continued to be led by the familiar band of women activists, but some women's organizations, including the YWCA, did support the attack on Indian rituals.[16]

Claims about sexual immorality became a powerful theme in the American Indian Survey, which implied that the seemingly charming dances of the Pueblos and other groups only masked various Nameless Horrors, usually of a sexual kind:

> According to statements by well informed people, [the secret dances] are characterized by unbridled license. . . . There is a report on file in the Indian Office concerning obscenities connected with the "religious" rites of the more backward Pueblos, and their barbaric cruelties when inflicting punishment, that is almost beyond belief. Thus far however, nothing has been done to eradicate these practices, probably on the ground that they belong to an Indian "religion."

Many of the complaints focused on the activities of the Koshare, the sacred clowns, who represented the forces of chaos and disorder. Various stories told of them fondling girls' breasts, of exposing themselves to women, of acts of sodomy. The secret dances of the Zuñis were "characterized by orgies similar to those noted as prevalent among the Pueblos." Among the Hopis, " 'special privileges' are accorded to the young men partaking in the dances." The implication is that these privileges were sexual, and the report stressed the peculiar dangers facing young Native girls. The Indian Bureau supported its claims of immorality with its book-length dossier of "unprintable, highly pornographic charges of wickedness in the religious practices," which was distributed to media outlets. These charges gained credence from contemporary allegations about Indian peyote use. If, as large sections of the public had come to believe, cocaine and marijuana inspired ungovernable lust, why should peyote not have the same effects?[17]

Charges of immorality and violence undermined the defense that suppressing the dances interfered with religious freedom. While the dances might be picturesque old customs, that did not mean that they should be immune from suppression or regulation. In India, the British had suppressed the equally venerable customs of Suttee (widow-killing) and child marriage, and the obscene rites attributed to the Pueblos should properly go the same way. Were the Indians' defenders really proclaiming an absolute right to religious freedom, regardless of their evil effects? As the *Missionary*

Review argued in 1925, it was naïve and dangerous of "a few authors, artists and ethnologists" to:

> decry any effort to eliminate tribal and racial art, traits and customs, even though such may be largely responsible for a peoples' poverty, ignorance and degradation. Apologists are found for polygamy, for the indecent in India's art and literature, for immoral African dances and for the American Indian's war dances, the weakening peyote worship and other degrading religious ceremonies.

If Indians were to emerge as Christian citizens, pagan rituals must cease.[18]

Indian Rights

These claims were enthusiastically preached by the long-established Indian Rights Association (IRA), which urged that tribal structures must be ended as the only means of bringing individual Indians to full citizenship in modern America. Association president Herbert Welsh wished to bring the Indians "out of a stone-age condition of human society by the spiritual force of Christian religion." According to Welsh, the Pueblos were in the midst of a full-scale pagan revival. Though dances might be picturesque, they were connected with features "that are held in secret that are of the most hideous, obscene and revolting character, dances the white people are never permitted to see." These secret rites might include actual human sacrifice. The Association claimed to hold sheaves of confidential reports and affidavits filled with unprintable details of these atrocious rites. "Children are being deliberately instructed in the most loathsome and vicious practices, under the plea that they are being initiated into the secret rites of a pure and beautiful religion."[19]

The critics' language has dated badly. Modern audiences instinctively suspect moralistic arguments using phrases like "hideous, obscene and revolting" and "loathsome and vicious." Herbert Welsh was a dubious source, given his strongly Protestant critique of the relatively tolerant Catholic missionary policies. Having said this, groups such as the Indian Rights Association had some worthwhile arguments to make, quite unrelated to either religious rivalry or sexual slanders. Their basic question was one familiar from contemporary debates in the African American community, namely, how did minority peoples survive and flourish in a white-dominated America? This was the core of the famous controversy between Booker T. Washington and W. E. B. DuBois. Was it better policy to assimilate, to embrace mainstream values, and, in effect, to become super-Americans? Or should one espouse cultural nationalism and separatism? The answer was by no means obvious, whether for Native or black Americans.

This debate had an added dimension for Indians, most of whom still lived in tribal or reservation communities. If they remained in their traditional communities, they would still have their ancient culture and rituals, but they would be denied any chance of individual enterprise, of economic modernization, of democratic participation. In this instance, religious pluralism ran directly into conflict with individualism and democracy. To quote M. K. Sniffen, an IRA official and one of the writers of the 1923 survey, preserving the old pagan order meant, in practice, "[letting] them remain in charge of the pagan *caciques* (high priests) of the respective pueblos whose rule shall be unquestioned even when it is autocratic and unjust by denying to the individual the right to think and act for himself." During the 1923 controversies, the bureau charged that pagan Pueblos were persecuting Christian neighbors, denying them their religious freedom. Though most Pueblos were indeed Christian, they expected strict conformity to tribal rituals and customs, and pressured dissenters. As the *Missionary Review* argued in 1925, this was the real threat to religious freedom: "the Indian chiefs, *caciques* and *gouvernors*, in an effort to keep alive these ceremonies, deny religious liberty to members of a community who refuse to participate. In other words, they punish and 'persecute' men, women and children who wish to break away from degrading rites."[20]

For critics like Welsh or Sniffen, those who defended Native rituals were dooming actual living Indians to live in perpetual slavery to repressive tribal systems, victims of the romantic white illusion of traditional society as naturally spiritual, aesthetic, and utopian. Particularly given the direction that U.S. Indian policy actually would follow over the next quarter-century, those were not foolish points to raise. Welsh and his allies added an effective rhetoric of individual rights to what was already a powerful indictment against the Indian rituals.

Resistance

Though the whims of BIA commissioners generally became government policy, in this case, the attack on the dances generated a real public fight.

The breadth and ferocity of the new resistance was stunning, massively larger than the limited complaints of the 1880s and 1902–1903. Participants in the 1923 controversies long recalled "the howl of protest which went up . . . [which] is still echoing in the Sangre de Cristo mountains."[21]

The Indian defense movement grew directly out of the existing resistance to the Bursum Bill, and it involved very much the same leadership, most with strong Taos connections. Commenting on the roots of the agitation, Alice Corbin Henderson wrote that "what happened last fall and winter, the storm of protest that flooded the press and astonished the still bewildered Indian Office, was altogether spontaneous and unexpected; but the roots of this outburst were far-back and full-grown." Again, John Collier played a leading role, as did Mabel Dodge. By 1923, Collier had a good deal of experience in reaching the media, and in winning sympathy for the Indians as exploited victims of hypocritical bureaucrats. One effective tactic devised by Collier and Dodge was a publicity tour of Pueblo representatives to New York and Chicago, where they performed dances in venues that included the New York Stock Exchange. Collier's activism would spawn a more lasting organization, in the American Indian Defense Association, AIDA (the older Society of American Indians had ceased to operate by 1923).[22]

But for all his celebrity, Collier was by no means a lone crusader. Other activists were poet Mary Austin and archaeologist Edgar Hewett, who had both long fought to defend Native arts and antiquities. The two met in Santa Fe in 1918, where Hewett headed the School of American Research. Between them, they had a wide network of friends and supporters. Both agreed that the BIA's proposed policies were a massive act of cultural vandalism, in addition to religious repression. Another visible leader was William S. Hart, one of the best-known cowboy film stars of the day, who had a deep and enduring interest in Native societies, and reputedly knew several Indian languages.[23]

From 1921 through 1924, BIA policy was widely attacked in the media, and charges against the dances were rebutted in visible outlets like the *New York Times*. Alice Corbin Henderson wrote that the movement "came largely from men and women deeply interested in the cultural life of the Indians, from scientists who have devoted their lives to a study of this culture, and from American artists and writers who have more recently come under the spell of Indian art, poetry, and music." Anthropologists joined artists, bohemians and tourists to protest the possible destruction of Native culture. A Los Angeles-based National Association to Help Indians aspired "to preserve ancient customs, beliefs and rites."[24]

The cause found allies among the intellectuals and bohemians who had traveled west with a strong predisposition to favor the primitive over bourgeois civilization. Some of the new arrivals also brought with them novel political attitudes, and experience in activism, whether that was socialist, feminist, or prolabor. In understanding the cultures from which they derived, in New York and other great cities, we might think of the second decade of the century as a prototype of the 1960s, in which radical political, social, artistic, and sexual ideas were manifested in new techniques of community organization, mass action, and simple rabble-rousing. In some ways, the year 1915 looks like a plausible dry run for 1968, and that was the political setting the bohemians had left behind them in New York. Most of the intellectual arrivals liked Indian cultures; and a number of them also knew valuable ways to publicize and defend them. BIA bureaucrats now found themselves facing protesters as obstreperous and determined as their better-known successors in the 1960s. Arguably, this was the first example of a mass cultural intervention in American politics.[25]

From the outset, the debate revealed a fascinating geographical slant. The BIA policy was initiated by people familiar with the Plains Indians, especially the Lakota; this was true of Burke himself, and also the activist missionaries. In public debate, though, the policy was discussed almost exclusively in terms of southwestern Indians, mainly the Pueblos. Reading the major newspapers, one could be forgiven for assuming that Arizona and New Mexico accounted for almost all the nation's Indians, rather than somewhat less than 20 percent. The media scarcely mentioned conditions in the Dakotas, Montana, or Minnesota, and devoted little space to Oklahoma, which was home to over one-third of America's Indians. Since few white tourists had ever visited these other Indian communities, they could easily be persuaded to believe the worst about the rituals of (say) the Plains Indians. But many whites, especially upper class and educated individuals, had by now visited the pueblos, however fleetingly. They relished the tourist opportunities there, and were enchanted by the romantic myth of the primitive. They were horrified at the threat that, as the *New York Times* lamented, "another year will bring to an end the Hopi Snake Dance, the Flute Dance, the Corn Dance of Santo Domingo, San Felipe, and other pueblos of the Rio Grande, the Festival of San Geronimo at Taos, the Shalago of Zuni, the Deer, Buffalo and Antelope Dances, besides other *beautiful religious ceremonies* [my emphasis]."[26] Repressing minorities is easy when the groups under attack do not have influential friends and sympathizers in the dominant community, but by this stage, the Pueblos emphatically did.

Defending Indians

Anti-BIA rhetoric operated at several levels. Most basically, the need was to rebut charges about the evils of pagan rituals and specifically the sexual allegations, and this was not hard to do. But linked to this, a novel and much more ambitious rhetoric asserted the right of Indians to practice a pagan religion if they wished, and to define that religion on their own terms, rather than just to select those practices that white observers found congenial. Their religion was indeed ancient, dark, and mysterious, but now, terms like those were regarded as high praise rather than condemnation. Some advocates advanced the revolutionary idea that Indian culture might be superior to that of the white West; and because of the intense publicity, these daring notions now achieved unprecedented visibility in national magazines and the most prestigious newspapers. Equally important, perhaps, is what was not generally said in these polemics. Through all the commentary in magazines and newspapers, virtually no critic was prepared even to give lip-service to the idea of Christianizing Indians, even as a long-term goal. Though the idea was not dead, it was possible to ignore it in respectable public discourse.

Much of the writing in this controversy was targeted against the ill-proven charges of sexual immorality and abuse. The Indians' defenders asserted either that the immorality did not exist, or that, if it did, it had been imported recently under white influence. Some sympathizers were cautious about asserting a right to religious practices that might include sexual elements. In the *New York Times*, Alida Sims Markus wrote that even if sexual improprieties were reported in any of the rituals, "it is likely enough a taint brought in from outside civilization and not one conceived by the mind of the Indian." Frederick W. Hodge, one of the nation's most distinguished anthropologists, argued that all the stories of immorality and violence were bogus, the result of the well-known Indian desire to give the gullible white listener anything he wanted to hear, "but what fun they had the next moment among themselves!"[27]

A few writers, though, were prepared to confront and even defend the possibility of sexual rituals, a concept made easier by the awareness of recent developments in anthropology. Frazer's *Golden Bough* had made the concept

of fertility rituals familiar to a mass audience, and related ideas appear in
T. S. Eliot's *Waste Land*, published at just this time (1922). Defending the
Pueblos on behalf of the AIDA, Elizabeth Shepley Sergeant noted that "in
the primitive world, sex is a part of the necessary and right order of the universe, and sexual and vegetational symbolism are not far apart." If sexual
symbols were wrong, what about familiar European customs like the May-
pole, or even Easter-egg rolling on the White House lawn? Helena Huntington Smith thought that "the [Pueblo] ceremonies are indubitably of a phallic
nature, but they are histrionic and not real, so with a little broad-mindedness
there is no cause for alarm."[28] Few now denied that Indian religion was anything but an authentic religion. As the Indian Defense Association declared,
"these Indian dances are collective religious expressions . . . the various Indian
holy days and holy seasons have been fixed for many centuries and are held in
as great honor as are Easter and Christmas among Christian peoples."[29]

If in fact the dances were part of a religion, then the U.S. government
was engaged in a savage policy of religious persecution, which deserved to be
condemned as a violation of American and particularly Protestant principles. Mary Austin, who claimed to know firsthand the mystical possibilities
of Indian spirituality, blamed the persecution on the "missionary mind." She
linked current policies with the mass destruction of Native texts and objects
by the Spanish conquistadors in Mexico. American policy might not be so
blatant, but "stupidity and neglect worked obscurely and less effectively to
the same end." This kind of religious repression echoed the Inquisition, a
new deployment of the ever-useful rhetoric of anti-Catholicism, which was
running rampant in the early 1920s. Charles F. Lummis argued that "the Indian Bureau is in effect trying to establish this Inquisition, which denies freedom of religion to the Indian parent, and imposes upon the Indian child
some alien creed which it is psychologically impossible for him to grasp."
John Collier agreed that Indians were facing "an actual Inquisition." Meanwhile, international events brought religious persecution and genocide into
the national headlines. Recent reports of religious and ethnic cleansing in Ot-
toman lands during and after the Great War raised awareness of minority religious rights. In 1922, Harry Emerson Fosdick alluded to the continuing
Armenian atrocities in his famous sermon "Shall the Fundamentalists Win?",
suggesting a direct linkage between religious intolerance and state violence.[30]

Also novel was the involvement in these debates of Native groups themselves, who spoke out for "our religion and religious rights," as a group of
Pueblo leaders wrote to the *New York Times* in 1923:

We want to keep our religion as any other white people would like to keep his. . . . The religious beliefs and ceremonies and forms of prayer of each of our Pueblos are as old as the world and they are holy. . . . To pass this religion, with its hidden sacred knowledge and its many forms of prayer on to our children is our supreme duty to our ancestors. . . . There is no future for the race of the Indians if its religion is killed.

Indians had expressed such sentiments often enough in the past, but rarely in the pages of the major newspapers and political magazines.[31]

Critics made effective use of analogies in white society. Did the Indians have secret rituals? Well, so did the Freemasons, who were then at the height of their popularity and prestige (President Warren Harding was a Mason). And Masonic rituals involved secret regalia, passwords, and even blood-thirsty oaths. Nor did the courts demand that Mormons end their exclusion of all nonchurch members from their closed rituals. Did the Indians have their own customs that set them apart from white society? So, too, did the dozens of ethnic groups who had crowded into the United States over the previous quarter-century, and the festivals and religious services of Italians or Poles continued uninterrupted. Even "progressive" Indians committed to Americanization saw no difficulty in keeping the old ceremonies alive as a sign of cultural pride. "They feel that they have a right to perform their old and often beautiful ceremonies, and that these rites do not interfere with their 'civilization.'" As long as mainstream American schools taught folk-dancing, whites had no reason to criticize Indians. In 1923, the *Literary Digest* argued that "religious freedom should be the same for him as for the white man. . . . No churches should be allowed to coerce him, and 'it should not be assumed without proof that a ceremony is immoral or unsanitary without expert evidence to this effect.'"[32]

This rhetoric of religious freedom was widely accepted. Such defenses moved the *New York Times* editorial page to criticize "the well-meaning 're-formers' who are so anxious to stamp out the Indians' culture and religion. . . . There are more ways than one of worshipping. Why not grant to others the right to live and worship after the manner of their fathers?" To quote Carl Moon's story in the *Times*, the Navajos were asking, "What sort of Great White Father is it that will put the taboo on a fellow's religion?" The Navajos "do not understand why it is so important to the white people that institutions centuries older than the white man's occupation of America should be banned by the power of a great government." Many critics of official policy cited the antiquity of Indian religion. The *Literary Digest* complained that "dancing has been a religion with the Indian for uncounted centuries; but he is given a year to think of some other way of expressing his religious emotions, or else. . . . The threat is left unexpressed." A cartoon in the *New York Tribune* mocked the busybody attitude of the BIA toward dances "about as barbaric as the Virginia Reel." While a BIA figure demands an end to "barbaric dances" that make Indians too emotional, the response is: "Sure! And send some missionaries out to teach them the Charleston!"[33]

An Old Dark Religion

For the white activists, ending the Indian rituals would be nothing short of a cultural catastrophe. Just as the nation had recognized the need to preserve Mesa Verde or the Grand Canyon, so Indian religion should be defended as a comparable treasure. Alida Sims Markus wrote of the tragedy of "those doomed Indian dances." These dances were good in themselves, "not only pageants of beauty but an inexhaustible fund of material for study; study that reveals the continuity of human development through living representatives of a prehistoric race." In his much-quoted paean to the aesthetic achievements of Native peoples, artist Marsden Hartley had written, "I cannot imagine what would happen to the redman if his one racial gesture were denied him, if he were forbidden to perform his symbolic dances from season to season." As Jung would argue, "the Pueblos as an individual community will continue to exist as long as their mysteries are not desecrated."[34]

Activists tried to present religious values in Indian terms, and in the process, they offered a very attractive picture. In the *New Republic*, Elizabeth Shepley Sergeant offered a lyrical description of the Pueblo religion, stressing the broad definition of concepts of sanctity, which extended to all mountains and canyons. On reservations where Native rituals had fallen into disuse, the society had itself fallen into decadence:

> While the dance ritual survives, even in modified or derived form, some legendary ghostly image or breath of the old free primordial red man's life will still haunt desert and prairie, and hold our red brothers in thrall. When it shall be wholly eliminated, red man and white will lose that last lovely vision of their country's Golden Age. For with the dances will die Indian costume and handicraft and decorative symbolism, Indian rhythm

and music and song, Indian worship and communal consciousness. Then will every Indian surely prefer the YMCA to the kiva, the corner to the tombé, and the movies to the Deer Dance.

Her article was entitled "Death to the Golden Age." Indian religion was essential to the Indian people, and a common phrase used to describe official policy was "taking the Indianism out of the Indian."[35]

These views reflected badly on the missionaries, who had long been the heroes of Protestant culture. As the *New Republic* wrote soon after these events, the missionary venture was questionable at the best of times, but attempts to convert America's Indians were particularly ham-fisted. Perhaps domestic evangelistic activities attracted inferior people, while the best sought adventure in Africa or China. These domestic missionaries

have been responsible for much of the stupid and narrow official attitude displayed toward, for example, the ceremonial dances of the desert Indians of the southwest, which they are all too prone to dismiss as unimportant "heathen ceremonies," overlooking the fact that these ceremonies mean quite as much to the Indian as Easter or Christmas means to the most devout Christian, and infinitely more than they do to 99 percent of the members of the average Church.[36]

Some activists urged that Indian religion contained treasures that the whites still had to discover, and pointed to the spiritual emptiness in Western culture. Anthropologist and poet Jaime De Angulo wrote:

They dance sullenly in the Pueblos for the whites are watching. The whites have forbidden the dances. The whites understand nothing. They think the Sun is just a shining plate. . . . They think only with their heads. They have lost their hearts. . . . The factories whir incessantly with fire in their engines. The white men run about, crazy. They have lost something.

In the *New York Times*, D. H. Lawrence argued that:

the Indians keep burning an eternal fire, the sacred fire of the old dark religion . . . let us try to adjust ourselves again to the Indian outlook, to take up an old dark thread from their vision, and see again as they see, without forgetting that we are ourselves. For it is a new era we have got to cross into. And our own electric light won't show us over the gulf. We have to feel our way by the dark thread of the old vision.[37]

John Collier declared that white Americans were too spiritually unsophisticated to comprehend the truths of the Native faiths. Far from being a shadowy precursor of Christianity, Indian religions contained within themselves much that Christianity had lost, or failed to learn. Familiar as these ideas sound today, they were radical in the context of the time. Though not entirely new, the pagan dance controversy allowed them to reach an unprecedented audience.

Collier's rhetoric about Indian religion was uncompromising:

> Substantially all of the Indian dance-drama ceremonials are religious. But the religion is of a kind that our modern unsophisticated mind knows little about, and it includes so much that ascetic Christianity has cast out from religion and committed to the world and the devil that it has been natural for our white missionaries and Indian Agents to believe they were dealing merely with barbaric social amusements. They actually have not known that they were thrusting themselves with contempt and violence into a holy of holies; they have not known that they were forcibly persecuting a religion whose waters were being drawn from the very fountain head.

Collier's demand for toleration extended to controversial rituals such as the Sun Dance, "a merging of every individual with the annually resurrected tribe in a social cosmic worship"[38] Indian religion was simply necessary to their survival as a people. As Collier wrote, "The Indians are deeply and universally religious. They still know how as tribes to follow ancient paths leading to the water of heaven. United in this life of religion, they can still stand up together as men, and they can still cling to their coveted remnants of soil." One of the glories of civilization is the recognition of "the sacredness of primitive religion to the primitive, and the beauty and nobility of it to the eyes of the informed civilized man." "Forcible Christianization" was unacceptable.[39]

Aftermath

Ultimately, the BIA's suppression policy failed. In 1926, Congress rejected a bill that would have allowed the bureau's commissioner to suppress religious practices of which he disapproved. The recent agitations also had political consequences, since a 1924 law gave Indians a new status as U.S. citizens. Indians now had full First Amendment protections, though it would be decades before the full effects of this change became apparent.

Not only had the enemies of Indian religions failed on this occasion to impose religious uniformity, but it was unlikely that conditions would ever be more favorable in the future. Liberal Christianity was in the ascendant in the mainline churches, and intolerance was condemned by the experience of the Ku Klux Klan movement of the mid-1920s, the Scopes trial of 1925, and the resurgence of anti-Catholicism during the 1928 presidential election. Indians were unlikely to face an officially sponsored missionary crusade to convert them forcibly. As Alice Corbin Henderson wrote, "There can be no doubt that public interest is now thoroughly roused, not only to the obvious necessity of keeping faith with our Indian wards, but also to the involved responsibility of preserving a primitive art and culture which, once destroyed, can never be restored."[40] So many were the defenders of Indian religions, and so well placed socially, that it became controversial to make what would once have been obvious remarks about the failings of Indian culture or religion. To do so invited condemnation as a bigot, a fundamentalist, an inquisitor.

During the late 1920s, public interest in Indians shifted away from explicitly religious affairs, but the social, economic, and political reform of Indian administration was now definitely on the agenda. The visibility that Collier received made him a national figure, the leader of an increasingly visible AIDA, which found ever more grounds for activism in new exposés and investigations. In 1928, the cause of Indian reform received a boost from a report, *The Problem of Indian Administration*, edited by Lewis Meriam, which exposed the mismanagement of Indian administration and the extreme poverty that it had either caused or failed to cure. Complaints about BIA abuses were not new, nor was the exposure of scandals, but this was far more systematic. In 1929, crusading journalist Vera Connolly published a muckraking attack on Indian administration in *Good Housekeeping*, exposing to a mass audience the extent of poverty and child exploitation in Indian communities.[41]

By the time Franklin Roosevelt was elected President in 1932, sweeping Indian reform was firmly part of the liberal agenda, and the New Deal relied heavily on the blueprint set out by the Meriam report. One of Roosevelt's key supporters was Harold Ickes, a veteran of the struggle against the Bursum Bill, who now became Secretary of the Interior. In choosing someone to oversee a total revision of Indian policy, Ickes turned to John Collier. This was a natural choice based on Collier's public reputation, but a remarkable decision given his mystical religious beliefs and his glorification of the primeval. In 1934, Collier became BIA Commissioner, and he personally remained the nation's most cited authority on Native affairs well into the 1950s. Collier was chosen to oversee a social revolution, which was mainly aimed to eliminate abuses in material conditions—in economic arrangements, in land rights, in educational policy, in political self-determination. But he believed that such a change could never come about unless rooted in "spiritual rehabilitation," and in a wholly new approach to Indian religions.

6

※

Brave New Worlds
1925—1950

We speak now as representatives of the most heroic race the world has ever seen, the most physically perfect race the world has ever seen, the most spiritual civilization the world has ever seen.

—Ernest Thompson Seton

During the 1920s and 1930s, Native spirituality established itself in the American consciousness as a valid religious tradition. Mainstream attitudes toward Native cultures became significantly more respectful and admiring. In 1934, George Cronyn noted the revolutionary change of attitudes that had occurred just since he first published his *Path on the Rainbow* in 1918. "At the very moment when the rich racial heritage of the Red Man seemed destined to vanish into archaeological obscurity, his vast, complex and poetic-cultural contribution approaches the recognition it deserves among all those who cherish the spiritual treasures of the human race."[1] Radical ideas popularized by John Collier about the superiority of Indian religions became commonplace, regularly presented in books and the news media. Cultural sensitivity toward Indian ways became sharply more obvious at the beginning of the 1930s, a time when many perceived a crisis of confidence in Western values. In the early 1930s, books sympathetically presenting Indian culture and beliefs were appearing at a rate that would not be matched again until the 1970s. New marketing practices promoted a favorable image of Indians, partly through the sale of artifacts and Indian crafts, but also through the dissemination of Indian spiritual wisdom.

113

Mending the House

When John Collier was seeking a historic precedent for the world he found
among the Indians, he cited the Teutonic community portrayed in William
Morris's *House of the Wolfings*. That story ends when the pagan Germanic warriors have driven off the Roman invaders and begin the task of restoration:

> Now when all this was done . . . the Wolfings gathered in wheat-harvest,
> and set themselves to make good all that the Romans had undone; and
> they cleansed and mended their Great Roof and made it fairer than be-
> fore, and took from it all signs of the burning. . . . But the Wolfings
> throve in field and fold, and they begat children who grew up to be
> mighty men and deft of hand, and the House grew more glorious year by
> year. The tale tells not that the Romans ever fell on the Mark again.

That account of purging the curse of civilization may have been in Collier's
mind when he became overlord of federal Indian affairs in 1934.[2]

Under his guidance, Congress passed the Indian Reorganization Act, the
Wheeler-Howard law, which reversed the past fifty years of U.S. Indian policy. Over the next decade, tribal structures were restored and reinvigorated as
the government encouraged communal patterns of social organization and
land ownership. In a massive departure from earlier practice, Indian education was reformed to stress Indian culture, and even to preserve Indian languages. The new legislation removed the power to regulate Native ceremony
and ritual, which could now operate openly. BIA Circular 2970, "Indian Religious Freedom and Indian Culture," ordered that "no interference with Indian religious life or ceremonial expression will hereafter be tolerated." As
Collier boasted, "Dead is the centuries-old notion that the sooner we eliminated this doomed race, preferably humanely, the better."[3]

Through the 1930s, Native communities were rent by debates over the
new federal policy, debates which followed exactly the lines sketched by
Herbert Welsh and the Indian Rights Association during the furor over pagan dances. Americanized Indians rejected the return to tribal structures,
fearing that a romantic view of tribal society would create a kind of segrega-
tion, blighting hopes of modernization and democracy. In Collier's mystical
vision of organic communities, Western concepts of democracy were irrelevant, since Native societies already possessed those values through natural
inheritance. At Acoma Pueblo, Collier wrote that its

social organization, its magical and animistic worldview, its racial aims are from of old. That earth shall go on, and the inseparable Race, the tradition and spirit and subliminal power of the Race, is the unchanging preoccupation of Acoma, a democracy of very complex institutions whose pinnacles gleam with a wonder-light and whose foundations rest in a secrecy inviolable.

From this perspective, modern systems of electoral democracy were irrelevant.[4]

Attacks on the new communalism were not limited to hidebound defenders of old-guard BIA policies. Skeptical liberals worried about the plight of individuals whose wishes might contradict those of the "inseparable Race," and religious issues proved divisive. Collier had successfully defended the right of the Pueblos to practice their own religion, but what happened when the now-autonomous Pueblos themselves restricted the rights of other believers, namely peyote believers? Could the Pueblos demand that tribal members participate in kiva rituals? A series of embarrassing disputes followed through the 1930s, and much to the amusement of his old enemies, Collier occasionally interfered in tribal affairs in just as arbitrary a way as his despised BIA predecessors. Clashes over individual rights grew during the 1940s, as Native veterans returned to their hidebound communities. As the *Nation* complained of one famous community in 1950, "Taos is ruled by a self-perpetuating clique of old men who permit no freedom of speech or religion, and no voting."[5]

Pagan Revival?

With all the intense disputes over communalism, land rights, and tribal government, the ambitious program of religious liberalization received strikingly little attention, all the more remarkable since this was such a keystone of Collier's approach. This in itself may testify to the declining influence of traditional evangelical concerns since, at a stroke, the federal government was legalizing pagan practices. No doubt, the social collapse of the 1930s served to shift public priorities to economic issues.

Recalling just how crucial the missionaries had been to Indian policy since Grant's time, their sudden eclipse was shocking. Even after the dance controversy, the Meriam report of 1928, so daring in many of its conclusions, still relied on missionary opinions for its religious discussion. Admittedly, Christian clergy were criticized for their sweeping attacks on all aspects of traditional culture. This was described as ill informed and counterproductive, but largely because it failed to build on the proto-Christian ideas that the investigators believed to lie in Indian religions. "A religion founded upon belief in a Supreme Spirit, the divine origin of the universe, immortality of the soul, and the immediacy and responsiveness of the Deity to human needs has basic factors which can very readily find a home in the great religion which the missionary brings." As before, the goal was still "the conversion of the race to Christianity," and missionaries should still try and persuade Indians away from the temptations of magic and the occult. Though overt repression was condemned, investigators were still far from recognizing Indian religious freedom. Even this committee still felt that Indian superstitions would give way before the march of science. "Once the Hopi is reasonably supplied with water by the government engineers, as he will be some day, the Hopi rain god, the Snake, will depart to return no more." And that, presumably, would be a good outcome.[6]

By the mid-1930s, in contrast, missionary opinions were conspicuously absent from the debates over federal Indian policy. Indian religious affairs were rarely discussed by the mainline churches themselves. As Martin Marty notes, "Theologians paid almost no attention to Native North American religion."[7] This neglect might have been considered a blessing, in that, for the mainline churches, missionary fervor toward Native peoples declined. In religious terms, the old white American triumphalism fell out of favor, at least in the major newspapers and magazines. Christians were acting almost as if the long-expected Indian extinction had actually occurred.

This did not mean that evangelical attitudes vanished overnight. Religious journals like the *Missionary Review of the World* offered a predictable attack on the toleration of paganism, but such protests rarely surfaced in mainstream newspapers or magazines. In 1935, one critic complained that Collier "proposes to resurrect all the old religious ceremonials with their immorality and statutory offenses," which would "debauch every Indian boy and girl" and destroy missionary efforts. But the protest had little effect.

One gauge of change was the lack of reaction to the writings of Elaine Goodale Eastman, the wife of Charles Eastman. From 1935, she wrote some powerful attacks on the new Collier regime in visible religious outlets such as the *Christian Century*, but, again, to no avail. This was striking, given her credentials as an authority on Indian matters and her extensive firsthand knowledge. She had pioneered reservation-based schools as an alternative to

sending children to the controversial boarding schools. In 1937, she produced perhaps the most systematic condemnation of Indian religious practices written since colonial times. Her catalogue of Indian religious abuses
included the peyote cult, polygamy, the ritual isolation of the menstruating
woman, "the occult arts and weird incantations of the medicine men," the
universal belief in witchcraft, "saturnalia" like the Snake Dance, and "rites
involving public torture and mutilation" such as the Sun Dance. She condemned "the new school of Nature-worshipers," white romantics like Collier who idealized this primitive and destructive faith. She pointed to recent
outbreaks of worrying "pagan superstition" like the Wendigo scare in the
northern woods, and asked whether the BIA would stand by while women
were sought out as witches. At any previous time, her account would have
had a real impact, but by the late 1930s, it stood so far removed from the
new social orthodoxies that it was largely ignored.[8]

Respect

Certainly white attitudes to Native faiths did not change overnight, in the
sense of treating them as equivalents to Christianity and Judaism: Willi
Herberg's famous 1955 book about multireligious America was not called
Protestant, Catholic, Jew, and Animist. Nor, despite the formal establishment
of Indian religious freedom in 1934, did the Indian schools end the infor-
mal enforcement of a Christianization policy. Nonattendance at Christian
services remained a serious matter into the 1960s. Throughout the period,
also, we still find examples of disrespect for Native attitudes, all the more
startling for the casual disregard for Indian sensitivities. In 1941, *Natural
History* published the account of a herpetologist curious about the snakes
used in the Hopi ritual. In order to find out if the snakes were defanged, he
had "hastily . . . liberated" one of the animals, that is, stolen it from the
heart of a cherished ritual, and taken it for analysis. The snakes are not actually worshipped, but the disrespect is amazing, all the more so since the
article included not a word about ethical issues. Nobody in the same years
contemplated stealing a consecrated Host from a Catholic church to test
whether it had actually been transformed into flesh and blood.[9] Meanwhile,
the trade in Indian relics and remains continued unabated. In 1955, *Natural
History* published an article headlined "WANT TO COLLECT INDIAN RELICS?
FINDING MEMENTOS OF THE ANCIENT PAST ADDS UNLIMITED ZEST TO

OUTDOOR RAMBLING." Through the 1960s, *Hobbies* magazine ran a regular column, "Indian Relics."[10]

Despite this, mainstream attitudes clearly did change from the mid-1920s onwards, as the ideas that had originated among the intellectuals acquired wider currency. A number of social trends in these years encouraged cultural relativism. Above all, the Crash of 1929 and the following Depression raised doubts about the superiority of urban and industrial Western civilization and its ability to survive. Following so shortly after the shock of World War I, the economic crisis raised grave questions about Western culture. These events naturally aroused interest in alternative arrangements, which were often sought in pre-industrial communities. In 1930, the manifesto *I'll Take My Stand* lauded traditional southern agrarian society. Others looked to America's Native past. In 1934, Collier claimed that the white race was "physically, religiously, socially and esthetically shattered, dismembered, directionless," and that hope lay with the Indians, those "harborers of a great age of integrated inwardly seeking life and art." The fact that such radical ideas about Indian culture were heard so commonly in the early 1930s does much to explain the lack of public objection to the new religious freedom policy. Hopes for Western civilization became even more tenuous as fears grew of another world war.[11]

During the 1930s, moreover, left-wing and radical opinions spread rapidly, with predictable effects on attitudes to social minorities. Familiar narratives of Western and Christian expansion no longer seemed so infallibly correct in the face of growing liberal guilt. Reviewing John Neihardt's *Black Elk Speaks* in 1932, John Chamberlain lamented the Wounded Knee massacre as "one of the many sins for which Manifest Destiny has to answer." *New York Times* critic R. L. Duffus recalled Wounded Knee and Sand Creek as "cruel and wanton massacres." In 1934, George Cronyn remarked how, since 1918, the Indian had come to be regarded as "a suppressed minority." *Newsweek* stated simply that "probably the worst and most insulting blunder the Federal government ever committed in its treatment of the Indian was its attempt to 'Americanize' him."[12]

By the height of the Depression, commentators were noting a popular American cult focused on the Indian, who was viewed as a symbol of the pagan and primitive, rather than as raw material for civilizing. In 1930, novelist Harvey Fergusson wrote in *Scribner's*, "Never since he left the warpath has the Indian filled so large a place in the public eye as he does today." This change reflected mixed motives:

There is a motive of commercial exploitation which has put the Indian dances on the stage like a vaudeville act, and filled the pueblos with dust and tourists and auto busses, a scientific motive which has moved tons of earth in a search for the buried aboriginal past, and a third motive, more elusive but perhaps the most important of all, which may be described as sentimental, philosophical or aesthetic, according to the view-point of the describer.

This was the new primitivism, the interest in Darkness, whether cultural or racial, the quest for societies more in tune with primal realities and primal spirituality than the corrupted civilization of the West: "Harlem and the Congo profit along with Taos and Cochiti." Margaret Mead's imaginative celebration of primitive simplicity, *Coming of Age in Samoa*, appeared in 1928.[13]

The most systematic statement of Native cultural superiority was *The Gospel of the Red Man* (1936), by veteran Indian advocate Ernest Thompson Seton. Seton believed that "the civilization of the white man is a failure; it is visibly crumbling around us"; and agreed with Collier that the solution lay in a return to Indian values and religion, a "universal, basic and fundamental" faith. Seton uses the familiar missionary argument that Indians share basic moral values with Christians, but suggests that it is the white Christians that have to advance to the Indian stage of moral development rather than the other way round. "The culture and civilization of the White man are essentially material. . . . The culture of the Red man is fundamentally spiritual." Indians practiced a superior monotheism, followed the Great Oversoul, lived the Ten Commandments, and practiced a thorough socialism. Women had a high role in Indian society, which dealt practically and immediately with social problems such as crime and poverty. Indians represented "the most spiritual civilization the world has ever seen." Such idealization would have been inconceivable if American self-confidence had not imploded.[14]

Writing Indians

By the 1920s, white audiences proved open to sympathetic accounts of Native cultures and religions as they really were, rather than as providing the raw material for Christian expansion. White readers now had access to major anthropological accounts of Native peoples, like George Grinnell's account of the Cheyenne (1923) or the Coolidges' description of the Navajos (1930).

Grinnell, in particular, would have an enormous influence on later accounts of Native society and spirituality, with his detailed descriptions of ceremonies and religious customs. Meanwhile, North American archaeology experienced a minor revolution as new discoveries confirmed that human beings had been living on Turtle Island far longer than had ever been supposed. The common nineteenth-century view held that Indians had occupied America for perhaps five thousand years, but from the mid-1920s, this dating was pushed back to at least twelve thousand years, to the end of the last Ice Age. Popular archaeology texts now showed that Native American roots extended back to the days of the European cave paintings, and so, presumably, did their religions.[15]

Several classic accounts of religious life appeared in these years. These included Gladys Reichard's *Spider Woman* (1934) and her *Navaho Religion* (1950), Ruth Benedict's *Zuñi Mythology* (1935), and Elsie Clews Parsons's *Pueblo Indian Religion* (1939). Reading such books, it was no longer possible to doubt the authenticity of American Indian religion or its value as an alternate spiritual path. Writing of Zuñi, Ruth Bunzel remarked on the "great public and esoteric rituals whose richness, variety, and beauty have attracted the attention of poets and artists of all countries. . . . The Zuñi may be called one of the most thoroughly religious peoples of the world." Such books sometimes offered Native societies as models and exemplars for white America. In 1934, Ruth Benedict's *Patterns of Culture* used Native societies as types of several cultural distinct patterns, each valid in its own way, and each offering something that Western society had lost. Zuñi was a model of Apollonian society, emphasizing balance and integration, the ancient principles of "nothing in excess," which offered such an attractive contrast to modern American individualism and competitiveness.[16]

Throughout the media coverage, we find much less confidence about the claims of Christianity. In 1932, John Neihardt published *Black Elk Speaks*, a book that would come to be regarded as an American spiritual classic. It was not viewed in such awed terms on its first appearance, and sales were disappointing, but the book was treated with respect, and considered quite equal to a Christian devotional work. Reviewing the book in the *New York Times*, John Chamberlain treated Black Elk as a serious intellectual figure, "a philosopher with a serenity to be envied . . . a sort of Indian Platonist." Though he admitted to not appreciating the details of the spiritual experiences described, Chamberlain was careful not to dismiss them. "The story of Black Elk's 'vision' is amorphous and vague, but possibly the ritual of the Catholic or the high Episcopal church would be just as nebulous to the Indian intelligence, so we can hardly blame Black Elk or Mr. Neihardt on that score."[17]

Black Elk Speaks was part of a growing genre of books highly sympathetic to Native peoples, and white reaction to them was overwhelmingly favorable. In 1929, Oliver La Farge's Pulitzer Prize–winning novel *Laughing Boy* presented a Navajo hero in a thoroughly Indian world, in which whites largely appear as bizarre outsiders, presiding over sinister institutions such as the jail. LaFarge contrasts the material squalor of Navajo life with the culture's overarching goal of achieving beauty and harmony, internal as much as external. The descriptions of Navajo religious practices are lyrical and profound, while the Jesus Road has at best a tenuous hold on its Native followers. After a series of personal disasters, the hero finds harmony once again through performing traditional rituals, and he is redeemed by dancing and singing with the gods. "Laughing Boy felt a deep sense of peace, and rejoicing over ugliness defeated. The gods danced before him, he felt the influence of their divinity . . . The past and the present came together, he was one with himself. The good and true things he had thought entered into his being, and were part of the whole continuity of his life." Henceforward, his life would be "Never alone, never lamenting, never empty, *Ahalani*, beautiful." The success of this book encouraged a new genre of novels by Indian writers themselves, notably D'Arcy McNickle's *The Surrounded* (1936). This book builds on the traditional Western format, but it also delves into spiritual themes, and the conflict of values faced by modern Indians. Though the hero faces Christian pressure to abandon his "barbaric" rituals and beliefs, Native ways are treated sympathetically.[18]

Other books of these years included memoirs or autobiographies of Indians themselves. These included Paul Radin's *Crashing Thunder* (1926; Winnebago), Walter Dyk's *Son of Old Man Hat* (1938; Navajo), Clellan Ford's *Smoke From Their Fires* (1941; Kwakiutl), and Leo Simmons's *Sun Chief* (1942; Hopi). We cannot always be sure that the autobiographies were quite as purely the work of the Indian subjects as they appeared: editors like Neihardt were quite capable of putting their own interpretation on the materials they collected. What mattered, though, was that Native cultures were now being presented at first hand, and not viewed through the missionary lens.[19] These memoirs were published by mainstream publishing houses, rather than by quirky occult or ethnographic presses, and they were well received. They also gave a startling amount of detailed fact and commentary about religious life. *Sun Chief* explains Hopi customs that had usually been closed to outsiders, including the kachinas, the secret societies; the proceedings in the kivas; and the cycle of the ritual year.

In 1933, Houghton Mifflin published *Land of the Spotted Eagle,* the memoirs of Luther Standing Bear, of the Lakota people. Like Black Elk, Standing Bear offered an exalted picture of his people's spirituality, stressing the relationship with Nature and the Earth:

> The old people came literally to love the soil and they sat and reclined on the ground with a feeling of being close to a mothering power. . . . Kinship with all creatures of the earth, sky and water was a real and active principle. . . . Only to the white man was nature a "wilderness" and only to him was the land "infested" with "wild" animals and "savage" people. To us it was tame. Earth was bountiful and we were surrounded with the blessings of the Great Mystery.

He argued that attitudes to Nature gave a decisive superiority to Native peoples: "The white man does not understand the Indian for the reason that he does not understand America."[20]

Even the most benevolent reviewers were suspicious of this glorious picture. They were skeptical of the Indian Utopia, "whose happy citizens went share and share alike . . . and in which generosity, courage and mercy flowed like the gentle rain from heaven." Yet reviewers felt the need to avoid criticizing the author too much, to avoid reproducing "the absurd mis-statements and misinterpretations of the Indian culture." It was now common to respond respectfully to accounts of Indian religion, to dismiss accusations of their primitive or savage qualities as mere bigotry.[21] If primitive or unsavory practices were to be described, the reporter had to avoid any impression of claiming superiority. This embarrassment is suggested by a 1932 review of a book on Pueblo beliefs:

> Naturally, the Acoma had their superstitions, believing in witchcraft, in portents, and in omens which brought bad luck. None of these superstitions . . . seem at all sinister. The Pueblo Indians had, in fact—and to a degree still have—an indigenous civilization of their own, which compared favorably in many respects with that of the white man as they first knew him.[22]

Cultural sensitivity had arrived in earnest.

Toward Toleration

Some writers on Native societies actively praised the syncretism or lack of intolerance that would earlier have been condemned as a deplorable lapse from authentic Christianity. In an article titled "What the Sioux Taught Me," Mari Sandoz held up the religious message of Native culture as a model for a white-dominated world torn by political and racial strife. America could learn much from a vision of the natural forces and elements as "the Great Powers in whom man and nature are united in brotherhood. In such a philosophy, hatred can never be harbored, not even hatred of an enemy." Christians should copy the gentle tolerance of this society: "These Indians still do not take Satan and hellfire very seriously, or the concept of an avenging God. The idea of building up fear is alien to their philosophy." She reports seeing a young Sioux man ritually dedicating a shirt to sky and earth, and then wearing it to attend a Catholic Mass.[23]

Even some progressive missionaries tried to distinguish between the strictly religious message they were seeking to give and its cultural implications. The media reported favorably on such experiments. On the Wind River reservation in Wyoming, a 1926 story told of "the sympathetic transfusion from the Indian religion to Christianity." The mixing of traditions was obvious in the chapel: "On the door, emblazoned in flaming colors, are the symbols sacred to the Arapahoe: the eagle, which sees and knows all; the sun, which is translated to them as Christ, the Sun of Righteousness; the Thunder Bird the bird of mystery. This is not the first time in the history of the world that similarities in faiths have been reconciled." Such comments suggest a dramatic growth of religious sensitivity, and a willingness to retain traditional symbols as a kind of civic religion rather than elements in demonic worship.[24]

In this new social environment, preserving Native cultures appeared a powerful virtue. Gleeful accounts of the decline of tribal customs were largely replaced by laments about the destruction of valuable old customs and lifestyles. In 1927, the *New York Times* headlined an article "ALASKAN FOLKLORE IS DYING, SAYS SMITHSONIAN EXPERT . . . FINDS NEW GENERATION ADOPTING MODERN WAYS." Of course, the U.S. government had spent a century trying to ensure that exact outcome, and newspapers such as the *Times* had hymned the progress of Americanization. In this story, however, ethnologist Herbert Krieger was quoted lamenting a cultural tragedy: "Only the old people remember these things and if they are to be preserved these old people must be interviewed before they die."[25]

Christianity and Totemism and Ancestor Worship

Christianity was itself affected by the new atmosphere of crisis and doubt. While fundamentalism was discredited, liberals wondered about the future of their religion in a world dominated by totalitarian ideologies, in which materialist science provided a substitute to traditional faith. Far from feeling confident about the right to impose a religion on Native subjects, Christians might face a future in which their own beliefs and practices appeared dated and irrelevant, and might themselves become ancient memories half-recalled by the very old.

Indian culture and religions provided a rhetorical counterpoint to un-wanted trends in American civilization, and especially the dehumanizing growth of mass society and the corporate state. In 1932, Aldous Huxley's novel *Brave New World* depicted an Indian reservation as one of the last holdouts of traditional human society in a global community dominated by a benevolent scientific dictatorship. (Though the reservation is usually described as Zuñi, the rituals also draw on Hopi traditions.) For citizens of the future scientific utopia, Indian society is multiply chilling in its retention of barbaric customs like marriage and the nuclear family. The reservation is a land of "absolute sav-ages [who] still preserve their repulsive habits and customs . . . marriage, if you know what that is, my dear young lady; families . . . no conditioning . . . monstrous superstitions . . . Christianity and totemism and ancestor wor-ship . . . extinct languages, such as Zuñi and Spanish and Athapascan."[26]

But nothing is quite so unspeakable as its fervent and fanatical religious practices, which are seen through the horrified eyes of the enlightened mod-erns, Bernard Marx and Lenina Crowne. From the kivas, there emerges:

> a ghastly troop of monsters. Hideously masked or painted out of all sem-blance of humanity, they had tramped out a strange limping dance round the square; . . . first one woman had shrieked, and then another and an-other, as though they were being killed; and then suddenly the leader of the dancers broke out of the line, ran to a big wooden chest which was standing at one end of the square, raised the lid and pulled out a pair of black snakes. A great yell went up from the crowd.

Men are dressed as ritual animals, amidst scenes of flagellation and bloodlet-ting. Even more incredibly, for the sophisticated visitors, a literate young Savage actually regrets that his white skin has prevented him from participating in the ceremony. " '*I* ought to have been there,' the young man went on. 'Why wouldn't they let me be the sacrifice? I'd have gone round ten times— twelve, fifteen. Palowhtiwa only got as far as seven. They could have had twice as much blood from me. The multitudinous seas incarnadine.' " He would have welcomed the opportunity to bleed and die, "for the sake of the pueblo—to make the rain come and the corn grow. And to please Pookong and Jesus. And then to show that I can bear pain without crying out. Yes . . . to show that I'm a man . . . Oh!"

The reader sympathizes with the Indians rather than with the bloodless puritans Bernard and Lenina. After all, the very Natives who practice the curious religion are also the ones who hold our own "revoltingly viviparous" values of family and parenthood, who retain a humanity that is lost in the world of science and hygiene. Huxley's portrait of Pueblo religion is all the more subversive because he deliberately picks all the aspects of Native culture that had most repelled even sympathetic observers in earlier decades— veneration of serpents, flagellation, hypnotic drumming, ritualized bloodshed, and human sacrifice. This is not Hiawatha on a mountaintop nobly communing with the Great Spirit, or even the Indian dancer imagined as elegant aesthete. By implication, even the "fanatical" practices of the Savage Reservation are as natural and fundamental a part of our humanity as, say, the parent-child bond, or the idea that there is more to human emotion than just neurochemistry. As Huxley points out, Christianity itself has often been associated with the same fanaticism, the same obsession with blood and sacrifice. Perhaps Christians needed to reimagine their own religion through Native eyes.

Encounters

Cultural and social changes created a greater openness to Native religions, a new willingness to see ceremonies as valid and beautiful experiences. At the same time, there were far more practical opportunities to encounter Native religions, through tourism, and through seeing and owning Native-made goods and crafts. The taste for Indian craftsmanship and ritual that in 1920 had been a prerogative of the white cultural elite would, by the 1940s, become democratized, as Indian art and religion were mainstreamed and merchandised.

A growing number of white Americans had the opportunity to see and admire Native cultures at first hand, especially along the well-trodden tourist route of the Southwest. In 1925, Charles F. Lummis published *Mesa, Cañon and Pueblo*, one of many books which now celebrated the Southwest, "its marvels of nature, its pageant of the earth building, its strange peoples, its centuried romance." By the 1920s, Lummis-inspired tourist-oriented books about the Southwest had become a whole publishing niche, always stressing familiar themes of mysterious landscapes, noble Indians, and pious Penitentes.[27] Tourism increased after Route 66 through New Mexico opened in 1926, and the railroads developed excursion travel. By 1929, John Marin was writing from Taos that the Harvey Company "take[s] loads of visitors to see the Indians at the pueblos. How do the Indians like it? They have no say in the matter." And the industry grew larger as New Mexico and Arizona built up tourism as a means of overcoming economic malaise. California and western states again grew steadily during the 1940s, in consequence of defense production and military expansion, and that meant more and more Americans passing through the Southwest. By 1950, Taos Pueblo was "of course, one of the most famous 'sights' in the United States."[28]

In cultivating tourism, advertisers freely stressed the ancient and pagan cultures that appeared so exotic. This meant the processions of the Penitentes, but the great religious festivals of the Indians had become big business. In 1939, New Mexico officials were "cooperating with local tourist bureaus in an intensive drive to familiarize summer vacationists with the Southwest's foremost attraction—the Indians." By this time, the Hopi Snake Dance was attracting audiences seven hundred strong, and that was only one event among many. Such gatherings were now reported in respectful tones. *Out West* characterized the Snake Dance as "a weird ceremonial enacted with extreme solemnity and devotion and carrying deep significance to the Hopis."[29]

Thousands of tourists sought out ceremonies that had a powerful religious content, but which were viewed as richly exotic cultural performances rather than as frightening heathenism. When, in 1938, *Readers Digest* published an account of the intertribal ceremonial at Gallup, the emphasis was on the traditional religious ceremonies, which were presented as intoxicating, even glorious. "Night lengthens. The dancing keeps on. The Kiowas with syncopated jerking rhythm fascinate with hypnotic charm. The Pueblos give their hunting dramas, their prayers for increase. The devil dance of the Apaches is sinister. The war dance of the Utes sets the heart pounding and the blood racing."[30] Some travel-writing made a heroic effort to describe the religious values underlying these popular displays, and in so doing, brought current anthropological observations before a mass audience. In 1940, an article in the popular magazine *Travel* discussed Native pantheism:

For the Indian, confusedly, the world, life and its secrets are a living whole, mysterious and vibrating. To be a part of this great natural force and to be conscious of one's being, it is necessary to be silent on the summit of a hill where the air is purified of worldly odors. Thus the Indian stores up power, the power that comes from the earth to his naked body; that comes to him during the ceremonies at which he dances to the rhythm of his beating heart and of the world, his bare feet in contact with the soil he calls his mother.[31]

Nor was Indian tourism confined to the now-familiar lands of Arizona and New Mexico. The boom in the Southwest was paralleled in other areas fortunate enough to have conspicuously nonassimilated Indian communities near big cities, or conveniently close to travel routes. And as in the Southwest, the more "pagan" the community, the greater the attraction. At least by the 1920s, the Seminole people of Florida were deeply involved in tourism. This industry became ever more significant as Florida grew in economic importance over the next three decades. Some areas that lacked authentic Native ceremonials now did their best to acquire them. In 1937, Palm Springs deliberately created such a new tradition, where "the Indians will enact their ancient tribal ceremonies and weird rites for the first time." By this point, the word "weird" is meant to be tempting rather than frightening. (The influential fantasy magazine *Weird Tales* first appeared in 1923). Also in the late 1930s, New Hampshire acquired the bizarre archaeological site known variously as Mystery Hill and America's Stonehenge. According to taste, the site is a warren of colonial root cellars, an ancient Druidic or Megalithic site, or the remnants of a lost Indian civilization with advanced astronomical skills. Whatever its true origins, subsequent marketers have stressed ritual and religious elements, including an alleged altar designed for human sacrifice.[32]

North by Northwest

The popularity of the Southwest encouraged aficionados of things Indian to look further afield, and especially to the societies of the Pacific Northwest, to the Kwakiutl, Haida, Salish, and Tlingit. The discovery of Northwest Coast art was not new, because at least since the 1870s, it had attracted and excited museum curators and connoisseurs. Natalie Curtis included Kwakiutl songs and artistic motifs in *The Indians' Book* (1907), while the film *In the Land of the Headhunters* had appeared in 1914. At least for the sophisticated market, the Northwest had been picked clean of its best objects before the First World War. But material from this region enjoyed new mass popularity in the 1930s, and articles about it now proliferated in popular magazines dealing with travel, tourism and the arts. Indians of the Northwest Coast attracted white attention for their ceremonials and their evidently "primitive" art, symbolized by their masks, animal carvings, and totem poles, which made for sensational illustrations. Once again, the aesthetic discovery promoted awareness of the exceedingly rich religious and mythological life of the Northwest Coast, with its shamanism and shape-shifting, its fascination with exotic animals like orcas, seals, and sharks, and the central role of Raven, the local trickster-figure. And legends of not-far-distant cannibalism and headhunting added a frisson.[33]

Especially powerful was the notion that human and animal worlds could be so strongly interconnected. As Alice Henson Ernst wrote in 1939:

On the Northwest Coast the lines between its three interlocking worlds have always been very thinly drawn: the human world, that middle territory in which man dwelt insecurely, confused between the voices and visions from a terrifying superhuman territory above the spirit world, and that much more cheerful but still frightening sub-human terrain beneath: the animal world. Civilized man, today, has progressively lost two of these worlds. . . . Ignoring—or distrusting—the elusive powers above him, he has also put Brother-Animal strictly in his place.

These ideas, too, would become part of the popular concept of Indian religion.[34]

Anthropologists such as Franz Boas had been writing extensively on the Northwest Coast since the turn of the century, but this work was popularized in the 1930s through Ruth Benedict's widely read *Patterns of Culture*. Benedict's portrait of the Kwakiutl was anything but flattering, with its emphasis on their acquisitive and competitive society and their Dionysian values, but it helped draw attention to the region. As writers and artists explored the societies of the Northwest Coast, many praised it in terms that recall the earlier discovery of the Southwest. In 1939, Alice Ernst described a ritual in language that recalls John Collier or Marsden Hartley. "The full-voice chorus from all corners of the room added its own primal force of assertion, running back like an undertone of racial heritage—a long, long way into the beginnings of human consciousness—or of human sophistication, if it so means for man to become aware of his own mental process."[35]

By 1941, *Travel* reported on Indian rituals in terms guaranteed to excite potential tourists and collectors:

Equipped with wooden helmets and armor of hides, they fought fiercely with clubs, and wearing fantastic masks they paid homage to their mythological deities in wild, tense dramas. . . . The masks reproduced on these pages are symbols of a world that has passed—barbaric, superstitious, but filled with a tremendous gusto and energy that found expression in hunting, fishing, warfare, prodigious ceremonies and feasts, and artistic activities as original as any ever done by the aboriginal inhabitants of this continent.

John Collier himself was rather irritated by the shift of interest away from his cherished Southwest, arguing that "the Northwest coast art is of a dead time . . . but Pueblo and Navajo art is of a living social age that wants to go on." But the new vogue for Northwest art proved enduring.[36]

Indian Crafts

Travel and tourism generated interest in Native material culture and vastly expanded the collector market for goods and handicrafts, ranging from cheap souvenirs to highly priced *objets d'art*. Indian crafts became fashionable during the 1920s. In 1925, Calvin Coolidge's wife wore Indian jewelry at her husband's inauguration, stirring interest in women's magazines. (The piece in question seems to have stemmed from the Smoki tribe, that is, from white re-enactors of Native rituals.) Few of those who collected Indian objects would have any interest or commitment to the religious principles underlying jewelry or kachina figures, but at least they would have a more favorable view of the art and the society that produced it, and would object vigorously to any further attempts at cultural interference. Attempts to preserve and promote Native culture now became just as widespread as the older efforts to stamp out what had been viewed as vestiges of pagan savagery.[37]

The "friends of the Indian" who had arrived in the Southwest in the early years of the century played a pivotal role in encouraging this trade, training Native artists, and marketing their products. In 1922, Edgar Hewett helped sponsor the first annual Southwest Indian Fair, an effort by local artists and anthropologists to promote and sell Native crafts. In addition to economic development, the goal was to preserve "the priceless heritage of distinctive Indian art," a heritage that could not be separated from its cultural and religious roots. In 1925, an Indian Arts Fund was founded in Santa Fe in order to collect and promote Native pottery. Soon after its foundation in 1928, Flagstaff's Museum of Northern Arizona was sponsoring Indian craft days, with the goal of giving local communities a wider market, of preserving and extending traditional skills.[38]

Alarmed at the erosion of old ways, Indians themselves tried to restore and adapt their religious practices, often in alliance with white anthropologists. A key figure in the preservation of traditional Navajo culture was Hosteen Klah, who had served as an informant to Washington Matthews, and who became a medicine man in 1917. He pioneered the daring idea of taking the hitherto-transient images from sandpaintings and preserving them in permanent form as rugs, which would attract an avid collector market. Until then, this kind of art had been regarded as a sensitive secret, rich in religious and ritual symbolism.[39]

Navajo sandpainting now reached a white public. One early publicist was Laura Adams Armer, whose lavishly illustrated magazine articles described the ceremonies underlying the visual displays. In 1929, sandpaintings were the subject of an effusive article by popular writer Manly P. Hall, complete with illustrations by Hosteen Klah himself. Hall wrote passionately of "these crude but complicated designs which, when completed, inspire the beholder with a sense of barbaric wonder." Just as impressive was what the paintings taught about the subtleties of Indian religions: "How at variance with our preconceived notions concerning the religious ignorance of supposedly half-savage peoples is the attitude of the Navaho toward the subject of idolatry." When the grand new El Navajo Hotel opened in Gallup, New Mexico, to accommodate the tourist trade, its lobby was decorated with murals based on sandpaintings. In the late 1930s, Alice Henderson and her husband cooperated with Hosteen Klah and Mary Cabot Wheelwright in creating the House of Navajo Religion, a cultural museum shaped like a Navajo hogan.

The institution evolved into Santa Fe's distinguished Wheelwright Museum of the American Indian.[40]

Not only did the fashion for Indian crafts survive into the 1930s, but it would actually be fostered by the federal government. In 1935, John Collier's Indian Bureau sponsored an Indian Arts and Crafts Board, to expand the market for "the products of Indian art and craftsmanship." (The Board's name may well commemorate Collier's long-standing interest in William Morris and his movement.) The measure attracted little public comment, not surprisingly, given all the other New Deal legislation flowing forth at this time, but one irony deserves attention. A federal board was now sponsoring and encouraging the production of items drawing heavily on "heathenish" Indian rituals and customs, giving a literal stamp of approval in the form of an official trademark warranting authentic Indian-ness. The attempt to promote Native culture reflected Collier's awareness of Mexican *indigenismo*, the official revival of Indian arts and culture, an endeavor that impressed American intellectuals. As V. F. Calverton wrote in 1936, while Americans had tried to annihilate Indian society, "the Mexicans have not only dedicated themselves to preserving Indian culture in its pristine form, but have come to worship the Indian, who remains to this day the dominant root-force out of which the Mexican nation has derived its being, its beliefs, its purpose." In Mexican culture, too, the glorification of Indianism was the corollary of anticlericalism and anti-Christianity, an idea that appealed to New Deal radicals.[41]

By the 1930s, also, an interest in the primitive still attracted avant-garde artists, who often chose religious or ritual themes. Looking back at the early years of the Taos circle, Marsden Hartley was struck by the growing fashion for Indian themes: "The Indian was not so popular as he is now among the esthetes," for whom terms like "primitive" represented high praise. John Marin reported attending an Indian dance, which he found "my greatest human experience—the barbaric splendor of it was magnificent." Maynard Dixon spent decades painting southwestern Indian subjects, and in 1931 he painted one of his best-known works, the *Round Dance,* depicting six Pueblo Indians in a ritual. When John Chamberlain reviewed *Black Elk Speaks*, he praised the illustrations, "excellent examples of a primitive art that is good in spite of (or perhaps because of) its disregard for realistic canons." Precisely because it was primitive, Native art was popular, modish, and profitable. When, in 1931, New York held its Exposition of Indian Tribal Arts, *New York Times* art critic Edward Alden Jewell was enthusiastic: "We

seem at length very much aware of a Western culture reaching back centuries before the discovery of the New World." Though Americans might
fully not understand its religious implications, "it is easy just to accept it as
esthetic material, especially since so much genuine artistry has gone into the
business of giving life to these strange and fascinating forms." The exposition was titled "The first exhibition of American Indian art selected entirely
with consideration of esthetic value."[42]

In the new mood, emphasizing the primitive and tribal qualities of Indian culture might be a sound marketing tactic. When, in 1932, John Neihardt presented his *Black Elk Speaks*, he selected his material to present his
hero as the remnant of an ancient paganism, excluding Black Elk's evolution
into a faithful Christian layman. Not mentioned was Black Elk's heroic attempt to reconcile the seven traditional symbols of the Lakota faith with the
seven sacraments of the Catholic Church, nor his claim that the two religions were essentially the same. In the 1930s, Catholic Indians were scarcely
interesting, but staunch pagans definitely could be.[43]

Mainstreaming

As Indian culture became fashionable, it could be sampled outside the tribal
homelands, as cultural and artistic exhibits now went on the road. In 1931,
the Exposition of Indian Tribal Arts included Navajo sandpaintings and
tribal dancers. News coverage dwelled on the quirks of the quaint Indians
visiting the big city—they were said to be bothered by elevators—but generally, the response was respectful. According to the *New York Times*, sandpaintings were "religious pictures, it was explained. . . . So when painted for
the white observers here, they will not be carried to absolute completion so
that this religious art will not be profaned." This is the newly standard language of "religious art," of sacred and profane.[44]

Under federal sponsorship, major Indian exhibits appeared at some of the
nation's major cultural venues, including San Francisco's Golden Gate Exposition of 1939, which Edward Alden Jewell termed "a very considerable . . .
eye-opener." In 1941, the Department of the Interior organized an exhibition
of Native art at New York's Museum of Modern Art, one of the largest of its
kind ever displayed. For Jewell, this show proved irrefutably that "the North
American Indian had a culture of deep significance and stirring power." The
New York Times devoted a full page to illustrating treasures from the show,

an awe-inspiring collection of masks, chiefly from the Pacific Northwest. The clear message for any culturally literate observer was to proclaim the vigor and creativity of Indian cultures. "In less than a generation, the definition of . . . Northwest Coast pieces has changed from 'ethnographic specimen' to 'fine art.' "[45]

Indian motifs appeared in surprising contexts. It was in the 1920s that southern California acquired a wave of Maya-style architecture, incorporating Mesoamerican themes into a familiar Art Deco tradition. This included hotels, churches, department stores, and a Masonic temple, as well as the celebrated Aztec Hotel (1925). The mass adoption of Indian artistic themes, though in wholly secularized forms, is evident from the pages of *School Arts*, a magazine aimed at schoolteachers. From the mid-1930s onwards, the magazine popularized Indian themes like sandpaintings. In 1939, an advertisement suggested what teachers could draw from Pueblo and Navajo themes, including kachina dolls. In 1949, *School Arts* published a photographic feature on "Ceremonial Dances," to provide themes for painting and drawing, but also to supply models for folk-dance activities in white schools. Throughout, the lack of comment about the religious or spiritual content of the performances is striking. One caption explains that "the tall horned figure is the famous Shalako God of Zuñi, who like our Santa Claus, brings gifts to all good children of the year." Just as folklorized were sandpaintings, described in detail in a 1949 issue. Children might be encouraged to create pictures of Father Sky and Mother Earth, but free of any suspicion that they were dabbling in another religion. In 1951, the magazine recommended sand painting as "an applied design activity suited to intermediate and upper grades."[46]

Given the massive evidence for the Indian fashion of these years, it seems odd that specifically cultural and religious aspects of Indian life do not appear in the cinema, which was the principal popular culture medium of the time. During the 1930s and 1940s, some movie depictions of Indians were admittedly crude and racist, but others were subtler and more perceptive. John Ford, in particular, shows immense respect for Indian peoples. In *Fort Apache* (1948), the Indians emerge as tough, dignified, and intelligent, and they are evidently fighting to defend themselves against brutal white exploitation. An impressive Geronimo is explicitly introduced as a medicine man. Yet the films of the era virtually never present an exploration of Indian religion in the way that would appear so regularly in the 1960s and 1970s. This lacuna is explained by the censorship policies of the Hayes Code years, dominated as they were by Christian and especially Catholic figures, who frowned on explorations of any non-Christian religious tradition. Otherwise, Native religions might well have been treated in the films of Hollywood's golden age.

Largely through the cultivation of ethnic tourism and Native crafts, Indians became a much-better-known part of American culture by the Second World War, and this gave an immunity to their religious customs. If customs like sandpainting were appearing in American high schools, then it is reasonable to speak of a mass constituency. In the same years, we also see the developing notion of Indian spiritual superiority, which was first manifested during the religious freedom debates of the 1920s. So popular would this theme become that, already by the 1940s, we can see the broad outlines of the New Age neo-Indianism of recent years.

7

⅍

Before the New Age
1920–1960

*For these men, the Navaho yei, the Pueblo katsinas, the Buddhist yogins,
the Christian saints, are but the vanguard of all mankind. We too are
slowly traveling the evolutionary Road of Life back to its source.*

—*Frank Waters*

Much of the popular material available today on Indian religions assumes,
often wrongly, that these traditions are closely aligned to esoteric and alternative spirituality, that they are part of a mystical New Age continuum.
However inaccurate, this long-established idea helps explain the growing acceptance of Native faiths from the 1920s onwards. For many Americans in
this era, Native religious practices were not just harmless old customs; they
contained great spiritual truths from which whites could learn. Even as Native culture was gaining mainstream acceptance, therefore, it was doing so in
a distinctive and perhaps distorted form. The modern New Age Indian thus
has an impressively long pedigree. In fact, the idea was so strong by mid-
century that the mystery is perhaps not how the modern synthesis appeared
but, rather, why it did not emerge decades earlier.

The Esoteric Boom

Esoteric and mystical ideas enjoyed enormous popularity in the 1920s
and 1930s, when there was a publishing boom in subjects like astrology,

Rosicrucianism, reincarnation, spiritualism, prophecy, and extra-sensory perception, as well as the mystical study of lost continents and the Great Pyramid. A wide-ranging public enthusiasm for esoteric matters gave rise to many small occult sects and study groups. National movements such as Psychiana and Mighty I AM used modern techniques of mass advertising and merchandising, and brought the esoteric message to millions of Americans. These movements themselves rarely endured, but the individuals and the ideas they represented survived long enough to provide a linkage between this first New Age and the counterculture of the 1960s and 1970s.[1]

Though Indians were not as central to esoteric thought before World War II, the idea of the Native as Natural Mystic exercised its appeal. We have already seen German colonists claiming some kind of Indian origin for their magic arts under the name of pow-wowing. During the nineteenth century, spiritualist mediums regularly claimed that their spirit guides were Indians, usually chiefs or medicine men, who would have had a special link to the Otherworld. In New Orleans, flourishing African American spiritualist churches claimed the special patronage of Chief Black Hawk. Spiritualist claims had a special appeal for women, who represented a sizable majority of mediums: women, presumably, possessed the psychic sensitivity needed to reach the higher spiritual planes occupied by Native peoples.[2]

Non-Native sympathizers had their opinions buttressed by some Indian writers themselves, especially Charles Eastman. Of course, he claimed, Indians believed firmly in an afterlife, and in reincarnation. "Certainly the Indian never doubted the immortal nature of the spirit or soul of man. . . . Many of the Indians believed that one may be born more than once, and there were some who claimed to have full knowledge of a former incarnation." Eastman did nothing to discourage the romantic idea of the Indian as peculiarly attuned to the mystic forces: "It is well known that the American Indian had somehow developed occult power. . . there are well-attested instances of remarkable prophecies and other mystic practice." If this was indeed the authentic voice of an Indian intellectual, he was speaking words well calculated to win the sympathies of educated white listeners. Ernest Thompson Seton regarded Indian occult powers as proven medical fact. Citing Eastman, he stated that "all their great leaders were mystics" who practiced second sight and clairvoyance.[3]

For Theosophists, Red Indians represented survivors of ancient continents like Atlantis or Lemuria. Helena P. Blavatsky believed that Indian pictographs were not rudimentary attempts at writing, but rather the survival of an ancient and universal system that dated back to Atlantis. Her disciples found the origin of the name "Atlantis" in the Nahuatl term for water. Quite reputable scholars tried to track the remnants of that Old-World order in archaeological sites and in contemporary "primitive" cultures. Seeking to explain Ohio's Serpent Mound, that "American Sphinx," enthusiastic writers drew analogies to the serpent worship of esoteric Hinduism. Interest in lost-continent theories reached new heights in the 1930s, with the excitement over the prophecies of Edgar Cayce and the new focus on the supposed continents of Mu and Lemuria. For New Age theorists and Theosophists, such connections provided a scientific basis for occult powers, for claims to prophecy or psychic powers. However bizarre and inexplicable these ideas might seem, they represented the lost science of the sunken continents. Mesoamerican cultures such as the Mayas and Aztecs were especially promising for such linkages, given their mysterious writings and great pyramids, and one mail-order esoteric cult of the 1930s claimed to be distributing secret Mayan wisdom to its paying customers.[4]

But North American Indian cultures also had their mystical devotees. Just how extensive was the occult lore surrounding the Indians is apparent from Mabel Dodge's account of her preparations to make her first trip to New Mexico. One friend told her stories of Native abilities to command levitation, tales "that touched the love of power that is latent in us all." That Indians had mysterious powers was confirmed by the existence of the great civilizations of Mesoamerica. Another friend brought a collection of volumes on Aztec and Mayan religions, and added, "I doubt very much whether the great stones of these Mayan temples were raised by hand. . . . Possibly they had hold of some law we have replaced by mechanical invention." She also consulted Ignatius Donnelly's "Story of Atlantis," that is, *Atlantis, or the Antediluvian World* (1882), the book that revived the Atlantis legend for the modern world. She was then fully equipped to approach modern Native American culture.[5]

The lost civilization theme recurs often—recall John Collier's *Red Atlantis*. A major early study of the mystical significance of Navajo sandpaintings was published by one of the greatest American occultists, Manly P. Hall. Hall believed that "no place upon the earth do we find a more curious or remarkable ritualism than that enacted in the hogan, where the secret mysteries of the first ages are still revealed by the sand priests and the tribal philosophers." Hall believed that "the North American Indian is by nature a symbolist, a mystic and a philosopher." In the 1930s, American Nazis stated that the swastika was not, as was claimed, an imported European symbol, but rather an ancient mystical symbol taken from Native American religions, and perhaps from antediluvian civilizations. They received some support in this from some Indian factions whose hostility to Collier and the Indian New Deal led them into a bizarre alliance with the white ultra-Right.[6]

Frank Waters and the 1940s

One intriguing pioneer of New Age Indianism was Frank Waters, whose work links the speculations of the 1930s and 1940s to the more modern esoteric movements. He is best known for his *Book of the Hopi* (1963), which exercised a vast influence over the counterculture of the 1960s and 1970s. All subsequent neo-Indian spirituality owes a vast debt to *Book of the Hopi*, which was as familiar a fixture of student dorm rooms as the *Tibetan Book of the Dead* or Jack Kerouac's beatnik odyssey, *On the Road*. In fact, Waters symbolizes a significant trend in American cultural history, namely, the connections among those eras of explosive social and political radicalism that occur periodically. As we have seen, much of what we associate with the radicalism of the 1960s had older precursors, especially in the second decade of the century and the milieu of the early Taos colony. Another wave of radical cultural and religious experimentation can be seen in the late 1940s. In fact, the connections between this era and the 1960s are strikingly close. It is almost as if currents of thought welled up in the 1940s, went underground through the following decade, and then returned to full view in the mid-1960s.[7]

The Second World War was followed by an era of social and intellectual ferment. This was the era of the Kinsey Report (1948), which did much to foster the sexual revolution; it was a time of rapid progress in civil rights and racial integration; and modern environmentalism also has its roots in these years, with the publication of Marjory Stoneman Douglas's *The Everglades* (1947) and Aldo Leopold's *Sand County Almanac* (1949). *On the Road* records a road trip undertaken in 1948–1949, when the Ginsberg-Kerouac circle was already speaking in terms of a "Beat" movement. The UFO scare that began in 1947 would become a major element of later New Age and esoteric speculation. So would the Jungian system of myths and archetypes popularized in Joseph Campbell's 1949 book, *The Hero with a Thousand Faces*. Campbell popularized the Native myths discovered and translated by ethnographers like Washington Matthews and Alice Fletcher. He would also describe *Black Elk Speaks* as "the best example . . . in our literature" of a guide to shamanism and the shamanic universe. Robert Graves's *White Goddess*, a key source for later neopagan and feminist spirituality, appeared in 1948.[8]

In such an atmosphere of questioning and experimentation, Indians could not fail to arouse romantic interest, and particularly in spiritual matters. As the United States became more technologically and socially advanced, more involved in the world's problems, the more Americans sought out the traditional and nonscientific spirituality of Native peoples, which offered a refuge from modernity. In 1947, *Travel* remarked that "while watching the ancient rites of the red man, the visitor will be made aware of the fact that despite the world's entry into the atomic age, an ancient culture is still to be found, a culture based upon religious ritual of thanksgiving, prayers for help to gods of rain, abundance and peace."[9]

The idea of presenting Native societies as spiritual exemplars flourished anew. In 1944, Paul Radin argued, "The last twenty years that have seen the break up of European civilization, ushered in so hopefully and optimistically in the sixteenth century, have also witnessed the dawn of a new era. . . . People and races whose course appeared to be run, and lost, only a generation ago, hope to play a new role." Against that background, he was prepared to envision an Indian Renaissance. In 1947, John Collier's *Indians of the Americas* restated his vision of the mystic glories of Native America, North and South, in a book that long remained *the* standard popular text on Indian affairs.[10] And as white Americans sought out potentially superior Native communities, their eyes turned yet again to the Zuñi, who received new attention in the writings of Edmund Wilson, and to the Hopi. One book in particular, *The Hopi Way* (1944), by Laura Thompson and Alice Joseph, made a powerful impact in a world weary of war and political extremism. According to one reviewer, "an intense and manifold scientific scrutiny" shows the Hopi community to be "an 'ideal republic,' a pure achieved democracy, intensely nurturing an ancient spiritual culture, intensely nurturing and socializing its young. . . . The Hopi live richly, intensely and peacefully, and the substance of their lives is spiritual, not material," in contrast to Western civilization, with its "unworkable materialism." The Hopi example offered "a healing message to minds drenched in the terror and pity of world tragedy, oppressed by the specter of vast and unpredictable change." It was "our indigenous Shangri-La."[11]

Appropriately, then, Frank Waters's career was well under way in the 1940s, when he was part of the Taos circle around Mabel Dodge. His major

books from that period include the novel *The Man Who Killed the Deer*
(1942), and *Masked Gods* (1950), an encyclopedic view of "Navaho and
Pueblo Ceremonialism," written in 1947–1948. Waters's works show how
easily available quite detailed studies of southwestern cultures had now become. *The Man Who Killed the Deer* explores the political dilemmas of the
Pueblo reservations during the Collier era, and the overwhelming pressures
to tribal conformity faced by Indians who sincerely wished to assimilate and
Americanize. Throughout the book (which is dedicated to "Mabel and
Tony"), Waters gives intricate descriptions of Pueblo religion, its rituals, beliefs, and dances.[12]

Masked Gods

Masked Gods powerfully demonstrates the growing integration of Indian
thought into the esoteric system. Already in the 1940s, Waters's work is
based on several "New Age" assumptions: American Indians belonged to a
common cultural and religious tradition that included the Mesoamerican
world of the Mayas and Aztecs; both North American and Mesoamerican
cultures grew out of very ancient societies on lost continents; both shared
core cultural elements with Asian religious and mystical traditions, especially Buddhism. Native Americans also had access to advanced powers that
must be understood in the light of the most modern Western science; and
their religious and spiritual traditions reflected the most modern insights of
psychology and psychotherapy. None of these ideas was new with Waters—
witness the Theosophists, and the pre–First-World-War circles of Mabel
Dodge—but it was Waters who most creatively synthesized these ideas and
applied them specifically to North American Indians.

Though Waters ostensibly gives a scholarly account of Pueblo and Navajo
rituals, he uses them as a vehicle for his personal mythology. He strays far
from the scientific methods of scholarly anthropology: introducing the
book, Harvard anthropologist Clyde Kluckhohn remarks how often Waters
makes him "wince." In his autobiography, Waters makes no secret of the
personal agendas driving his work. His own mystical experiences included a
vision of the Mexican metropolis of Teotihuacán as it would have stood a
thousand years ago (the visions sound very much like peyote experiences).
In trying to make sense of these "periodic deviations from the usual aspects
of reality," Waters immersed himself in Hindu, Tibetan, and Taoist thought,

and in the writings of Jung. He read "dozens of such books. All revealing mankind's ages-old search for the Otherworld under different names, and by different disciplines."[13]

The most powerful contemporary influence on his work was Russian mystic George I. Gurdjieff, who so often emerges as a prophet of the later New Age. Waters was introduced to Gurdjieff's thought by Mabel Dodge, who had known the guru since his first American tours in the 1920s. Gurdjieff taught an influential esoteric system designed to awaken humanity to full spiritual consciousness, the next stage of spiritual evolution (Gurdjieff's system closely recalls that of Richard Bucke, whose idea of Cosmic Consciousness was cited by John Collier). In order to create this fully conscious human being, Gurdjieff stressed the need to integrate mind, body and emotions. Part of his method was an emphasis on sacred dance, on gesture and ritual movement, features which had been lost in Western religion but which evidently survived in Native traditions.[14]

Jung is another powerful influence throughout. Reporting the Deer Dance of Taos Pueblo, Waters sees:

the two deer mothers symbolizing the female imperative, the instinctual forces of the unconsciousness of the earth. And the deer dancers, the men trying to break free from the circle, symbolizing the masculine intellect, the forces of the will of man. So there's a bi-polar tension here—whoops and yells, scrambles in the snow, as one breaks free and is brought back by the deer watchers, etc. A lot of fun, a drama of what takes place inside of us.

The "mystery play" of the Deer Dance proved the greater psychological sophistication of the Pueblos, their superior psychic integration. In contrast, "we excessively rational white, Anglo-Americans by our force of will can't break free from the forces of the unconscious, from the realm of instinct embodied within us."[15]

Waters's treatment of Native symbolism is wholly syncretistic. If Navajos or Pueblos accept a dualism of light and darkness, he promptly finds parallels in the Chinese concept of yin and yang, in Jungian thought, or cites Gurdjieff. He delves into esoteric Christianity and the Gnostic gospels, speculates about the mystical teachings of the Essenes and the secret learning that Jesus allegedly acquired in Egypt, India, and elsewhere. He already knows Graves's *White Goddess*, and probably his *King Jesus*.[16]

But by far the most frequent references are to Asian and specifically Buddhist sources. Like many other esoteric theorists of the time, Waters was also fascinated by Tantric theories, and especially by kundalini yoga. According to this tradition, the material system of a human being is paralleled by a spiritual or etheric body, structured around seven chakras, "wheels," centers of spiritual power. At the lowest chakra, located at the base of the spine, there lies a potentially vast source of spiritual energy, kundalini, which is symbolized by a sleeping serpent. Through meditation and mystical exercises, the adept can awaken the serpent, which rises through the higher chakras until it reaches the highest "wheel" at the top of the head. At this explosive moment, when the serpent is fully uncoiled and the highest chakra is energized, the adept experiences total awareness and spiritual illumination. In the English-speaking world, the kundalini system was popularized by the work of Sir John Woodroffe ("Arthur Avalon"), who linked the spiritual body of Tantrism with the physical anatomy as understood by Western medicine. (The highest or Crown Chakra thus corresponds to the pineal gland). His 1919 book *The Serpent Power* heavily influenced both Jung and Gurdjieff. Woodroffe's ideas can also be seen in another long-influential text, the *Tibetan Book of the Dead,* published in 1927 by W. Y. Evans-Wentz (Woodroffe contributed a foreword to the book). Waters would later work personally with Evans-Wentz.[17]

Though superficially these various writers say nothing about Native American matters, for Waters, these Asian insights are critical. He claims extensive similarities between the Native eschatologies he describes "and its parallels found in the *Bardo Thodol,* the Tibetan *Book of the Dead,* in the *Secret of the Golden Flower,* the Chinese *Book of Life,* and in the Egyptian *Book of the Dead.*" The Hopi myth of emergence through successive worlds is compared to the Tibetan myth of the world-mountain, Mount Meru. The tale reflects stages of spiritual and psychological consciousness, so that evolutionary progress through worlds symbolizes personal evolution, as described by mystics like Gurdjieff and Ouspensky. "It is only by such a synthesis of Eastern religious-philosophies and Western sciences with Navaho and Pueblo ceremonialism that we can see clearly the intent and meaning of the latter . . . it is not the purpose here to present the main principles of Mahayana Buddhism beyond an elucidation necessary for fuller understanding of Pueblo and Navaho ceremonialism." (Waters is comforting: one does not need a *total* understanding of Mahayana Buddhism to understand southwestern cultures, just a working knowledge.) All these ideas are integrated into a New Age synthesis that was largely novel in 1950, but which now reads like the commonplaces of a thousand New Age bookstores scattered across the United States. It was Waters above all who made the Ganges flow into the Rio Grande.[18]

Waters is sympathetic to alternative archaeology, to stories of Atlantis and other lost continents. Discussing the origins of the Hopi, he challenges the official version of migration across the Bering Strait to suggest that perhaps, as they claimed, they had always lived in America. Or possibly they came from "a submerging yet unverified but certainly sometime existent continent that lay in the Atlantic." In *The Book of the Hopi*, Waters would suggest that ancient lost continents might correspond to the various bygone Hopi worlds of emergence. He speaks further of "a legend of continental migrations that stem back into the remote prehistoric past," and asks, "From what ancient race of world mankind did the Hopi spring?"[19]

Occult and New Age writers then and now commonly present their ideas in pseudoscientific form, suggesting that the mystic forces they portray are based in a science that we have not yet learned to appreciate. Already in 1942, in *The Man Who Killed the Deer*, Waters depicts a group of elderly Pueblo men worshipping in a kiva as precisely analogous to whites operating an electric generator, each in their way manipulating objective forces and power sources:

> Calling up through the little round opening in the floor the warmth and power of the sleeping earth-serpent. Calling up from the depths of their own bodies, from the generative organs, the navel center and the heart, their vital life force. . . . And all this infusion of strength and power, grace and will, they loosed as if from the sagittal suture on the crown of the head, covered by the scalp lock—from the corresponding aperture at the top of the kiva. As one, powerful, living flow, they directed it upon the focus of their single concentration.

The description is pure kundalini yoga, though Waters sees the mobilization of inner power as the generation of literal, objective energies. "Who doubts the great magnetic currents of the earth, or the psychic radiations of man?" As to what Indians might accomplish with these powers, this was "a race that had raised pyramids by ways now unknown to man . . . [who had] developed a civilization whose ancient mysteries still defied the probings of modern minds."[20]

In later books, Waters's notion of occult science becomes still more explicit, not least in his constant reiteration of evolutionary thought. His account of the Hopi universe draws from Einsteinian thought. The Indian is one "who by his own space-time concept of reality refutes as illusory and irrelevant all that we have here so far learned about him." Despite its apparent primitivism, the Hopi held a scientifically sophisticated view of the universe as "an inseparably interrelated field or continuum." Discussing the idea of the Sun god, Waters suggests close connections to modern science: "It may not be wholly a coincidence . . . that the Los Alamos atomic research laboratory is located on 'The Hill,' above the old pueblos of Jemez, Santa Clara and San Ildefonso, so close to that Navaho Mountain of the East, sacred to the sun." The laboratory's builders must have been responding to deep archetypes in the American unconscious. The connections are, he feels, intuitively obvious: "Los Alamos and Mesa Verde, Project Trinity and the ancient sun temple, the Essenes, the prehistoric cliff-dwellers and the laughing new Clementines strolling by him in the moonlight."[21]

Pioneers

In part because it was published by an academic press, *Masked Gods* did not reach the mass audience that Waters would find with the *Book of the Hopi*. Even so, he was certainly not alone in his esoteric vision of Indian ways. One well-known victim of pseudo-Indianism was Henry Wallace, formerly Franklin Roosevelt's Vice President, and the candidate of a quixotic campaign for the presidency in 1948. Wallace had a notorious affinity for gurus of all sorts, and one of the most influential was "a faux-Indian medicine man" named Charles Roos, who addressed Wallace as 'Poo-Yaw' and 'Chief Cornplanter.' " (Wallace had served as Secretary of Agriculture). The two men bought land in Minnesota as a base from which they could explore the religious aspects of the coming New Age.[22]

Also illustrating the esoteric appeal of Native culture was Leslie Van Ness Denman, who came from a great San Francisco family. She has recently earned some historical attention because of her influence on her husband, Judge William Denman, in one of the leading religious-freedom cases of the 1940s. This was the trial of Guy and Edna Ballard for allegedly operating their Mighty I AM cult as a cynical money-making racket. Leslie's influence helped enlighten her husband about the mind-set of New Age believers, and prevented what could have been a devastating legal blow against fringe religions. But she was not a dispassionate observer. Already in the 1940s, she was thoroughly immersed in Indian and pseudo-Indian lore in a way that would be thoroughly familiar today. Every year, in lieu of a Christmas card, she would mail to friends a pamphlet based on tribal lore, with titles such as *A Chant, A Myth, A Prayer: Pai-Ya-Tu-Ma, God of Dew and the Dawn*; *Sh'a A-La-K'o Mana: Ritual of Creation*; or *The Flute Ceremonial, Hotevila and Snake Antelope Ceremonial of the Hopi Mesas*. In 1957, she edited *The Peyote Ritual*, celebrating the movement and praising its insights. She believed that the peyote worshipper "prays to the great Light to understand the light within himself."[23]

Other figures from this era illustrate the complex relationship between esoteric and occult traditions and what purported to be an objective recording of Native ways. In Joseph Epes Brown's *The Sacred Pipe* (1953), Black Elk offered a systematic account of the rituals of his people, written and arranged in such a way that they could in theory be adopted by imitators, whether Native or white. The book is the ultimate source and inspiration for many of the modern practitioners who attempt to copy Native rituals like the Vision Quest or the sweat lodge. By applying feminine names and titles to spiritual beings, the book also offers rich resources for later feminists. Potentially, the book is both a New Age bible and a manual of pseudo-Native spirituality for a movement yet to be born. As with Neihardt's work, though, it is difficult to know how much of the thought-world attributed to Black Elk is authentically his, and how much arises (consciously or not) from the esoteric ideas of the editor. Brown himself was working at exactly the same time as Waters, collecting his material in 1947–1948. Like Waters, he was deeply involved with esoteric speculation, in this case the Traditionalist movement based in Western Sufism, which looked to the ancient spiritual traditions common to all humanity. *The Sacred Pipe* may be a manifestation of Western mysticism as much as of the pristine religion of the Native peoples of the Plains.[24]

Doors of Perception

The strongest connection between the older esotericism and the later New Age comes through the use of peyote and the attendant idea of shamanism. We have already seen that peyote had some limited white use early in the century. Even during the grimmest years of repression for peyote users, the drug's use was well known to a mass public through journalistic writings. A ceremony is described at length in *The Man Who Killed the Deer*. Generally, the accounts were sympathetic to peyote worshippers, and balanced official claims about its harmfulness with rival statements that it had no lasting effects. Some writers went much further, recalling the findings of respected pioneers such as Havelock Ellis and Weir Mitchell, who had written alluringly of "brilliant visions," "a vast field of golden jewels, studded with red and green stones, ever-changing."[25]

Experimentation was inevitable, especially in academic settings. With so many anthropologists studying Indians, some were bound to try the drug, and were so impressed that they spread its use among their colleagues and friends. When Alice Marriott recorded her peyote experiences in the *New Yorker*, she could find no words adequate to describe the effects. It was "Paradise. . . . It's like seeing the door to life swing open." The academic link was especially fruitful in the San Francisco Bay area: Berkeley had one of the nation's most prestigious anthropology programs, with many graduate students, in a setting conveniently close to experimental urban subcultures. By the late 1940s, "a small band of white peyote users emerged, and peyote was easily available in San Francisco." In Southern California, one peyote advocate was the astonishing Jack Parsons, a pioneer of modern rocket science, as well as a renowned occultist, and the local representative of Aleister Crowley's mystical order, the *Ordo Templi Orientis*. At least by the early 1940s, Parsons' group was using peyote in occult rituals, which included kundalini techniques.[26]

Drug use as such does not necessarily have any spiritual connotations, but the peyote experiments of the 1940s soon acquired mystical and shamanic dimensions, which users saw in the context of American Indian myth and belief. One evangelist was Jaime De Angulo, who neatly spans the generations between the great anthropologists of the early twentieth century and the later figures of the counterculture. A brilliant linguist, he worked at Berkeley in the 1920s under Paul Radin and Alfred Kroeber, though Kroeber soon found him irresponsible and erratic. De Angulo spent time in the Dodge-Luhan circle at Taos, where he was close to D. H. Lawrence and Robinson Jeffers, and he protested the suppression of the pagan dances. He acted as Jung's interpreter with his Pueblo informants, and at Berkeley, De Angulo was among the first to teach Jungian psychiatry. From the mid-1930s until his death in 1950, he was a legendary countercultural figure in Northern California, an exponent of shamanism and peyote, and reputedly a member of the Native American Church. De Angulo loved the image of Coyote, the creator-trickster figure, one who traveled between the worlds. In 1949, De Angulo delivered a dazzling series of radio talks, "twenty hours of story, poetry and song broadcast over KPFA radio in Berkeley," which became the basis of his book *Indian Tales*. Through his work, the nascent Beat movement learned the connections between peyote use, shamanic theories, Jungian ideas, and trickster imagery. Gary Snyder described him as "a now legendary departed Spanish shaman and anthropologist [who] was an authentic Coyote medium." De Angulo's disciple Robert Duncan described himself as a poet-shaman.[27]

Peyote played a role in Beat culture reminiscent of what LSD would later be for hippies. Allen Ginsberg composed *Howl* during a peyote-inspired vision in San Francisco. Some of the rising literary figures were also deeply interested in Indian cultures. Kenneth Rexroth loved Native cultures for their verse as much as for their communitarian values. Gary Snyder may have been the most thorough convert, due to his early immersion in the Woodcraft books of Ernest Thompson Seton, reinforced by his later admiration of De Angulo. At Reed College in 1950–1951, his senior thesis applied the mythic theories of Jung and Campbell to a Haida swan-maiden story.[28] Snyder's experiences working on the Warm Springs Indian reservation inspired his poem *Berry Feast*, which drew both on a tribal first-fruit ritual and the legend of Coyote the trickster. Both these Indian images are set against the cold conformity and ecological devastation of white America, the "dead city." This was the poem he read in 1955 at the start of what would become famous as the San Francisco Poetry Renaissance. Allen Ginsberg described him as a "peyoteist . . . hungup on Indians," though increasingly, his major interests were shifting to Zen Buddhism. Not surprisingly, given this résumé, Snyder claimed to find little new in the neo-Indian spirituality of the late 1960s, since he had been living these ideas for two decades. Nor was he alone in his obsessions. When Michael McClure published his *Peyote Poem* in 1958, he wrote, perhaps mocking Snyder: "And the Indian thing. It is true! / Here in my apartment I think tribal thoughts." The vision of interconnectedness and unity attained through peyote led McClure to an early awareness of ecological concerns.[29]

Through the 1950s, some published accounts of peyote were not merely sympathetic—astonishingly so given the violently antidrug climate of the time—but they specifically located the drug in a mystical and spiritual context. In 1954, Native use of peyote was sympathetically described in *The Doors of Perception*, Aldous Huxley's pioneering text on drugs and altered consciousness. For Huxley, such drugs represented an authentic doorway to spiritual experience, albeit one neglected by mainstream Western societies. "Christianity and alcohol do not and cannot mix. Christianity and mescaline seem to be much more compatible." Huxley spoke warmly of peyotists: "In sacramentalizing the use of peyote, the Indians of the Native American Church have done something which is at once psychologically sound and historically respectable." Peyote use gave Indians "the best of both worlds, indeed of all the worlds—the best of Indianism, the best of Christianity, and the best of those Other Worlds of transcendental experience, where the soul knows itself as unconditioned and of like nature with the divine. Hence the Native American Church." These passages would be much read during the 1960s.[30]

But studies of peyote also appeared in many strictly mainline newspapers and magazines, including *Life, Look, Travel,* the *New Yorker,* and even *Hobbies.* Some articles suggested that peyote might authentically have the ability to open the mind to new psychological states. The claims of shamans to wander between worlds might have a basis in objective fact, a wonderful notion for fantasy writers. In 1958, science fiction author Cyril Kornbluth published his much-imitated story "Two Dooms," in which a scientist slips into an alternate world dominated by victorious Axis powers. This transformation is wrought through God Food, the peyote-like hallucinogen supplied by a Hopi medicine man.[31]

Particularly influential in the post–Huxley popularization of peyote was a lengthy 1957 *Life* article by R. G. Wasson, "Seeking the Magic Mushroom." Describing the stunning visions obtained through the drug, Wasson speculated on their psychological foundations, and on the very nature of mind. The lesson once again was that shamans had a rich psychological understanding that modern science could not yet fully comprehend. Perhaps the mushrooms might "prove of help in coping with psychic disturbances"? Significantly for later developments, Wasson's guide through the ritual was a woman, a Mexican *curandera,* whose words sound as if they derived from a Goddess-oriented text written forty years later. She declares: "I am a creator woman, a star woman, a moon woman, a cross woman, a woman of heaven. I am a cloud person, a dew-on-the-grass person."[32]

Shamans and Scientists

So much of what we think of as the contemporary New Age was already in place no later than 1950, the year of Waters's *Masked Gods* and De Angulo's death. These components included ideas of shamanism and altered states of consciousness; an interest in Indian prophecies and lost continents; a thorough mingling of Native American and Asian beliefs; and the mass importation of Mesoamerican mythologies. Within a few years, other ideas that at least potentially could form part of this package included chemical experimentation, psychological self-exploration, environmentalism, and even religious feminism, a mélange that was intoxicatingly different from the orthodox religious currents of 1950s America.

We even find the overlap between esoteric and therapeutic ideas that would appear in modern-day pseudo-Indian movements, and in neo-shamanism. The title *Masked Gods* is meant to suggest the actual masks of figures like the kachinas, but also the concealed personality traits that emerged during psychoanalysis. Waters was fascinated by developments in contemporary psychiatry, and found linkages between the buried forces in the unconscious and the mystic powers claimed by occult writers. His speculations gained support from the academic study of American Indian mysticism by reputable theorists, who were influenced by psychoanalysis, and by psychosomatic interpretations of disease. These accounts praised exactly those features of traditional religion that nineteenth-century observers had condemned as irredeemably primitive: the works of shamans and medicine men. Some suggested that the music and chanting that characterized Indian rituals might actually contribute to curing psychosomatic illnesses, while perhaps Indians had pioneered modern discoveries in the medical uses of hypnosis. In 1936, an article in the *American Journal of Psychiatry* examined "Some points of comparison and contrast between the treatment of functional disorders by Apache shamans and modern psychiatric practice." In 1941, *Psychiatry* reported a study of Navajo religion by Alexander and Dorothea Leighton, who praised the effectiveness of traditional healing rituals, with their emphasis on group and community support, and on shared emotional experience. Whether the Navajos knew it or not, they were practicing effective psychotherapy.[33]

Indian rituals were now being treated as worthy of serious investigation, and even as a valid kind of alternative science or medicine. Also, this was occurring long before the dramatic growth in popularity of alternative medical treatments from the 1970s onwards. In 1948, sociologist Elizabeth Ferguson argued in the *Scientific American* that "witch doctors have a great deal in common with modern physicians, no offense intended." Moderns could learn much from the methods of American Indians, and especially from the

Navajo. The article's main illustration was a Navajo sandpainting, "one of many psychological treatments in primitive medicine." Throughout, Ferguson praised "medicine men" for their "amazing shrewdness," even praising the very tricks that for earlier generations had just proved how cynically deceptive medicine men were. When a shaman pretended to suck at a body and draw forth a worm or a thorn, this would have a positive psychosomatic effect on the patient, who would see the cause of the illness visibly removed. "Primitive medicine learned long, long ago what modern medicine is just rediscovering—that distinctions between the mind and the body are artificial." Traditional medicine had much to teach in its cultivation of herbal remedies, since through trial and error, tribal practitioners had built up "a body of empirically sound treatments." And ancient medicine had not forgotten that the patient had to be treated "as a social being as well as a biological organism." Conversely, modern scientists were faulted for failing to learn from these precedents. Of course, Ferguson and her contemporaries were not praising Native religion *as religion*, but were treating it as an intelligent and worthwhile aspect of human culture, which deserved preservation and study.[34]

By the 1950s, the heyday of Freudian prestige in America, Native treatments were acquiring a remarkable respectability. Admittedly, some writers were still complaining of traditional medicine as an obstacle to progress, an "iron curtain of superstition," but others were seeing positive features in the old religions. In 1958, Anthony Wallace claimed that the Iroquois had invented the psychoanalytic theory of dreams long before their first contact with Europeans. When, in the same year, *Time* published the story of Mary Grey-Eyes, a Navajo woman healed by modern Western medicine, this was no longer a simple tale of the triumph of science over superstition, of Western light illuminating Indian darkness. A section of the story headed "Mind and Body" told how the reservation clinic worked closely with traditional healers, because "Navajos have some sound ideas about health," especially in their emphasis on harmony. "They recognize no dichotomy between mind and body; so all their medicine is in a sense psychosomatic." At every point, the tone of the story was far friendlier to Native practice than it might have been thirty years before. *Time* concluded by noting that when a new clinic was dedicated in 1956, two medicine men were invited to perform rituals: "It looks as though the magic of both races has been effective."[35]

Also supporting Indian claims were other kinds of Western science that have since been largely discredited, notably parapsychology. In the 1930s,

J. B. Rhine received national attention for his experiments that gave credence to extrasensory perception, so perhaps Indian claims to supernatural powers were not as far-fetched as they appeared? In 1948, an otherwise unexceptional article on the peyote religion in *Travel* remarked that recent experiments showed that the drug could indeed unleash precognition and other psychic powers. These "chemical keys" could "open doors deep within the complex labyrinth of the human mind." Scientific discoveries were used to support the argument commonly made by the admirers of Indian spirituality, namely, that Native peoples had access to secrets yet to be uncovered by over-sophisticated white people.[36]

Forgetting the Indian?

The question must then arise: why did the modern New Age view of Native spirituality not emerge in the 1950s, rather than the 1960s and 1970s? Why did *Masked Gods* not become the scriptural authority that the *Book of the Hopi* would later be? It is intriguing to ask whether Jaime De Angulo or one of his disciples might have fulfilled the role that Carlos Castaneda would later play as the guru of New Age shamanism. In fact, the slowness of Native spirituality to gain a mass following by the late 1950s was striking. Except for the continuing exploration of peyote, little seemed to remain of the older interests, which were confined to bohemian circles in major cities like San Francisco; the Beat movement remained strictly on the cultural fringe. So complete was the oblivion that counterculture radicals of the 1960s thought they were the first generation to recognize Indian achievements. They assumed that all previous generations had shared the racist contempt of the early settlers, the dismissal of Native religions as crude devil worship.

This view was quite wrong. The contemporaries of John Collier, Ernest Thompson Seton, and Frank Waters needed no instruction about the glories of Native spirituality. To some extent, the counterculture's misperception of earlier generations was an inevitable feature of insurgent radical movements, which commonly exaggerate the intellectual gap between themselves and their predecessors. But the generation of the 1960s was right to contrast its own attitudes with those of the decade immediately preceding. Their mistake was to assume that the attitudes of the 1950s were essentially those of all previous eras of American history.

Though Indian culture had indeed been fashionable for many years, public interest did decline during the 1950s, remarkably so given its recent vogue. Perhaps the shift is not amazing, though, if indeed the perennial American interest in Indians grows and shrinks in inverse proportion to satisfaction with mainstream society. In 1920 or 1930, deep disaffection with Western culture naturally led to an idealization of Indian culture. Conversely, when discontent was relatively low, as in the booming 1950s, it made sense for Americans to seek satisfaction in their own communities. Americans simply had much less need for idealized Indians. Social changes had a particular impact on women, who so often constitute a primary market for alternative spirituality. In the 1940s, an unprecedented number of women had been in the workplace, but in the following decade, changes in social mores and in employment patterns led to a new emphasis on home, family, and domesticity. Statistics for churchgoing and church membership reached new heights. Demography also helps explain the contrast between the conformist 1950s and the experimental 1960s. In the 1950s, there were simply far fewer Americans in the teenage and young-adult cohorts, the sort of people most likely to become starry-eyed over promises of mystical enlightenment. And the young people who were active in the 1950s had nothing like the disposable income and free time that their counterparts would a decade later.[37]

In hindsight, too, perhaps the scale of that earlier cultural vogue for Indians was part of the problem. By the 1950s, things Indian were falling out of fashion, not because they were considered primitive or revolting, but rather because the culture had been so overexposed. The mass tourism of the interwar years had commercialized Indian crafts and ceremonials, and purists feared that both were hopelessly compromised. In practice, selling to tourists and collectors seemed to have meant selling out to tourists and collectors. Reporting on the handicrafts on show at the Gallup Inter-Tribal ceremonial in 1956, *Newsweek* commented that "the prizewinning items however had a cosmopolitan chic which had as much to do with tribal lore as a solid gold Cadillac." And art that is taught in high schools is unlikely to excite the cultural elite.[38]

Books claiming to present the truths of Native spirituality were seen as equally clichéd, and devalued. Brown's *Sacred Pipe* would be crucial for later enthusiasts, but when it was published, although the book was respectfully received, it had little public impact. When Oliver La Farge reviewed it, he had to reassure his nervous readers: "To report that a book deals with the mystic side of Sioux religion as expounded by the oldest surviving Sioux priest is to risk frightening away readers. Many believe that American Indian religion is unworthy of serious consideration." The second sentence would have sounded as amazing in 1930 as it would today. Nobody seemed to care any more.[39]

During the 1950s, too, the political idealism of the Collier years was fading. The continuing desperate poverty of Indian communities led to new prescriptions for reform, most of which called for a renewed attempt to bring Native peoples into the social mainstream. A new federal policy aimed at eliminating Indian cultural differences and ending the reservation system under a program worryingly described as "termination." In the mid-1950s, the Eisenhower administration initiated a new era of assimilation, more benevolently intended than the previous one, but potentially just as devastating. Under a policy announced in 1953, federal jurisdiction over tribes would be ended, and tribal members subjected to full U.S. jurisdiction. At the same time, the government launched an ambitious scheme to relocate Indians to urban areas. The new policies had excellent intentions, namely, moving Indians from the demeaning status of wards to full and effective citizenship. For all their noble goals, though, both plans were soon judged to be utter failures.[40]

The termination policy was unpopular. Recalling Helen Hunt Jackson's campaigns of the 1880s, John Collier titled his protest, "Back to Dishonor," and Native activists such as D'Arcy McNickle opposed the changes.[41] Debate rumbled on through the 1950s. What is striking, though, is that the disruption of ancient communities, and the physical removal to cities, could have been contemplated with nothing like the mass opposition that had surfaced during the 1920s. Though Indian causes still commanded liberal sympathy, this was expressed in terms of supporting social and economic development, rather than the defense of idealized prehistoric societies that safeguarded great spiritual truths. For the time being, Red Atlantis had foundered.

8

❧

Vision Quests
1960—1980

In my vision I saw people returning to the land with a new humbleness and respect for the Earth Mother. I saw new ceremonies coming out of the old.
—Sun Bear

Through American history, romantic Indian images are most sought after in eras of alienation and crisis. Not surprisingly, then, the greatest surge of interest in things Indian to date occurred during the 1960s, as Native issues became inextricably linked with other critical social and political concerns. Quite rapidly, sympathy for Indians was transformed into an active interest in pursuing Native spirituality, a quest that soon unearthed rich materials from earlier eras of enthusiasm: the works of Frank Waters, the accounts of Black Elk offered by John Neihardt and Joseph Epes Brown, the diverse visions of the Indian as Natural Mystic and Child of Nature. Culturally, most modern attitudes toward Indian culture and religion can be traced to the traumatic circumstances of America *circa* 1970.

But this surge of interest differed from its predecessors in one crucial way, namely, that sympathy soon transformed into active imitation. The notion of whites copying Indian rituals was anything but new: witness the peyote ritual in Progressive-era New York, the white snake dancers at the Astor Hotel, the Smoki pseudotribe, Ernest Thompson Seton's Woodcraft movement. In earlier periods, though, there had been no serious attempt to base these activities in authentic Indian religious beliefs. Even Seton, that evangelist of the Indian gospel, was preaching a mystical form of liberal Christianity, and spoke little of actual rituals: he never suggested practicing shamanism, or building a sweat lodge. However enthusiastic the Smokis, they never thought their snake rituals might have any effect on the climate. By the 1970s, though, Native spirituality was repackaged in a way that made it feasible for adoption by white observers, in however generic or deceptive a form. Once that shift had occurred, once it was possible to live a neo-Indian religion, that change could not be reversed. Once launched, the movement acquired its own dynamic, and it would quickly develop as part of the emerging New Age movement.

Indians and Insurgents

During the 1950s, Indians attracted the sympathetic attention of liberal activists, for whom they symbolized both racial exploitation and grinding poverty. In addition, the continuing interest in genocidal Nazi policies through these years raised disturbing questions about America's own history of extermination and mass-population transfers. In 1949, Carey McWilliams's account of California's Indian policy drew the obvious European analogies, with "liquidation" as the means to "solve the problem." Discussion of the concept of "genocide" was kept alive by the Adolf Eichmann trial of 1961.[1]

In media portrayals of the time, Indians had the advantage that their struggles were not quite as desperately controversial as were those of African Americans. For instance, despite the pervasive racism Indians have encountered, sexual liaisons between whites and Indians have rarely had the same explosive power to shock and offend as black-white relationships. Even the most conservative Americans delight in claiming traces of Indian ancestry in a way they would never do with African roots. Films used Indian characters to depict racial injustice, while similar stories of black victims might arouse resentment and even boycotts in southern states. In the 1960 western *The Magnificent Seven*, the heroes forcibly desegregate a cemetery by burying a dead Indian: the message of tolerance and equality would have been less widely accepted if the black-white issue had been addressed directly. Largely because of the national awareness of racial issues, Indian issues were treated more sympathetically. Indians benefited from the enhanced awareness of civil-rights issues as defined and defended by the courts. In 1964, the

Supreme Court of California struck down the conviction of three Indians
for peyote use on the grounds that the prohibition constituted a violation of
religious freedom.

In the 1960s, as widespread social liberalism increasingly became radical-
ized, Indians served as symbols of cultural resistance, as icons for what
would come to be known as the counterculture. In 1962, Ken Kesey's classic
novel *One Flew Over the Cuckoo's Nest* used as its narrator the severely disturbed Indian "Chief Broom." In this mirror-image world, Broom's diag-
nosed insanity is a symptom of his utter alienation from the proper
standards of white America. If anything, his madness symbolizes his cultural
superiority, his greater humanity. (Kesey's choice of an Indian narrator reflected his own use of peyote as he was writing the book.) Also at this time, an
official report, *The Indian: America's Unfinished Business,* suggested that, far
from being a lethal obstacle to inevitable progress, Indian values and attitudes offered much that white society could copy. The report challenged notions that Indians had been held back by their lack of thrift, diligence, and
punctuality. Indians held these values as much as they needed to, but combined them with other more important principles, such as communalism,
cohesion, cooperation, an ideal of unity, and reverence for nature. By the
time the report appeared in print in 1966, this message attracted a growing
number of white admirers.[2]

As Philip Deloria remarks, "For whites of all classes, the quests for personal autonomy and identity often involved forays into racial Otherness." In
the late 1960s, hippies spoke of themselves as "tribes," and pseudo-Indian
styles of dress and hair became fashionable. Setting the trend in these matters was San Francisco, where the new drug culture built upon the older subculture of beatniks and peyote aficionados. The legendary "Human Be-In"
in San Francisco in 1967 was a "gathering of the tribes." *Life* magazine reported at length on the "Happy Hippie Hunting Ground," claiming that
some young utopians were already living in tipis and hogans, some attempted to live off the land in Indian fashion, trying to learn "how to find
wild vegetables and herbs, how to raise corn and rabbits, how to weave baskets, even how to stalk game and tan hides. They seek out the old men who
remember the tribal patterns, for hippies are tremendously attracted to the
Indians' communal society, where all is shared . . . where there is a sense of
group ceremony and ritual." According to this supportive piece, Native
leaders themselves lauded these efforts. "Militant chief" Rolling Thunder
said that the hippies "are the reincarnation of the traditional Indians who

have fallen. They are the ghosts of warriors who have come back to reclaim their lands." This looks like a potent commercial for the nascent neo-Native spirituality movement.[3]

In the late 1960s, New Mexico especially had become a popular destination for hippie travelers, and also a center for communes, some of which built tipis for shelter. By 1974, Gary Snyder was praising the willingness of young people, "longhairs," to return to the land, to live in Indian style. He denied that this trend involved any nostalgia, but was rather necessary for planetary survival: "Here is a generation prepared to learn from the Elders. . . . Loving and protecting this soil, these trees, these wolves. Natives of Turtle Island." Older generations of Natives, however, remained unimpressed. Conflicts developed when hippies tried to move into Native communities, which they saw as islands of communal pacifist values and alternative spiritualities. Residents found the sexual behavior of the newcomers so shocking that most were soon expelled. For their part, white radicals were puzzled by the fervent patriotism of most Native communities, and their pride in military service. Reservations are awkward places to show disrespect for the American flag.[4]

As the counterculture became more politicized, Indians were idealized for their stubborn resistance to white authority, their maintenance of traditional, communal values. A best-seller of these years was Dee Brown's epic of the Indian wars, *Bury My Heart at Wounded Knee* (1970), avowedly an *Indian* history of the American West. In fact, Indians seemed to be prototypes of the then-idealized guerrillas of the Viet Cong. At Berkeley, an image of Geronimo became a logo for the free-speech movement, which spawned the underground newspaper the *Berkeley Tribe.* One television movie of the era was *Tribes,* the story of a conflict between a hippie conscript and a sadistic drill instructor. Though the film has no explicit Indian content, the suggestion is that the counterculture was seeing itself as a tribe at war with mainstream America.[5]

The Hollywood productions of these years illustrate the changing attitude to Native peoples. It is possible to exaggerate the simplistic portrayals of Indians in earlier cinema, since many films of the 1940s and 1950s offered sympathetic and well-rounded Native characters. By the 1960s, though, such complexities had given way to a simpler and wholly admiring stereotype. In *Cheyenne Autumn* (1964), Indians are victims reminiscent of the Jews and other persecuted and displaced populations of the Second World War. Idealization of Indians crested at the end of the decade. Vietnam analogies were explicit in *Soldier Blue* (1970), in which the historic 1864 slaughter of the

Cheyenne village at Sand Creek becomes indistinguishable from the recently exposed My Lai massacre. These films depicted Indian societies highly favorably, often using the device of showing a white person being absorbed into these different traditions. In *A Man Called Horse*, (1970), Richard Harris achieves the status of manhood in the Lakota nation through the agonizing Sun Vow ceremony, in which cords are passed through his chest. In *Little Big Man* (1970), Cheyenne society is idyllic in its relaxed ways, its sexual freedom, and even (a first in Hollywood's Wild West) in tolerating homosexual lifestyles and gender-bending. This film also introduced the sacred figure of the "contrary," the figure known to the Lakota as *heyokah*, a name that has had a long afterlife in New Age spirituality. The Indian society of such films is all the more attractive when contrasted with the violent, repressed, and hypocritical world of white America.

Some films explicitly linked the counterculture to Native realities. In the *Billy Jack* trilogy (1971–1977), the hero is an outrageously idealized amalgam of images who blatantly appeals to the wish fulfillment of the white audience. Billy Jack is a half-Indian ex-Green Beret, who uses his martial arts skills to defend local hippies against racism and police brutality. He also travels to his home kiva to explain to the tribal elders that young white people are sincerely seeking spiritual truths and moving on paths parallel to those of the Pueblo people. Another hippie homage appeared in *Easy Rider* (1969). The heroes make their pilgrimage across an American West marked by ancient Indian sites, however degraded by the modern world: they fill their tanks at Arizona's Sacred Mountain gas station. One of the movie's stars, Dennis Hopper, purchased the Taos house of Mabel Dodge, that earlier apostle of Indian cultural glories.

Red Power

Making Indians even more congenial to white radicals was the activism of the Red Power movement, which was inspired by the black civil rights struggle. Like African Americans and Latinos, Indians seemed to be a local manifestation of the insurgent Third World on U.S. soil.

The new Indian activism began in the mid-1960s with several separate campaigns intended to defend and enforce treaty terms concerning practical issues like water rights and fishing rights, or the defense of Native lands against flooding for dam projects. The sit-ins of the civil rights movement inspired "fish-ins." Spontaneous local campaigns merged into a more generalized liberation movement, inspired by texts such as Vine Deloria's "Indian manifesto," *Custer Died for Your Sins* (1967). The American Indian Movement (AIM) was founded in Minneapolis in 1968, and drew heavily on the ideas and urban-guerrilla style popularized by the Black Panthers. The Red Power movement achieved global headlines with its occupation of Alcatraz Island from 1969 to 1971. It also became involved in notorious confrontations on the Pine Ridge reservation in South Dakota. A 1973 occupation at Wounded Knee led commentators to ask, semiseriously, if Richard Nixon might not be the first president since 1890 to have a full-scale Indian war on his hands. When AIM supporters engaged in a bloody confrontation with federal agents, this in turn led to celebrated trials and worldwide agitation on behalf of Native political prisoners. In 1973, Marlon Brando created a sensation at the Oscar ceremonies when he refused to accept his award personally, preferring to send a Native woman to denounce the exploitation of Indian peoples.[6]

While overt radical activism faded during the 1970s, the Red Power years had a lasting impact on Native culture and especially Native religions. In drawing attention to Indian grievances, activists showed the immense public sympathy that existed and the collective guilt for past atrocities. This created the opening for the legislative reforms of the 1970s, which revolutionized official attitudes to Native religious freedom and land rights. Also, Red Power differed from Black Power in that the heady days of radical advance were not followed by any significant backlash. For most white urban communities, Native peoples were sufficiently far removed that no immediate conflicts over crime or housing would interfere with the process of romanticization.

A new cultural self-awareness encouraged Native writers, who found that their ideas appealed powerfully to a mainstream audience. The modern renaissance of Native American writing dates from the publication of Scott Momaday's Pulitzer Prize–winning novel *House Made of Dawn* in 1968, that banner year of Native radicalism. Like many other books from the new wave of Native writing, Momaday's work often draws on religious themes, which further raised public awareness abut Native spirituality. Finally, the Red Power movement itself promoted a revival of traditional religion and ceremonies. As with Black Power, the decline in confrontational activism during the 1970s did not mean that radicalism had vanished, but rather that it was transmuted into cultural nationalism, and a quest for cultural and religious roots.[7]

Creating Neo-Native Spirituality

As the U.S. role in the Vietnam War wound down from 1971, white activists shifted their concerns away from political radicalism and into broader cultural issues like feminism and environmentalism. Many young people gravitated toward religious and spiritual interests, which most felt could not be accommodated within the framework of existing churches and denominations. Both Protestant and Catholic churches tended in the radical 1960s to look askance at mysticism, contemplation, or individualistic devotion, which detracted from social activism, with the result that seekers looked elsewhere. Fringe religions and study groups now flourished. Some groups acquired the reputation of cults, with authoritarian spiritual leaders who often claimed supernatural powers, and fears about excesses provoked a full-scale anticult panic by the end of the decade. A national trend toward "turning within" led to a boom in therapeutic and self-help movements, many of which acquired spiritual aspirations. To borrow Steven Tipton's phrase, these various movements all contributed to the process of *Getting Saved from the Sixties*.[8]

In all these developments, the new and often overlapping interests in ecology, gender, spirituality, and self-help, Native American themes would be critical. Given the precedents of the 1920s and 1930s, it was scarcely surprising that the crisis years around 1970 would lead to a rediscovery of idealized stereotypes of Indians, or that this vision would acquire specifically religious dimensions. In fact, the degree of romanticization would far surpass earlier precedents. This was partly due to the depth of the social crisis in the late 1960s, but also to the role of the mass media in disseminating a sense of fear and national fragmentation. While riots and racial strife were anything but new in American history, only in the 1960s were they brought into every living room through the medium of television. In other ways too, social trends made the disaffected more aware of radical social alternatives than they might have been in earlier eras. We can attribute this to the upsurge of higher education in the post–World War II years, and the vastly increased market for popular books on religion, anthropology, psychology, and social issues. But whatever the reasons, from about 1970, an innovative and syncretistic spiritual movement sought authenticity and authority in Native teachings.

Frank Waters and the Fifth World

The idea that Indians had a special mystical link to the forces of nature and the environment owed much to Frank Waters's immensely influential *The Book of the Hopi* (1963), a sequel to his 1950 book *Masked Gods*, on the Pueblos and Navajos. Building on his earlier themes, the new book presented the mystical Indians as the prophets both of imminent crisis and of the eventual coming of a glorious era, the "New Age." In his daring synthesis of esoteric and scholarly materials, framed in a prophetic and apocalyptic vision, Waters recalls that other great religious innovator, Joseph Smith. Waters, too, may have intended the *Book of the Hopi* as a prophetic or scriptural text.

By the time he lived on the Hopi reservation, from 1959 through 1963, Waters had a thorough grounding in New Age and mystical thought, and he knew exactly what he thought he would find in his new home. While on the reservation, he received his own dreams and mystic revelations, for which he found validation in the Hopi thought-world. However sophisticated the Hopi culture and its religious dimensions—as they undoubtedly are—the book should not be taken as a simple record of what the Indians told him spontaneously. Even if Waters did not ask leading questions, the Hopi by this stage had decades of experience dealing with white anthropologists, and in shaping the information they supplied to the needs and interests of their listeners. A considerate people, the Hopi do not like to turn visitors away empty-handed. Like *Masked Gods*, the book betrays on every page Waters's particular interests and obsessions.[9]

The new title arrived at an opportune moment in American cultural history, and it became steadily more popular as the decade progressed. In fact, much of the thought and activity of New Age spirituality can be seen as an extrapolation of the *Book of the Hopi*, sometimes verging on plagiarism. So many of the themes and ideas found in the book have become commonplace that some effort is needed to imagine how exciting it was for its early readers. The book was presented not as the work of one white author, but rather as the collective voice of thirty Hopi elders from the aboriginal inhabitants of America. In a decade when millions claimed to be seeking an authentic America, free of contemporary abuses and injustices, this offered a demanding claim to authority. Hopi culture was multiply appealing for white readers. These ancient and authentic Americans aspired to practice peace and lived communally, in harmony with the natural world. Even the word "Hopi" meant "peace." Through Waters's work, mainstream readers found that the Hopi held "a world view of life, deeply religious in nature, whose esoteric meaning they have kept inviolate for generations uncounted. Their existence always has been patterned upon the universal plan of world creation and maintenance, and their progress on the evolutionary Road of Life depends upon the unbroken observance of its laws."[10]

The Hopi showed how to live alongside a warped American culture, "suffering American domination with aloofness and secrecy, and keeping at bay the technological civilization swirling around them." They offered a practical model to the communal movement of these years. However, the world was approaching a crisis in which the Hopi and their values might not remain obscure much longer. As the "psychic chasm" separating white America from the rest of the world was growing ever wider, "who can doubt the signs that a transition to another great new age has begun?" Equally geared to contemporary American concerns was Waters's praise of "this message of peace, this concern with helping to preserve the inherent harmony of the universal constituents of all life," and what man could achieve "if he can but find a way of self-fulfillment." Such a way was not to be found among the genocidal peoples of WASP America, "cold-blooded, deeply inhibited, and bound by their puritan traditions."[11]

The Hopi worldview, as Waters presented it, resonated with prophetic and apocalyptic ideas that had been popular in American religious thought since colonial days, and which had regularly inspired new religious movements. Much of the *Book of the Hopi* expounded the people's mythological structure, with its story of how humanity had emerged through several successive worlds, until reaching the present realm of reality, the Fourth World. Apart from its cosmic significance (says Waters), each world corresponds to a stage of psychophysical development. Our present Fourth World is a transient evolutionary moment—fortunately, since we now live under the "full expression of man's ruthless materialism and imperialistic will." But before long, first individuals and then the whole world will move from materialism to spiritual consciousness, moving toward "the wholeness of all Creation, whence he sprang." The book ends with a discussion of the alleged Hopi prophecies, which seem remarkably suited to the precise political conditions of the world in 1963, the age of Cold War tensions and Third World decolonization. The United States would perish in a nuclear holocaust, leaving the Hopi communities to survive. Gradually, "the humble people of little nations, tribes and racial minorities" would begin "the Emergence to the future Fifth World," a transition that had already begun.[12]

Consistently, this sounds more like Waters's old mentor Gurdjieff than Hopi wisdom. Gurdjieff had taught that human evolution was at a perilous phase, and that the world could be saved only by reconciling the wisdom of East and West. To accomplish this, Gurdjieff taught his esoteric system, which would include the old mystical emphases on body, emotions, and mind, but which would rise above them. The world could thus be saved only by his "Fourth Way," which would mark a leap in evolutionary consciousness. The Fourth Way sounds like the Fifth World.

In other ways, too, Waters imposed his own views on the raw materials he was finding among the Hopis. One aspect of this was Waters's evident interest in Mesoamerican matters. He believed that the Hopi shared common cultural and ethnic roots with the Maya, and Maya themes featured in the mystical dreams he experienced on the Hopi reservation. Perhaps the Hopi had originated as "a small Mayan branch, possibly a religious cult, which migrated north to the Four Corners area of our own southwest?" The claim is historically dubious, not to say inconsistent. If Hopi traditions are so worthy of respect, then Waters should have acknowledged their claim to have originated ("emerged") much closer than southern Mexico, namely, in the Grand Canyon. But the Mexican Connection allowed Waters to integrate Mayan lore and prophecies into the popular picture of Hopi thought and culture. This foreshadowed the modern New Age tendency to draw on the great civilizations of Mexico when trying to understand North American Indian religions.[13]

Throughout this complex work, interested readers could find myths and images relevant to their own changing needs. As interest grew in feminine spirituality, readers could focus on powerful female characters such as Spider Woman, who was so critical to organizing the new creation, and to Mother Earth and the Corn Mother. Just as appealing to contemporary spirituality was Waters's immersion in esoteric thought. In the *Book of the Hopi*, he directly compares Hopi wisdom with the Asian religious themes then so much in vogue; as in *Masked Gods*, we hear about Tibetan Buddhism and Tantric mysticism, and, of course, he uses the mythology of Atlantis and other lost continents. Though presented as a record of traditional teaching, Waters's commentary transforms the *Book of the Hopi* into a survey and an overview of occult and esoteric teaching as it had flourished in the United States since the late nineteenth century.

Natural Indians

Mystical views of Indian culture gained popularity as confidence in mainstream white civilization crumbled at the end of the 1960s. Critical to the
new cultural awareness was a veneration for nature, land, and environment,
a set of beliefs in which Indians played a unique symbolic role. When the
heroes of *Easy Rider* bed down in the ruins of an Anasazi settlement, their
guide reminds them, "The people this place belongs to are buried right under you. You could be a trifle polite. . . . It's a small thing to ask." This sense
that the Indians were the rightful owners of the land went beyond the limited scope of that one pueblo and its cemetery. In 1974, Gary Snyder argued
that the nation's problems could be resolved only when its inhabitants renounce "the European word 'America' and accept the new-old name for the
continent, 'Turtle Island.'"[14]

Today, one common stereotype of Indian spirituality holds that Native believers are lovingly attuned to Mother Earth, in contrast to the rapacious urges
sanctified by Judeo-Christian faiths. Native spirituality is seen as holistic, inte-
grating spirit and nature, mind and body. This theme is not new, since the
Mother Earth concept appears in the famous speech of Smohalla, popularized
by John Collier, but it was restated vigorously in the 1960s. One key influence
was Mircea Eliade, who in the 1950s and 1960s was the world's most quoted
authority on shamanism. After he took an academic position in the United
States at the University of Chicago in 1958, his writings shaped the emerging
academic study of religion. Particularly influential was *The Sacred and the Profane*, which appeared in an English edition in 1959. For all its sober academic
language, the book carried an angry, antimodernist agenda that would have
rung true with Collier. (Like Joseph Epes Brown, Eliade's intellectual roots lay
in Traditionalism.) For Eliade, the symbolic structures of primal religions
offered their believers a richly satisfying worldview, an integrated cosmos, in
which place, time, and nature all enjoyed sanctified status. In contrast, secularized moderns—and especially Westerners—lived in a state of chaos, a de-
sacralized and demythologized world without meaning, in which nature was
effectively dead. To illustrate the completeness that moderns have lost, Eliade
quoted Smohalla, whose words carried "incomparable freshness and spontaneity." Without such a spiritual concept of the natural world, modern humanity
lacked hope, and this anomie caused pervasive depression and anxiety.[15]

By the 1960s, the poverty of modern concepts of nature had become so familiar as to be almost clichéd, as had the veneration for Indian nature worship.

The report *America's Unfinished Business* stressed "their idea of unity and their reverence for Mother Earth" as the core of Indian values and attitudes. "The spiritual attachment to nature . . . has brought the Indian into an intimate accord with the elements. . . . Land is believed to be part of a benevolent mother and like her, vital to life. Among Indian tribes, it was generally considered to be not a merchantable product but one the user had the natural right to enjoy."[16]

Devotion to Mother Earth acquired a political dimension with the emergence of the environmental movement. Rachel Carson drew attention to the notion of imminent ecological crisis in 1962, but as the decade progressed, other observers increasingly placed the problem in a religious context. In 1967, Lynn White delivered a much-quoted address, "The Historical Roots of Our Ecological Crisis," which explicitly blamed the biblical injunction to conquer and subdue the earth.

Especially in its Western form, Christianity is the most anthropocentric religion the world has seen. . . . Christianity, in absolute contrast to ancient paganism and Asia's religions (except, perhaps, Zoroastrianism), not only established a dualism of man and nature but also insisted that it is God's will that man exploit nature for his proper ends. . . . What we do about ecology depends on our ideas of the man-nature relationship. . . . By destroying pagan animism, Christianity made it possible to exploit nature in a mood of indifference to the feelings of natural objects.

The destruction of paganism was not just a cultural or aesthetic tragedy, it had created the necessary preconditions for the rape, and perhaps the murder, of Mother Earth. White's speech foreshadows later writing on Native spirituality in its rhetorical use of idealized paganism in order to condemn the Judeo-Christian West. The contrast between the two is presented so starkly, with the pagans so good and the Western Christians so irredeemably evil, that it looks like a manifestation of the gross dualism he himself scorns.[17]

Given the religious context of 1967, White did not discuss the logical solution to this problem, namely, a return to explicit paganism. Instead, he hoped for a renewal of earth-centered spirituality within Christianity, which might grow out of the Franciscan tradition. Within a few years, though, concern about Mother Earth was grounding itself in the traditions of historic paganism, and particularly of Native American spirituality, as the Indian became the symbol of ecological restoration. In 1971, a legendary television commercial depicted the tears shed by Indian chief Iron Eyes

Cody as he witnessed the plague of litter polluting the nation. (In yet another example of "playing Indian," Cody himself proved to have been of Italian American heritage.)

The same year, an ABC television film about ecology introduced the now world-famous speech in which Chief Seattle supposedly presented his sophisticated view of the interconnectedness of Nature and all living things. Seattle reportedly declared:

> The earth is our mother. . . . The white man's dead forget the country of their birth when they go to walk among the stars. Our dead never forget this beautiful Earth, for it is the mother of the red man. We are part of the Earth and it is part of us. . . . Man did not weave the web of life—he is merely a strand in it. Whatever he does to the web, he does to himself.

Although the speech continues to circulate, it is bogus, at least in the form that it developed during the 1970s. It was created by scriptwriter Ted Perry to make an imaginative point about ecological concern, and despite Perry's protests, it was promptly circulated as if it were an original document. Its obvious historical inconsistencies did not prevent it from winning instant credibility. To take one problem, a Native American who lived on Puget Sound would scarcely have reported that "I have seen a thousand rotting buffaloes on the prairie, left by the white man who shot them from a passing train." The reference to white people walking among the stars suggests the contemporary space program.[18]

In fact, the speech represents an apt symbol of the white appropriation of Native culture. Some words spoken by the historic Chief Seattle in 1854 were translated, very freely, by a white observer, who modified them according to the views and standards of a nineteenth-century American. This "authentic" speech then became the foundation for the document that emerged in 1971. For all its artificial quality, though, the Seattle speech acquired a life of its own as the scripture of a spiritually oriented ecological movement, in which the Chief himself became a venerated saint. It became a canonical scripture of the Native spirituality movement.

Into the Plains

Other texts helped shape attitudes toward Indian spirituality, and suggested ways in which ordinary consumers could participate directly. One was

Robert Heinlein's 1961 science fiction novel *Stranger in a Strange Land*, which on its surface does not mention Indian themes at all. The hero is a human being raised among Martians, who brings to Earth people a new communal religion founded upon a mystical bond with nature, and sacraments based upon sharing water. If this sounds suspiciously like the *Book of the Hopi*, or the Savage reservation of *Brave New World*, this is because Heinlein was drawing on the Zuñi culture as portrayed in anthropological studies. Also like Heinlein's Martians, the Hopi had a host of cultural taboos concerning water and thirst. The *Stranger* mythology served as another entry point for Native and especially southwestern traditions into the counterculture.[19]

Also critical was *Black Elk Speaks*, a book that originally appeared in 1932, but which remained fairly obscure for decades. The book enjoyed a massive revival following its discovery by Carl Jung, and a new edition appeared in 1961. The book's fame spread after Black Elk was heavily quoted in *Bury My Heart at Wounded Knee*, and a popular edition appeared in 1972. Thereafter, the book became a mainstay of college courses on Native Americans and, often, on comparative religion. Reading *Black Elk* initiated a generation of young, white Americans into the mythical and ritual universe of the Plains Indians, and familiarized them with such ideas as the sweat lodge, the sacred pipe, and the Vision Quest.[20]

The commercial success of *Black Elk Speaks* and *Bury My Heart at Wounded Knee* encouraged publishers to reprint most of their older Native titles, while a number of new autobiographies also appeared with a heavy emphasis on the Plains cultures. In 1972, *Lame Deer, Seeker of Visions* offered another systematic account of Plains religious customs and rituals, though the story was now brought up to date to acknowledge the upsurge of Indian political activism. Other titles from these years included Joseph Medicine Crow's *Memories of a White Crow Indian* and *Sanapia: Comanche Medicine Woman*. Brad Steiger's *Medicine Talk* foreshadowed many later New Age texts in offering "a guide to walking in balance and surviving on the Earth Mother."[21]

In the long run, the most influential of the new books was *Seven Arrows* (1972), by Hyemeyohsts Storm, who rarely receives the credit he deserves as a key progenitor and popularizer of the New Age. Storm himself claims mixed roots, his parents respectively from German stock and from the Northern Cheyenne people of Montana. He asserts that, "beginning in my youth, I had the greatest fortune to become the apprentice of the brilliant and powerful Zero Chief, and Holy Woman, Estcheemah. She was a Mayan

Breed Indian who was born during the bloody and sorrowful Indian Wars of
the late 1800's. She was one of the wisest and most powerful Medicine
Chiefs of her time, and a Carrier and teacher of the Medicine Wheels."
Storm's Indian credentials have been assailed by many Native activists—
though he received an imprimatur from Vine Deloria, Jr., who in 1973
praised the book as one of the few efforts "made by Indians to educate
Americans on the complexities of living with a particular land."[22]

Seven Arrows is a lavishly illustrated volume, consisting of tales of Plains
Indian peoples, but its most important innovation was the Medicine Wheel,
which provides an organizing framework for the whole text. The symbol recurs throughout the work, and is presented as the cardinal structure of Native
religion. At the outset, the book declares that "the Medicine Wheel is the
very Way of Life of the People. It is an Understating of the Universe. . . . The
Medicine Wheel is everything of the People. The Medicine Wheel is the Living Flame of the Lodges, and the Great Shield of Truth written in the sign of
the Water. It is Heart and Mind. . . . The Medicine Wheel is the Total Universe." And so on. The importance of these ideas will be discussed later, but
at present, it is enough to say that the Wheel would provide the basis for a
rich mythology. And at least in its well-known form, the Wheel originates
with Seven Arrows, though it derives something from older traditions.[23]

One effect of the new wave of books was the growing interest in the spiritualities of the Plains Indians, as opposed to the older stress on the kivas and
dances of the Pueblo and Navajo, and the world of the Anasazi. Partly this
change was political, since radicals were attracted by the heroic resistance of
the Lakota and Cheyenne against U.S. military forces: unlike the Hopi, these
were not "peaceful people." But also, this was a longer-term cultural shift that
dates back to the 1930s and the regular use of Plains themes in Hollywood
Westerns. These visual images shaped white expectations of what "real" Indians were supposed to do, and how they were meant to appear. This resulted
in some oddities, as the actors recruited to play Indian characters were often
southwestern, so that a film that claims to describe Plains conditions often
has Cheyenne or Lakota characters clearly speaking Navajo, on the assumption that white audiences would neither know nor care.

In turn, white expectations shaped Indian behavior. By the 1950s, anthropologists were noting the spread of Plains customs like the war bonnet and the
war dance, and the emergence of pan-Indian imagery. When intertribal cultural events occurred, such as the great annual meetings at Gallup, "a close-to-
aboriginal Navaho or Apache dance receives only a scattering of applause, but

a Plains-type war dance enjoys a thundering ovation from the white audience, regardless of whether the dance is performed by the Kiowas or the Zuñis! The result is that more and more tribes are adopting Plains styles of dancing, and pan-Indianism proceeds apace."[24]

These changes would have a profound impact not just on non-Native attitudes toward Native spirituality, but on the practices of the New Age movement. In addition to broadening the available repertoire of religious practices and styles, the shift to the Plains made Native ways easier to emulate for individuals and small groups. Already by the 1950s, works like Joseph Epes Brown's *Sacred Pipe* gave a structure to perform such ceremonies. *Seven Arrows* also located the exotic and mystical firmly in the Plains cultures rather than in the mesas and deserts of the southwest. Now, as young white people were delighted to learn, one could go beyond merely admiring the religions of the Indians; instead, one could actually participate.

Enter the Shaman

Other writings in these years reinforced the linkage between Native spirituality and occult or mystical powers. This movement grew out of the popular fascination with the Native use of peyote and mind-altering drugs, and their spiritual potential. This interest in drugs would in turn generate an influential literature on shamanism, that other means of voyaging between the worlds. (Again, Eliade's writings contributed mightily to this enthusiasm.) These explorations offered further ways in which non-Native practitioners could participate fully in Native spirituality. Though these themes were not necessarily connected with other enthusiasms of the day, such as Hopi mysticism or Plains rituals, the different elements would coalesce.

We have already traced the continuing interest in peyote through the 1950s through visible mainstream works like Huxley's *Doors of Perception* and the Wasson article in *Life*. The Wasson article in particular was a source for another text that popularized Native spirituality, namely, Carlos Castaneda's 1968 book *The Teachings of Don Juan*. This told of Castaneda's years-long apprenticeship to a *brujo*, a wise man or shaman, who was also an expert on medicinal plants and hallucinogens. The book attracted a vast following, and Castaneda quickly followed up with other titles: *A Separate Reality* and *Journey to Ixtlan*. The initial reception was highly favorable. *Don Juan* was published by the prestigious University of California Press, and in 1973, *Journey to Ixtlan* earned Castaneda a doctorate in anthropology from UCLA.[25]

Over the years, Castaneda's work has been repeatedly challenged as a work of creative fiction rather than an actual memoir or investigation, and the existence of a real Don Juan Matos is doubtful. Problems appear on every page. This purports to be the tale of a Yaqui from the northern state of Sonora, yet he uses a sacred mushroom found far to the south in Oaxaca. Skeptics claim to have found the direct literary sources around which the Don Juan myth is constructed, included the Wasson articles in *Life* and Andrija Puharich's 1959 book *The Sacred Mushroom*. Also dubious are the claims made throughout the books for actual magical experiences that seem to have occurred in the real world rather than on the spiritual plane of the shamanistic universe. Did Castaneda's characters really fly, transform themselves into animal shapes, or levitate? Did he fight a *diablero*? [26]

For all their transparent problems, Castaneda's books raised expectations about what an inquirer might find from new religious movements, and from acquiring pseudo-Indian status. While inner peace or spiritual progress were both desirable qualities, these books seemed to promise the believer true magical and psychokinetic powers. These ideas appealed in the mid-1970s, when a national social and political crisis raised widespread doubts about official explanations and interpretations for almost anything. Quite ordinary people became prepared to accept what would hitherto have appeared bizarre theories about assassinations, government conspiracies, and UFOs. In 1974, responsible media outlets gave respectful coverage to Uri Geller's claims of mystical powers. Psychic powers and occult theories achieved widespread credibility, especially when these were linked to lost civilizations. Though Castaneda himself does not delve into the ancient roots of his alleged tribal shamans, followers were quick to draw connections with the lost worlds of Aztecs, Mayas, and especially the Toltecs. The recent New Age boom in Toltecs, who now constitute a substantial presence on the Internet, can be traced directly to Castaneda. For modern theorists, the historical Toltecs have the additional virtue that they never developed the sophisticated writing systems associated with Mayas or Aztecs, so statements about them can be neither checked nor disproved.[27]

Castaneda generated a genre of books in which Native shamans and medicine men are credited with authentic supernatural powers. The title of Doug Boyd's 1974 book *Rolling Thunder* recalled a well-known Indian text from half a century before, Paul Radin's story of *Crashing Thunder*. That was, incidentally, another story of redemption through peyote. In *Rolling Thunder*, however, accounts of inner spiritual experience have been transformed into claims of miraculous intervention in the real world. Boyd's book was "a personal exploration into the secret healing powers of an American Indian medicine man," which made astonishing claims for the reality of the powers claimed by one shaman. Most incidents would qualify as "miracles," including a healing successfully performed on a man with a severely infected leg. Boyd made no attempt to explain these acts, which seemed beyond the scope of Western science, but which were accommodated within the higher spiritual wisdom of Native peoples. He writes that "the concepts of agents and spirit power do not fit comfortably within the confines of our accumulated knowledge. To understand these things we will need a wider grasp of the reality and the life force whence physical representations and their accompanying physical facts are made manifest." People needed to understand that the earth was truly alive: "the earth was a being, an individual with health problems." These were basic facts, reflecting the realities of nature. By that standard, "Indians were the most natural of people, and the most supernatural people in the world might well be found among white establishment technologists who, as far as nature is concerned, know so little."[28]

Foreshadowing so many books of the next thirty years, *Rolling Thunder* is as much a generic New Age manifesto as it is a discussion of any given Indian tradition. Following in the tradition of the *Book of the Hopi*, Rolling Thunder's biographer locates him in a spiritual tradition parallel to those of India and Tibet, and compares him to equally preternaturally gifted swamis. Apparently, karma is a concept as fundamental to American Indians as to Indian Indians, and it is often invoked by the Native American shaman. Rolling Thunder reputedly traced the history of Indian nations to lost continents, and he supported the claims that ancient animals such as Yeti and Bigfoot did exist, having survived the primeval catastrophes.

Making a Religion

Medicine men, shamans, sweat lodges, Vision Quests, Native prophecies, a return to tribal values—all these ideas were so powerfully present in the culture by the early 1970s that it was only a matter of time before entrepreneurs grasped the opportunity to package them in a form attractive to consumers. One innovator was Hyemeyohsts Storm, whose rich Plains mythology presented the Medicine Wheel as an Indian structure that virtually anybody could build in any setting and use as a plausible basis for rituals.

Among the most influential of the new wave of salesmen was former film actor Sun Bear (Vincent LaDuke), an Ojibwa. Sun Bear began his mission to white America during the *annus mirabilis* of 1970, when he preached Indian spirituality to colleges and universities in the Sacramento area. Like many of the era's new gurus, he organized his converts into a network of communes. Like his counterparts, too, he found that these efforts failed, largely because of the effects of drug abuse. However, Sun Bear persevered, and founded "the Bear Tribe Medicine Society, a non-profit, multiracial organization that teaches about earth healing and earth-centered spirituality." It was this institution that makes Sun Bear such a departure in the selling of Native spirituality, because what he was offering his white clientele was not just books or lectures, but the promise of authentic participation in Indianness. He offered membership in a pseudo-Indian religion that drew from the actual rituals and beliefs of many separate traditions.

Sun Bear's movement successfully bridged the quite-different worlds of early 1970s utopianism and the more sophisticated New Age movement of the 1980s. Originally, Sun Bear taught the kind of ecologically sensitive communalism that had been popularized in films like *Easy Rider*. His manifesto argued that:

> the dominant society has created imbalances because of ignorance and irresponsibility. We know that during this time small groups of people will begin again to live together in love and harmony. This is the vision of the Tribe: to teach people they can live in a manner that will allow them to understand the changes that are occurring on Mother Earth and to take their places as Her Caretakers.

Presently, Western civilization was in crisis, facing dangers of resource-exhaustion, violence, and pollution. The Tribe offered a *Self-Reliance Book*, a manual for communal living dealing with such basic realities as composting, recycling, and building root cellars. By 1975, the Tribe acquired a communal base near Spokane.[29]

Though the commune movement went into sharp decline after the *Easy Rider* era, the notion of withdrawal to the wilderness became attractive once again with the new survivalism of the mid-decade. Urban industrial civilization seemed fragile in these years, with recurrent war scares in the Middle

East, the oil shortages of 1973 and 1979, and the twin crises in Iran and Afghanistan in 1979–1980. A return to the land seemed an attractive alternative to imminent apocalypse, while peaceful hippie communes were largely supplanted by well-armed survivalist compounds. In giving a distinctly Indian flavor to communalism, Sun Bear's message seemed highly relevant and, moreover, it retained the peaceful idealism of the hippie years.

The explicitly religious quality of Sun Bear's message resonated with a generation deeply familiar with the *Book of the Hopi*. He claimed to have experienced a trance vision recalling that of Black Elk, warning of crisis and renewal. He now popularized the Medicine Wheel as a core symbol of Native spirituality, although it was quite foreign to his own Ojibwa roots. His apocalyptic vision was supported by prophecies and teachings drawn indiscriminately from the Hopi, Iroquois, and other peoples. Sun Bear was not merely a commune leader, but the shaman and teacher of the Bear Tribe. As his publicity declared, "Sun Bear is looking for Spiritual Warriors. Become an apprentice."

In 1981, the shaman began leading Medicine Wheel rituals with the support of existing and emerging New Age groups. One pioneering Wheel ceremony in the mountains above Malibu was "co-sponsored by the Bear Tribe Medicine Society; the Deer Tribe Medicine Society; with support from the Hutash Community of Human Dimensions Institute West, Ojai; the Heartlight Community, Calabasa; the Healing Light Center of Glendale; and NAMA the National American Métis Association." Another ritual followed in Seattle, and within a few months, the most successful event took place in the Bay Area, at Camp Royaneh, in Sonoma County. Almost a thousand reportedly attended, including "masked dancers . . . each carrying a rock to form the circle round the sacred Buffalo skull, placed in position by Sun Bear. Other dancers followed, with rocks for the twelve moons, different clans, qualities, etc." Reportedly, since then, tens of thousands have participated in related rituals.[30] After Sun Bear died in 1992, leadership passed to his non-Indian "medicine helper and spiritual partner," Wabun Wind. Sun Bear's reputation lives on through his daughter Winona LaDuke, an environmental activist who in 2000 ran as Ralph Nader's vice-presidential candidate.[31]

Sun Bear's career was deeply controversial, especially among Native activists themselves, who were in these same years passionately engaged in exploring their own spiritual roots. The non-Native activities were so shocking because they drew freely on authentic practices, yet with marginal involvement or authorization by Natives themselves. As a common joke held, the only Indian in the Sun Bear Medicine Society was Sun Bear himself. Some white observers were equally cynical. In 1980, the film *Serial* parodied the New Age faddery of the Bay Area, and inevitably it mocked the predilection for Native American religion. When a worldly white businessman dies, his family buries him with a ludicrously inappropriate Plains Indian ritual held on the shores of the San Francisco Bay, complete with chanting medicine men in full headdresses.

But Sun Bear's success spawned imitators. Already in 1980, a group of Traditional Elders was protesting that "various individuals are moving about this Great Turtle Island and across the great waters to foreign soil, purporting to be spiritual leaders. They carry pipes and other objects sacred to the Red Nations."[32] By this time, white interest in Native spirituality had crossed a crucial threshold, namely, that non-Natives were no longer content to admire at a distance. Now, they wanted to be part of this highly idealized spirituality of earth and land, of balance and equality. Usually despite their sharpest objections, Indians became central symbols of the New Age.

9

🌱

The Medicine Show

Don't dream it—be it.
—*The Rocky Horror Picture Show*

By the mid-1970s, Indians were established as countercultural icons. Indians had already been mass marketed in films like *Little Big Man*, and the quest for authentic Native voices was manifested in the success of later books and television productions, such as Ruth Beebe Hill's novel *Hanta Yo* and the novels of Jamake Highwater. But the nature of the merchandising was changing. While Indian culture and art had long since reached a mass audience— at least by the 1930s—it was now Native spirituality that proved most exciting to consumers.[1]

Native themes became more readily accessible than ever before, and religious angles were much in evidence. Some of the best writing available was now from Native writers themselves, like Scott Momaday, Louise Erdrich, and Leslie Marmon Silko, while new cultural theories made suspect the once standard practice of white authors writing about Native societies.[2] Yet having said this, some non-Native writers continued to have a massive impact on popular attitudes to Native spirituality. One much-loved text was Margaret Craven's novel *I Heard the Owl Call My Name*, the tale of a Christian minister who at the end of his life comes to admire the profound spirituality of the Kwakiutl people. Though the book appeared in Canada in 1967, it reached a mass U.S. audience only in the early 1970s, at the height of the Indian boom; and for thirty years, Craven's book has been a popular choice for young adult readers.

It was in 1970, that great year for Indian rediscovery, that Tony Hillerman published *The Blessing Way*, the first of his many thrillers set in Navajo country. Hillerman never accepts the reality of the supernatural, or allows actual magical or religious devices to shape his plots, but he uses witches and religious leaders as characters, and his heroes discuss religious beliefs at length. As a result, millions of his readers have by now acquired a thorough acquaintance with terms such as the *chindi*, the troubled spirit that remains near a corpse; or the skinwalker, the evil witch who transforms into the shape of other beings. Readers also encounter the concept of *hozho*, harmony within and without, a concept that has attracted white readers since the time of Washington Matthews. In other novels, Hillerman explores the beliefs of other tribes: the Zuñi, for instance, in *Dance Hall of the Dead*. Hillerman sensitized a generation of mystery readers to Native perspectives and concerns in matters like the protection of sacred sites.

Interest in Native spirituality was perceptibly shifting from the counterculture to the social mainstream, and this movement continued even as both the counterculture and social radicalism faded. A remarkable publishing boom during the 1980s and early 1990s indicates not just a mass interest in Indian religions, but a change in the response that commercial marketers were expecting from the public. Many of the books that now appeared were not just serious academic studies, or even romanticized fictions to provide the stuff of fantasy. They were intended to inspire involvement and participation, to allow ordinary consumers, however implausibly, to share the Native religious experience. Accompanying the books were subsidiary markets in art, videos, tarot cards, music, and, of course, tourism. The selling of Native spirituality acquired a strong economic foundation, which means that the phenomenon is unlikely to fade for the foreseeable future. No longer was the fascination with Indian-ness confined to eras of disillusionment with mainstream America: the fantasy was now firmly part of the commercial landscape.

Though the new Indianism was built upon long-established romantic and esoteric traditions, it was also shaped by several new factors that had gained force during the 1970s. Originally, these ideas were quite separate—neopaganism, Goddess feminism, neoshamanism, UFO belief, archaeoastronomy—but increasingly, between about 1979 and 1981, they merged into a New Age synthesis. These ideas created a demand for guides and gurus, for texts that could offer near-scriptural authority.[3]

Medicine Women

In colonial times, the worst charge that could be made against Native religious practices was that they were clearly allied with paganism and witchcraft. By the end of the twentieth century, that was perhaps their greatest attraction. Parallel to the 1970s boom in Indian spirituality was a general interest in paganism and the occult, and these other trends helped shape white concepts of Native religion. Pagan, Druidic, and Wiccan traditions all gained a following, buoyed by enthusiasm for feminist spirituality. Across the spectrum of New Age groups and activists, Indian themes were much in evidence, not least in the adoption of pseudotribal names. Starhawk was the pagan witch whose influential 1979 book *The Spiral Dance* marked "a rebirth of the ancient religion of the great goddess."[4]

The year 1979 marked the publication of several other texts that would profoundly influence the new feminist spiritualities. This included Elaine Pagels's *The Gnostic Gospels*, a study of feminist and mystical strands in early Christianity, and the collection of readings entitled *Womanspirit Rising*. Like *The Spiral Dance*, each book in its way indicted the dominant Christian tradition for fostering oppression and inequality. Each also urged the exploration of alternate spiritual paths more closely attuned to the feminine, the intuitive, the mystical. Margot Adler's *Drawing Down the Moon* surveyed the new pagan upsurge, but the book also popularized and coordinated the diverse strands of the movement. Feminist spirituality, with all its neopagan connotations, now acquired institutional foundations in universities and colleges—in Women's Studies programs—in seminaries, and in women's religious organizations.[5]

Native themes coexisted easily with these paganizing trends, and in its rhetoric, a group such as the Bear Tribe closely resembled the new sects. Also, neo-Native and pagan groups shared a common enthusiasm for shamanism. In 1980, Michael Harner's book *The Way of the Shaman* inspired a new interest in shamanism not just as something interesting that "they" (Native peoples) did, but as something white Americans could also explore. Harner himself wrote not just as an academic anthropologist, but as "an authentic white shaman."[6]

These underlying interests explain the phenomenal success enjoyed by Lynn Andrews's 1981 book *Medicine Woman*, which catered to pre-existing markets for feminist spirituality, shamanism, and Native cultures. Like the *Book of the Hopi* in its day, the book arrived at precisely the right historical moment. *Medicine Woman* purports to record the experience of a white woman who during the mid-1970s finds herself threatened by an evil sorcerer, Red Dog. She gains the help of two medicine women from the Canadian Cree tradition, who teach her Native shamanism. She achieves victory after a series of dreams and visions in which Native and Mesoamerican traditions are thoroughly confounded. One key scene involves a pyramid, a Grand Jaguar Temple, and the southwestern trickster figure, Kokopelli.[7]

Central to Andrews's work through the years was the Sisterhood of the Shields, which she describes as a female shamanic society. The idea stems from *Seven Arrows*, and Hyemeyohsts Storm actually appears as a character in *Medicine Woman*. According to Storm, twelve sacred shields originally existed, guarded by twelve "keepers of the shields of light," a sacred office: they were "healers, diviners and teachers." Each shield corresponded to one of the peoples of the earth. In addition, each individual had his or her own particular shield. In Andrews's books, the Sisterhood plays an increasing role, with the shield as a psychic and material weapon that symbolizes her womanhood. Her website explains that "the ancient teachings taught by the Sisterhood of the Shields . . . embrace the study of global shamanic cosmologies and sacred art technologies."[8]

The book itself has been much criticized. It was subsequently the focus of a lawsuit by Andrews's partner David Carson, who claimed that he had devised the mythology she publicized. Also, much of the Native culture described is implausibly drawn from multiple tribal traditions, and derives from known literary sources. The Cree medicine women use Hopi and Lakota language and concepts in phrases like "What is the voice of woman but the voice of the kachina?" Though the book was sold as nonfiction, it is better seen as a work of imagination. But such doubts about authenticity did not prevent Lynn Andrews from going on to a remarkable publishing career over the following decade, with titles such as *Star Woman, Crystal Woman,* and *Windhorse Woman.* She runs instructional workshops, and "Lynn's Mystery School" offers degree programs.[9]

The commercial triumph is not difficult to explain in the context of the time. Apart from exploring fashionable spiritual themes, the book offered many readers, especially women, a clear wish fulfillment. Not only could they fantasize about heroic magical exploits against oppressive male exploiters, but they could enter wholly into the mysteries of the much-admired Native peoples. As Andrews's mentor tells her, "Lynn . . . you have come to me as a rainbow warrioress. You are a bridge between the Indian world and the white world, a bridge on this great Turtle Island." What sensitive modern white person would not wish to hear such an affirmation? Lynn Andrews's success showed publishers just how large the audience was for books of this type, books that taught Native spirituality, rather than just *about* it.[10]

Healing

By the mid-1980s, such manuals were reaching flood tide. Native traditions contributed to another booming publishing genre of these years, namely, the interest in therapy, self-help, and recovery. The therapy boom reached its height in the decade after 1986, and focused on recovering from healing traumas suffered during childhood, often from abuse. This was the time that the phrase "dysfunctional family" entered popular usage. The concept of "codependency" appeared in 1987 with Melody Beattie's *Co-Dependent No More*; the widely read self-help manual *The Courage to Heal* appeared the following year. Meanwhile, the pop psychology boom revived interest in the Enneagram, another device that can be traced to the fertile mind of George Gurdjieff. Healing and shamanic themes emerged strongly in the Native spirituality books, with a plethora of titles like *Spirit Healing, Native Healer, The Dancing Healers, Navaho Symbols of Healing*, or *Healers on the Mountain*. Sandra Ingerman's *Soul Retrieval* concerned "mending the fragmented self through shamanic practice." The potential of Native American healing techniques received an official imprimatur of sorts in 1992, when a massive report to the National Institute of Health discussed the possible value of different kinds of alternative medicine. (The authors stressed that discussing these ideas did not mean endorsement, but even mentioning such coverage in a federal report carried a symbolic message.) These alternative techniques included "Native American Indian health care practices," such as sweating and purging, herbal remedies, and even shamanic healing. The report was open to considering such methods, though suspending judgment about their value: "Among Native American Indians living today there are many stories about seemingly impossible cures that have been wrought by holy people. However, the information on what was done is closely guarded and not readily rendered to non-Native American Indian investigators."[11]

Native spirituality meshed closely with secular trends in therapy and recovery. The idea of the Vision Quest exercised a powerful influence, with the concept of finding oneself, achieving wholeness and reintegration, through a solitary experience in the wilderness. As early as 1973, a scheme to rehabilitate troubled youths through wilderness adventure programs chose the name Vision Quest. The late 1980s witnessed a fashion for returning to the primitive, for recovering one's authentic identity by escaping the evil trappings of civilization. In 1989, *The Roaring of the Sacred River* discussed "The wilderness quest for vision and self-healing," drawing on Native sources like Hyemeyohsts Storm and Fools Crow. Throughout, the book drew on pseudo-Native language and concepts, including the adoption of Indian-style names such as Gift Bearer and Night Stalker. The party proceeded "step by step through the wilderness to the Sacred Mountain," undertaking various rites of passage en route. "The candidate has much ritual material at his disposal: singing, chanting, drumming, rattling and all the other ways to make music." Alongside Native themes, the book uses a standard array of New Age and mystical writings, including the *I Ching*, Buddhist scriptures, the Sufi poems of Rumi, and the (spurious) Essene Gospel of John.[12]

The therapy fad became linked to gender issues and the rediscovery of one's authentic sexual identity. In 1990, Robert Bly's *Iron John* advocated a rediscovery of masculinity through a new men's spirituality, which might involve returning to the wilderness and participating in communal rituals with a powerful Native feel. The aim was to recover the "Wild Man," who "encourages a trust of the lower half of our body, our genitals, our legs and ankles, our inadequacies, the soles of our feet, the animal ancestors, the earth itself." Bly's work inspired a new men's movement, which promoted male bonding and fellowship through Native practices like drumming and the sweat lodge. In 1992, Clarissa Estes explored the Jungian "wild woman archetype" in her *Women Who Run with the Wolves*. Both Bly and Estes spawned many imitators. If ideas such as these had mainstream status, as indicated by their presence in magazine articles, television talk shows, and PBS specials, that legitimized the pseudo-Indian works that advocated similar notions of primitivism.[13]

The Book Boom

By the mid-1990s, anyone seeking Indian spiritual teachings could find a host of offerings from authors like Brooke Medicine Eagle, Mary Summer Rain, Kenneth Meadows, Bobby Lake-Thom, and Steve Wall. Though these works covered a wide variety of approaches, and varied in their faithfulness to Native teachings, their general themes can aptly be summarized by the title of Thomas Mails's 1988 book, *Secret Native American Pathways: A Guide to Inner Peace*. These authors were purporting to offer a distinct spiritual tradition, a Red Road hitherto closed to non-Natives, but now opened by Native teachers or whites specially privileged to bear the revelation. Furthermore, this Native tradition promised things that, many believed, could not be found in conventional Western religion, an inner peace, a wholeness, and an integration with the earth and nature.[14]

Partly, the new wave of spirituality books stemmed from specialized New Age publishers, such as Inner Traditions International, with its related imprints Destiny and Bear & Co.; Shambhala; Element; and the well-established occult press Llewellyn. Over the past twenty years, these presses have produced dozens of titles on themes like Native American prophecy, shamanism, and earth-centered mysticism. Though the presses are relatively small, their titles sometimes go into many printings and editions. Ted Andrews's book *Animal-Speak: The Spiritual and Magical Powers of Creatures Great and Small* (Llewellyn) has reportedly sold over three hundred thousand copies to date.[15]

For all the efforts of the fringe presses, the principal force in popularizing Native religions was the mainstream powerhouse of Harper San Francisco, which now emerged as the Goddess's direct representative in the publishing world. Harper produced *Womanspirit Rising, The Spiral Dance, The Way of the Shaman, Soul Retrieval,* and *The Dancing Healers,* as well as *Medicine Woman* and other Lynn Andrews titles. Harper's enthusiasm for Native titles reached its height between 1989 and 1994, when the press published Lynn Andrews's *Teachings Around the Sacred Wheel,* Ed McGaa's *Mother Earth Spirituality* and *Rainbow Tribe,* Joan Halifax's *The Fruitful Darkness,* and *Mayan Vision Quest.*[16] Between 1990 and 1994, Jamie Sams published several Harper titles, including *Other Council Fires Were Here Before Ours* and *The Thirteen Original Clan Mothers*. She also produced the *Sacred Path Cards,* including a lavish deck of tarot-style cards that claim to epitomize Native spiritual teachings. Cards include such familiar motifs as Pipe, Sweat Lodge,

Vision Quest, Peyote Ceremony, Standing People, Sun Dance, Medicine
Wheel, Kokopelli, Moon Lodge, Heyokah, Stone People, Shaman's Death,
and Hour of Power. (The work is complemented by a *Sacred Path Workbook*
and an album of *Sacred Path Songs*.) Sams's medicine cards were designed in
collaboration with David Carson, Lynn Andrews's former partner.[17]

In most cases, the authors were writing as believers and advocates. Sams
presents herself as a spiritual teacher. Sandra Ingerman writes as a shaman,
who "teaches workshops on shamanism around the world and was formerly
the Educational Director of the Foundation for Shamanic Studies directed
by Michael Harner. Sandra is recognized for bridging ancient cross-cultural
healing methods into our modern day culture addressing the needs of our
times."[18] Though Joan Halifax is primarily a Buddhist teacher, her work
draws on both Mexican and Native American spiritual leaders.

Merchandise

The proliferation of books was only a small part of the commercialized spirituality boom. Mystical Indians could easily be encountered in the cinema or
on television. In 1980, *Altered States* used the Castanedan idea of the anthropologist experimenting with Native hallucinogens. The early 1990s were particularly prolific in Indian images, with a powerful stress on Native
spirituality, in films such as *Black Robe* (1991) and *Last of the Mohicans* (1992).
The 1990 film *The Doors* portrayed an Indian holy man as spiritual guide
through the alternate realities made available through LSD and peyote. (The
original Doors took their name from Aldous Huxley's *Doors of Perception*.)
The idealized portrait of Lakota society in *Dances with Wolves* (1991) popularized ideas of totemism, not to mention the belief in the Indian as friend of
the environment. Another benevolent and powerful medicine man featured
in *Thunderheart* (1992), this time in the context of a militant Indian movement struggling against the oppressive federal government. As in *Dances with
Wolves*, *Thunderheart* was accessible to the mainstream audience since, although the portrait of white society was very negative, it was still possible for
a sincere white to convert to Native ways and religion, to discover the inner
Indian. And like Kevin Costner's Lieutenant Dunbar, the hero of *Thunderheart* also experiences mystical revelations of Native truths.[19]

Also on offer were practical aids for meditation and divination. Jamie
Sams's tarot deck is only one of many with a Native focus, all of which have

been created since the late 1980s. Theme tarot decks now available include *Medicine Woman, Native American, Rock Art, Santa Fe,* and *Southwest Sacred Tribes.* That is in addition to several divination decks that depart from the traditional tarot structure. In this category we find *Cards of Winds and Changes, Lakota Sweat Lodge Cards, Medicine Cards, Sacred Path, Shaman Wisdom Cards, Spirit of Truth Native American Reading Cards, White Eagle Medicine Wheel,* and *Wolf Song Cards.* Leita Richesson's *Shaman Wisdom Cards* are "inspired by Native American tradition, medicine and religion. Empowers users to develop their own healing power as they journey through life." Cards are grouped into what would normally be termed suits, including Moon Tribes, Animal Sisters, Plant Clans, Tree Brothers, and Sacred Stone Societies.[20]

A related industry offers music and art inspired by Native spiritual traditions. Much recent music stems from Native artists themselves, and represents an important cultural revival, but alongside this, we also find a vast market of more questionable roots. In a typical New Age store, a section of CDs and albums presents ostensibly Native artists and groups whose atmospheric music mixes Native themes with a strong dose of contemporary electronics. A typical album includes titles like "The Shaman's Dream," "Vision Quest," "Star People," and "Ancient Stones." Brule offers "Sunrise Offering," "Warrior's Circle," "Dream Shield," and "Vision Circle." Some groups draw more on contemporary Native societies, as interpreted by popular modern writers, while others hark back to the imagined glories of lost civilizations. *Anasazi* by Geodesium is characteristic in its combination of various musical traditions, drawing on synthesizers, pan flutes, drums, wind chimes, harp, and voices. Tracks include "Call of the Canyon" "Water Prayer," "Chaco Twilight," "Summer Solstice," and "Stars Over the Pyramid." Musician Rusty Crutcher offers a series of such albums, each based on a shrine such as Chaco, Machu Picchu, or the "Isle of Avalon" (the English Arthurian site of Glastonbury). His *Chaco Canyon* album offers "environmental sounds digitally recorded in Chaco Canyon primarily during solstices and equinoxes." Suggesting the almost ritual nature of the performance, one reviewer praised it for expressing "just the right shamanic intensity." The same artist's "Serpent Mound" "blends Native American sensitivity with modern technology. He builds upon three major themes—an acoustic piano dirge, a synthesizer drone, and Lakota flute melodies—to explore the spirituality of the Adena."[21]

A visit to a New Age–oriented store, especially in the West or Southwest, will illustrate the sheer volume of lifestyle items related to Native spirituality, quite apart from the more standard realm of art and jewelry. Centers like

Sedona abound in such emporia, and this town's Crystal Castle claims the title of the "metaphysical department store." Naturally, given the location, the store does a good trade in crystals and rocks, each linked to a particular sacred location, to one of the town's famous spiritual vortices. Other popular items in New Age stores include dreamcatchers, suitable for mounting in the home or over rearview mirrors. Medicine bags are small pouches containing stones, crystals, twigs, fetishes, or herbs. They are marketed as containing spiritual powers, part of the shaman's essential toolkit, and they bear titles such as the "shaman's bag" or "spirit bag." We also find mandellas, ornamental versions of traditional battle shields. These days, though, they are so debased from their original heroic context that they are velvet faced and decorated with big-eyed wolves. As one firm advertises:

> The Mandella is one of the most powerful American Indian items there is. There is big medicine in this descendant of the plains dance shield. Prayers for survival, spiritual blessings, strong visions, physical protection, and long life go into the making of the traditional Mandella. As well as lessons which can teach of the circle of life, the interconnectedness of creation, and the beauty and importance of diversity in Mother Earth.

A fine line separates the marketing of art and that of spirituality. What in fact are people buying when they seek out Hopi Kachinas or Native fetishes, whether originals or tawdry imitations? The merchandising process is symbolized by the image of Kokopelli, the Anasazi flute player who so often features in rock painting and petroglyphs. Usually, he is shown as a phallic figure, but the phallus is modestly suppressed in the countless images that have made him an unofficial symbol of the southwest. Desexed, he appears today in pendants, T-shirts, bumper stickers, and tattoos. By the 1990s, the *High Country News* was offering the satirical greeting, "Have a Kokopelli day!" Other rock art features prominently on posters and T-shirts, where it is given suitably mystical titles, like the "shaman's flight."[22]

Doing It Yourself

For those not content just to observe the spiritual scene through reading or listening, an overwhelming range of practical opportunities now became available. From the mid-1980s, many of the available books were specifically intended as how-to guides, almost always for the individual practitioner. Ed McGaa's *Mother Earth Spirituality* describes the seven major Lakota rituals specified by Black Elk, adding that "reviving these ceremonies in this time of crisis will, it is hoped, bring forth a new found perception and respect for the natural elements. I hope that the reader will attempt to do some ceremony in order to carry on that position of stewardship." McGaa provides detailed descriptions of the techniques involved in performing the peace pipe ceremony, building a sweat lodge, and undertaking the Vision Quest, so that the reader can, ideally, become a virtual Lakota.[23]

One prolific writer is Wolf Moondance. She is "a Native American visionary . . . drawing on her Osage and Cherokee heritage and training in human development," whose books include *Rainbow Medicine, Spirit Medicine, Star Medicine,* and *Bone Medicine.* Like other contemporary authors, her work describes rituals that the ordinary reader can actually perform. Most begin with smudging, that is, burning sage and sweet grass and passing through it all the objects that the ritual may demand. These might include a medicine blanket, "to be used in ceremonial work as a shield of safety," literally a spiritual safety blanket; or one can build a personal dream catcher. A shaman's necklace can be made out of gold and silver thread. She recommends creating a spirit medicine bundle, a larger version of the medicine bag, made up of special objects appropriate to one's personality and spiritual calling. This might mean flowers, rocks, cloths, sweet grass, and sage. The bundle can provide the basis for a domestic altar that serves as the spiritual center of the home, very much like the practice of Hinduism or Latino Catholicism. The altar is here named a "prayer mesa," a name that reflects the literal meaning of the word "mesa," namely, "table." In this context, it is obviously meant to imply the great southwestern mesas that are home to peoples such as the Hopi, and to give a Native grandeur to a humble kitchen table.[24]

Wolf Moondance's books largely consist of manuals for rituals, appropriate for different seasons and intentions. In one description, the practitioner is told: "You will be building a cornmeal circle. Start by honoring the sun, standing in the east. . . . Raise a pinch of cornmeal above you, giving thanks to the spirits of the East and to Great Spirit for all that comes from the East. Honor the eagle, the spring, the morning and the beginning." After centering the mind in an act of concentration, "We are going on what is known as a guided journey. It is shamanic journeying. . . . The path will take you to a place known as your tranquility center." This ceremony is representative of much of the literature in its use of common New Age themes and symbols. The central mythology is Indian, with the cornmeal and rattles, and the particular forms visualized. "I see the dark eyes of the raven that sits in the room. I see the earth medicine of raven as well as its personal totems. There are horses and deer, wolves and eagles. There are arrows and hawks." But most of what we see here is best described as popular psychology and meditative self-examination. Virtually everything is familiar from traditional Western occultism, with its emphasis on visualization, and the creation of a sacred circle. Qabalistic influences are also evident. This is traditional esoteric practice, as popularized by early twentieth-century authors such as Dion Fortune.[25]

The elements of Wolf Moondance's ritual life—smudging, the medicine bundle, the home altar—appear in many of the do-it-yourself texts. Brooke Medicine Eagle's *Buffalo Woman Comes Singing* also recommends techniques for creating a sacred space, for smudging, and for fasting. Every chapter includes workbooks, lists of questions and activities of the sort that had become popular in self-help and therapeutic manuals during the previous few years. Readers might list "the nine most powerful sacred objects you own," how each object was obtained, when it was first used, and so on. Then "choose one of the sacred objects on the list and perform a special ritual with it—one appropriate to its teachings. Record your experience and your feelings about it in your journal, along with any results." The book includes an "Earth Medicine Contract" with which the reader can "make a sacred pact to reconnect with Mother Earth and All Life from the depths of my being and to give action and beauty to this commitment." Sometimes, the Indian elements look like a thin veneer. What most people would describe as a support network here becomes a "support hoop."[26]

Wheel of Dreams

Though the practices and ideas on offer are very diverse, some symbols are used consistently, and they help us understand the principles underlying neo-Native spirituality. One common symbol in the new literature is the Medicine Wheel, a device that originally held little significance for most Native peoples. As we trace the wheel's evolution through the neo-Native thought-world, we can see the powerfully syncretistic nature of the movement.

In their original context, Medicine Wheels are stone circles that com-memorate the sacred places of various Plains nations. Though they can be found in remote locations across the Northern Plains of the United States and into Canada, the best known is the Bighorn Medicine Wheel, which stands on the Wyoming-Montana border. This structure takes the form of a circle with a stone cairn at its circle, and twenty-eight "spokes" emanating from the center of the wheel. Despite the numinous power of the site, the Bighorn Wheel historically received little attention even from white enthusi-asts about mystical Native spirituality, largely because the location is so inac-cessible. To get there still means a long drive west of Sheridan and a hike to the actual site. Before the 1970s, the Bighorn Wheel remained little known except to professional archaeologists, in contrast to sites such as Chaco Canyon and Mesa Verde, which had long been fixtures on the tourist circuit. Even the Sheridan Chamber of Commerce did not offer a guide to the Wheel till 1940. As the New Age movement developed, though, the Bighorn Wheel was attracting speculation about its origins. In 1959, even the re-spectable *New York Times* reported claims that the structure was built either by Aztecs or by some mysterious lost race, and speculations grew during the 1970s. If it was built by a lost race, "what strange fate overcame them, and why did they suddenly vanish into the strange, dark night of history?" Be-sides the great stone wheel, we also see the influence of Cheyenne wheels, basically wooden hoops used in games described by classic authorities like James Mooney and George Grinnell. Also, Sun Dance rituals used wheel symbols divided into four sections, representing compass points, winds, and elemental forces. In the 1970s, Hyemeyohsts Storm grafted these portable sun symbols onto the megalithic original. Shortly afterwards, Sun Bear adopted the wheel as the central symbol for his new Native movement, the basis for his system of earth astrology.[27]

Linking the wheel symbol to the actual megalithic site encouraged specu-lation about many issues of great interest to the New Age and metaphysical subculture. Just how were these directional orientations connected to the mystic powers of earth and heavens? And the wheel's resemblance to the an-cient Tibetan symbol of the mandala raised questions about crosscultural parallels: might such figures be relics of ancient globe-spanning civilizations? Such linkages were encouraged by the parallels between Navajo and Tibetan sandpainting. Evelyn Eaton sees the wheel as "a Cosmic Blueprint, a Man-dala of the Greater Medicine Wheel of the Universe." Soon, dozens of books were devoted solely to the wheel symbol, while the image recurs in

hundreds of other texts: Lynn Andrews's website uses it as a logo. Readers of
Wolf Moondance are encouraged to build their own wheels, each requiring
exactly sixty-eight rocks. These are divided into one central rock, symbolizing the Creator, and then lesser categories of song rocks, direction rocks, and
so on. Such amateur building has become a primary activity of pseudo-Native religious practice. At sacred times like solstices and equinoxes, stone
wheels proliferate around Western sacred sites, to the annoyance and puzzle-
ment of Indian residents.[28]

While the Bighorn Wheel was just divided into twenty-eight small sections, and the Sun Dance wheel into four quarters, Storm and Sun Bear
popularized a division into four major quarters, each of which was later sub-
divided into three units. This made the Wheel usable as a device for divination and for character analysis. (This closely recalls the symbol of the
Woodcraft Way, as devised by Ernest Thompson Seton in the 1920s, which
was likewise divided into four groups of three "Native values," all emanating
from a central figure of the Great Spirit.) In this new model, the wheel en-
closed a kind of Celtic cross pointing to the four compass points, allowing
enthusiasts to relate the wheel to cardinal points, seasons, personality types,
zodiac signs, or, basically, whatever they wanted. "The stones can be taken to
represent anything, everything, nations, problems, peoples, qualities." Each
quadrant of the wheel might represent a direction and a color, and thus symbolizes a phase of consciousness. The twelvefold division allowed theorists to
apply the long-familiar methods of European astrology, though rebaptized
with suitably Native American characters. Writers could then apply the directional mythologies of Western occultism to use the Medicine Wheel for
divination, character analysis or contemplation, all apparently founded
upon an authentically ancient "Native" tradition. The wheel bore teachings
that the disciple could learn and internalize.[29]

One active theorist is Kenneth Meadows, author of several books on
"earth medicine." For Meadows, the wheel is a universal symbol, a map of
the year, with its equinoxes and solstices, but also of the corresponding
phases of growth and contraction within the human being. The year is divided into twelve phases, such as awakening, growing, flowering, long
days, or ripening. Each individual has a character type corresponding to
the location of the birth date around the wheel, and thus to the dominant
animal that presides over that time: the Beaver, Salmon, and so on. The
books mix classical astrology with pseudo-Native language and a diluted
totemism. In this system, "a totem mirrors aspects of your nature and un-

locks the intuitive knowledge that lies beyond the reasoning capacity of the intellect."[30]

As Meadows's books promise, you can "identify your personality profile and determine your life destiny through the Native American Medicine Wheel." Individual Beavers and Salmons can find more detail about their character and destiny from subsidiary texts devoted to each animal type. "Otters are friendly, lively and perceptive"; "practical and steady, Beavers have a capacity for perseverance." "Forceful and flamboyant, Salmon people, like their totem animal, are not easily daunted. . . . If your birth totem is Salmon, you are a warm and exciting friend." Each type also received advice on relationships. A Salmon considering a Falcon should know that "this volatile couple will find romance and excitement, but there may be hurt pride from time to time." Beaver with Falcon, on the other hand, is "not an easy relationship." Such analyses suffer from the familiar flaws of Western (or Chinese) astrology, namely, the extreme improbability that the human population can be categorized into a dozen or so categories divided according to birth date. Another objection is that this system has nothing particularly Indian about it, and that a Beaver, for instance, sounds much like an old-fashioned Euro-American Aries.[31]

Other writers use the turning of the wheel as a pattern for religious or psychological development, and an amazing volume of writings is devoted to explicating these rival systems. In Storm's original book, the four cardinal points were north (wisdom; the buffalo; the color white); east (illumination; the eagle; yellow); south (innocence; the mouse; green); and west (introspection; the bear; black). A cycle begins in the north, the realm of matter and the cold, and proceeds through the east (knowledge and enlightenment) and south (the spiritual realm) before reaching the west, the realm of introspection.[32] This pattern has been widely imitated. At the center of Brooke Medicine Eagle's wheel stands the "Great Mystery, All that is Self." "Whether it is a day, a year, a project, a lifetime, or any other human cycle, it is represented on the Medicine Wheel. We travel round and around the wheel in our Earth walk, and if we remember to spend as much time in the releasing and quieting quadrants as in the sprouting and doing quadrants, we find a balanced way."[33]

Jamie Sams's *Dancing the Dream* explores four paths of mystic initiation, each corresponding to a direction on the wheel. Throughout, her lessons are framed in terms of her Indian teachings and visions, and her inheritance from venerated elders like "Grandmother Twylah." But as with Wolf Moondance, the result is a familiar mixture of Western occultism and popular psychotherapies. For Sams, the Western spoke of the wheel corresponds to initiation. This is the "place of introspection and listening," which "teaches us about healing and contains many lessons that help us reclaim the fragments of ourselves that may have been wounded or denied at various times throughout our lives." Here, we are empowered to heal "addictions, old pain or trauma, physical illness, emotional instability, unhealthy psychological patterns, childhood issues, manipulation or control behaviors, dysfunctional relationships, and any other forms of imbalance." This psychologizing extends to the spiritual death and rebirth required for the making of a shaman. In the traditional view, this death involved a traumatic visionary experience, perhaps with major physical symptoms, but for Sams, the terminology refers only to "the death of false ideas, [the] end of destructive illusions."[34]

In *The Thirteen Original Clan Mothers,* Sams adds a powerful feminist element. Each wheel segment represents one of the "clan mothers" that is also a personality type. Their names include Setting Sun Woman, Weaves the Web, and Listening Woman, while at the center of the wheel is the thirteenth mother, the blue moon of transformation. Each mother also represents life lessons, so that Listening Woman is "the keeper of discernment and guardian of introspection," the one who teaches us "how to HEAR THE TRUTH."[35]

Tribes

All these teachings can be explored individually, but organized and communal activities are also available. In the past twenty years, workshops and training programs on Native spirituality have become a significant enterprise. Brooke Medicine Eagle describes the evolution of such training sessions. She writes that "by the late seventies, I had been given enormous amounts of information through vision," and decided to offer it to the public. She chose a theme, organized it in a two-day seminar, and offered it in ten cities across North America. All had Native titles, such as "Dancing Buffalo Woman's Dream," "That We May Walk Fittingly," or "The Looks-Within-Place." All, though, drew heavily on contemporary psychological and therapeutic concepts. "The Body of a Warrior" "used techniques including Feldenkrais work to awaken participants to a fuller sensing through their bodies and thus to create an awakening of their spirits." In the early 1980s, under the influence of Sun Bear, Brooke Medicine Eagle expanded her repertoire to include the Medicine Wheel.[36]

Some training programs are directly connected with one of the well-known authors, or else use that association as a kind of brand name. If not run by a particular expert, they are in his or her tradition. Jamie Sams is cited as the inspiration for New Mexico's Heyokah Center, run by two of her pupils on the site at which Sams first offered her Healing Camp in 1989. The Center offers space for "Women's sweat lodge ceremonies, retreat space, support groups, learning circles, and Native American Women's studies." It "provides quality Healing Quests, mountain retreats for spiritual contemplation, open dialogues in women's circles, as well as the teachings from Jamie's many books."[37]

Some of these programs focus on particular aspects of Native spirituality, like shamanism or Vision Quests, while others are more comprehensive. A number of groups and entrepreneurs offer training in shamanism. In 2003 Bill Brunton held a workshop in Minneapolis-St.Paul on "The Way of the Shaman." Brunton is "an anthropologist, shamanic practitioner and a member of the faculty of the Foundation for Shamanic Studies." Participants would "be initiated into shamanic journey, aided by drumming and movement techniques that induce a shamanic state of consciousness and can awaken dormant spiritual abilities and connections with Nature." The foundation offers its "rigorous training" to five-thousand clients each year. Other courses in 2003 included "Five-Day Soul Retrieval Training with Sandra Ingerman" in Santa Fe, while San Francisco was host to "Five-Day Harner Method Shamanic Counseling Training." Those registering for soul retrieval are warned that before registering, "please make sure that you have been having success in contacting your power animals and/or teachers on your own and that you feel confident about your journey skills." Another workshop "will introduce you to common shamanic practices; we will discuss and create sacred space, discuss shamanic practices, and journey to meet our power animals. (If you are inclined, feel free to bring an object to place on our altar)."[38]

Recalling the Bear Tribe of the 1970s, other enterprises try to offer a complete Native experience. One of the most ambitious is the Arizona-based Deer Tribe Metis Medicine Society, founded in 1986 by Harley Swift Deer Reagan. According to its website, tribal leaders "are modern day representatives of an ancient lineage of sacred knowledge of universal laws, ceremonial alchemy, healing techniques, alignment and communication with the elements of nature, magick, controlled dreaming, spiritual awakening and determination. Like the arcane mystery schools of the Sufi, the Druidic and Celtic, the Tibetan, and other Great Power traditions, the Sweet Medicine Sun Dance Path has evolved over thousands of years." (The spelling of "magick" indicates the influence of modern European occultism, specifically the ideas of Aleister Crowley). The Deer Tribe traces its origins to the Twisted Hairs Medicine Society, a "magickal mystery school," dating back in the Americas to 1250 BC (though Reagan has claimed that the underlying ideas can be traced back over a hundred thousand years). In the 1970s, the group reportedly designated Swift Deer to bear its message to the modern world. Deer Tribe members participate in a wide range of activities, including rite of passage ceremonies, longhouse programs, seasonal and pipe ceremonies, healing rituals, and martial arts. Controversially, the group also advertises its "*Chuluaqui Quodoushka* spiritual sexuality teachings . . . based on sacred shamanic traditions that integrate spirituality and sexuality into your life." Allegedly, these Q rituals represent an amalgam of Cherokee and Mayan traditions. Dozens of local Deer Tribe lodges and study groups are scattered across the United States and Canada, but are also found in Germany, Australia, and England; the movement might claim five thousand followers in all. Lodges bear names such as Lightning Snow Wolf Lodge, Clan of the Dragon Riders, The Eagle's Dream Study Group, and the Warrior Dreaming Youth Study Group.[39]

Finding such ventures has been made vastly easier by the coming of the World Wide Web. Minimal searching will demonstrate the abundance of such activities, through search terms like "sweat lodges," "medicine wheels," "shamanism," "moon lodges," "medicine bags," "smudging," "crystals," and "heyokah." Examples are legion. In Phoenix, the GoldenWind Dreamers sweat lodge advertises that "We are a Metis Sweet Medicine Sundance lodge. We provide Full Moon Women's lodges, Brotherhood lodges and Community lodges where men and women can sweat together. This is done with the utmost integrity and honoring of each other." (The lodge is affiliated with the Deer Tribe.) In New Mexico, we find an "Earth Sky (sweat) Lodge at Spirit of Nature Retreat with Raven. Are You Ready for a Deeper Spiritual Connection? Getting in touch with Nature and Mother Earth is the best way!" In Missouri, the Ozark Avalon Church of Nature promises a Medicine Wheel experience: "We will learn how the Medicine Wheel at Ozark Avalon was constructed, the various pathways of the wheel (the center circle, the spirit paths, the moon and totem paths, the spirit keepers), building a personal Medicine Wheel, and how to utilize the Medicine Wheel for your spiritual path-working."[40]

Though these ideas can be encountered separately, the interested seeker commonly discovers them as a New Age package, which combines shamanism, medicine wheels, sweat lodges and the rest. On a typical website, the California-based *www.thewildrosenet*, we find detailed offerings about ceremonies, the Drum Team, sweat lodges, the Eagle Dance, dream symbols, the Medicine Wheel, alternative healing, planetary alignment, and Tibetan Buddhism. This particular group offers a full ritual life: "Several times a year, The Wild Rose Dreamers Lodge holds a ceremonial weekend in which participants are sent out on various vision quest ceremonies. . . . The Night on the Mountain of Fear is the first major individual ceremony." A full-day Eagle Dance is also available. Shamanic classes include "teachings and healing techniques from Native American, Celtic, Hebrew, Chinese and East Indian cultures." Maine's Standing Bear Center for Shamanic Studies offers similarly varied activities, including shamanism, drumming, and smudging. Individual programs include "Snake Medicine and the South Position on the Medicine Wheel Mandala"; "Talking with Trees" ("trees are powerful sources of shamanic wisdom and teachings"); and a "Women's Shamanic Council and Closing Drumming Circle." A Florida program included an "Experiential Workshop of Smudging, Drumming, Shamanic Journeying, Medicine Wheel Building, and Crystal Grid Meditation and Fire Ceremonies."[41]

Alongside organized commercial operations, we also find countless local activities, classes, and workshops that advertise in New Age bookstores or on college campuses. One typical handbill for an evening program available in Pennsylvania advertises "Native American Wisdom and Tradition and Spirituality," offered by an Oklahoma Cherokee who "has worked with the healing aspects of drumming and the usage of crystals for the past twelve years." Lessons offered included smudging ("a potent form of medicine"), prayer ties, drumming, and face painting. Participants are advised to bring drums and/or rattles. A great many individuals travel the country, claiming to offer Native spiritual secrets, and varying in the degree of authentic tradition that is merged into a nonspecific New Age potpourri. Aware that a claim to full medicine man status might be easily disprovable, a number claim the less-specific rank of "pipe-carrier." The opportunities available to such entrepreneurs have vastly increased in the past decade with the rise of the Internet.

Spiritual Tourism

Another means of exploring the Native spiritual realm is through travel to sites regarded as extraordinarily sacred. Tourism to sites such as Chaco Canyon and Mesa Verde can be traced to the late-nineteenth century, and "the mystic Southwest" was a selling point before World War I. Today, the tourist industry is a well-established fact across Native America. Some Indian nations, like the Navajo, use the lively interest in Native sites to generate income, but also as a form of public education, allowing outsiders to see the real glories of Native homelands and cultures. Usually, these operations will present religious sites and themes, but in a knowledgeable and nonsensational way.

Since the 1970s, though, more speculative spiritual interests have become powerful attractions for visitors, and tourist opportunities have developed to accommodate them. Indian communities have long offered some kind of spiritual experience, perhaps through faux medicine men: the Seminoles have a long history of such showmanship. More recently, certain special places attract awed observers in quest of a spiritual encounter. It is open to debate whether such travel can properly be termed pilgrimage, a word usually associated with a known and respected religion, or mere tourism, with its implications of dilettantism and commercialism. The seriousness and intensity of many visitors suggests that the more respectful term "pilgrimage" is in order.[42]

The principal venues are found in the West and Southwest. Both Chaco and Mesa Verde were prominently featured in the *Book of the Hopi*, as were other Anasazi remains, and spiritual interest grew during the 1970s. California's Mount Shasta reputedly has a spiritual energy that is "so powerful that it has been called the 'Epcot Center' of sacred sites." (As it does so often, the modern New Age is here building on old foundations: already in the 1930s, Mount Shasta had reputedly been a haunt of the Ascended Masters, the spiritual giants who inspired Guy Ballard to form his Mighty I AM movement.) The height of New Age tourism at both Chaco and Mount Shasta occurred during the Harmonic Convergence of August 1987, when the planets were experiencing a rare alignment that occurred only every few centuries. In order to share the surge of cosmic energies, some three thousand gathered at Chaco in a "psycho-spiritual, meta-historical expression," with the goal of "awakening to ancient memories and future visions and discovering their personal destinies through the experience of sacred space and time."[43]

The Native connotations of these places were obvious, and the same was true of other popular sites located throughout the United States: Cahokia in Illinois, Serpent Mound in Ohio, Enchanted Rock in Texas, or Aztalan in Wisconsin. Elsewhere, pilgrimage places emerged primarily for reasons unconnected with past or present Native realities, but they were increasingly absorbed into the neo-Indian mythology. Sedona offers rich resources for a New Age audience, and a local esoteric community emerged in the late 1950s. Most of the growth came from the mid-1970s onwards, after psychics lauded the area's spiritual vortices. Five- or ten-thousand people visited Sedona for the Harmonic Convergence.[44]

Today, this spiritual metropolis flourishes on the strength of its "vortices of spiritual power," its rock tours, and it boasts an abundance of crystal gazers and New Age bookstores. Sedona attracts four- to five-million visitors annually, making it Arizona's leading tourist attraction after the Grand Canyon. Neo-Indian spirituality is very much in evidence and, as elsewhere, little attention is paid to exact cultural affiliations. Though the main Native groups in the locality are Yavapai, Apache, or Hopi, the rituals most popular among white consumers are Medicine Wheel ceremonies, together with Plains customs such as sweat lodges and Lakota purification rites. Adrian Ivakhiv describes one typical event thus: "Plains Indian (Lakota) rituals are thus being offered by a tour leader with a Slavic name at a place—far from the Plains—that 'the Native Americans' consider sacred ground; all for those willing to pay the price." Earth Wisdom Jeep Tours includes in its repertoire a Medicine Wheel tour, "an in-depth journey that merges myth, meditation, native plants and sacred pilgrimage traditions." Scenic Vortex tours are also available. One bus tour from the city promises, "You'll also receive a blessing from your Native American guide at the healing springs of Montezuma's Well."[45]

Traveling to such sites can involve either being an isolated tourist seeking ambience, or as part of a group performing rituals or organized meditations. At special seasons, especially around astronomical occasions like solstices, these sites attract large numbers of New Age pilgrims. Specialized firms offer spirituality tours, in which authentic Native sites are presented indiscriminately with generic New Age attractions. A New Mexico tour organized by the firm Luminati includes Anasazi sites such as Chaco Canyon and Bandelier Monument, as well as New Age encounters. One day's highlights include "brunch with Takara 'The Dolphin Lady' performing a Dolphin Essence Ceremony, evening visit to the Star Dreaming Ranch with ten stone temples, Nine Fires of Truth Ceremony with Raven, Native American musicians." Such enterprises are commonplace around the well-established pilgrimage sites. Sedona Soul Adventures urges travelers, "When you feel Sedona calling, count on us to be your guides. Allow our many healers, intuitive guides and spiritual artists to usher you into the experience of a lifetime. We would love to arrange a customized, one-of-a-kind soul adventure especially for you."[46]

Whether through buying books and CDs, attending workshops, or visiting sacred sites, some people are clearly spending a great deal of money on exploring Native spirituality. The plethora of programs would not exist if they were not attracting paying patrons. But why? What are they seeking from the Medicine Wheel or Sedona that they cannot find in established religions or philosophies?

When studying fringe religions, observers often quote the remark that "Cults live on the unpaid bills of the churches," which is to say that new religious movements arise to meet demands not being satisfied by existing providers. In the case of the new Native spirituality, the scale of public interest, and the marketing infrastructure that has arisen to meet it, suggests a very substantial demand that had not been fulfilled by Christianity or Judaism, or even by secular therapeutic movements. Partly, this might mean that in American culture, social movements tend to assume a religious coloring that they would not in other more secular societies like those of Western Europe. But the need for religious experience did not have to express itself as strongly as it did through Indian models and stereotypes. The question again arises: Just what were people finding in the largely imaginary world of shamans and totems, of Kokopelli and Medicine Wheels, that they were not finding in the mainstream Western religions, above all, Christianity? What dreams were they trying to catch?

10

🌿

Thinking Tribal Thoughts

By listening to nature through nature-based ceremonies, we can be like the
Sioux.

—Ed McGaa

The wave of books and related materials on Native spirituality is diverse in
its content, and in many cases, the actual relationship to any Native tradition past or present is tenuous. Nobody enforces orthodoxy in neo-Indian
spirituality, and certainly not accuracy. Still, we can trace certain themes,
which appeal to what is obviously a substantial audience. Though we do not
have anything as neat or systematic as a creed of neo-Indian spirituality, certain core ideas and themes run throughout these various cultural manifestations and the broader social movement they represent.

The appeal of Indian-ness needs little explanation in general, but the
specifically religious package has features that make it particularly attractive
to a modern audience. One, clearly, is its repackaging in terms that are already familiar from the Western New Age. While the images and names are
relatively new, the underlying ideas are old friends: occult, metaphysical, and
pseudoscientific concepts that in various forms have demonstrated their appeal to American audiences for perhaps the last 150 years. The literature on
neo-Indian spirituality is rife with notions that have little in common with
most authentic Native religious practices, including astrology, reincarnation,

197

crystals, vegetarianism, meditation, and holistic medicine. But this in itself raises more questions: if people have access to these ideas through familiar Western texts, why do they need to go to Indian sources to discover them once more?

Neo-Indian spirituality illustrates a familiar paradox of contemporary religious movements, namely, the issue of authority. Many who reject the traditional structures of organized religion do so because of a dislike of hierarchy, dogma, and traditional authority, and prefer to base themselves on principles of individualism, spontaneity, and self-reliance. Yet there remains a residual notion that religion must claim authoritative status, whether that authority stems from tradition, charismatic power, revelation, or—a popular option—from alternative scriptural sources. Many Americans unhappy with traditional Christianity look to heretical documents like the Gnostic gospels. If religious texts do not exist to justify contemporary trends, then such scriptures are invented or appropriated as needed. The popular *Course in Miracles* is a case in point, as is *The Celestine Prophecy*. To use a literary analogy, poets are pained to hear the question, "Is that a real poem, or did you write it yourself?" The implication is that a "real" poem must be old-established, approved, and canonical, and cannot just be produced by one individual. Equally, lone thinkers, however brilliant, cannot be expected to produce real religious truths. Spiritual things cannot be "invented," a term which suggests making something fake or artificial. Religious truth is transmitted, not invented.

What makes the Indian packaging of New Age ideas so attractive is the appeal to authority and antiquity. It offers a connection with the primitive that also implies a grounding in fundamental human realities. In this quest for the authentic, consumers seek out and accept the authority of spiritual leaders and teachers, who are accorded great respect because of their supposed credentials within a particular tribal tradition. Jamie Sams claims to speak less through her individual inspiration than because of her membership in the "Wolf Clan Teaching Lodge." By grounding contemporary New Age beliefs and practices in Native cultures, these ideas are given an aura far outweighing that of the Bible or other mainstream sources of religious authority. And according to some theories quite widespread in neo-Indian thought, these old-new ideas might be even more ancient than they appear, with origins in lost ancient civilizations, in this world or beyond.

Something in the Blood

Popular presentations of Native spirituality imply that authority is derived from racial identity, from the genes: lineage matters. Commonly, authors use names that will sound Indian to a mainstream public, whether or not these are assumed. Recent authors include Wolf Moondance, Nancy Red Star, Beverly Hungry Wolf, Brooke Medicine Eagle, Eagle Man (Ed McGaa), and so on. Book covers virtually always supply a brief biography of the author that emphasizes their tribal origins, and this fact does much to determine how seriously the reader is likely to view the contents. ("Ed McGaa is an Oglala Sioux lawyer, writer, and lecturer who has introduced thousands to Native American spirituality and rituals.") The author is presumed to be speaking not just for her- or himself, but unveiling the secrets of a given tradition. Ideally, the book is supported by brief recommendations from other tribal-sounding names. If not Native, the author must cite the chain of tradition that he or she is tapping into. Loren Cruden is "a midwife and herbal healer, [who] worked for many years with a Potawatomie medicine man to develop her spiritual practice. She now leads shamanic workshops and sweat lodges in the Pacific northwest."[1]

The issue of tribal identity is sensitive. Indian activists complain that most of those marketing Native spirituality have little or no claim to Indian-ness, and are thus engaged in cultural theft. (A different kind of rage is directed against entrepreneurs who are unquestionably Indian, who are denounced as quislings and sell-outs.) Certainly, ethnic identity can be difficult to prove. If a person claims to be Cheyenne or Navajo, that can usually be settled definitively by reference to tribal records, but many of the key writers and gurus speak more generally of a heritage which is often traced to multiple peoples. The virtue of that claim is that it is basically immune to disproof.

Since the 1970s, purveyors of Native spirituality have made much use of the concept of Métis, the mixed race "tribe." The word is parallel to the Spanish "mestizo," though Metis is also an ancient Greek goddess of wisdom, mother to Athena. Métis are a genuine and significant historical phenomenon in Canada, where people of mixed French and Native stock survive in large numbers. But the popularity of the term in the modern literature can be traced to Hyemeyohsts Storm, a founding member of the National American Métis Association. This group declares that they are a "Native stock and Mixed Heritage. . . . Soon, all the Reservations will be Métis and certainly most of our inner cities are Métis now. There are at least

85,000,000 of us here in the United States today." If everyone is in some sense Indian, then no one has the right to assert exclusive Indian-ness, or to protest the appropriation of Indian spirituality and the attendant rituals. The near-infinite expansion of Métis status is anathema to Native activists, but it is tempting for anyone wishing to adopt Native identity and heritage and claiming authority to transmit Native mysteries. Since the share of Métis stock is undefined, the claim is open to anyone who wishes to assert it. Among recent writers, Evelyn Eaton claims to be a Métis shaman and Brooke Medicine Eagle claims Métis heritage. Harley Swift Deer Reagan runs the Deer Tribe Métis Medicine Society.[2]

Tapping into Nature

Indian heritage matters because Native peoples are presumed to have a special link to nature, the natural world, and the environment. Native writers or spiritual leaders are, in a sense, speaking for nature and the land, as well as for their tribes and peoples. Native peoples, like members of other primal religions worldwide, are one with the landscape below and the heavenly forces above. "Native American Indians learned how to live with the earth on a deeply spiritual plane." Indian religion is believed to work on the attractive principle that Hopi thought summarizes as "blending with the land and celebrating life." This special relationship gives the potential to acquire occult or supernatural powers, to know and manipulate the environment.[3]

By accepting and practicing Native spiritual teachings, disciples are acknowledging their proper place in the universe. Responding to the modern growth of environmental awareness, ecological theorist Thomas Berry comments, "We are returning to our native place after a long absence, meeting once again with our kin in the earth community." Our models should be the Native people of America, with "one of the most integral traditions of human intimacy with the earth, with the entire range of human phenomena, and with the many living beings which constitute the life community." This return to the truth of nature means that, as Gerald Hausman writes, "we must learn the language of Native America and become a part of our own natural history. Doing so we will hear our universal heart—the one God intended us to hear when the world was new." A distinguished center of the New Age movement is California's Esalen Institute, founded in 1962. The institute takes its name from the region's Esselen Indians, and integration with nature is at the core of that idea:

> Here at Esalen, in our attempts to create meaningful ritual—symbolic ceremonies to mark our days, to deepen our sense of connection with the earth, the heavens, and all of the living beings with whom we are inextricably interwoven—we, 'the supplanters,' have often borrowed from Native American traditions: the talking stick, the sweat lodge, the fire circle, the drum, the rattle. We long for the unstrained unity, belonging, and reverence that we imagine our predecessors possessed. . . . In this regard, our own cultural heritage of meaningful ritual seems like a well run dry.

In contrast to Native peoples, white Americans live *In the Absence of the Sacred*, to use the title of a 1991 book.[4]

Many people feel a special relationship with nature, and feel energized or inspired in the presence of natural beauty, but common to neo-Indian spirituality is a belief that the mystical powers of nature have an objective basis. The sacredness of landscape goes far beyond a Romantic love of wild nature, since particular places are said to hold in themselves an inherent power or sanctity, regardless of whether observers recognize this fact. A Native sacred place is not holy because of its historical or cultural connotations, or because it is a place where prayer has been valid: rather, its sanctity is innate. These are "places where the veils are thin between planes and forces, where the three dimensional and the more dimensional sometimes meet and merge." When Native people erected Medicine Wheels or cut earth-figures, they were acknowledging this pre-existing holiness. As the website *www.newagetravel.com* claims, "The Native people of North America knew about the powers of sacred places long before the continent was invaded by Europeans. Some of the sacred sites of the continent's First Nations are identifiable by great mounds, cliff dwellings and rock art."[5]

Fundamental to Native spirituality texts is an absolute contrast between Western and Native attitudes toward nature, a split with vast religious and cultural implications. According to current writings, while Native peoples treat the earth as a mother to be venerated and respected, the Judeo-Christian tradition incites its adherents to subdue and exploit it. Westerners have simply lost the power to see the natural world, to understand the sanctity of places and natural projects that is so characteristic of the Native. (The

critique recalls Eliade's *The Sacred and the Profane.*) At the start of the twentieth century, a sizable number of Americans believed that the confrontation
between Christianity and Native religions was a struggle between clearly
defined good and evil. Christianity offered liberation from spiritual ignorance, from the ways of darkness and death. A hundred years later, a number
of Americans believe similarly that the two traditions are far from equal, but
now, it is rather the Native faiths that offer liberation and healing, individual
and global. The view of Native societies is utopian, while Christianity appears as a patriarchal blight on the landscape.

Modern proponents of Native spirituality posit an extreme contrast between the utopian life credited to Indian peoples before Contact and Conquest, and the grim consequences wrought by the unspiritual Europeans. So
marked is the change, in fact, that Contact is better described as "the Fall."
According to Thomas Mails, around 1100 the Hopi received the teachings of
Maasaw, the "awesome Guardian of the Earth," and "for the next 750 years,
the people blended and celebrated, living in peace and happiness." Spanish
intrusions proved marginal, and change only came in the twentieth century,
for when "the White government steadily turned the people away from
Maasaw's teachings, peace and happiness was turned away with it." For
Mails (a Lutheran pastor), Maasaw was a figure of divine authority, "the Savior of the Hopi, just as Jesus Christ is the Savior of the Christian world."
Perhaps he was Jesus in Indian guise? Whatever his identity, the Hopi people
lived in a paradisial state so long as they hearkened to his teachings.[6] White
people can share this glory so long as they adopt Native ways, which, in the
contemporary context, usually implies a strong environmentalist stance. As
Ed McGaa comments, "The bright rainbow . . . is now blooming among the
environmental and spiritual gatherings of enlightened peoples that have begun to flourish across the land." For radical activists like Earth First!, this
affection for Native values goes as far as forming a special order of Mudhead
Kachinas, sacred clowns founded on Zuñi precedent.[7]

The Edenic idea of Native America has been widely popularized, but
never to such a mass global audience as in the 1995 Walt Disney cartoon *Pocahontas.* This film had few pretensions to historical accuracy, but less important than the factual errors (such as the relative ages of the characters) were
the attitudes attributed to the two cultures, Native and English. English culture is exploitative, cruel, barbaric: it is European, Christian, and irredeemably masculine. These greedy explorers have come to exploit and
conquer the land. On the other side, the Indians are environmentally sensi-

tive and gender-equal. In her song "Colors of the Wind," the lovely Pocahontas states her creed that every animal, every rock and tree, "has a life, has a spirit, has a name." Her special friends include a raccoon, a hummingbird, and Grandmother Willow, a spirit residing in a sacred tree. In the film, John Smith gradually learns these lessons, though the main features of Powhatan religion that the historical Smith recorded, five years after meeting Pocahontas, were that her tribe feared and worshipped the devil, and sacrificed children to him. Perhaps the Disney corporation is saving that material for a sequel.[8]

Totems and Shamans

The natural relationship extends fully to animals, so that Natives do not acknowledge a rigid barrier separating humans and animals. Throughout Native legend and mythology, animals interact with humans; they speak and act much as humans do. At least for a century, white observers have been familiar with the commonplace tales featuring the trickster Coyote, stories of shape-shifting, and the easy passage between the human and animal realms.[9]

Central to the modern Native spirituality synthesis is the idea of a special relationship between a human and a particular animal, which represents a guiding spirit. We often hear of the "totemic animal," but this concept is fluid; not surprisingly, since the idea of totemism is so highly debated with the world of academic anthropology. In one view, totemism only makes sense in the context of a society or community, in which a number of people united in a kin relationship claim descent from a particular animal, with whom they claim a special link. The fact that people are united in this way defines their relationship to people of other clans with other totems. In the neo-Indian literature, totemism has a rather different and more individualistic sense, which owes more to memoirs like Black Elk's. In this view, the personal totem animal is discovered or acknowledged in a special shamanistic vision. In *Dances with Wolves*, the Lakota recognize the special quality of the Kevin Costner character because of his close relationship with a wolf. This theme often overlaps with the idea of the Vision Quest, an idea popularized by Parkman and made famous in modern times by Joseph Campbell. Even an episode of *Star Trek: Voyager* showed a Native American officer helping a colleague meditate in order to find her animal spirit guide.

This kind of individual totemism is the model offered in books like Brad Steiger's *Totems: The Transformative Power of Your Animal Totem*, Timothy

Roderick's *The Once Unknown Familiar: Shamanic Paths to Unleash Your Animal Powers*, or Nicki Scully's *Power Animal Meditations: Shamanic Journeys with Your Spirit Allies*. The use of the term "familiars" in this literature indicates the neopagan context. In European witch lore, accused witches were said to possess an animal given to them by the devil, a demon in animal form. The neopagan interpretation of these charges is that the witches of the early modern period were authentic pagans still versed in ancient lore, who still retained the knowledge of the totemic animal. Just as some enthusiasts claim that authentic mystic forces manifest themselves in holy places, so totemism is portrayed as an actual perception of occult forces. Kenneth Meadows writes that "a totem is a symbolic sensor that serves as a connector between different levels of being, different life forms whether human, animal, vegetable, mineral or celestial, and different levels of the mind. . . . Totems are links also with formative forces that are otherwise beyond the range of consciousness and can only manifest within."[10]

Shamanism is another term that means something different to academics than to ordinary consumers of New Age spirituality. In modern usage, Native American "shamanism" has acquired many of the complexities not just of the classical practice outlined by Eliade, but also of questionable parallels drawn from other primal cultures, including the ancient Celts of Western Europe and the British Isles. In its modern New Age version, a shaman is an individual in touch with spirits or spiritual states. The term covers a spectrum of practices and behaviors, varying greatly in how literally the adept takes the boasted powers. True, the shaman travels to other spiritual worlds, but are these located in some other spiritual dimension, or within the mind or soul? In some teachings, shamanism means deploying inner psychological powers, manipulating trance states, for instance, in order to achieve alternate states of consciousness. "A shaman is one who walks between the worlds, a person who, through various practices, is able to visit realms of reality that are often negated by the Western worldview. A shaman is also a healer and protector of the community."[11]

Yet as in the case of totemism, much of the literature also suggests that the shaman taps into real objective powers beyond those recognized by science. In these descriptions, pseudo-Native spirituality bases itself on the ideas of Western occultism, on Theosophy and Spiritualism, and before that on the ethers and spiritual fluids suggested by Mesmerism. Like Frank Waters before him, Kenneth Meadows taps a whole pseudoscience of auras and energy fields, in which the physical body coexists with other unseen structures. "The 'organs' of the energy body around which it is built and sustained are circular whorls of spiraling energy which are generally called chakras. . . . The American Indian shaman saw them as swirling discs of energy spinning at different rates and in different directions." The astral body, meanwhile, consists of "a very fine substance which interpenetrates physical matter." The astral plane is the place you visit in your dreams. The fact that the Sanskrit term chakra literally means "wheel" naturally allows analogies to be drawn to Native American themes.[12]

Other authors speak a kindred language of pseudoscience. For Wolf Moondance, smudging is "a powerful tool that is used in contemporary shamanism . . . which clears the etheric realm. This is the energy field surrounding your body that is known as 'your space.' Your feelings extend up to a hundred feet beyond your 'physical body' and make up part of the etheric realm." Jamie Sams describes unseen energies that can be tapped or manipulated by the shaman or seer. In *Dancing the Dream*, she asserts that "a Seer is a person who can access the unseen worlds of spirit and energy while in waking states. A Seer can follow the lines of energy in those realms to receive information and can locate the areas where those energies manifest themselves in our physical world." The worlds of "physicality and intangible energies" are bound together by "a grid of energy lines operating like a radio wave or frequency, without visible form."[13]

The use of pseudoscientific language is characteristic of occult and New Age movements, which for two hundred years have popularized and exploited contemporary advances in science and technology. Major advances in science have often been appropriated by occult or metaphysical movements, which claim to deploy parallel powers. The Mesmerism of the early nineteenth century echoed discoveries in electromagnetism; Spiritualism was influenced by progress in telegraphy; and twentieth-century movements used mongrelized concepts like "psychic radio." Frank Waters appropriated Einsteinian space-time language. This kind of borrowing is rhetorically useful because it allows occult movements to boast that they are at the cutting age of progress, that they are both drawing on the perceptions of modern science and surpassing it. Such claims are all the weightier when the groups argue that they are reviving ancient lost arts that prevailed in Atlantis. To paraphrase Arthur C. Clarke's famous dictum, any sufficiently misunderstood science is indistinguishable from magic. In its use of the rhetoric of science, modern neo-Indian spirituality clearly distinguishes itself from authentic Native traditions.

Reclaiming the Feminine

In the modern synthesis, Native religion is Earth religion, which is Mother religion and Woman's religion. Much neo-Indianism is directed toward a female audience, a somewhat surprising idea given the subordinate role of women in at least some historical Indian societies. Contemporary appropriations of Native spirituality place great store on its particularly feminine aspects, and stress the linkage with the Goddess, Mother Earth. Brooke Medicine Eagle writes that "North America—Turtle Island—is a feminine place."[14] If in fact Native religion is so female in its orientation, and this represents the authentic spiritual Way grounded in nature, then contemporary feminist spirituality is far more in tune with reality than its patriarchal counterparts. Instead of asking why white Americans are turning to Native beliefs, the better question would be why women of all races remain in religions that ignore or despise the feminine. Once again, Native tradition gives a decisive authority to contemporary religious trends.[15]

Just how strong was the Native belief in Mother Earth has caused some controversy. Based on texts such as the speech of Smohalla, the assumption over the past century has been that Native religions generally accepted a Father God coexisting on equal terms with the Earth Mother. When Tecumseh was negotiating with U.S. forces in 1810, he is reported to have declined a chair, saying, "The sun is my Father and the earth is my Mother, and on her breast will I lie." James Mooney believed that this idea lay "at the base, not only of the Smohalla religion, but of the theology of the Indian tribes generally." However, scholars like Sam Gill have challenged the belief in a central Earth Mother figure, finding few texts to support the idea.[16]

Such doubts, however, have little effect on current popular writers, for whom Native religion is feminine in its essence. Paula Gunn Allen writes:

> In the beginning was thought and her name was Woman. The Mother, the Grandmother, [is] recognized from earliest times into the present among those peoples of the Americas who kept to the eldest traditions. . . . Old Spider Woman is one name for this quintessential spirit, and Serpent Woman is another. Corn Woman is one aspect of her, and Earth Woman is another, and what they together have made is called Creation, Earth, creatures, plants and light.

The creation story is one of Cosmogyny, Allen's invented term that feminizes cosmogony. Allen's vision incorporates Pocahontas as a near-messianic figure, a spiritual leader and medicine woman who was the founding Mother of America, virtually an incarnation of these goddess figures. Mary Summer Rain writes of "Nature. Teacher. Both terms being interchangeable. Grandmother Earth, the wise Old Woman of the Woods, the greatest Teacher of all." "Nature belongs to the Creatrix who breathed life into all God physically manifested in the Beginning."[17]

Native peoples are literally children of the earth, and that realization is believed to shape their conduct toward nature and the environment. Wallace Black Elk argues, "Our body is made of fire, rock, dirt, earth. Because we drink water, and we eat green, we are part earth. So the fire, rock, water, and green—that's what rules me. That's how come we are earth people." Once again, this gives a spiritual underpinning to contemporary ecology movements. Advocating a "Mother Earth spirituality," Ed McGaa asserts that Native spirituality and ritual is the only correct response to the endangerment of the Earth Mother: "Why not turn to ceremony, at least to get the feeling, the message that our planet must live? She is speaking to us quite strongly already. Let her speak also in ceremony. . . . Mother Earth cannot heal herself alone. She needs our help."[18]

Logically, neo-Indian religion offers women ample opportunities as shamans and adepts, and a potent belief in special women's mystic orders and rituals has flourished ever since Lynn Andrews first revealed her Sisterhood of the Shields. Jamie Sams's book *The Thirteen Original Clan Mothers* bears the subtitle "Your sacred path to discovering the gifts, talents, and abilities of the feminine through the ancient teachings of the Sisterhood." Sams claims an explicitly feminine spiritual inheritance, offering access to "the Traditions that were allowed to live because of the refusal of these people to give up their connection to the Earth Mother. . . . [This is] the basis of these stories. I am truly grateful for this Woman's Medicine." This is "a powerful new method for honoring and incorporating native feminine wisdom into our daily lives." Her system deploys the terminology of feminist spirituality, aspiring "to continue weaving the web of the Sisterhood and make it strong," to promote "the nurturing of healed women." As often in these books, feminine spirituality is associated with the Earth, and with the defense of the environment.[19]

The Spirituality of the Body

In terms of current religious practice, the greatest appeal of Native spirituality is in its powerful sense of physicality, of the body. Here again we find the

familiar contrast with the evils of Judeo-Christian religion, which emphasizes the cerebral and the textual, while condemning sexuality and the body.
For neo-Indians, any authentic spirituality must integrate body and spirit,
and Westerners have much to learn from Native traditions of dancing and
drumming, through which a worshipper can achieve altered and even ecstatic states of consciousness. Linked to these holistic ideas is a stress on healing
of mind and body, of reintegration. The popular practice of the sweat lodge
offers purification and healing of mind and body. Though the exact symbolism varies, some take the lodge ritual to signify death and rebirth, as a participant enters and leaves the dark, wet interior.

Women play a special role in these new approaches. Since the 1970s, feminist and neopagan spirituality has evolved a range of practices and rituals,
some of which claim Native roots. One is the moon lodge, an example of
adapting what initially seems an unattractive aspect of Native tradition. In
their origins, moon lodges indicated a powerful suspicion about women's
ritual contamination during the menstrual period. Such an idea is found in
other religions, including Judaism, in which sexual intercourse is prohibited
for a set time following a woman's period, and ritual purification is demanded. Native societies, however, carried this principle a good deal farther.
As Alfred Kroeber wrote in 1907, "The menstruating woman was every-
where regarded as unclean, and excluded especially from acts of worship.
Not infrequent was the conception that she contaminated food, especially
meat." Women needed to be exiled to special quarters outside the community, a moon lodge.[20]

Some modern pagans have revived the idea of the moon lodge, the
monthly women's gathering, but in a context of celebration rather than
purging impurity. "Traditionally, the Moontime is the sacred time of
woman when she is honored as a Mother of the Creative Force." Brooke
Medicine Eagle speaks positively and mystically of Grandmother Moon,
and the ceremonies appropriate to her time. Again, moon lodges are easily
available through the workshops and retreat centers that proliferate across
the United States, usually alongside other neo-Indian rites such as sweat
lodges, drumming, and shamanic training:

> We gather to talk, chant, make magic, eat, create art, share women's mys-
> teries and wisdom, tell stories, play with herbs, and make music. Whether
> you are bleeding, ovulating, or neither, this is a sacred time to come to-
> gether with other magical women. By forming circles at each moon-lodge

we are reclaiming our bodies, our blood, and each other. It is also simply a great time to meet other fabulous women!

Some groups go further than others in their explicitly religious symbolism, speaking of "the offering of menstrual blood to the Earth."[21] Native spiritual traditions give religious significance to what was neglected or despised in mainstream Western thought. In Native spirituality, at least as currently reconceived, women not only are treated as equals in spiritual matters, but can claim a special power. In addition, sexuality is presented more respectfully, in contrast to what are seen as world-denying and repressive faiths like Christianity.

Besides women, gay groups seek a spiritual foundation in Native beliefs. Gay spirituality draws on the idea of the berdache, the man who voluntarily assumes a female role in society, and who is fully accepted as a woman. The berdache certainly existed, and was much described in European travel writing and early ethnography. Such characters also appear in fictional works, including *Little Big Man*. In the late twentieth century, though, the spiritual aspects of the berdache fascinated gay writers.[22]

Native traditions spoke respectfully of the Two-Spirit person, in whom masculine and feminine aspects were balanced and reconciled. If this is indeed an ancient belief, that gives added authority to claims that homosexuality should today be validated and treated as fully authentic. As Patricia Nell Warren writes:

> Traditionally considered as gifted medicine people, the feminine and the masculine dances together in them, as it does in all things. . . . The Two-Spirit ought to be not merely accepted, but celebrated as in those days of old. That experience of twoness as one is a key stage of our journey to learn what it means to be human. Maybe the Two-Spirit person is closer to truly human than the rest of us.

In an age when religious denominations are divided over gay issues, the tolerance of homosexuality in the ancient earth-rooted religions offers inspiration.[23]

Earth and Stars

Neo-Native spirituality looks down to the earth, but also up to the heavens. As we have seen, some recent writing underplays the explicitly religious or supernatural content of Indian culture, offering theories and advice that are scarcely distinguishable from secular therapies. Shamanism is portrayed more as a kind of psychotherapy than an authentic supernatural experience. Other interpretations, though, not only portray Indians in the familiar image of superspiritual mystics, but also point to direct connections between Native spirituality and the stars and heavenly bodies, and to extraterrestrial forces. This perception, which can be traced to the 1970s, transformed attitudes to Indian lore and the sacred sites. Though these ideas originated in reputable science and astronomy, they were absorbed into occultism and astrology, and it was in these forms that they gained a mass audience. Indian holy places came to be seen as centers of mysterious spiritual forces, which were likely connected with alien powers. These radical ideas rooted Native spirituality in the culture and science of superior ancient civilizations.

This new interpretation originated in the respectable academic study of the ancient European stone monuments known as megaliths. Looking at sites like Stonehenge, scholars argued that their arrangement followed astronomical alignments, so that (say) an observer looking from one critical stone to another would have been able to record the rising or setting of the sun or moon on particular days, and thus to commemorate heavenly events such as solstices. Soon, American archaeologists were finding similar alignments in abundance in Central America and at U.S. sites. In 1972, the Bighorn Medicine Wheel was found to be "a simple yet sophisticated astronomical observatory that was built to mark the summer solstice": it may also be aligned to the summer rise of the brightest and most significant stars. Cahokia in Illinois is the site of several sun-calendar structures, which have been named "Woodhenges" after the equivalent British sites.[24]

One spectacular find was made at Chaco in the late 1970s. Mysterious carvings in a cave marked the exact position at which, on the summer solstice, the sun shining into the cave would cast a convincing image of the so-called Sun Dagger. (Other equally precise effects occurred at the two equinoxes.) Archaeological discoveries were popularized through films and television documentaries, such as Nova's *The Mystery of the Anasazi* (broadcast on PBS in 1973) and *The Sun Dagger* (1982), and they gave a new fascination to sites like Chaco. Through the 1970s, the Anasazi world regained the glamour it had possessed during the age of discovery almost a century earlier, boosted still further by the new scientific findings. In 1974, Gary Snyder's collection of poems, *Turtle Island*, began with his "Anasazi," devoted to that ancient people, "up to your hips in Gods."[25]

Other observations in these years showed the importance of looking not just at specific sites, but also their wider environments. Chaco lies at the center of a vast network of ancient pathways or roads stretching many miles into the distance, and uniting the main canyon complex with lesser settlements. Most of the "roads" are too rudimentary to be compared with the great transportation systems of the Romans or the Incas, and they should rather be seen as marking lines of spiritual or symbolic power. Whatever their meaning, such road networks were once quite common, and would, for instance, have stretched over much of southern Ohio, linking the great mounds and carved earth figures of the region. For New Agers, these routes recall the ley lines said to connect ancient monuments and sacred sites across Western Europe. The more such vast systems came to light, the more they (apparently) demonstrated the spiritual energies with which Native peoples had invested their environments. To quote one enthusiastic writer,

> The Serpent Mound is one of those rare loci of the planet's topography where the consummate joining of terrestrial magnetism with astronomical alignments serves to astonish one at the accomplishments of our ancestry's knowledge of Earth and Heaven . . . This powerful energy rising from the depths of the earth–body is the energy of transformation, the energy that destroys blockages and barriers to the higher states of consciousness. It is the energy charted by shamans of every primary culture, the energy inherent in every human body. The ancient Hindu yogis named it kundalini, the Serpent Power.[26]

Extraterrestrials

Most of the new study of ancient sites was reputable and scholarly, and no one disputes that heavenly alignments can be found, though one might quibble over specific claims. What the recent discoveries prove is that early Native peoples were profoundly attuned to the natural world, were close observers of the skies, and recorded their observations as accurately (and beautifully) as they could, none of which involves any claims about supernatural powers. The emergence of archaeoastronomy happened, though, to coincide with other more controversial kinds of research. From the late 1960s, belief in UFOs became popular, and the idea of extraterrestrial visitors came to be associated with ancient remains and archaeological sites. In works such as *Chariots of the*

Gods (1968), Erich von Däniken suggested that evidence of UFOs and ancient astronauts could be found around the world, particularly among New World cultures like the Mayas and Incas. Also influential were John Michell's books *The View Over Atlantis* and *City of Revelation*, which incorporated ley lines and sacred geography into theories about UFOs, lost continents, prophecy, and numerology. Throughout Michell's work, too, runs the theme of the Serpent Power, the suggestion that the sacred lines and megalithic sites focus the earth energies commonly symbolized by the snake or dragon.[27]

The UFO linkage was reinforced by Native spokesman Vine Deloria, Jr., whose 1973 manifesto *God Is Red* demonstrated a powerful affinity for fringe science. Deloria writes sympathetically of the bizarre theories of Immanuel Velikovsky, who proposed that catastrophic cosmological events might have affected human history. Deloria argues that Native American tales might also recall these disasters. "What we might have previously been pleased to call creation stories might not be such at all. They might be simply the collective memories of a great and catastrophic event through which people came to understand themselves and the universe they inhabited." The Hopi claimed to recall the creation and destruction of several earlier worlds, in which great wars were fought with flying machines, specifically flying shields "made from hide propelled by some unidentified power." Should such stories be credited? Or rather, what right did anyone have to challenge them?[28]

The issue again was one of authority. The conventional scientific worldview is that modern humanity emerged in Africa some two hundred thousand years ago, and that human beings migrated to North America relatively recently, within the past twenty thousand years. Legends or folktales about tribal origins may well contain elements of historical truth, but are not likely to be reliable beyond a few centuries at most. All these statements flatly contradict the traditional bases of Indian culture and religion, which assert that Native peoples are truly aboriginal, having lived in a particular region literally since the Creation. Also, Native cultures commonly assert that different worlds and races have risen and fallen over long eons, and that records of these events are accurately preserved in extant myths. Most Indian peoples have no difficulty in seeing their myths as symbolic and nonhistorical, just as nonfundamentalist Christians commonly understand the chronology of the book of Genesis.[29] But in the radical 1970s, Indian activists demanded to know why Indian "myths" should not be as credible as the official worldview, which was presented as objective and scientific. If Indian stories spoke of lost ancient civilizations, cosmic catastrophes, and ancient flying machines, why were they automatically suspect? And if a respected activist like Deloria was prepared to support doctrines so congenial to New Age doctrines, that gave them a credibility that could never have come from the standard white authors. Taken together with the writings of von Däniken and Waters, *God Is Red* offered an influential foundation for later speculations about the otherworldly context of Indian religions.

UFO beliefs reached new heights in the mid-1970s, as massive public distrust in government and official institutions produced widespread sympathy for alternative science, for New Age and occult ideas. In 1977, the film *Close Encounters of the Third Kind* showed alien spaceships arriving at Wyoming's Devil's Tower, a site sacred to several Indian nations. Against this intellectual background, claims about the astronomical connections of other Native sites supported the linkage between Indian religions and otherworldly forces. Perhaps when Indian shamans boasted of walking among the stars, they were not speaking metaphorically.

Interest in extraterrestrials raised questions about just why Indian sites had the heavenly alignments that they did. Looking at Chaco Canyon or the Bighorn Medicine Wheel suggested parallels with other mystic and monumental objects around the world, which supposedly were intended to draw the powers of the earth or connect human communities with the forces of the stars and heavenly bodies. Perhaps these American sites exemplified not just primitive or primal religion, but a whole alternative science attuned to the powers of the earth and the heavens.

Prophecies

The notion of extraterrestrial contact is rhetorically useful because it can explain why faith should be placed in the always-popular native prophecies and apocalyptic warnings. Why, for instance, should we attach any significance to the date 2012, in which the complex Maya Long Count calendar comes to an end? Perhaps the world will end in this year, or will pass through an epochal transformation of some kind, but in either case, believers know that the ancient Maya had access to sophisticated astronomy, and had accurate foreknowledge of cosmological events. The prophecy thus relies on information derived from a higher civilization, from this world or beyond.[30]

Prophecy continues to be a major component of the neo-Indian texts. This interest can be traced to the *Book of the Hopi*, but it has roots in the wider New Age culture, as exemplified by the popularity of Nostradamus and Edgar Cayce. The attraction is not hard to understand. Though many people are fascinated by glimpses of the future, the Judeo-Christian prophetic tradition is unpopular with many for whom it is associated with political and social conservatism. Indian prophecies, which usually carry comparable millenarian messages, are acceptable because they lack this cultural affiliation. In Nancy Red Star's *Legends of the Star Ancestors*, "Wisdom-keepers" claim to speak for tribal communities around the world. Reputedly, "keepers around the world have seen signs occurring, signs that were predicted by ancient prophecies," and these tell "how Earth's environmental and social crises are part of a larger cosmic plan for the planet's transition into an enlightened age."[31]

The Hopi are still popular sources of prognostication. Thomas Mails claims to pass on the secret teaching of a Hopi elder, which, when he first heard it, he immediately recognized as standing "with the most important revelations ever given by the Creator. . . . This secret includes awesome prophecies, sublime instructions, and dire warnings, that together make up a unique survival kit." The Hopi message draws on the familiar idea of successive worlds, the Fourth of which is in its closing stages and is about to yield to a Fifth, following a time of tribulations, a Great Purification. First there will be an alignment of planets, followed by harrowing changes in climate, and a returning Ice Age. At the end, Maasaw will return to lead his people. Then "a new age will appear; there will be a new dawn of time when the world will bloom into peacefulness." In the final crisis, Hopi land will survive as a shelter for mankind. Mails notes that many of these forecasts have close connections with the ideas of Nostradamus, who likewise made "incredibly accurate predictions."[32]

Remarkably, claims Mails, ancient prophecies have repeatedly been fulfilled in our modern world. This includes the coming of "roads in the sky," "moving houses of iron," and "horseless carriages"; also, "women's skirts will be raised above the knee, devaluing the sacred body of the female." The Hopi are said to have foretold the building of a house of glass, which corresponds to the United Nations building. Reportedly, they predicted two great wars, following the invention of a great "gourd full of ashes," believed to be the nuclear bomb. Obviously, these predictions would be more convincing if they had not first been recorded at the end of the twentieth century, at which point they have a distinctly retroactive quality. Also, the specific elders who gave these prophecies may or may not have been presenting tribal wisdom, as opposed to their own personal ideas. Indians also read bizarre UFO texts and watch trash television, and contrary to stereotypes of ancient wisdom, even some elders might be credulous.[33]

Indians from Space

By the 1980s, ancient Indian communities had been absorbed into the common myth of the lost scientific civilization, a variant of the Atlantis myth. The fact that the Anasazi had apparently vanished offered an extra bonus for speculation. The notion of "disappearance" is hotly disputed by Pueblo people themselves, who plausibly claim the so-called Anasazi as lineal ancestors, and most modern archaeologists agree. But in contemporary New Age lore, the Anasazi vanished somewhere into the Great Cosmic Beyond. One website claims that "in the northwestern corner of New Mexico there exists the remnants of an ancient civilization that developed architecture, engineering, social organization, mathematics, geomancy, cosmic astronomy and large-scale ritual to a high art. They may even have mastered the technologies of anti-gravity and time travel as well." The Chacoans "took the big leap forward. They journeyed fearlessly into sacred space, transected galactic time and never looked back." Among the various theories, "the Anasazi had been lifted off in space ships; they had discovered portals into other dimensions of space and time; or they had mastered nodal energy centers that are scattered around the whole region." The vortices of Sedona might themselves represent such power centers.[34]

Popular culture has helped spread such ideas. In a 1995 episode of *The X-Files*, "Anasazi," Agent Fox Mulder receives a computer disk with full information about government UFO cover-ups, but it is encoded in Navajo. Mulder's translator explains to him the story of the Anasazi, a term here translated as "ancient aliens," whose sudden disappearance from the historical record indicated a mass alien abduction. Similar ideas and characters returned in later episodes, including the idea of mysterious and alien-related texts that need to be translated from Navajo. In another episode, Mulder is healed by the Navajo ceremony of the Blessing Way, during which his spirit travels the bridge between the worlds. In passing, his Navajo mentor reports a good deal of now-familiar Native legend, including the Plains belief about Buffalo Woman.[35]

However much these ideas may appear to belong to the far fringes of speculation, they have reached a wide audience because of the occult and

UFO-oriented backgrounds of some of the best-known popularizers of Native spirituality. Jamie Sams offers an example. In her earlier works, published by small presses, she emerges as an explicit enthusiast for UFO lore,
views that reappear more discreetly in her mainstream writings with Harper.

In 1988, Sams published what is presented as a spiritual autobiography titled *Midnight Song* with Bear & Co. Sams claims to have been psychically
gifted since childhood. About 1973, while she was in her early twenties, a
Mexican shaman initiated her into her career as a medicine woman who
could recall her previous lives. Some years later, she received spectacular revelations from a Voice, which explained to her the extraterrestrial history of
the area near her home in Palm Springs. "There was a terrible war here
15,000 years ago and you were witness to it. . . . Seven cities were lost and the
myth of this is still recorded by the Native Americans who are the remnant
race of Lemuria, called Mu, or the Motherland." These ancient metropoles
were the Seven Cities of Cibola—communities that mundane archaeologists locate in the historical pueblos of the Four Corners region—and they
were destroyed in interstellar warfare, by the use of "nuclear laser bombs."
The Voice also offers a detailed political history of these archaic struggles
("the dark beings of Orion had infiltrated Atlantis") and the affairs of the
still-extant Galactic Confederation. Sams records that "I have traveled
through time to seek the vanished ones—the ancients that colonized our
earth—and met them in the physical world high in the Andes." Other
earthly places contain gateways to interstellar space, including (naturally)
the Bermuda Triangle.[36] Sams's book contains a laudatory introduction from
"academic shaman" Jose Arguelles, one of the prime movers of the 1987
Harmonic Convergence. His book *The Mayan Factor: Path Beyond Technology* "teaches us how to connect directly, sensuously and electromagnetically
with the Galactic Synchronization Beam, a time wave that is now triggering
a new phase of galactic evolution."[37]

Books such as *Midnight Song* are commonplace, and there is no reason
why Sams should not present her claims of psychic revelation. But according
to any kind of consensus view, they are located at the extreme edges of New
Age thought and UFO-logy, and this background casts a different light on
her later publications with the mainstream press Harper. Though the more
startling extraterrestrial claims are toned down in the later Harper books,
they are definitely present. In *Dancing the Dream*, Sams claims that, "according to the teachings of my Seneca Elders, Grandpa Moses Shongo and his
granddaughter Twylah Nitsch, we have experienced the Fourth World of

Separation for the last sixty or seventy thousand years" (Twylah Nitsch had been a friend of the Sun Bear community).[38] In *The Thirteen Original Clan Mothers*, the Mothers sometimes appear as psychological symbols of aspects of the feminine personality, but are also portrayed as near-goddess figures who have in the past intervened to create new worlds.

Just as enthusiastic for ancient civilizations and alien contacts is Kenneth Meadows. After describing some of the great earth mounds built by Native peoples, he asks, "Were some of the massive figure-like mounds a means of communicating with beings from another planet? Or were they perhaps a method of alignment with certain cosmic energies and of bringing cosmic power from the stars down to earth?" Noting how often various tribes report having come to their historical homelands from another place, he speculates that perhaps they came from some other world entirely, "or were they from lands now vanished beneath the waves?" Allegedly, the oral teachings of the Cherokees claim that human beings came to this planet 250,000 years ago from a planet of the star Sirius, and that in their language, the word for "stars" is the same as that for "ancestors." Harley Swift Deer Reagan of the Deer Tribe claims that Native Americans descend from Star People who arrived from another planetary system almost a million years ago.[39]

Crystal Skulls

Extraterrestrial ideas also appear in other texts not overtly concerned with UFOs or related lore. One vehicle for such ideas is the eccentric but quite commonplace tale of the "Crystal Skulls." The story has its roots in the 1930s, in the writings of archaeologist F. A. Mitchell-Hedges, whose Central American travels have an Indiana Jones quality. He believed that Central America had a stronger claim to be the cradle of civilization than the Middle East, and argued that this region retained traces of lost civilizations harking back to ancient Atlantis. During the 1920s, his daughter Anna reportedly discovered a remnant of archaic culture in the form of a stunningly modeled crystal skull found in the ruins of a Mayan city in Belize. Critics argue that the whole account of the discovery was fictional, and that the item was actually purchased at auction years later. The skull itself is certainly a modern creation, as are the many others that have appeared subsequently. Nevertheless, Mitchell-Hedges made the skull the focus of some baroque legends, linking it to Mayan human sacrifice rites, and portraying it as "the embodiment of all evil." By the 1970s, the crystal skulls entered New Age mythology as potent relics of ancient Atlantis, and they even acquired a canonical number: there were exactly thirteen skulls.[40]

None of this would have anything to do with North American Indian matters, if the skulls had not attracted the attention of some of the most active New Age writers. In *The Medicine Way,* Kenneth Meadows cites and illustrates the skulls, and presents maps of ancient Atlantis and Mu, the supposed precursors of modern Indian spirituality. In *The Thirteen Original Clan Mothers,* Jamie Sams traces Indian lore to the very ancient times before Turtle Island broke into continents, presumably tens of millions of years ago. The thirteen Crystal Skulls were then scattered around the world, but "the Stone People are the libraries of earth and hold all records of the Earth's true history." Each skull is associated with one of the Clan Mothers. In 1999, Sams wrote in *Dancing the Dream* that "the ancient Native American wisdom of the Crystal Skull and White Buffalo Dreaming Societies, both of which I have been a part of, has been held in secret for centuries." In her view, "The potential that exists for human beings to become fully conscious and clear is represented by the original thirteen crystal skulls given to the people of Earth by another culture that came from beyond the stars. The Mayans call these people the 'Sky Gods.'" Collectively, these skulls symbolize "the thirteen hertz that will be experienced by everyone on earth in the year 2012." The scientific meaning of this phrase is questionable because a hertz is an arbitrary unit that depends on Western concepts of timekeeping, and it is puzzling why the number should have seemed so critical to ancient astronauts.[41]

Natives Old and New

After thirty years of enthusiastic cultural work, the Native spirituality movement has become a complex and multifaceted reality, and it would be futile to try to analyze its every aspect, still less to challenge it. It scarcely seems profitable to confront all the claims about lost continents and UFOs, all the mystical beliefs about auras and crystals.

Despite this, some broad points do deserve to be critiqued. The first, obviously, is that much or most of what is currently presented as Native spirituality simply should not be so described, at least in the sense that it represents or reproduces the practice of any historical community. Much of the synthesis is historically recent and, at least in its present guise, largely artificial. This is true most obviously of themes like the crystal skulls and the tarot cards, but also of the Shield mythology, the Medicine Wheel, and much contemporary shamanism. These are the products of a generation of creative spiritual entrepreneurs. Most of the "Native" lore also owes much more to the generic New Age context than to anything truly Native. Much could equally well have been presented with the trappings of some other culture if that had had the same cachet during these same decades. For a New Age believer, the close resemblances between (say) Celtic, Native American, and Tibetan spirituality suggests that each in its way partakes of universal human powers and instincts, and perhaps indicates that each tradition traces its origins to a common ancient culture.[42] A cynical observer would suggest that each of these traditions is being packaged in ways that are congenial to a Western audience, with little reference to the authentic character of Native American, Celtic, or Tibetan cultures.

Also troubling is the contrast between the fundamental assumptions underlying Native and neo-Indian spirituality, especially in matters like individuality and community. Native traditions are firmly based in the community, and Native religions make no sense except in a communal context, often linked further to a particular landscape. What gives any "primal" religion its essential quality is that it does not relocate successfully, or at least, not without great difficulty. When uprooted, such religions can easily perish. This is quite different from the world of the neo-Indian practitioner, who is assumed to be a lone individual, or at best a member of a small, transient group. Historically, shamans, for instance, were inextricably linked to a particular community, the interests of which they serve. Modern shamans, in contrast, are profoundly individualistic, and shamanism is usually a practice for sole practitioners engaged in personal spiritual endeavors. Equally, New Age practitioners treat the Vision Quest in terms of the integration of the individual, and not as originally conceived, the preparation of the individual to fulfill his or her role in the community.

False Contrasts

Throughout recent writings, we find a view of Native societies that is highly problematic. In order to assert the value of Native spirituality, writers consistently idealize their subjects, past and present, ignoring or underplaying those aspects that they might find unsettling or inconvenient. Just as a hundred years ago, missionary authors could find nothing good to say of traditional Native religion, their New Age counterparts today can find little that is less than perfect.

Particularly suspect is the theme of blaming a patriarchal Judeo-Christian ideal for such modern evils as warfare, religious intolerance, and the rape of the environment. This is not to deny that Europeans or Americans have committed such crimes, or that their actions toward Native peoples have often been abominable. Even historians thoroughly familiar with the horrors of white-Native interactions can usually find some new atrocity that if anything makes the picture even worse than previously assumed. Anyone who thinks the Plains warfare of the 1870s involved unconscionable white conduct should look back to the arguably worse behavior by U.S. forces during the Seminole wars of the 1830s. But it is questionable to argue that such horrors are necessarily connected with Euro-American civilizations, or, as is commonly argued today, with their religious foundations.

History does not support the idea that Earth-based religions like those of Native America had any advantages in these matters over their Christian counterparts. We are not dealing with a confrontation between Native light and European darkness. Native and Christian religions each had the potential for violence and abuse, but Europe had the dubious blessing that its surging economic and military power permitted it to dominate the globe, and thus had more opportunities to carry out exploitation on a wider scale.

At every point, the comparative indictment of Judeo-Christian values is weak. If Europe was a war-torn continent, so was pre-Columbian America, North and South. Warfare was rife, and destructive, in tribal societies. In the Southwest especially, archaeologists through the decades have gone to great and unconvincing lengths to provide peaceful interpretations for what are almost certainly fortifications erected by a conflict-ridden society living in constant fear of attack. Only recently has the extent of war in Anasazi society been fully acknowledged. Across North America, quite independently of European intervention, tribes and peoples were exterminated or driven far from their traditional lands: regions were ethnically cleansed. In Central America, too, early interpretations of the Maya as peaceful astronomer-kings lasted only until the decipherment of their written texts, which reveal a tenuous system of rival city-states engaged in near-constant warfare and massacre. Slavery was also widespread in Native American communities. Though it attained nothing like the scale or harshness of the plantation systems of the nineteenth century, neither did premodern Europe possess anything of this magnitude.[43]

The alleged contrasts between bloody Europe and peaceful Turtle Island are at their least plausible during the era of Contact, when a widespread popular mythology portrays the Christian world as a nest of superstition, intolerance, and genocide, symbolized by evils such as the Inquisition and the witch hunts. In terms of modern New Age texts, Christian Europe is symbolized by a woman burning at a stake, while across the Atlantic, Native women were honored for their spiritual gifts. The contrast is perverse. Until modern times, most Native American religions had a powerful belief in the human ability to inflict harm through supernatural means, that is, in witchcraft, and antiwitchcraft movements have repeatedly flourished. Given the relative scale of the populations, there is no evidence that Native societies were any more merciful to suspected witches than their transatlantic counterparts. And if Europe burned people at the stake, so did many Native societies, whether in mass ritual sacrifices (as in the southeastern states), or as part of the cruel ritual tortures that were so widespread. Even seventeenth-century Europe, so familiar with religious violence and persecution, found the accounts of torture among the Huron and Iroquois almost beyond belief. We should certainly be awed by the sophisticated cultures that produced the stone cities of the Southwest or the mound communities of the Mississippi Valley; but we should not ignore the violence and bloodshed that would have been routine parts of their ritual life. Such acts did not discredit their culture or their religions, any more than the sporadic outbursts of religious violence in contemporary Europe should be taken as necessary characteristics of Christianity.[44]

Even the standard idea of the ecologically sensitive Indian, appalled at the wholesale slaughter of wildlife, looks increasingly tenuous. While Native cultures acknowledged the spirits of their game animals, they also thought it wrong to decline the gift that the animal spirits were offering to the people, and they killed as long as they had the opportunity to do so. The legendary vast herds of buffalo on the Plains were probably a temporary phenomenon, existing on that scale only in disputed no-man's-lands in which no tribal group exercised political or military supremacy.[45]

To argue that Native America was not a utopia obviously does not justify conquest, enslavement, or any of the later acts of brutality or betrayal. But it does raise questions about the persistent rhetorical use of Native societies and their values as the virtuous opposites of a deeply tainted European Christendom, and about the use of historically dubious claims that magnify European sins. Perhaps the most far-reaching claim is the argument that contact with Europeans precipitated a population drop in the New World on a scale that constituted the worst act of genocide in human history. While Native numbers did decline following the importation of new diseases, the genocide claim can only be sustained if one accepts extraordinarily high estimates for pre-Columbian populations, which may exaggerate the real figures by an order of magnitude. However widespread the historical myth, the notion that tens of millions of Native peoples perished as a result of the Columbian contact is credited because it confirms an ideological tendency to paint Europe and the West in the bloodiest colors.[46]

The extreme moral contrast between Christian and Native societies is a myth, in the sense of something that is false or misleading, but we can also use that word in its correct technical sense. A myth is also a story used to teach a higher truth, often one with religious significance. In this context, exalting Native societies and spiritualities helps to proclaim their superiority to the West and to Christianity. People interested in the new spirituality believe they have found in Native culture all the values they believe are lacking in conventional Christian or Jewish traditions, values of environmentalism and gender equality, of a mysticism that does not reject the bodily world. As often in the past, these wishes and dreams were projected onto Native cultures without too much concern about whether they reflected historical or social realities.

Through most of American history, Native peoples themselves have had little opportunity to respond to the shifting images that white people applied to them. In the late twentieth century, though, just as the new spirituality movement was becoming so influential, America's Indians were acquiring unprecedented self-confidence, which was manifested in political influence and (a real first) in economic power. If the rise of neo-Indian spirituality represented an irresistible force, then in recent decades, it has on occasion collided with an immovable object, in the shape of the Native desire to fight cultural appropriation.

11

⚜

Returning the Land

The religion of the Indian is the last thing about him that the man of another race will ever understand.

—*Charles Eastman*

In 1970, President Nixon signed a bill returning the sacred Blue Lake to the Pueblo of Taos, righting what was commonly seen as a historic injustice. This one measure symbolizes a radical change in both popular and public attitudes toward Native peoples, and especially toward their cultural and religious beliefs. By the end of the twentieth century, Native religions had acquired a recognition and prestige that they had never possessed before. Despite complaints that legal acknowledgment had not gone far enough— for instance, in the use of peyote—Native religions now enjoyed a full-scale revival. Also in contrast to earlier years, these ideas were now developed and presented by Native peoples themselves, rather than by their would-be white advocates. As America's Indians entered a period of cultural revolution, their new self-confidence inevitably expressed itself in growing protests against those non-Natives who tried to appropriate their spirituality.[1]

Native Power

By the late 1960s, Indian activism faced a promising political situation. While liberals and radicals naturally sympathized with Red Power rhetoric conservative politicians also supported Native causes to a degree that many found surprising. Though few Americans hold fond memories of Richard Nixon, his reputation endures in Native communities, and that despite the Wounded Knee confrontation. Barry Goldwater was another strong supporter of Native land claims. (Goldwater's lifelong sympathies with Indian culture made him a significant collector of kachina figures.) Nixon favored a generous policy of Native self-government, removing Indians from federal control without depriving them of federal support, thus offering the best of the termination policy but without its drawbacks. He aimed "to strengthen the Indian's sense of autonomy without threatening his sense of community," a strategy that culminated in the Indian Self-Determination Act of 1975.[2]

Though the results were patchy, tribal self-determination allowed some nations to make major economic gains. Some profited spectacularly by exploiting their natural resources. The Southern Utes, for instance, became rich from their natural gas reserves: a tribe less than fourteen hundred strong now commands assets worth $1.45 billion.[3] For many peoples, though, the road to prosperity involved gambling. In 1988, reservation gaming was legalized by the Indian Gaming Regulatory Act, and a national boom was soon under way. By 2001, 290 casinos were scattered over twenty-eight states, earning a combined revenue of $12.7 billion, including $5 billion in profits. Indian gambling operations have been deeply problematic, and not just on moral grounds. While some tribes have profited greatly, and have distributed the windfall fairly among their members, many of the poorest groups have received next to no benefit. Some 44 percent of revenue derives from casinos in just three states, namely California, Connecticut, and Florida, while little revenue flows to states with such large Indian populations as Montana, the Dakotas, and Oklahoma. Yet for all the criticisms, gambling gave Indian interests across the United States an unprecedented political and economic clout. For the first time, Indian lobbyists were major players in the nation's state houses.[4]

One token of success was the substantial growth of Indian population numbers, a change that had little to do with the normal mechanisms of demographic change. Being Indian was now fashionable and, in some cases, profitable. Like other Americans, few Natives can claim racial purity, and so some degree of subjective choice is involved in their self-identification. At a time when Indian blood was a handicap, many with Native ancestry would be unlikely to identify as Indian if they could claim white status. From the 1960s, though, the romanticization of Indians encouraged many of partial ancestry to admit and even exaggerate their Native claims. By the end of the century, a claim to Native status was likely to bring real advantages, in terms of minority status for employment, or access to gambling profits. The scramble to build and run casinos even led to the resurrection of some tribes, sometimes on shaky historical grounds. Particularly controversial was the revival of the Mashantucket Pequot tribe, owner of the lucrative Fox-woods casino complex in Connecticut. Whatever the reasons, the U.S. census suggests a population explosion in self-defined American Indians from the 1960s onwards. Native population grew from 250,000 in 1900 to 524,000 in 1960, but then expanded to 2 million by 1990 and 2.5 million by 2000.[5] Despite all the continuing poverty and deprivation in many reservations, many felt these were good times to be Indian. (The growth of Indian autonomy in the United States fell far short of what was accomplished in Canada, where the First Nations made remarkable progress in achieving sovereignty over vast stretches of the land).[6]

Just how radically the political environment had changed was apparent in 1992, during the quincentennial commemoration of the arrival of Columbus. In different circumstances, such an event might have been expected to mark a demonstration of American patriotism and solidarity, but in the event, it proved deeply divisive. Native activists took the lead in protesting or boycotting events celebrating what they saw as the invasion of America, and the subsequent genocide. The anniversary provoked an outpouring of books and articles demanding justice for Native peoples.[7] Often, this rhetoric specifically focused on the evils of Christianity as the ideological weapon of the conquerors, who thought their religion justified every atrocity. Long after the actual coming of Europeans (in this view), Christianity continued its war of conquest in Native hearts and minds, demanding the extirpation of their rituals and beliefs. "After the ravages of European-borne diseases, the religion of the Europeans was the single most dangerous force the Indians across the entire hemisphere would ever face."[8] America's Indians could no longer be ignored; nor could their religions.

The New Old Religion

These social and legal changes gave immensely added momentum to the revival of Native religious life. In the 1970s, political activism expressed itself in cultural and spiritual revival, and the recovery of lost and threatened rituals. Once again, Vine Deloria, Jr., served as the prophet of the new movement, with his influential 1973 book *God Is Red*. Indian communities across the country experienced a revival of religious traditionalism. On the Mohawk reservation, the new spiritual emphasis was reflected in the newspaper *Akwesasne Notes,* which developed a circulation of some seventy thousand. The paper reached out to "Native and Natural Peoples," including white neopagans. In 1977, representatives of the Iroquois Confederacy presented to the United Nations a sweeping declaration of Native religious grievances, a document later published as the *Basic Call to Consciousness*. The *Call* demanded a return to Native spiritual traditions, which were portrayed as survivals from a more ancient Earth. Only thus could the planet be saved from apocalyptic ruin. ("The way of life known as Western Civilization is on a death path on which their own culture has no viable answers.")[9]

Meanwhile, the return of Blue Lake began a wider official policy of responding to Indian concerns on land issues, and more generally of recognizing cultural concerns. In 1978, the American Indian Religious Freedom Act acknowledged that "the religious practices of the American Indian . . . are an integral part of their culture, tradition and heritage, such practices forming the basis of Indian identity and value systems." The federal government recognized that, through the years, the "abridgement of religious freedom for traditional American Indians" had been a persistent problem.[10]

The religious revival has been an enduring theme in the work of the Native writers who occupy such a central place in the modern American literary tradition. This could scarcely be otherwise, since so many of these authors are struggling with issues of cultural identity and the rival attractions of traditional Native roots and modern American society. In *The Way to Rainy Mountain*, Scott Momaday returns to his Kiowa roots through his memories of his grandmother and the eclipse of her religion with the end of the Sun Dance: "She was a Christian in her later years, but she had come a long way about, and she never forgot her birthright." So rich are these materials that it is hardly possible to offer anything more than a sketch here, but recent fiction did much to shape views of Native religion among educated white people, not least because of the strong representation of such works on college syllabi.

Momaday's *House Made of Dawn* stresses the survival of Native religion beneath the veneer of Euro-American civilization. Describing a Pueblo community, he writes, "The invaders were a long time in conquering them; and now, after four centuries of Christianity, they still pray in Tanoan to the old deities of the earth and sky. . . . They have assumed the names and gestures of their enemies, but have held on to their own secret souls; and in this is a resistance and an overcoming, a long outwaiting."[11] Part of the process of cultural survival is the religion of peyote, and a peyote ceremony is intricately described. Later authors would draw extensively on Native traditions and images, for instance, in Louise Erdrich's *Tracks* (1988), with its explorations of Ojibwa ideas of sorcery and totemism. Erdrich revives the once clichéd figure of the Wendigo in *The Antelope Wife* (1998). The trickster appears in such Native novels as Thomas King's *Green Grass, Running Water.*

Some writers not only used Native religions, but speculated about wholesale revivals of primal and pagan tradition, in books that recall Lawrence's *Plumed Serpent.* These ideas seemed all the more plausible given the apocalyptic threats of warfare and ecological crisis during the 1970s and early 1980s. In 1978, Native American writer Gerald Vizenor published *Darkness in St. Louis* (later known simply as *Bearheart*), a fantastic tale of survivors fleeing across a collapsing America. Whites seek salvation among the Indian communities that offer the last chance for survival. Eventually, the characters find refuge in Chaco Canyon, in the awe-inspiring Anasazi settlement of Pueblo Bonito. This is the gateway to the Fourth World, entered during the mystic time of the winter solstice.[12]

Equally pessimistic about Euro-American civilization is the *Almanac of the Dead* (1991) by Leslie Marmon Silko, whose ancestry is part Laguna Pueblo. Her vast novel imagines the collapse of white America before the march of the Native peoples of North and South America—a theme that harks back to John Collier's ideas of hemispheric Native solidarity. Silko gives a racial emphasis to two leading political issues of the day in which the United States was entangled with Latin America, namely, the guerrilla wars in Nicaragua and El Salvador, and cocaine trafficking. In both cases, Native peoples were striking back, while America itself was collapsing through urban decay and environmental crisis. The cities would die, eco-terrorists would destroy the dams. After the apocalypse, the buffalo would reclaim the Plains, and America would be Native once more.

However, the main thrust of the novel, and the struggle it describes, is religious. Christianity had failed in the Americas: "The Europeans . . . had gone through the motions with their priests, holy water, and churches built with Indian slave labor. But their God had not accompanied them. The white man had sprinkled holy water and had prayed for almost five hundred years in the Americas, and still the Christian God was absent." The old religion survived, and was returning—and its symbols were the serpents. As a

Hopi prophet declares, "The giant snakes, Damballah and Quetzalcoatl, have returned to the people. . . . The snakes say this: From out of the south the people are coming, like a great river flowing restless with the spirits of the dead who have been reborn again and again all over Africa and the Americas, reborn each generation more fierce and more numerous."[13] The book culminates with a messianic vision of insurgent Native American armies led by two mysterious brothers with their sacred macaws, through whom they receive messages from the spirit world. The reference is to the Hero Twins of the *Popol Vuh*—by implication, America's true and only Bible.

Christian and Pagan

Despite manifestations of pagan triumphalism, white observers sympathized with the Native religious revival, and not just New Age followers. Religious relativism had long been a strong force among liberal churches, and seemed all the more necessary with the expansion of American religious diversity at the end of the century. Liberal churches now explicitly acknowledged that Native peoples had their own authentic way to the divine. In 1987, leading clergy of the major Christian denominations in the Pacific Northwest, including Roman Catholics, Lutherans, and Methodists, issued a declaration to the Native peoples of the region, formally apologizing for "the destruction of traditional Native American spiritual practices." The declaration defended Native religions, asserting that "The spiritual power of the land and the ancient wisdom of your indigenous religions can be, we believe, great gifts to the Christian churches. . . . May the God of Abraham and Sarah, and the Spirit who lives in both the Cedar and Salmon People, be honored and celebrated."[14]

Some liberal Christians brought elements of Native practice into their own ritual life, as a means of incorporating concerns about environmentalism and racial diversity. One radical activist in the 1980s was Matthew Fox, then a Dominican priest, who earned notoriety by recruiting the pagan witch Starhawk for his Institute of Creation Spirituality, based at California's Holy Names College. A Lakota spiritual teacher founded a sweat lodge for the diverse faculty. Fox's spirituality drew ever more heavily on Native traditions, with the appearance of a tipi, dancing, drum rituals, and his own Vision Quest.[15] Although Fox represented an extreme wing of liberal Catholicism (he later left the church), he was by no means unique in his willingness to explore Native traditions. At one Catholic seminary in the early 1990s, an experimental liturgy included the familiar Indian sacred symbols of corn and pollen, earth and water. The ritual included a prayer ultimately derived from Black Elk:

All is a circle and a hoop within me . . .
Look inside the circle and the hoop
You will see your relation and nations
Your relation to the four legged
And two legged
And the winged ones
And the Mother Earth
The Grandfather Sun
The Grandfather Moon
The Direction and the Sacred Seasons
And the Universe.[16]

Most Christian believers never encountered such syncretism directly, but they did hear from their clergy about the environmental insights of Native peoples, as the alleged speech of Chief Seattle became a popular sermon text. In mainline denominations, they also heard that all the different religious traditions, including Native ways, were equally valid.

Such a shift of attitudes raised acute dilemmas for Native Christians themselves. A substantial majority of Indians are Christian, representing most of the main American denominations, while independent and Pentecostal churches have a strong presence on many reservations. Most Christians were prepared to accept and celebrate Native culture, while Native Christian theologians offered thoughtful suggestions for reconciling the old and new ways. Some Christians, though, were troubled by the new tolerance for syncretism, not to mention the overt anti-Christianity of some recent writings on Native religion and history.[17]

Indian Religions and the Law

By the end of the century, few doubted that Native religions were authentic and worthwhile faiths, entitled to the same rights and protections as any other and, arguably, to even more consideration than mainstream creeds.

Ever since the Religious Freedom Act of 1978, American courts have faced the dilemma of trying to accommodate Native interests when they clashed with those of the wider society. At the same time, the courts had greatly expanded the bounds of religious freedom. Under the key decisions of *Sherbert* and *Yoder*, religious conduct could be regulated only when a "compelling state interest" could be established, and when there was "no alternative form of regulation." As the nation's religious diversity increased due to immigration, so did the courts' willingness to respect newer traditions. In 1993, a case involving the Afro-Cuban religion of Santeria prevented cities from prohibiting animal sacrifice.[18] In such a laissez-faire environment, Native American issues were certain to receive special consideration.

Most of the resulting decisions by courts and official agencies show a massive cultural shift toward supporting and even favoring Native religious traditions. In some famous cases, pro-Native official policies have attracted the strongest criticism from white environmentalists who traditionally saw Native peoples as allies. One traumatic example not directly concerned with ritual involved the assertion by the Makah people of their right to hunt whales. Just as sensitive was the claim by other nations to collect eagle feathers for ritual purposes. In both instances, cherished values came into direct conflict, as the defense of Native rights ran contrary to the protection of endangered species.[19]

Conflicts over Native religious rights often arose in prison. Until the 1960s, American prisons made little or no allowance for the religious needs of inmates except for Christians and Jews. Even when minority needs were notionally met, authorities followed the conventional view that formal religious practice was confined to specified days and times, rather than being integrated into everyday conduct. We also see vestiges of the old division between Indian "religion" and "superstition." Indians were welcome to gather for worship, but not to use ritual objects like eagle feathers, sacred pipes, special herbs, and certainly not peyote. Long hair was another divisive issue, raising yet again the distinction between religious and cultural attributes. Many traditional-minded inmates insisted that this was a religious requirement rather than a fashion style. Prison authorities prohibited long hair on grounds of hygiene, and also of safety, since the hair provided a place to conceal weapons.[20]

Over the last quarter century, the courts have heard many complaints about prisoners' rights, and generally, the religious rights of Indian prisoners have been established far more clearly than ever before. Prisoners could participate in sweat lodges, and could demand access to Native spiritual advisers just as Christian or Jewish inmates could expect access to their own chaplains. American moves to recognize religious rights do not match what has been done in Canada, where new facilities offer custom-designed sweat lodges. Even so, American courts now mandate that Native religions must be treated seriously as religions.[21]

NAGPRA

The most important Native-related law in these years was the Native American Graves Protection and Repatriation Act of 1990 (NAGPRA), which provides a telling measure of the shift in mainstream attitudes toward Indian religious issues. In the legal environment created by NAGPRA, the government is now criticized for bending over backwards to support Native religious positions uncritically, exactly the opposite of the policies for which it was criticized fifty or one hundred years ago. We have truly come full circle.

NAGPRA was a response to a glaring social abuse, namely the ghoulish exploitation of Native remains in museums and even popular tourist attractions. Seeing the bones of one's recent ancestors displayed for an audience prepared to pay the price of admission would be a harrowing experience for anyone, but it was all the more dreadful for Native peoples, who have a strong religious regard for the material remains of the dead. Ancestors occupy a special place in many religious systems. NAGPRA called for the repatriation of such Native human remains. Indian bones that had long been gathering dust in various museums were to be restored to their tribes of origin, and special obligations were laid upon archaeologists who might come upon such remains in future. Any "Native American cultural items" found on federal land were to be restored to the "lineal descendants" of the peoples concerned, or where that could not be determined, to the tribe on whose land these remains were found.[22]

NAGPRA initiated a revolution in both the American archaeological profession and the practice of museum-keeping. Museums accepted the letter of the law, but in many cases went far beyond strict legal requirements to meet Native demands. Not only were remains returned, but henceforward, all displays that might potentially offend Indian sensibilities were altered or purged, with the Native community concerned having the final word. Controversial items might include photographs of excavations in which skeletons were featured. New concepts of Indian sovereignty meant that archaeologists wanting to maintain access to sites had to give enthusiastic support to at least the principle of cooperating with Native peoples, to pay attention to Native traditions and legends that they might otherwise have dismissed. The interpretation of such sites has to tread a very fine line between reflecting what archaeologists believe to be factual and acknowledging the beliefs of local people. This is all the more difficult when neighboring tribes tell mutually inconsistent myths.

The original grievances that NAGPRA was meant to remedy were so outrageous as to prevent criticism of what was in fact a truly radical measure, which went far toward establishing in federal law certain doctrines of Native religious thought. The problems with NAGPRA became apparent with a series of conflicts over archaeological discoveries, the most famous being the so-called Kennewick Man discovered in Washington State in 1996. Kennewick Man was deeply problematic because, ethnically, the nine-thousand-year-old remains had no connection with historic Indian populations. He represented a distinct racial type, probably from the western Pacific. Nor did he represent an isolated case, since all the very oldest remains found in North America belong to this non-Indian racial type, long-skulled and narrow-faced.[23]

Kennewick Man and his ancient counterparts have generated much speculation about the earliest settlement of the Americas. They challenge the long-established orthodoxy that ancient Paleo-Indians migrated across the land bridge from Siberia some fifteen thousand years ago, their path across the continent being marked by the Clovis spear points they left. Accumulating evidence now points to "pre-Clovis" settlement dating back to twenty thousand years or before and, crucially, suggests that settlement was ethnically diverse, being drawn from Eastern Asia and even, some believe, from Western Europe. If true, this could mean that the ancestors of modern-day Indians were not in fact the first Americans, and even that they might have displaced older stocks.

Contemporary Native leaders deeply resented these explosive theories. Under NAGPRA, however, and a sympathetic federal government, Indian activists were in a position to prevent such controversial research. NAGPRA explicitly established in law the doctrine that all human remains prior to 1492 must be ethnically Indian, and therefore that they are presumptively connected with some modern-day tribe. If human remains are discovered and dated to ten or twelve thousand years, the government must treat seriously the claim of the local Native people who claim him or her as an ancestor, so that the body must be given to that tribe for reburial, usually in secret, without detailed scientific analysis. This has been the fate of some of the oldest and most critical remains, including the 10,600-year-old Buhl Woman found in Idaho in 1989, and buried shortly afterwards by the Shoshone-Bannock tribes. Other remains are closed to scientific investigation during legal conflicts that can continue for many years. In the case of Kennewick Man, the nearest claimants were the three confederated tribes of the Cayuse, Umatilla, and Walla Walla, whose website explicitly states, "Since time immemorial, we have lived on the Columbia River Plateau."[24] On that basis, they requested the remains of someone they believed to be their distant ancestor.

In such hearings, a legal claim to remains could be staked by "the Indian tribe that is recognized as aboriginally occupying the area in which the objects were discovered."[25] But in this context, "aboriginal" is a questionable notion. Though many Native peoples have creation stories asserting that they have lived in a particular region since the beginning of time, historical or archaeological evidence often suggest a much shorter residence, perhaps of only a few centuries. Historical evidence might also suggest that tribal identities were much more fluid than Native traditions suggest, and that a given tribe emerged relatively recently. But in the new legal environment, authorities were required to treat seriously tribal claims to have lived in particular lands since the beginning of time, so that oral histories and creation myths both acquired a surprising credibility.

This approach receives academic support from Vine Deloria, Jr., whose book *Red Earth, White Lies* argues that alternative scientific approaches validate Native claims to extreme antiquity. To take an extreme example, he notes that local Native traditions parallel scientific accounts of the formation of Oregon's Three Sisters, the remnant of a giant volcano named Mount Multnomah. This would not be surprising if the events recalled dated back some centuries, but in this case, Mount Multnomah vanished in a giant eruption perhaps twenty-five million years ago. Deloria suggests either that the scientific geology is wholly wrong about dates, or that Indians have in fact been in America for millions of years. In either case, tradition should count as much as scientific theory. Based on such arguments, American Indian Creationism has become a serious force.[26]

Official respect for "aboriginal" claims is striking because of the implied attitude toward religious sensibilities. No government would consider prohibiting the investigation of dinosaur remains on the grounds that the findings might outrage Creationists, still less that such embarrassing bones be buried secretly to avoid giving offense; but NAGPRA comes close to limiting archaeology in the name of religious faith.

Setbacks?

Not all the legal conflicts during these years resulted in Native victories, and activists complain about the courts' failure to extend proper protection to Indian religious practices. We hear repeatedly about courts "chipping away at religious protections." In fairness, though, many of the disputed cases illustrate just how far Native peoples had come in terms of self-assertiveness, since they were making claims that would never have been contemplated a generation previously.

Many of the issues concerned public lands, which since the early twentieth century had been regarded as a national patrimony, to be conserved in national parks and monuments. By definition, such public treasures were not reserved for private use, but the designated lands included countless sites held sacred by Native peoples. Though Indians had no formal right of ownership to these sites, how far could they exercise control over their use? Since the 1970s, conflicts have erupted over many sites that Native peoples consider sacred, including Bear Butte in South Dakota, California's Mount Shasta, and Arizona's San Francisco Peaks.

One persistent issue involves Wyoming's Devil's Tower, which in 1906 was designated America's first national monument, and which has long been a magnet for climbers and campers. For Indians, though, the site is holy, and should not be climbed except for ritual purposes: "the rock represents a part of creation which we respect and honor."[27] Prior to the last quarter century, Native protests would have been ignored, but in the new mood of the 1990s, some judges were prepared to ban commercially led climbing, at least during sacred seasons. A white climbing guide responded that banning climbers was in practice a federal establishment of Indian religion. He also claimed to consider climbing an expression of his own spirituality. The National Park Service compromised by requesting a voluntary climbing ban during sacred seasons. Though apparently a defeat for Native religious activism, official willingness even to consider these demands marked a major change of sensibilities.

Other conflicts involved setbacks for Native peoples. While it was not difficult to convince a court or agency that a landmark such as Devil's Tower was a sacred site, what could be done about seemingly ordinary lands targeted for change or development? Conflicts arose over proposals to flood lands on which Native peoples traditionally had sacred places and burial grounds, or to build roads through forests in which Natives pursued their Vision Quests. In such cases, the Indian right to pursue their religion was indeed being impaired, and the courts admitted as much. On the other hand, given the lack of direct ownership, Indians had no right to protest official actions, whether as individuals or as nations. Federal courts generally refused to hear such broad attempts to veto development, and Indian claims received setbacks in cases like *Lyng v. Northwest Indian Cemetery Association,* when a majority of justices accepted that "government simply could not operate if it were required to satisfy every citizen's religious needs and desires."[28]

Logically, too, if Indian nations received recognition in such cases, might not their right to veto development extend to the whole country? For a religion based on the natural world, just which mountain or forest, what river or canyon, is *not* sacred land? Or which housing development is not standing on what was once pristine forest? And who decides? Many Indian nations remain deeply factionalized, and the concept of religious orthodoxy does not exist. Anyone can claim to declare a patch of ground sacred territory, and that will carry weight with some groups. No master list of known and accepted sacred sites exists, partly because many peoples treat such special locations as secret.

This problem of authority has emerged over major scientific projects such as the attempts to build telescopes on Arizona's Mount Graham. Although planners initially made every good-faith effort to ensure that no sacred lands were being infringed, activists soon argued that holy ground was being violated, that Mount Graham had a sanctity comparable to that of Sinai or Ararat, and therefore that "the telescope project violates the human rights and religious freedoms of Apache people."[29] Yet it is far from clear that the mountain ever enjoyed a holy status, and when asked for evidence that the site had any traditional sanctity, advocates responded that the decision relied on tribal mysteries too secret to be divulged. For liberals and environmentalists in the United States and Europe, the Mount Graham project was represented as a naked violation of Indian religion. Telescopes have been built, but only after protracted legal warfare that consumed both time and money. Nor was this case unique. In the Hopi country, a wrenching controversy in the 1990s involved the quarrying of Arizona's Woodruff Butte, which contained perhaps a dozen shrines of great sanctity. The Hopi, however, refused to identify these sites specifically, to the frustration of the white landowners, who countered (unfairly) that claims were being invented as needed.[30]

The only issue in which Native religions failed to win decisive advances was in the use of peyote, and that is admittedly a large exception. Even in the new atmosphere sympathetic to Indian religious rights, claims to use a hallucinogenic drug were still controversial, all the more so at the height of the war on drugs that defined criminal justice policy during the 1980s. The key legal decision was *Smith*—more fully, *Employment Division, Department of Human Resources of Oregon v. Smith* (1990). Two Natives fired for peyote use were denied unemployment compensation because their dismissal was the direct result of their misconduct, that is, their drug use. The U.S. Supreme Court upheld the decision, despite a number of earlier decisions demanding that government must show a "compelling interest" in regulating religion. By reducing the "compelling" standard, the court opened the way to much greater regulation of all religions, creating a backlash among many mainstream religious denominations. The ensuing legal and political battles echo to this day, but for present purposes, *Smith* showed once again how often Native religious practices establish the boundaries of what is and is not acceptable religious conduct.[31]

The issue involved some of the dilemmas familiar from NAGPRA disputes, and brought government close to giving active preference to Native religion. In 1994, Congress attempted to defend the right to peyote use while avoiding a legalization that would open the drug to all users. It stated that "the use, possession, or transportation of peyote by an Indian who uses peyote in a traditional manner for bona fide ceremonial purposes in conjunction with the practice of a traditional Indian religion is lawful, and shall not be prohibited by the United States or any State." The plausible-sounding defense of "traditional" religion is weakened by the fact that the peyote religion is only around a century old, making it younger historically than (say) Christian Science. This issue demonstrates once again how difficult it is for governments to define what is proper or bona fide in religious matters.[32]

Counterattack

The resurgence of Native religion was accompanied by intense conflict with those who believed themselves to be following Native ways. There is an obvious irony here. In 1900, Indians faced an enormous danger of repression and cultural annihilation from those who despised their spiritual traditions, which they could not or would not understand. A century later, many Indians felt instead that their greatest enemies were those white people who were striving so hard to imitate and adopt those same rituals and beliefs. Whereas Indian religions had once been stigmatized as "cults," that is, as bogus religions, Native peoples now deployed that very same loaded term against the white wannabes.

Indian criticisms of neo-Native activity developed during the 1980s, originally in pamphlets and newspaper articles, but soon spreading to direct action. Seminars and ceremonies organized by figures like Sun Bear met with protests and disruption. More commonly, New Age leaders were attacked in the activist press, and extensively on the Internet as this became more widely accessible. Simple polemics were accompanied by exposés of particular leaders and groups. New Age entrepreneurs may be outnumbered by the activists seeking to expose and condemn them, including groups such as Cherokees Against Twinkies (CAT), which targets what it regards as bogus websites. One activist website offers tips on "how to recognize an exploiter":

> Leaders who demand exorbitant lecture fees and offer to travel all over to country to spread their spiritual 'knowledge' should be avoided at all costs. Native American spiritual practices are specific to geography. Legitimate teachers *do not leave their communities*. Our spiritual practices vary greatly from region to region. . . . Plastic Shamans who travel all over the world are usually cult leaders. . . .Use of the term "Shaman" alone is a good indicator of fraud. Native leaders don't use this term. . . . Mention of UFO's, Earth Changes or government cover-ups. . . . Positive comments from Europeans, especially Germans, almost always indicate a fraudulent site.[33]

A "Wall of Shame" claims to "sound the alarm on Nuage swindles!" The site seeks to expose most of the leading New Age activists, charging them variously with deceptive practices (falsely claiming Native heritage), greed, or simple foolishness. "Many of them hang around legitimate Native communities like sharks, looking for any little detail that can make them look credible and help them polish their cons." Typical descriptions of entrepreneurs include "a most offensive attempt to completely assimilate Native American spirituality into the whitest-of-the-white, squeaky-clean-Christianity. . . . Another plastic medicine woman who went through past lives regression and found spirit guides to tell her to move to New Mexico and start looking for that sucker that's re-born every minute." Such condemnations look mild when compared with the vituperative attacks on genuine Indians who have reached out to white audiences, like Wallace Black Elk.[34]

The most comprehensive and aggressive of the activist statements was the *Declaration of War Against Exploiters of Lakota Spirituality*, published by traditional spiritual leaders in 1993.[35] The elders complained about:

> the unspeakable indignity of having our most precious Lakota ceremonies and spiritual practices desecrated, mocked and abused by non-Indian "wannabes," hucksters, cultists, commercial profiteers and self-styled "New Age shamans" and their followers; . . . with horror and outrage we see this disgraceful expropriation of our sacred Lakota traditions has reached epidemic proportions in urban areas throughout the country . . . our precious Sacred Pipe is being desecrated through the sale of pipestone pipes at flea markets, powwows, and "New Age" retail stores . . . sacrilegious "Sun Dances" for non-Indians are being conducted by charlatans and cult leaders who promote abominable and obscene imitations of our sacred Lakota Sun Dance rites.

In response to these abuses, the elders "hereby and henceforth declare war against all persons who persist in exploiting, abusing and misrepresenting the sacred traditions and spiritual practices of our Lakota, Dakota and Nakota people." Native peoples should identify and resist these activities "utilizing whatever specific tactics are necessary and sufficient—for example demonstrations, boycotts, press conferences, and acts of direct intervention." This zero-tolerance policy extended to Native leaders who tried to authorize "the expropriation of our ceremonial ways by non-Indians." Any such leader should be regarded merely as a "white man's shaman."

Neo-Native teachers reacted strongly against these criticisms, and a lively rhetorical war proceeds on the Internet. One target of the attacks is Brooke Medicine Eagle, a friend of both Sun Bear and Wallace Black Elk. She rejects the criticisms as "stunning examples of just the kind of fighting and separation the prophecies had urged us to forsake in order to pursue unity and a New Age of harmony among All Our Relations."[36] But calls for unity seem doomed to failure when Native groups utterly reject any claim that the New Agers share in their cultural inheritance.

Roots of Resistance

Why was the resistance so fierce? The reasons were partly practical but largely symbolic. Native activists were disturbed to see outsiders apparently stealing their treasured rituals and practices, often in such a crude and inaccurate form that they constituted a kind of blasphemy. Pipes and other sacred symbols were not to be bandied around as commercial objects. The offense was worse when entrepreneurs, white or Indian, were profiting from this merchandising, demanding admission fees to Medicine Wheel ceremonies or training workshops. In the 1980s, Sun Bear charged $100 for participation in his Medicine Wheel ceremonies, $150 for a Vision Quest. And this at a time when, even allowing for all the recent economic advances, most Native communities still live in a state of economic devastation. Much of the hostility against white adoptions of Native rites grew from deep-rooted class resentment.

From the point of view of Native activists, a solid indictment could be mounted against neo-Nativism. They could argue, plausibly, that the package in which Native religion was marketed was deeply untrue to the original, and that the New Age borrowings often looked trivializing and downright flaky. Lisa Aldred remarks that "some of the incidents denounced as most offensive include Sun Dances held on Astroturf, sweats held on cruise ships with wine and cheese served, and sex orgies advertised as part of 'traditional Cherokee ceremonies.'" The last reference is to the controversial encounters organized by the Deer Tribe Métis Medicine Society, meetings that detractors have denounced as a "New Age sex club." Native activists were furious when HBO's adult series *Real Sex* presented these activities as authentic Cherokee tradition.[37]

Since the rise of the modern Red Power movement in the 1960s, Indian activists have often used a strategy of "How would you like it?," imagining alternative realities in which white people were confined to squalid reservations and denied the right to worship in their own churches and synagogues. In the case of the pseudo-Indian groups, the analogy might run as follows. Imagine a society in which people who know next to nothing about Christianity are proclaiming themselves as priests, or more likely as popes and bishops. Suppose further that they use the sacred symbols of the faith, such as the Eucharist, in trivial or blasphemous ways, mixed with the rituals of a dozen different systems, sacred and secular. In such a setting, it would be no defense to claim that the would-be popes had received the imprimatur of someone claiming Christian credentials, least of all if that person was known to sell certificates of popehood to anyone who asked.

And what a simple religion the Native tradition must be if it can be picked up so easily! As Andy Smith argues in an article aimed at "all those who were Indian in a former life":

> Nowadays, anyone can be Indian if she wants to be. All that is required is that a white woman be Indian in a former life or that she take part in a sweat lodge or be mentored by a 'medicine woman' or read a 'how to' book. . . . A few days spent on a reservation, and a few hours reading a book about our ceremonies, do not authorize a person to put on imitation Sioux rituals.

The popularity of such events could deceive outsiders into thinking this eclectic and deeply money-oriented movement had anything substantial to do with Indian realities. "Ceremonies are crossing tribal boundaries and mixing until it is hard to tell which rituals are authentic and which ones are made up." One Onondaga leader argues that "non-Indians have become so used to all this hype on the part of impostors and liars that when a real Indian spiritual leader tries to offer them useful advice, he is rejected. He isn't 'Indian' enough for all these non-Indian experts on Indian religion." At a time when authentic Native religions had only recently established their legal validity, it was all the more necessary to resist imitators who threatened to discredit them. Claims to sacred sites might be weakened if these same places also became venues for New Age extravaganzas.[38]

Native activists portrayed the neo-Native leaders as confidence tricksters and their customers as their gullible marks. One satire of neoshamanic commercialism offers a mock handbill with the slogan "Become an Urban Shaman! . . . This is the antidote to alienation you've been waiting for: your direct line to the Nature Spirits! . . . Your life will be transformed or your Mana back!"[39] A trenchant parody of white wannabes is found in the 1995 Canadian film *Dance Me Outside* (based on a story by W. P. Kinsella). Robert is a white Toronto lawyer married to Illiana, a Native woman. When the couple visit the reservation, the mother plots to bring Illiana together with her (Indian) old flame, but to accomplish this Robert has to be gotten out of the way for a night. A group of Illiana's young relatives accomplish this by promising to initiate Robert into the tribe, through a series of ludicrous rituals that they are clearly making up as they go along. (When the men state their sacred totemic names, the best one can offer is "I am the Walrus.") At every stage, Robert not only devours every piece of bogus ceremonial, but obviously knows far more about it than the native youths. When told to seek his animal spirit, Robert is happy to dance naked through the woods, issue blood-curdling shrieks as he becomes one with his inner wolverine. He shouts and chants his pleasure at the thought of hunting and tearing the flesh of small mammals. Watching the performance, the young men are delighted: "Where did you find this guy? He's *excellent.*"

Apart from causing emotional offense to believers, the imitation of Native spirituality poses immediate practical dangers. The more non-Indians convinced themselves that they were following Native ways, the more inclined they were to seek out Native holy places, and to perform rituals or other actions there that were offensive to traditional people. Nudity and sexual freedom were a frequent complaint. For New Age visitors to sacred sites like Mount Shasta, nudity represents a return to innocence, and a joyous celebration. For Indians, though, the same activities suggest disrespect or blasphemy: would white visitors behave in this way in a church or synagogue? Other possible offenses include burying objects on sacred land or—a serious atrocity—burying the remains or distributing the ashes of a dead loved one. In white culture, such an action indicates respect, leaving the deceased in a place of beauty and holiness. In many Indian cultures, the same action amounts to desecration, while corpse-powder is the weapon of the most threatening witches.

Cultural Theft

By the 1980s, a visceral reaction against white imitators was grounded in scholarly theories, especially postcolonialism, with its critique of cultural appropriation or, rather, expropriation: cultural theft. The argument was based on power, of the exploitation of the weak by the strong. For a century, the dominant culture had tried to destroy Native society and its faiths. Now, having failed, members of that same culture were trying to steal what did not belong to them. To quote a 1994 protest against New Age sweat lodges at a Wellness festival:

> European-Americans have stolen Native lands, Native resources, Native children, Native cultural images, and more recently Native profits. Now,

some New Agers are taking Native American spirituality too. All of these thefts constitute violations of Native sovereignty—the inherent right of indigenous nations to govern themselves, and keep the lands, cultures, and economies that belong to them.

While empires stole raw materials from their occupied territories, white Americans were trying to steal the most basic cultural possessions from their subject peoples. No matter that the action was presented in terms of envious imitation; it was still theft.[40]

Equally troublesome for Native critics was the whole idea of whites' identifying with Indians, from relatively trivial actions such as adopting pseudo-Indian names, all the way to inventing whole pseudotribal identities and spurious revelations. Though presented as a tribute, a kind of solidarity with Indians, the adoption of Indian-ness is highly selective, and ignores most of the all-too-practical pressing issues facing Indian peoples in the modern world. As Andy Smith argues, "White 'feminists' want to become only partly Indian. They do not want to be part of our struggles for survival against genocide; they do not want to fight for treaty rights or an end to substance abuse or sterilization abuse. They do not want to do anything that would tarnish their romanticized notions of what it means to become an Indian." Smith and other critics were raising the complex issue of the relationship between race, class, and gender. Many of the white women attracted to Native spirituality saw in it a means of liberation from their own historical oppression. To achieve this, however, they were invading the cultural territory of the far-more-comprehensively oppressed, of disinherited races and nations. For these critics, pseudo-Indian-ness is in itself a form of anti-Indian racism, through which white people can deny accountability for their own past misdeeds:

> While New Agers may think that they are escaping white racism by becoming "Indian," they are, in fact, continuing the same genocidal practices of their forefathers/foremothers. . . . These people don't realize that genocide is more than the killing of the physical body, it includes the destruction of the culture and spirituality. And taking the spiritual practices and blending them with other culture's practices does effectively kill the spirituality.

Whites need to recall, humbly, that "Native Americans owe us *nothing*. Our culture's spiritual poverty is our own responsibility to explore and address creatively." Activist Russell Means complains, "When [whites] wanted our land, they just announced they had a right to it and therefore owned it. Now, being spiritually bankrupt themselves, they want our spirituality as well."[41]

Central to the postcolonial critique is the issue of voice, of who has the right to speak for an oppressed community. Indians have never lacked voices, in the sense that outsiders have usually been prepared to speak for them, to interpret them to the outside world. The difficulty is that even well-wishers have claimed the right to determine the Indians' best interests, regardless of their own wishes and feelings. Mabel Dodge effectively tried to rule Taos Pueblo, while on a larger scale, John Collier knew unquestioningly that his ideal vision was the correct path for all America's Native peoples. Sometimes such paternalism was beneficial, but generally, few things have harmed America's Indians more than the actions of those who thought they knew what was in their best interests. Today, non-Indians not only seek to practice Indian spirituality themselves, but to determine what is or is not appropriate to that tradition. Native activists still complain that New Age neo-Indians led opposition to Makah whaling. The more pseudo-Indians speak on such issues, the greater danger that the general public will mistake their voices for the authentic views of Native peoples, so that once again, Native voices will be silenced.

Yet even against such convincing arguments, a case can be made that neo-Native spirituality is a rather more positive development than its critics claim, and may well have a solid claim to be a legitimate religious movement in its own right. Sometimes, for instance, we read the checklists that activists offer so that a potential consumer can decide whether a particular entrepreneur is offering authentic Native spirituality ("plastic shamans who travel all over the world are usually cult leaders," and so on). These lists are shrewd, and to the extent that they prevent exploitation, they can be useful. But they all make certain bold assumptions about the nature of religion; about the role of authenticity and historicity, and the potential for change and development over time. Even if neo-Natives are not reproducing Native traditions accurately, does that mean that what they are doing is necessarily spurious or deceptive, or that it can never become legitimate or accepted in its own right? To take a specific example: if we assume that the New Age Medicine Wheel is a novel and even spurious invention, at what point does it become the symbol of a legitimate religious practice?

Ironically, the critique of New Age Indian spirituality rehearses many of the same issues that in earlier decades had arisen concerning the religious practices of the Indian nations themselves. Once again, the central question involves the definition of religion, and of what constitutes a "proper" and "acceptable" religion. And, just as important, who has the power to determine these issues?

Conclusion

Real Religion?

All religions are true for their time.
— Joseph Campbell

Over the course of the twentieth century, Euro-American attitudes to Native spirituality underwent a thorough transformation, from puzzled contempt to awed respect. In some ways, though, the same basic questions remain, and are still unresolved. If we grant that religions deserve respect, or at least tolerance, we still have to decide what exactly constitutes a "religion." In 1900, the question applied to the dances, rituals, and ceremonies that characterized the practice of Indian religions, the ways of life that white observers all too easily dismissed as corruptions of a primitive ideal. Today, a similar issue of authenticity arises about New Age adaptations of Indian spirituality. Do they represent a legitimate spiritual practice, or are they, too, degenerate and harmful? Are they no more than a troubling parody of a "real" spiritual tradition, namely, the ancient Native faiths?

Though the consequences of the debate are different from a century ago—nobody is discussing the forcible suppression of Neo-Indianism—the basic arguments remain. And even if persecution is not on the horizon, writers on Native issues still devote a remarkable amount of venom to attacking the New Age traditions. From this perspective, what the pseudo-shamans are doing is silly play-acting or disrespectful blasphemy, rather than authentic religion.

But what does "authentic" mean in this context? Religions, not just of the Native variety, are often portrayed as if they possess an ancient, pristine core of reality, which remains despite all the inevitable change and development. Once we have agreed on this identifiable core, we can see that a given adaptation represents a distortion or betrayal, even a blasphemous intrusion. Looking at religions, though, we must be struck by their fluid, dynamic quality, so that it is often hard to tell just what that ancient core might be, and, by implication, whether adaptations might be legitimate outgrowths. Of course, to assert that a religion changes is not to assert that it is false. In Catholic Christianity, the theme of change and development is exalted as one of the hallmarks of the tradition.

By what standard can we say that neo-Indianism is not a legitimate variant of traditional Native religion? Or, indeed, that it is not an authentic religious system in its own right? Once again, the presence of Native spiritualities, so different from mainstream definitions of religion, presses us to define the limits of mutual recognition and respect. And there is every indication that values of mutual toleration are going to become still more necessary in years to come. If anything, the use and abuse of Native spirituality by outsiders will become ever more widespread.

Onions and Olives

In approaching religious traditions of all kinds, we encounter a paradox that bedevils recent postmodern thought. Postmodernism offers a general skepticism of all creeds, rejecting all overarching explanations or metanarratives. Historical and literary truths are ultimately subjective. The assumption is that all such statements are ultimately assertions of power, which acquire their privileged status from the social and economic status of those with the power to establish their views as authoritative. In a postmodern view, religions or cultural traditions are natural targets for deconstruction, to determine whether these might be "onions or olives." Scholars strip away outer layers of meaning, but when they have finished, they differ about whether they will be left with some kind of solid core, like the stone of an olive, or with essentially nothing, as when one has stripped the layers of an onion.

This skeptical view is epitomized by a scene in Philip K. Dick's novel *The Man in the High Castle*, in which a debate rages over an object that may or may not be a priceless antique. "One has historicity, a hell of a lot of it. As much as any object ever had. And one has nothing. Can you feel it? You can't. You can't tell which is which. There's no 'mystical plasmic presence', no 'aura' around it." So is the object genuine? The dealer explains: "I'd have to prove it to you with some sort of document. A paper of authenticity. And so it's all a fake, a mass delusion. The paper proves its worth, not the object itself." And the paper itself is genuine only to the extent that it is vouched for by another piece of paper. Hence, "the word 'fake' meant nothing really, since the word 'authentic' meant nothing really."[1]

Yet having rejected absolute truth, postmodernists find themselves in the position of accepting the authority of some claims, which stem from historically oppressed groups, especially racial minorities. The conclusion seems to be that all historical or religious claims are constructed fictions; but those made by the historically powerless, such as Native communities, must be given privileged status. Standard academic historical or anthropological approaches to Native cultures must be suspect, as tools of colonial exploitation; but historical statements from those communities themselves must be valued as far as possible. No voice is authoritative, but some are more authoritative than others. Native religions are authentic, traditional, legitimate, and might be subjected to the sins of cultural theft or appropriation.

In recent controversies over American Indian spirituality, Native activists have protested against New Age groups they believe to have misrepresented their ethnic identity. In some instances, we can legitimately speak of claims being fraudulent, as when someone falsely advertises an item as of Navajo or Pueblo manufacture. In other cases, though, the objection is that the religious system on offer is deceptive or fraudulent. In a protest against the Maryland-based Sweetgrass Lodge, the Red Road Collective urges supporters to complain to that state's attorney general, on the grounds that:

> they have deliberately misrepresented themselves as Native American women and falsely advertised ceremonial practices that have nothing to do with any legitimate Native American spiritual practices. In addition, the use of the word "Sweetgrass" in the name of the site is an unqualified use of tribal symbolism, not to mention deeply offensive to Native American women when used in the context of this web site.[2]

Put another way, the New Age religions are "onions," wholly fictitious creations, which stand in contrast to the truth of Native faiths.

Without addressing the particular groups concerned, the claims made in this letter, which are typical of recent Native activism, are troubling. Critical, of course, is the word "legitimate," in the context of religious or spiritual practice. Provided a religion does not violate criminal law—for instance, by practicing human sacrifice—it is difficult to see how any tradition can be described as either legitimate or illegitimate, in terms of being treated as a bona fide religion. That is quite distinct from arguing which if any religions have a claim to divine truth, a point on which neither lawmakers nor social scientists have any right to comment.

We can agree immediately that much of the New Age synthesis that claims to be Indian has very poor credentials, in the sense of accurately reflecting the spiritual life of any authentic Native community, past or present. Frank Waters's Hopi universe reflected Frank Waters as much as it does the Hopi; Native American tarot cards and crystals are pure New Age constructs, with at best tenuous roots in Native practice; and the UFO and space mythologies attached to so-called Indian works have no Indian origins whatever. Much recent writing that affects to offer Indian traditions of healing should more accurately be described as popular therapy at best, psychobabble at worst. Probably, at least some of the leading neo-Indian gurus have very weak claims to Indian status, whether genetic or cultural, and most of what they preach is of very recent origin. In some cases, it is hard to argue with derogatory labels like "flakes" and "twinkies."

But having said all that, we can still ask what difference any of this makes to claims of legitimacy. A religion is not less valid because it is newly minted, nor even because its early development may contain elements of deceit. Mormonism offers an example here. We can debate at length whether Joseph Smith received an authentic revelation or whether his whole system, together with its scriptures, was the product of his fertile mind. But even if we take the most negative view, and assume that Smith was a liar and mountebank, can anyone doubt that he founded a real and powerful faith, an authentic religion, for which followers would lay down their lives? Still younger faiths are Wicca and neopaganism, which largely trace their origin to the 1954 publication of Gerald Gardner's book *Witchcraft Today*. This was a wildly imaginative work that in many ways should be regarded as creative fiction rather than the revelation of ancient paganism that it claimed to be. (One theory holds that Gardner's ideas grew out of a splinter faction of the pseudo-Indian Woodcraft movement founded by Ernest Thompson Seton, but that is another story.)[3] Though many neopagans will comfortably acknowledge the synthetic nature of their tradition, they do not see it as any less valid a religion. Religious reality can be taken at various levels. For many liberal Christians who doubt the literal historical truth of the Gospel accounts of Christ's resurrection, that event still is a life-transforming symbolic truth.

Relevant here is the classic legal statement on religious toleration offered by Supreme Court Justice Robert Jackson in the *Ballard* case of 1944. From Jackson's perspective, the Ballards offered a blatant case of religious deception. They had organized a bogus and deceptive cult, Mighty I AM, which taught "nothing but humbug, untainted by any trace of truth." But having said this, and having admitted the potential harm to "over-credulous people," Jackson stated that "the price of freedom of religion or of speech or of the press is that we must put up with, and even pay for, a good deal of rubbish."[4] Government and courts should not intervene to prevent religious experimentation, even when that was actively dangerous, and certainly not when it merely appeared outlandish or nontraditional.

In short, a "real" religion is one that people are prepared to treat as such, regardless of the historical or scholarly grounds on which their views are based. By that standard, the neo-Native religion of the New Age groups is as valid as any other, and deserves as much respect.

Stealing Religion

Nor is a religion less valid if it adapts, or even plagiarizes, an existing system. To some degree, all new religions do something like this, because followers like to believe that their beliefs can be traced to some kind of antiquity, or else are rooted in an existing community. Sometimes existing scriptures of other faiths are adapted, or analogous documents invented. Alternatively, in order to give an impression of roots and traditions, the new religion will adopt the symbols and heroic figures of an older faith. Some New Age believers like to believe that what they are doing builds on the older foundations of venerated ancient movements like the Gnostics or the Sufis; others claim a Native American heritage.

Once religious ideas exist, they can and will be borrowed and adapted, though often not in ways of which their original adherents would approve. The history of primitive Christianity involved lengthy struggles against the Jewish communities who were appalled by the offensive claims of the so-called New Israel. Once they had established their separate identity, Christians themselves denied the claim of heretics to share the Christian title, and thus to use its rituals or sacred texts. As the Christian Father Tertullian complained of his Gnostic rivals, "not being Christians, they have acquired no right to the Christian Scriptures." In the past few years, the Roman Catholic Church has sued independent "Catholic churches" in American cities, accusing these upstart denominations of deceiving believers by their use of the word "Catholic." In such cases, the church is effectively struggling to defend its brand name, its trademark.[5] Modern Jews are angered by the activities of messianic Jewish congregations, and reject their claims to authentic Jewish status. Instead, messianic Jews are viewed as a deceptive cult, and the term "Jews" in this context is often placed in quotes.

Perhaps we cannot exactly say that religions cannot be copyrighted, since some newer faiths such as Scientology fight hard to defend their doctrines as intellectual property. Usually, though, such resistance is futile. As Gary Snyder argues, rebutting Native activists, "Spirituality is not something that can be 'owned' like a car or a house."[6] Ideas spread and faiths evolve, whether or not the parent religions approve. Usually, this is accepted as a fact of religious life, if not greeted with enthusiasm. Jews do not picket the Easter Vigil service of the Episcopal Church, which includes the proclamation, "This is the night when You brought our fathers, the children of Israel, out of bondage in Egypt," however inaccurate this statement might seem historically and ethnically. Nor do mainline Christians demonstrate outside churches of the Latter-day Saints, protesting their alleged falsifications of Christian doctrine.

If we press the delicate idea of legitimacy, no religion has anything like the immemorial antiquity that it claims. That old-time religion often isn't. Judaism has constantly reinvented itself while always claiming to be building on ancient roots. Radical monotheism and the monopolistic role of the Jerusalem Temple probably developed during the seventh and sixth centuries BCE, and both ideas were then retroactively attributed to ancient founders. Probably around the same time, the holy mountain of the faith, hitherto located in the "far north," was identified as Jerusalem's Mount Zion. To some extent, every religion maintains an illusion of antiquity, no matter how sweeping its modern transformations. Though Japanese Shintoism appears to be the immemorial religion of the land, it achieved its present form as recently as the eighteenth and nineteenth centuries. The Hinduism that proved so seductive to late Victorian Westerners had been transformed quite radically in recent decades, largely through contacts with Christianity and Western intellectual currents. Religious believers never like admitting that their practices or beliefs begin at a specific point of time, though they clearly do. One classic example of a novel movement claiming spurious ancient roots is the rigid fundamentalism that has developed, over the past century or two, among the scripture-based religions.

Ancient Roots

Since religions change over time, sometimes dramatically, we can reasonably ask what is the core tradition, the heritage from time immemorial, that neo-Natives are accused of violating when they pursue their own novel practices. Just as we can ask about the core identity of Judaism or Hinduism, we can explore what is "real" Native American religion. For oral and primal religions, such as the Native American faiths, it is difficult to determine just what their ancient core beliefs would have been, since we usually see them through the eyes of missionaries or ethnologists, and the presence of those aliens has already affected the society. This is a classic dilemma in anthropology as much as physics: the presence of the experimenter transforms the experiment.

Yet even if we could accurately reconstruct Indian religious beliefs and practices as they had existed prior to Contact—in 1400, say—this would not mean that we would have reached an authentic and immemorial core. In the Southwest, where the archaeological record is so rich, we can clearly trace the rise and fall of religious movements and practices. Though the Anasazi world clearly had kiva structures, they played a different social role than they did in the historical Pueblo world. And while it grew from older roots, the kachina cult itself reached maturity only around 1300. (The Hopi themselves believe that their religion already existed when they first emerged into the present Fourth World.)[7] As in any dynamic society, Native American religions have changed over time, and they have been influenced by new forces from external cultures.

We should not automatically accept claims that particular tribes have "always been" more or less where they first appear in the historic record, or that they have always venerated particular mountains, rivers, or natural features in that location. This is a controversial issue, since ancient land claims are so critical to contemporary debates over tribal rights, but these rights are well enough grounded without having to reject a great deal of historical and archaeological evidence. Time and again, we find that claims of being rooted in a particular sacred soil are made by tribes that we know moved to their present location relatively recently. The Navajo believe that the Creator gave them a special territory located between four sacred mountains in the Four Corners region, and that they have always lived within these boundaries. Many Navajos will also happily acknowledge that their ancestors migrated from the northwestern regions of the continent, and arrived within their sacred homeland only during the fifteenth century, perhaps around the time that Columbus set sail. That knowledge does not detract from the sacred quality of the four mountains, or suggest that there is anything "false" about the Navajo religious tradition. In practice, though, "time immemorial" can span just a few centuries.

Other claims about sacred landscapes are equally questionable. Though Lakota tradition firmly associates that people with the Black Hills, all evidence suggests that that people originated much farther east, until they were driven west by tribes armed with new European firearms. In the early eighteenth century, these nations were still concentrated in Minnesota. Nevertheless, modern activists hold that the Black Hills really have belonged to those tribes since time immemorial, and that anyone who claims to the contrary must be motivated by prejudice. And such claims acquire real foundations in a relatively short historical span: the Lakota fought desperately to keep whites out of their sacred Black Hills. Who can say that their beliefs were less than legitimate?

If antiquity is to be the criterion of authentic religion, then this would give New Age religions a definite advantage over some Native practices. Though the New Age movement as we know it today is a recent development, its components are centuries old, tracing back in some instances to nineteenth century Spiritualism and Mesmerism, in others to the esoteric world of the Renaissance. It is at least as old as the Native American peyote movement, which likewise draws on ancient practices, but incorporated into a ceremonial structure that began just over a century ago. Just as the Euro-American New Age borrows heavily from native cultures, so peyote congregations draw massively on Christianity. Like the New Age itself, peyotism is a classic new religious movement.

The Future

An excellent case can be made for putting up with the foibles and follies of other religions, including those that appear to trespass on one's own territory. Tolerance should become still more necessary in coming years, since there is no sign that mainstream white society is going to lose its fascination with Native religions. Also, any kind of neo-Indian movement that emerges in the near future will have at its disposal a still-wider repertoire of practices and themes than did earlier generations. In addition to the core ideas of Native spirituality, the pseudo-Native spiritual package now includes UFOs, reincarnation, channeling, tarot cards, and so much else that over the years has attracted the magpie collector instinct of the New Agers. (And, let it be said, these more arcane interests have been fed by Native writers themselves: flakiness is not a Euro-American prerogative.) Never before have consumers been offered such a staggering range of books and other products describing Native spirituality in such enthusiastic detail, while the Internet has made this cornucopia ever more widely available. Yet the more white people sympathize with Indians and try to show solidarity with them, the more they do so through forms of imitation that are seen as insensitive profanation rather than sincere flattery. We can reasonably assume both that new forms of playing Indian will emerge in a future social or economic crisis, and that the particular kind of play will be quite as troubling to Native peoples.

But any future disputes over the appropriation of Native spirituality will be different from those of bygone years. American Indians today are not just more willing to assert their rights—the consequence of four decades of militancy—but their newfound economic muscle also gives them the political clout to implement their demands. We are in a very different environment from the 1960s, when Indians watched in passive bemusement as the counterculture absorbed and imitated their religious practices. Here, too, the Internet has played its role, since it is no longer possible for non-Native gurus to organize their seminars and workshops without attracting the attention of Indian activists, and without drawing protesters, whether direct or electronic. The more pseudo-Indian tribes and lodges move online to draw consumers, the more easily they can be tracked and confronted.

Religious controversies might also be affected by looming political debates. Conceivably, Indian activism could increase dramatically over the coming years, as the tribes' sovereign character generates ever-more resentment, more legal and constitutional conflicts, and perhaps provokes demands to curb their autonomy. Indian sovereignty caused little debate when the tribes were pauperized, but their new wealth has made them alarming neighbors for states and cities, and bitter legal confrontations are only a matter of time. Before long, acrimonious debates over Indian political rights and cultural independence could spill over into religious controversies involving the control or proprietorship of spiritual practices, access to sacred lands, or challenges to claims of tribal identity.

We can imagine the disputes already. Who has access to this sacred mountain at a particular season? Can a tribe limit access to people holding correct ethnic credentials? If so, can an individual use genetic evidence to assert a right of access? And what about workshops on Native spirituality: by what right does this person claim to be a Cherokee or an Apache, or to teach the practices of that tribe? If she cannot document the claim, can she be prosecuted for fraudulent advertising? Might tribes invoke trademark protections for their sacred symbols? How far can spiritual information be defined as a saleable commodity subject to copyrighting and protection? Will courts assert rights of "cultural privacy," however much these might conflict with individual or commercial rights?[8] Such questions would have seemed absurd a few years ago, but the vast influx of gambling wealth gives the tribes access to unprecedented legal expertise, as well as political influence. The resulting confrontations will probably generate some intriguing case law, and yet again, the process of accommodating Native religious beliefs will stretch and redefine our concepts of religious liberty.

Still Dreaming

Beyond doubt, the lively non-Native interest in American Indian life sometimes expresses itself in ways that are rude, intrusive, or downright obnoxious. Examples are legion. When attending a sacred ceremony like a Pueblo dance, it beggars belief that so many tourists defy the repeated polite requests not to take photographs, or to stay out of restricted areas. Respect for religious sensibilities apart, the contempt for the community's hospitality is despicable. So many people brought up on reservations have comparable childhood memories, of white tourists wandering into private houses uninvited in order to gawp at the quaint Indians. Often, the appropriations of Native traditions that we see in books and workshops can be just as grossly insensitive, and have no motive beyond making money. Native people's anger at such behavior is easily understood.

Yet having said this, so much of the interest in Indian spiritual life has been positive in its tone and in its effects. Indians themselves have benefited immensely. If not for the passion for Indians as otherworldly mystics, as sons and daughters of Mother Earth, white attitudes through most of the past eighty years would not have been so largely favorable, and would not have supported the sweeping legal concessions of recent decades. If not for that underlying sympathy, those measures might well have provoked a widespread populist response. Sometimes, stereotypes can help as well as hurt.

Also, despite the instances of exploitation that undoubtedly have occurred, much of the non-Native interest has been sincere, respectful, and motivated by a real desire to learn from the spiritual powerhouse of Native religions, and, where possible, to absorb some of those strengths. The results of that encounter have been overwhelmingly positive, and have had an impact far beyond what might be expected from the very limited numbers of Native Americans. Ever since white Americans began to recognize the spiritual treasures to be found in these ancient communities, Native religions have offered new ideals, which have affected the aspirations of the mainstream faiths. However mangled or mistranslated their words, the ideas of Chief Seattle and Smohalla still provide powerful models that demand a response. Knowing of the existence of the primal faiths has forced Christians and Jews to ask themselves about their own attitudes to the natural world, to the sacred landscape, to the environment, to the spirituality of the body. Though at first, these ideas may be cultivated in new and fringe religions, those laboratories of American spirituality, ultimately they influence the mainstream institutions, with lasting consequences. And as long as the dreamlike image of the "white man's Indian" continues to evolve and mutate, there is no sign that this process of influence and adaptation will cease.

Notes

Abbreviations

AIQ	*American Indian Quarterly*
CC	*Christian Century*
JAF	*Journal of American Folklore*
MRW	*Missionary Review of the World*
NYT	*New York Times*

Chapter 1

1. Philip J. Deloria, *Playing Indian* (New Haven, Conn.: Yale University Press, 1998). Compare Elizabeth S. Bird, ed., *Dressing in Feathers* (Boulder, Colo.: Westview Press, 1996); Shari M. Huhndorf, *Going Native* (Ithaca, N.Y.: Cornell University Press, 2001).
2. C. Richard King and Charles Fruehling Springwood, eds., *Team Spirits* (Lincoln: University of Nebraska Press, 2001).
3. Robert F. Berkhofer, *The White Man's Indian* (New York: Vintage, 1978); Gretchen M. Bataille and Charles L.P. Silet, eds., *The Pretend Indians* (Ames: The Iowa State University Press, 1980); Jacquelyn Kilpatrick, *Celluloid Indians* (Lincoln: University of Nebraska Press, 1999); Peter C. Rollins and John E. O'Connor, eds., *Hollywood's Indian* (Lexington: University Press of Kentucky, 1999); Andrew MacDonald, Gina MacDonald, and Maryann Sheridan, *Shape-Shifting* (Westport, Conn.: Greenwood Press,

2000); Gretchen M. Bataille, ed., *Native American Representations* (Lincoln: University of Nebraska Press, 2001); Armando José Prats, *Invisible Natives* (Ithaca, N.Y.: Cornell University Press, 2002).

4. Catherine L. Albanese, *Nature Religion in America* (Chicago: University of Chicago Press, 1991); and Albanese, *Reconsidering Nature Religion* (Harrisburg, Pa.: Trinity Press, International, 2002).

5. In the history of American religion, the figure of "the Indian" has been almost as malleable as that of Jesus, who is similarly reinvented by each new generation: Philip Jenkins, *Hidden Gospels* (New York: Oxford University Press, 2001); Stephen Prothero, *American Jesus* (New York: Farrar Straus Giroux, 2003).

6. For the Smokis, see Etta J. Oliver, "Mystic Dances of the Painted Desert," *Travel* 47 (Jul. 1926): 27–29. The group operated from 1921 to 1990. For the existing Smoki Museum, in Prescott, Arizona, see *http://www.smokimuseum.org*.

7. Ed McGaa, *Mother Earth Spirituality* (San Francisco: Harper San Francisco, 1990); Thomas E. Mails, *Secret Native American Pathways* (Tulsa, Okla.: Council Oak Books, 1988); Jamie Sams, *Sacred Path Cards* (San Francisco: Harper San Francisco, 1990); Sams, *The Thirteen Original Clan Mothers* (San Francisco: Harper San Francisco, 1994); Paul B. Steinmetz, *Meditations with Native Americans: Lakota Spirituality* (Santa Fe, N.M.: Bear, 1984).

8. Sun Bear, Wabun Wind, and Crysalis Mulligan, *Dancing with the Wheel* (Lithia Springs, Ga: New Leaf Distributors, 1992); Vicki May and Cindy V. Rodberg, *Medicine Wheel Ceremonies* (Happy Camp, Calif.: Naturegraph Publishers, 1996); Marie Herbert, *Healing Quest* (Boston: Red Wheel/Weiser, 1997); Roy I. Wilson, *Medicine Wheels* (New York: Crossroad/Herder & Herder, 2001); E. Barrie Kavasch, *The Medicine Wheel Garden* (New York: Bantam, 2002); Kenneth Meadows, *Earth Medicine*, rev. ed. (Edison, N.J.: Castle Books, 2002); Marie-Lu Lörler, *Shamanic Healing within the Medicine Wheel* (Las Vegas, Nev.: Brotherhood of Life Books, 2003).

9. Rayna Green, "The Tribe Called Wannabee," *Folklore* 99(1) (1988): 30–55; Susan Mumm, "Aspirational Indians," in *Belief Beyond Boundaries*, ed. Joanne Pearson (Burlington, Vt.: Ashgate, 2002), 103–31.

10. Donald S. Lopez, *Prisoners of Shangri-La* (Chicago: University of Chicago Press, 1998). For Curtis, see "Lives 22 Years with Indians to Get Their Secrets," *NYT*, 16 Apr. 1911.

11. Ward Shepard, "Our Indigenous Shangri-La," *Scientific Monthly* 62 (Feb. 1946): 158–64, about the Hopi nation. The term "Shangri-La" stems from James Hilton's 1933 novel *Lost Horizon*.

12. Geary Hobson, "The Rise of White Shaman as a New Version of Cultural Imperialism," in *The Remembered Earth*, ed. Geary Hobson (Albuquerque, N.M.: Red Earth Press, 1978), 100–108; Alice B. Kehoe, "Primal Gaia: Primitivists and Plastic Medicine Man," in *The Invented Indian*, ed. James A. Clifton (New Brunswick, N.J.: Transaction Publishers, 1990), 193–209; Andy Smith, "For All Those Who Were Indian in a Former Life," *Cultural Survival Quarterly* (Winter 1994), at *http://users.telenet.be/gohiyuhi/articles/art00018.htm*; Terry Macy and Daniel Hart, *White Shamans and Plastic Medicine Men* (video, 1995); Christopher Ronwanien:Te Jocks, "Spirituality for Sale," *AIQ* 20(3–4) (1996): 415–31; Ward Churchill, *A Little Matter of Genocide* (San Francisco: City Lights, 1998); Churchill, *Fantasies of the Master Race* (San Francisco: City Lights, 1998); Laurie Anne Whitt, "Cultural Imperialism and the Marketing of Native North America," in *Natives and Academics*, ed. Devon A. Mihesuah (Lincoln: University of Nebraska Press, 1998), 139–71; Deloria, *Playing Indian*, 154–80; Laura E.

Donaldson, "On Medicine Women and White Shame-Ans: New Age Native Americanism and Commodity Fetishism as Pop Culture Feminism," *Signs* 24(3) (1999): 677–96; Lisa Aldred, "Plastic Shamans and Astroturf Sun Dances," *AIQ* 24(3) (2000): 329–52; Dagmar Wernitznig, *Going Native Or Going Naïve? White Shamanism and the Neo-Noble Savage* (Lanham, Md.: University Press of America, 2003).

13. For the very different Canadian story, see John Webster Grant, *Moon of Wintertime* (Toronto, Can.: University Of Toronto Press, 1984); James R. Miller, *Skyscrapers Hide the Heavens* (Toronto, Can.: University of Toronto Press, 1989); Boyce Richardson, *People of Terra Nullius* (Vancouver, Can.: Douglas & McIntyre, 1994); R. Bruce Morrison and C. Roderick Wilson, eds., *Native Peoples*, 2nd ed. (Toronto, Can.: Oxford University Press, 1997); Olive Patricia Dickason, *Canada's First Nations*, 2nd ed. (Don Mills, Can.: Oxford University Press, 1997).

14. The literature on the realities of Native religions is vast and authoritative. See Åke Hultkrantz, ed., *Belief and Worship in Native North America* (Syracuse, N.Y.: Syracuse University Press, 1981); Hultkrantz, *Religions of the American Indians* (Berkeley: University of California Press, 1981); Howard L. Harrod, *Becoming and Remaining a People* (Tucson: University of Arizona Press, 1995); Jace Weaver, ed., *Native American Religious Identity* (Maryknoll, N.Y.: Orbis, 1998); Lee Irwin, ed., *Native American Spirituality* (Lincoln: University of Nebraska Press, 2000); Joel W. Martin, *The Land Looks After Us* (New York: Oxford University Press, 2001); Joseph Epes Brown with Emily Cousins, *Teaching Spirits* (New York: Oxford University Press, 2001).

15. Carol Lee Higham, *Noble, Wretched, and Redeemable* (Albuquerque: University of New Mexico Press, 2000).

16. Kenneth R. Philp, *John Collier's Crusade for Indian Reform, 1920–1954* (Tucson: University of Arizona Press, 1977); Lawrence C. Kelly, *The Assault on Assimilation* (Albuquerque: University of New Mexico Press, 1983); Alvin M. Josephy, *Now that the Buffalo's Gone* (Norman: University of Oklahoma Press, 1985), 77–123.

17. John Thomas Noonan, *The Lustre of Our Country* (Berkeley: University of California Press, 1998).

18. Mark Stephen Massa, *Charles Augustus Briggs and the Crisis of Historical Criticism* (Minneapolis: Fortress Press, 1990); Washington Gladden, *Who Wrote the Bible?* (Boston: Houghton Mifflin, 1891); Charles Augustus Briggs, *The Authority of Holy Scripture*, 2nd ed. (New York: Scribner, 1891); *Essays in Modern Theology and Related Subjects* "gathered and published as a testimonial to Charles Augustus Briggs" (New York: Scribner, 1911). The impact of the new criticism on religious belief is suggested by Harold Frederic's novel *The Damnation of Theron Ware* (New York: Stone & Kimball, 1896). For the feminist critique, see Matilda Joslyn Gage, *Woman, Church and State* (Chicago: C. H. Kerr, 1893); Elizabeth Cady Stanton, *The Woman's Bible* (Boston: Northeastern University Press, 1993). James Mooney, *The Ghost-Dance Religion and the Sioux Outbreak of 1890* (North Dighton, Mass.: JG Press, 1996), 290.

19. Richard H. Seager, *The Dawn of Religious Pluralism* (Lasalle, Ill.: Open Court, 1993); and Seager, *The World's Parliament of Religions* (Bloomington: Indiana University Press, 1995); Philip Jenkins, *Mystics and Messiahs* (New York: Oxford University Press, 2000); Judith Snodgrass, *Presenting Japanese Buddhism to the West* (Chapel Hill: University of North Carolina Press, 2003).

20. Martin E. Marty, *Modern American Religion* (Chicago: University of Chicago Press), vol. 1, *The Irony of It All* (1986); vol. 2, *The Noise of Conflict* (1991); and vol. 3, *Under God Indivisible* (1996).

21. Jenkins, *Mystics and Messiahs.*

22. Carolyn N. Long, *Religious Freedom and Indian Rights* (Lawrence: University Press of Kansas, 2000); Garrett Epps, *To an Unknown God* (New York: St. Martin's Press, 2001).

23. R. C. Gordon-McCutchan, *The Taos Indians and the Battle for Blue Lake* (Santa Fe, N.M.: Red Crane Books, 1995).

24. Francis Parkman, *The Jesuits in North America in the Seventeenth Century* (Boston: Little, Brown, 1867), 83–87.

25. Roger Sandall, *The Culture Cult* (Boulder, Colo.: Westview, 2000).

26. John M. Oskison, "Making an Individual of the Indian," *Everybody's Magazine* 16 (Jun. 1907): 723.

27. Robinson Jeffers, "New Mexican Mountain."

28. Deloria, *Playing Indian,* 156.

29. Adele Heller and Lois Rudnick, eds., *1915: The Cultural Moment* (New Brunswick, N.J.: Rutgers University Press, 1991); Steven Watson, *Strange Bedfellows* (New York: Abbeville Press, 1991); W. Jackson Rushing III, *Native American Art and the New York Avant-Garde* (Austin: University of Texas Press, 1995); W. Jackson Rushing III, ed., *Native American Art in the Twentieth Century* (New York: Routledge, 1999); Sherry Lynn Smith, *Reimagining Indians* (New York: Oxford University Press, 2000). Not, of course, that Indians are the only group to be idealized when confidence in American values flags: see David Weaver-Zercher, *The Amish in the American Imagination* (Baltimore, Md.: Johns Hopkins University Press, 2001). For comparable black American uses of an idealized Africa, see Wilson J. Moses, *Afrotopia* (New York: Cambridge University Press, 1998).

30. Marsden Hartley, "Red Man Ceremonials; An American Plea for American Esthetics," *Art and Archaeology* 9 (Mar. 1920): 7–14; C. G. Jung, *Memories, Dreams, Reflections,* rev. ed. (New York: Vintage, 1965), 252; John Collier, *The Indians of the Americas* (New York: W. W. Norton, 1947), 15.

Chapter 2

1. Alvin M. Josephy, *Now that the Buffalo's Gone* (Norman: University of Oklahoma Press, 1985), 77–123; Nicholas Griffiths and Fernando Cervantes, eds., *Spiritual Encounters* (Lincoln: University of Nebraska Press, 1999); Ronald Niezen, ed., *Spirit Wars* (Berkeley: University of California Press, 2000); Daniel K. Richter, *Facing East from Indian Country* (Cambridge, Mass.: Harvard University Press, 2002).

2. Henry Warner Bowden, *American Indians and Christian Missions* (Chicago: University of Chicago Press, 1981); Clyde A. Milner II and Floyd A. O'Neil, eds., *Churchmen and the Western Indians, 1820–1920* (Norman: University of Oklahoma Press, 1985); Carol Lee Higham, *Noble, Wretched, and Redeemable* (Albuquerque: University of New Mexico Press, 2000). Catholic authorities could be very repressive, as with the kachina cult, but they tended to be more prepared to absorb and compromise. For the diversity of missionary responses, see Ramon A. Gutierrez, *When Jesus Came, the Corn Mothers Went Away* (Palo Alto, CA: Stanford University Press, 1991); Robert H. Jackson, *Indians, Franciscans, and Spanish Colonization* (Albuquerque: University of New Mexico Press, 1996); Carroll L. Riley, *The Kachina and the Cross* (Salt Lake City: University of Utah Press, 1999); Christopher Vecsey, *American Indian Catholics* (South Bend, Ind.: University of Notre Dame Press), vol. 1, *On the Padres' Trail* (1996); vol. 2, *The Paths of Kateri's Kin* (1997); and vol. 3, *Where the Two Roads Meet* (1999). For South American

policies, see Nicholas Griffiths, *The Cross and the Serpent* (Norman: University of Oklahoma Press, 1996).

3. *The True Pictures and Fashions of the People in That Part of America Now Called Virginia, Discovered By Englishmen,* at *http://etext.lib.virginia.edu/etcbin/jamestown-browsemod?id= J1009b* ; John Smith, *A Map of Virginia. With a Description of the Countrey, the Commodities, People, Government and Religion,* at *http://etext.lib.virginia.edu/ etcbin/jamestown-browse?id=J1008* . Roger Williams is quoted from Patrick Allitt, ed., *Major Problems in American Religious History* (Boston: Houghton Mifflin, 2000), 34; Jouvency from ibid, 31. In each English-language document, spelling has been modernized.

4. David Murray, "Spreading the Word," in Griffiths and Cervantes, *Spiritual Encounters,* 43–64; Norman Cohn, *Warrant for Genocide,* new ed. (New York: Serif, 2001); Debra Higgs Strickland, *Saracens, Demons, and Jews* (Princeton, N.J.: Princeton University Press, 2003). For the Indian response to the missionaries, see James P. Ronda, "We Are Well as We Are," *William and Mary Quarterly* 34(1977): 66–82.

5. Cotton Mather's "Though we know not *when . . .*" is quoted from Perry Miller, *The Puritans* (New York: Harper Torchbook, 1963), vol. ii, 503. The remark about Azazel is from Garry Wills, *Under God* (New York: Simon & Schuster, 1990), 140, and ibid., 138–43 for Mather's interpretation of the plagues. For "irradiated an Indian Wilderness" see Cotton Mather, *Magnalia Christi Americana,* eds. Kenneth B. Murdock and Elizabeth W. Miller (Cambridge, Mass: Belknap Press, 1977), 89. For the later influence of prophetic and providential ideas, see Christopher L. Miller, *Prophetic Worlds* (New Brunswick, N.J.: Rutgers University Press, 1985).

6. Mather's "horrid sorcerers and hellish conjurors" is quoted from Wills, *Under God,* 141. The descriptions of the *Powaw* are from Miller, *Puritans,* vol. ii, 505–7.

7. Alexander Whitaker, *Good News from Virginia Sent to the Counsell & Co. of Virginia, Resident in Virginia,* at *http://etext.lib.virginia.edu/etcbin/jamestown-browse?id=J1024.*

8. Spanish colonists were already deeply imbued with the conspiratorial view of witchcraft; see Fernando Cervantes, *The Devil in the New World* (New Haven, Conn.: Yale University Press, 1994).

9. Quoted in J. Manuel Espinosa, *The Pueblo Indian Revolt of 1696 and the Franciscan Missions in New Mexico* (Norman: University of Oklahoma Press, 1988), 33; Andrew L. Knaut, *The Pueblo Revolt of 1680* (Norman: University of Oklahoma Press, 1995); Peter Nabokov, ed., *Native American Testimony,* rev. ed. (New York: Penguin, 1999), 54. Joe S. Sando, "Popé, the Pueblo Revolt, and Native Americans in Early New Mexico," in *New Mexican Lives,* ed. Richard W. Etulain (Albuquerque: University of New Mexico Press, 2002).

10. Rev. 13: 13–14 (KJV).

11. Neal Salisbury, *Manitou and Providence* (New York: Oxford University Press, 1982), 137; Murray, "Spreading the Word."

12. Mary Beth Norton, *In the Devil's Snare* (New York: Knopf, 2002); Elaine G. Breslaw, *Tituba, Reluctant Witch of Salem* (New York: New York University Press, 1996).

13. Arthur C. Parker, *The Code of Handsome Lake, the Seneca Prophet* (Albany: University of the State of New York, 1913); Anthony F. C. Wallace, *The Death and Rebirth of the Seneca* (New York: Knopf, 1970). Jefferson's remark is from Russell Bourne, *Gods of War, Gods of Peace* (New York: Harcourt, Brace, 2002), 1.

14. F. G. Stevens, "Canadian Indians and the Great Spirit," *MRW,* Feb. 1917, 122

15. Howard A. Clark, "Conditions among the Navajo Indians," *MRW,* Dec. 1917, 917

16. "In a Neglected Country," *NYT,* 5 Oct. 1884. John Muir, *Travels in Alaska* (Boston: Houghton Mifflin, 1998).

17. "Alaska's Rise Told by Veteran Pastor," *NYT*, 28 Nov. 1927; Samuel Hall Young, *Alaska Days with John Muir* (New York: Fleming H. Revell, 1915).

18. Douglas Cole, *Captured Heritage* (Norman: University of Oklahoma Press, 1995), 30; W. Richard West, ed., *The Changing Presentation of the American Indian* (Seattle: University of Washington Press, 2000).

19. The Biblical reference is to Rev. 20: 1–3. The Spanish traveler is quoted in Curtis Schaafsma, "Pueblo Ceremonialism from the Perspective of Spanish Documents," in *Kachinas in the Pueblo World*, ed. Polly Schaafsma (Salt Lake City: University of Utah Press, 2000), 128.

20. John Gregory Bourke, *The Snake-Dance of the Moquis of Arizona* (New York: Scribner, 1884); "Dancing with Rattlesnakes," *NYT*, 2 Nov. 1884; Joseph C. Porter, *Paper Medicine Man* (Norman: University of Oklahoma Press, 1986). Compare C. Staniland Wake, *Serpent-Worship* (London: G. Redway, 1888); Wilfrid D. Hambly, *Serpent Worship in Africa* (Chicago: Field Museum of Natural History, 1931). The other southwestern phenomenon that shocked white Americans in these same years was the Penitentes: see "Painful Fanaticism," *NYT*, 22 Apr. 1876; "Purification by Torture," *NYT*, 26 Mar. 1883. Like the Snake Dance, their rituals would also become a popular tourist attraction.

21. Fanny Bandelier, *The Journey of Alvar Nuñez Cabeza De Vaca* (Chicago: Rio Grande Press, 1964). Early Spanish contacts in Florida are discussed in Marjory Stoneman Douglas, *The Everglades: River of Grass*, 50th anniversary ed. (Sarasota, Fla.: Pineapple Press, 1997); Ralph Linton, *The Sacrifice to the Morning Star by the Skidi Pawnee* (Chicago: Field Museum of Natural History, 1922).

22. W. H. Prescott, *History of the Conquest of Mexico* (New York: Harper, 1843).

23. "Find Tribal 'Murder Farm,'" *NYT*, 7 Jan. 1929; Paul S. Martin, *Lowry Ruin in Southwestern Colorado* (Chicago: Field Museum of Natural History, 1936). "Digs Up Ancient City of a Million Indians," *NYT*, 7 Sep. 1924. Cannibalism stories also emerged from the Pacific Northwest: see W. L. Beaseley, "Secret Cannibal Society of the Kwakiutl," *Scientific American*, 15 Aug. 1903, 120–22.

24. "Big Medicine Man Tortured," *NYT*, 12 Jan. 1902; Mary Hunter Austin, *The Land of Little Rain* (New York: Penguin 1997), 36–37; "Murder of Indian Medicine Woman," *NYT*, 20 Sep. 1903; Josephy, *Now that the Buffalo's Gone*, 77–123.

25. "A Peculiar Indian Custom—the Sun Dance," *NYT*, 22 Jul. 1871; "A Horrid Indian Festival" *NYT*, 16 Aug. 1882; for the Chicago event, see Cole, *Captured Heritage*, 129–30.

26. Frank Hamilton Cushing, *My Adventures in Zuñi* (Palo Alto, Calif.: American West Publishing Company, 1970), 50, 88.

27. Gilson Willets, "Most Un-American Part of the United States," *NYT*, 20 Aug. 1905.

28. F. W. Hodge, "Rites of the Pueblo Indians," *NYT*, 26 Oct. 1924.

29. Eliza McFeely, *Zuñi and the American Imagination* (New York: Hill & Wang, 2001), 68.

30. "Zuñis Torturing Witches," *NYT*, 9 Sep. 1897; "Indian Girl Poisoned for Witchcraft," *NYT*, 25 Nov. 1900; Mary Kay Morel, "The Zuñi Witchcraft Trial of Nick Tumaka," *Wild West* 11 (Feb. 1999): 24–28.

31. "Possessed of an insane desire" is from M. O. Scott, "Pagan Indians of Canada," *Canadian Magazine* 15 (Jul. 1900): 204–15; "Mounties on Long Trail to Barren Lands to Stop Chippewa Outbreak of 'Weetigo,'" *NYT*, 11 Feb. 1934. Algernon Blackwood's horror story "The Wendigo" appeared in 1910. Stories about Indian ghosts and superstitions were a media mainstay. See "Plan Dance to Lay Ghost; Seattle Indians Will Drive Away a Death-Dealing Spectre," *NYT*, 14 Jan. 1926; "Lake's Evil Spirit Is Near Coolidge; President's Route to Offices Skirts Domain of Old Black God Mudji Manitou," *NYT*, 8 Jul. 1928.

32. "Superstitious Neglect; Killed by the Treatment of the Medicine Man," *NYT*, 16 Nov. 1886; "Led to Death by Sorcerer," *NYT*, 17 Dec. 1909; "Buried His Baby Alive," *NYT*, 9 Nov. 1925; "Burial of Baby Alive Causes Second Murder," *NYT*, 2 Apr. 1925.

33. "The Klamath Indians; Something about the Modocs and Their Neighbors," *NYT*, 2 Jan. 1873; Peter Nabokov, ed., *Native American Testimony*, rev. ed. (New York: Penguin, 1999), 251–52.

34. "Find Tribal 'Murder Farm'."

35. "Indian Leader Dies Keeping Pagan Faith; 'Chief Isaacs' of the Onondagas Expires as Medicine Men Combat Evil Spirits," *NYT*, 1 Jun. 1929.

36. Audubon is quoted from Elémire Zolla, *The Writer and the Shaman* (New York: Harcourt Brace Jovanovich, 1973). Philip Jenkins, *The New Anti-Catholicism* (New York: Oxford University Press, 2003).

37. Garry Wills, *Witches and Jesuits* (New York: Oxford University Press, 1995).

38. Whitaker, *Good News from Virginia*; Robert Beverley, *History and Present State of Virginia*, ed. Louis B. Wright (Charlottesville, Va: Dominion Books, 1968), 211. For Lamaism, see Donald S. Lopez, *Prisoners of Shangri-La* (Chicago: University of Chicago Press, 1998).

39. For the enduring symbolic power of the Inquisition, see Jenkins, *The New Anti-Catholicism*.

40. James Mooney, *The Ghost-Dance Religion and the Sioux Outbreak of 1890* (North Dighton, Mass.: JG Press, 1996). Miller, *Prophetic Worlds*; R. David Edmunds, *The Shawnee Prophet* (Lincoln: University of Nebraska Press, 1985); Joseph B. Herring, *Kenekuk, the Kickapoo Prophet* (Lawrence: University Press of Kansas, 1988). Robert H. Ruby and John A. Brown, *Dreamer-Prophets of the Columbia Plateau* (Norman: University of Oklahoma Press, 1989); Greg Dowd, *A Spirited Resistance* (Baltimore, Md.: Johns Hopkins University Press, 1992). For "fanaticism," see Philip Jenkins, *Mystics and Messiahs* (New York: Oxford University Press, 2000).

41. "The Wisconsin Indian Scare," *NYT*, 25 Jun. 1878; "The Dance of the Dreamers," *NYT*, 5 Sep. 1881; John G. Bourke, "The Indian Messiah," *Nation*, 4 Dec. 1890, 439–40; M. P. Maus, "New Indian Messiah," *Harper's*, 6 Dec. 1890, 947; William E. Dougherty, "Indians of North America," *Overland* 19 (Mar.–Apr. 1892): 357–75; "Looking for the Messiah," *NYT*, 10 Oct. 1892; Michael Hittman and Don Lynch, eds., *Wovoka and the Ghost Dance* (Lincoln: University of Nebraska Press, 1998).

42. Jenkins, *The New Anti-Catholicism*. "Looking for the Messiah"; "Indian Uprising Feared," *NYT*, 18 Apr. 1898; M. O. Scott, "Pagan Indians of Canada," *Canadian Magazine* 15 (Jul. 1900): 204–15.

43. James Axtell, *The Invasion Within* (New York: Oxford University Press, 1986); De Crevecoeur is quoted in Bourne, *Gods of War, Gods of Peace*, 17. Red Jacket is quoted from Samuel G. Goodrich, *Lives of Celebrated American Indians* (New York: J. M. Allen, 1843). Red Jacket was an important leader and a significant thinker in his own right: see Wallace, *The Death and Rebirth of the Seneca*.

44. Washington Irving, *A History of New York, from the Beginning of the World to the End of the Dutch Dynasty, by Diedrich Knickerbocker* (New York: Inskeep & Bradford, 1809).

45. The Pope quote is from *Essay on Man*, I, 99. The Peace Commission is from Francis Paul Prucha, ed., *Documents of United States Indian Policy*, 2nd ed. (Lincoln: University of Nebraska Press, 1990), 107. Parker is quoted in G. E. E. Lindquist, *The Red Man in the United States* (New York: G. H. Doran, 1923), 47.

46. *The Song of Hiawatha: The Peace Pipe*.

47. "Legend of 'Redeemer' Found Among Indians," *NYT*, 17 Jul. 1932.
48. Bartram is quoted in Joel W. Martin, *The Land Looks After Us* (New York: Oxford University Press, 2001), 60. For the idea of Indians' Hebrew roots, see Josiah Priest, *Wonders of Nature and Providence Displayed* (Albany, 1826); George Catlin, *Letters and Notes on the Manners, Customs, and Conditions of the North American Indians,* vol. ii (New York: Dover, 1973), 232; William Apess, *On Our Own Ground,* ed. Barry O'Connell (Amherst: University of Massachusetts Press, 1992).
49. "The Iroquois had one god" is from R. R. Baker, "What Is the Educational or Moral Value for Boys and Girls in Reading the Books about the American Indian?" *Public Libraries* 27 (Jun. 1922): 323–26; Lindquist, *The Red Man in the United States,* xv. Lee I. Thayer, "Hopi Indians and Their Religion," *MRW* 40 (Jul. 1917): 507–13; "How an Old Indian Revealed a New Resurrection Myth," *Literary Digest,* 7 May 1927, 44–46.
50. Lindquist, *The Red Man in the United States,* vi.
51. At best, these practices might be colorful quaint customs, reliable fodder for newspaper readers on slow news days, but nothing like real religion. For this genre of news stories, see, for instance, "Celebrating the Indian New Year; Curious Customs of the Pagan Indians on the Tonawanda Reservation," *NYT,* 10 Feb. 1895; "Indians at Pow-Wow Observe Old Rites," *NYT,* 25 Nov. 1909.
52. Lindquist, *The Red Man in the United States,* 257 (the Mescalero), 297 (Papago), 287 (Hopis).
53. "The Navajos of Arizona," *NYT,* 24 Dec. 1888.
54. Taylor is quoted from Prucha, *Documents of United States Indian Policy,* 123–24. Owanah Anderson, *400 Years: Anglican Episcopal Mission Among American Indians* (Cincinnati, Ohio: Forward Movement, 1998).
55. Prucha, ed., *Documents of United States Indian Policy,* 157–58.
56. An excellent account of the cultural assimilation policy can be found in Josephy, *Now that the Buffalo's Gone,* 77–123. See also Sandra L. Cadwalader and Vine Deloria, Jr., eds., *The Aggressions of Civilization* (Philadelphia: Temple University Press, 1984); Janet A. McDonnell, *The Dispossession of the American Indian, 1887–1934* (Bloomington: Indiana University Press, 1989); Frederick E. Hoxie, *A Final Promise* (Lincoln: University of Nebraska Press, 2001); Frederick E. Hoxie, ed., *Talking Back to Civilization* (New York: Bedford/St. Martin's Press, 2001).
57. Prucha, ed., *Documents of United States Indian Policy,* 160–62. Teller's code is also found at *http://www.law.asu.edu/homepages/clinton/Ind1/CFRCt.htm.*
58. Douglas Cole and Ira Chaikin, *An Iron Hand Upon the People* (Vancouver, Can.: Douglas & McIntyre, 1990). For Canadian suppression of Native traditions, see Katherine Pettipas, *Severing the Ties that Bind* (Winnipeg, Can.: University of Manitoba Press, 1994).
59. Helen Hunt Jackson, *A Century of Dishonor* (Norman: University of Oklahoma Press, 1994); Mary Hershberger, "Mobilizing Women, Anticipating Abolition," *Journal of American History,* 86(1)(1999): 15–40; Siobhan Senier, *Voices of American Indian Assimilation and Resistance* (Norman: University of Oklahoma Press, 2001).
60. Sarah Barringer Gordon, *The Mormon Question* (Chapel Hill: University of North Carolina Press, 2002).
61. Prucha, ed., *Documents of United States Indian Policy,* 186–88; Grinnell is quoted from William Thomas Hagan, *Theodore Roosevelt and Six Friends of the Indian* (Norman: University of Oklahoma Press, 1997), 191
62. For the new Indian Offenses policy see Hagan, *Theodore Roosevelt and Six Friends of the Indian,* 129–30; Zitkala-Sa, *American Indian Stories, Legends and Other Writings* (New

York: Penguin, 2003), 237; "Sioux At Pow-wow Ban Tribal Dances; Christianized Indians Decide to Abandon Manifestations of Their Former Faith," *NYT*, 22 Aug. 1921.

63. John Collier, *The Indians of the Americas* (New York: W. W. Norton, 1947), 234. For the continuing religious traditions of the Seminoles, see Marjory Stoneman Douglas, *The Everglades*. "Regarding their ancient laws and customs" is quoted from Charles Francis Saunders, *The Indians of the Terraced Houses* (New York: G. P. Putnam, 1912).

64. "Utes to Placate Manitou," *NYT*, 28 Jul. 1912.

Chapter 3

1. Lewis Henry Morgan, *Ancient Society* (New Brunswick, N.J.: Transaction Publishers, 2000); Arturo J. Aldama, *Disrupting Savagism* (Durham, N.C.: Duke University Press, 2002). Throughout this chapter, I have used Scott Michaelsen, *The Limits of Multiculturalism* (Minneapolis: University of Minnesota Press, 1999).

2. Spencer Trotter, "Indian Fairy Book," *Popular Science* 76 (Jun. 1910): 565–69; Thomas C. Moffett, *The American Indian on the New Trail* (New York: Missionary Education Movement of the United States and Canada—Methodist Book Concern, 1914), 14, 19; Moffett, *The Bible in the Life of the Indians of the United States* (New York: American Bible Society, 1916).

3. Timothy Dwight, "The Triumph of Infidelity," in *The New Oxford Book of Christian Verse*, ed. Donald Davie (New York: Oxford University Press, 1981), 207; Bartram is quoted in Joel W. Martin, *The Land Looks After Us* (New York: Oxford University Press, 2001), 60, 59.

4. Henry Rowe Schoolcraft, *Algic Researches* (New York: Harper & Brothers, 1839); idem, *The Myth of Hiawatha, and Other Oral Legends, Mythologic and Allegoric, of the North American Indians* (Philadelphia: J. B. Lippincott, 1856); idem, *The Indian Fairy Book* (New York: Allen Bros., 1869). Cornelius Mathews, *The Enchanted Moccasins: And Other Legends of the American Indians* (New York: Putnam, 1877); Stith Thompson, *Tales of the North American Indians* (Bloomington: Indiana University Press, 1929). Michaelsen, *The Limits of Multiculturalism*.

5. Simon J. Bronner, *Popularizing Pennsylvania* (University Park, Pa.: Pennsylvania State University Press, 1996).

6. James O. Ashenhurst, "Difficulties in Missions to the Indians," *MRW* 31 (Jul. 1908): 516–19.

7. Frank Hamilton Cushing, *Zuñi Folk Tales* (New York: Putnam's/Knickerbocker, 1901). Thomas C. Parkhill, *Weaving Ourselves into the Land* (Albany: State University of New York Press, 1997).

8. Jesse W. Fewkes, "An Interpretation of Katcina Worship," *JAF* 14 (1901): 81–94.

9. John Smith, *A Map of Virginia. With a Description of the Countrey, the Commodities, People, Government and Religion,* at *http://etext.lib.virginia.edu/etcbin/jamestown-browse?id=J1008* . Robert Beverley, *History and Present State of Virginia*, ed. Louis B. Wright (Charlottesville, Va.: Dominion Books, 1968), 195.

10. This section is based on George Catlin, *Letters and Notes on the Manners, Customs, and Conditions of the North American Indians*, vol. 1 (New York: Dover, 1973), 155–84.

11. Catlin, *Letters and Notes*, 156.

12. Francis Parkman, *The Jesuits in North America in the Seventeenth Century* (Boston: Little, Brown, 1867), 60–61.

13. Ibid., 65.

14. Jesse Green, ed., *Zuñi: The Selected Writings of Frank Hamilton Cushing* (Lincoln: University of Nebraska Press, 1979); Green, *Cushing at Zuñi* (Albuquerque: University of New Mexico Press, 1990); E. Jane Gay, *With the Nez Perces*, eds. Frederick E. Hoxie and Joan T. Mark (Lincoln: University of Nebraska Press, 1981); Joan T. Mark, *A Stranger in Her Native Land* (Lincoln: University of Nebraska Press, 1988); Garrick A. Bailey, ed., *The Osage and the Invisible World* (Norman: University of Oklahoma Press, 1995); Katherine Spencer Halpern and Susan Brown McGreevy, eds., *Washington Matthews: Studies of Navajo Culture, 1880–1894* (Albuquerque: University of New Mexico Press, 1997); Sherry Lynn Smith, *Reimagining Indians* (New York: Oxford University Press, 2000). For the limits of objectivity in the new wave of scholarship, see James Clifford, *The Predicament of Culture* (Cambridge, Mass.: Harvard University Press, 1988).

15. The remark about the size of Smithsonian collections is from Frederick E. Hoxie, ed., *Talking Back to Civilization* (New York: Bedford/St. Martin's Press, 2001), 8. Joseph Henry is quoted from Douglas Cole, *Captured Heritage* (Norman: University of Oklahoma Press, 1995), 48.

16. Hoxie, *Talking Back to Civilization*.

17. Eliza McFeely, *Zuñi and the American Imagination* (New York: Hill & Wang, 2001).

18. Frank Hamilton Cushing, "My Adventures in Zuñi," *Century Illustrated Monthly Magazine* 25–26 (1882–83), 191–207, 500–511. John Gregory Bourke, *The Medicine Men of the Apache* (Glorieta, N.M.: Rio Grande Press, 1970); Franz Boas, *The Shaping of American Anthropology, 1883–1911*, ed. George W. Stocking, Jr. (New York: Basic Books, 1974); Curtis M. Hinsley, *Savages and Scientists* (Washington, D.C.: Smithsonian Institution Press, 1981); James Mooney, *Myths of the Cherokee* (Asheville, N.C.: Historical Images, 1992); Halpern and McGreevy, *Washington Matthews*; Don D. Fowler, *A Laboratory for Anthropology* (Albuquerque: University of New Mexico Press, 2000).

19. Christopher Cardozo, ed., *Native Nations* (Boston: Little, Brown, 1993); Cardozo, ed., *Sacred Legacy* (New York: Simon & Schuster, 2000). Other great ethnographic documentaries of Native life appeared in the silent era, including *Nanook of the North* (1922) and *Silent Enemy* (1930).

20. Cushing, *Zuñi Folk Tales*, xiv.

21. Walter McClintock, "Four Days in a Medicine Lodge," *Harper's Magazine*, Sept. 1900, 519–32; McClintock, *The Tragedy of the Blackfoot* (Los Angeles: Southwest Museum, 1930).

22. For the development of the concept of shamanism, see Mircea Eliade, *Shamanism: Archaic Techniques of Ecstasy* (Princeton, N.J.: Princeton University Press, 1964); Daniel C. Noel, *The Soul of Shamanism* (New York: Continuum, 1999); Piers Vitebsky, *Shamanism* (Norman: University of Oklahoma Press, 2001); Ronald Hutton, *Shamans* (London: Hambledon and London, 2001); K. Von Stuckard, "Re-enchanting Nature," *Journal of the American Academy of Religion* 70(4) (2002): 771–800; Graham Harvey, ed., *Shamanism* (London: Routledge, 2002). For the application of the concept in North America, see Washington Mathews, "The Prayer of a Navajo Shaman," *American Anthropologist* 1 (1888): 149–71; W. J. Hoffman, "Pictography and Shamanistic Rites of the Ojibwa," *American Anthropologist* 1 (1888): 209–29; Frank H. Cushing, "Remarks on Shamanism," *Proceedings of the American Philosophical Society* 36 (1897): 184–92; Alexander F. Chamberlain, "Kootenay Medicine-Men," *JAF* 14 (Apr. 1901): 95–99; R. Dixon, "Some Shamans of Northern California," *JAF* 17 (Jan. 1904): 23–27; John Lee Maddox, *The Medicine Man* (New York: Macmillan, 1923); Willard Z. Park, *Shamanism in Western*

North America (Evanston, Ill.: Northwestern University Press, 1938); Isabel Truesdell Kelly, *Southern Paiute Shamanism* (Berkeley: University of California Press, 1939).

23. Washington Matthews, "Songs of Sequence of the Navajos," *JAF* 7 (1894): 185–94; John Gregory Bourke, *The Medicine-Men of the Apache* (Washington, D.C.: Government Printing Office, 1892); Maddox, *The Medicine Man.* "Ancient Religion of Shamanism Flourishing Today," *NYT,* 17 Jul. 1904.

24. F. Monsen, "The Destruction of Our Indians," *Craftsman* 11 (Mar. 1907): 683–91; Lee I. Thayer, "Hopi Indians and Their Religion," *MRW* 40 (Jul. 1917): 507–13.

25. Boas, *The Shaping of American Anthropology.*

26. James Mooney, *The Ghost-Dance Religion and the Sioux Outbreak of 1890* (North Dighton, Mass.: JG Press, 1996), 290.

27. Mooney, *The Ghost-Dance Religion and the Sioux Outbreak of 1890,* 290–92. Mooney, *The Sacred Formulas of the Cherokees,* 7th Annual Report, Bureau of American Ethnology (Washington, D.C., 1891), 302–97. L. G. Moses, *The Indian Man* (Urbana: University of Illinois Press, 1984).

28. Daniel G. Brinton, ed., *Rig Veda Americanus. Sacred Songs of the Ancient Mexicans* (Philadelphia: D. G. Brinton, 1890); Brinton, *The Myths of the New World,* 2nd ed. (New York: H. Holt, 1876); Lewis Spence, *The Popol Vuh* (London: David Nutt, 1908); Ellen Russell Emerson, *Indians Myths: Or, Legends, Traditions, and Symbols of the Aborigines of America Compared with Those of Other Countries* (Boston: J. R. Osgood, 1884).

29. Daniel G. Brinton, *The Lenâpé and Their Legends* (Philadelphia: D. G. Brinton, 1885).

30. Washington Matthews, *The Mountain Chant,* 5th Annual Report, Bureau of American Ethnology (Washington, D.C., 1884), 379–467; Matthews, "Navaho Night Chant," *JAF* 14 (1901): 12–19.

31. Alice C. Fletcher, *Indian Ceremonies* (Salem, Mass.: Salem Press, 1884).

32. Andrew Lang, "Red Indian Imagination," *The Independent,* 18 Jan. 1900, 163; George William Cronyn, ed., *The Path on the Rainbow* (New York: Liveright, 1934); Amy Lowell, "Songs of The Pueblo Indians," *The Dial* 69(3) (1920): 247–51.

33. Austin is quoted from her introduction to Cronyn, *Path on the Rainbow.* "The most superior literary form" is from Mary Austin, "Aboriginal Fiction," *Saturday Review of Literature,* 28 Dec. 1929, 597–99; Alfred Riggs is quoted from G. E. E. Lindquist, *The Red Man in the United States* (New York: G. H. Doran, 1923), 51. For Harrington, see Cash Asher, "Pueblo Indians Fear for Their Religion," *NYT,* 13 Jul. 1924.

34. "With this knowledge": F. Millspaugh, "Corn in the Worship of the Indians," *Chautauquan* 31 (May 1903): 338–43; Alice C. Fletcher, "Prayers Voiced in Ancient America," *Art and Archaeology* 9 (Feb. 1920): 73.

35. Arthur Farwell, "Artistic Possibilities of Indian Myth," *Poet-Lore* 1 (1904): 53.

36. John Lloyd Stephens, *Incidents of Travel in Central America: Chiapas, and Yucatan* (New York: Harper, 1841). J. P. MacLean, "The Serpent Mound," *American Antiquarian And Oriental Journal* 7 (1885): 44–47; Frederick W. Putnam, "The Serpent Mound Saved," *Ohio Archaeological and Historical Quarterly* 1 (1887): 187–90; idem, "The Serpent Mound of Ohio," *Century Illustrated Magazine* 39(6)(1890): 871–88; Roger G. Kennedy, *Hidden Cities* (New York: Free Press, 1994).

37. Ernest Ingersoll, *The Crest of the Continent* (Chicago: R. R. Donnelly, 1885); Frank McNitt, *Richard Wetherill: Anasazi,* rev. ed. (Albuquerque: University of New Mexico Press, 1966); Reuben Ellis, ed., *Stories and Stone: An Anasazi Reader* (Boulder, Colo: Pruett Publishing Co., 1996); James Elliott Snead, *Ruins and Rivals* (Tucson: University of Arizona Press, 2001).

38. The School of American Archaeology later became the School of American Research.
39. Charles H. Lange and Carroll L. Riley, *Bandelier* (Salt Lake City: University of Utah Press, 1996); Adolf F. Bandelier, *The Delight Makers* (New York: Dodd, Mead, 1890); Henry Blake Fuller, *The Cliff-Dwellers* (New York: Harper, 1893); John N. Swift and Joseph R. Urgo, eds., *Willa Cather and the American Southwest* (Lincoln: University of Nebraska Press, 2002).
40. Charles F. Lummis, "Montezuma's Castle," *The Land of Sunshine,* vi (1896–97), 72.
41. "Digs Up Ancient City of a Million Indians," *NYT,* 7 Sep. 1924; "Find Amazing Relics of Mayas' Empire," *NYT,* 20 Aug. 1925; Kenneth W. Barr, "Tales of Maya Indians Recounted by Explorer," *NYT,* 30 Aug. 1925. For older attitudes about the origins of New World civilizations, see Stephen Williams, *Fantastic Archaeology* (Philadelphia: University of Pennsylvania Press, 1991); Kennedy, *Hidden Cities.*
42. James A. Leroy, "Indian Festival at Taos," *Outing* 43 (Dec. 1903): 282–88.

Chapter 4

1. Eliza McFeely, *Zuñi and the American Imagination* (New York: Hill & Wang, 2001).
2. For contemporary publicity material on travel to the Southwest, see Walter Hough, *The Moki Snake Dance: A Popular Account of that Unparalleled Dramatic Pagan Ceremony of the Pueblo Indians of Tusayan, Arizona* (Chicago: The Passenger Department, Santa Fe Route, 1899); Joseph Emerson Smith, *The Story of Mesa Verde National Park: America's Sublime Antiquity Has the Lure of a Mystery Greater than the Ruined Cities of the Old World* (Denver, Colo.: Denver and Rio Grande Western Railroad Co., 1910); Agnes C. Laut, *Through Our Unknown Southwest: The Wonderland of the United States—Little Known and Unappreciated—The Home of the Cliff Dweller and the Hopi, the Forest Ranger and the Navajo—The Lure of the Painted Desert* (New York: R. M. McBride & Co., 1915); Karleton Hackett, *A Pilgrimage to Mesa Verde* (Denver, Colo.: Denver and Rio Grande Western Railroad Co., 1917); *Come into Western Colorado: Mesa Verde National Park Circle Trip: See the Mystical Southwest* (Chicago: Denver and Rio Grande Western Railroad Co., 1922). See also George Wharton James, *The Indians of the Painted Desert Region* (Boston: Little, Brown, 1905); idem, *New Mexico: The Land of the Delight Makers* (Boston: Page, 1920). Marta Weigle and Barbara A. Babcock, eds., *The Great Southwest of the Fred Harvey Company and the Santa Fe Railway* (Tucson: University of Arizona Press, 1996); John F. Sears, *Sacred Places* (Amherst: University of Massachusetts Press, 1999); Sherry Lynn Smith, *Reimagining Indians* (New York: Oxford University Press, 2000); Marguerite S. Shaffer, *See America First* (Washington, D.C.: Smithsonian Institution Press, 2001).
3. Edgar Lee Hewett, "Ancient America at the Panama-California Exposition," *Art and Archaeology,* Nov. 1915, 65–102; Lawrence is quoted in *Stories and Stone: An Anasazi Reader,* ed. Reuben Ellis (Boulder, Colo.: Pruett Publishing Co., 1996), 154.
4. Catherine L. Albanese, *Reconsidering Nature Religion* (Harrisburg, Pa.: Trinity Press, International, 2002); Mary Hunter Austin, *The Land of Little Rain* (New York: Penguin, 1997). For Lummis, see Charles Fletcher Lummis, *The Land of Poco Tiempo* (Albuquerque: University of New Mexico Press, 1952); idem, *A New Mexico David* (Freeport, N.Y.: Books For Libraries Press, 1969); idem, *The Enchanted Burro* (Freeport, N.Y.: Books For Libraries Press, 1972); Kevin Starr, *Inventing the Dream* (New York: Oxford University Press, 1985); Patrick T. Houlihan and Betsy E. Houlihan, *Lummis in the Pueblos* (Flagstaff, Ariz.: Northland Press, 1986); Mark Thompson,

American Character (New York: Arcade Publishing, 2001). Barbara A. Babcock and Nancy J. Parezo, *Daughters of the Desert* (Albuquerque: University of New Mexico Press, 1988); Nancy J. Parezo, ed., *Hidden Scholars* (Albuquerque: University of New Mexico Press, 1993); Leah Dilworth, *Imagining Indians in the Southwest* (Washington, D.C.: Smithsonian Institution Press, 1996); Margaret D. Jacobs, *Engendered Encounters* (Lincoln: University of Nebraska Press, 1999).

5. Mark David Spence, *Dispossessing the Wilderness* (New York: Oxford University Press, 1999).

6. Gilson Willets, "Most Un-American Part of the United States," *NYT*, 20 Aug. 1905.

7. Jesse Walter Fewkes, "The Oraibi Flute Altar," *JAF* 8 (1895); and Fewkes, *Hopi Snake Ceremonies* (Albuquerque, N.M.: Avanyu, 1986); Charles Francis Saunders, *The Indians of the Terraced Houses* (New York: Putnam, 1912). For contemporary accounts, see Hamlin Garland, "Among the Moki Indians," *Harper's Weekly*, 15 Aug. 1896, 801–7; Hough, *The Moki Snake Dance*; "The Moki Snake Dance," *NYT*, 30 Sep. 1900; George A. Dorsey and H. R. Voth, *The Mishongnovi Ceremonies of the Snake and Antelope Fraternities* (Chicago: Field Columbian Museum, Chicago, 1902); Theodore Roosevelt, *A Book-Lover's Holidays in the Open* (1916; repr., New York: Scribner, 1925); D. H. Lawrence, "The Hopi Snake Dance," in Lawrence, *Mornings in Mexico, and Etruscan Places* (London: Heineman, 1956), 61–80. Pictures of the ritual in the 1890s can be found in Aby M. Warburg, *Images from the Region of the Pueblo Indians of North America*, tr. and ed. Michael P. Steinberg (Ithaca, N.Y.: Cornell University Press, 1995).

8. Thomas C. Moffett, *The American Indian on the New Trail* (New York: Missionary Education Movement of the United States and Canada—Methodist Book Concern, 1914), 270–71; Philip J. Deloria, *Playing Indian* (New Haven, Conn.: Yale University Press, 1998); H. Allen Anderson, *The Chief: Ernest Thompson Seton and the Changing West* (College Station: Texas A&M University Press, 1986).

9. "Society Studies Hopi Snake Dance," *NYT*, 11 Apr. 1914; Etta J. Oliver, "Mystic Dances of the Painted Desert," *Travel* 47 (Jul. 1926): 27–29; "Smoki at Sundown," *Rotarian* 68 (Jan. 1946): 19. For the existing Smoki Museum, see *http://www.arizonan.com/outdoorarizona/Smoki.html.*

10. James A. Leroy, "Indian Festival at Taos," *Outing* 43 (Dec. 1903): 282–88; "The dances held each day at the Grand Canyon": D. Maitland Bushby, "The Dance of the Snake," *Overland* 87 (Jun. 1929): 167.

11. Charles Eastman, *The Soul of the Indian* (Boston: Houghton Mifflin, 1911).

12. Saunders, *Indians of the Terraced Houses.*

13. Philip Jenkins, *Mystics and Messiahs* (New York: Oxford University Press, 2000), 90.

14. Erik Trump, "The Idea of Help," in *Selling the Indian*, eds. Carter Jones Meyer and Diana Royer (Tucson: University of Arizona Press, 2001), 162–63; Douglas Cole, *Captured Heritage* (Norman: University of Oklahoma Press, 1995), 124; Barbara Babcock, "Maids of Palestine," in *Art and the Native American*, eds. Mary Louise Krumrine and Susan Clare Scott (University Park, Penn.: Penn State Press, 2001), 246–67. For early cultural displays, see "Indian Displays Feature of Show; Relics and Antiquities of Tribes at Grand Central Palace Exhibition," *NYT*, 27 Dec. 1907.

15. The collecting boom in artifacts from the peoples of America's Northwest Coast now reached amazing heights as the objects came to be seen as artistic treasures in their own right, rather than merely anthropological curios. Cole, *Captured Heritage*; Ira Jacknis, *The Storage Box of Tradition* (Washington, D.C.: Smithsonian Institution Press, 2002).

16. Mary Austin, "American Indian Dance Drama," *Yale Review* 19 (Jun. 1930): 732–45.

17. Julian Ralph, "My Indian Plunder," *Scribner's*, Nov. 1896, 637–45; Walter McClintock, "Four Days in a Medicine Lodge," *Harper's Magazine*, Sep. 1900, 519–32; A. L. Kroeber, "Ishi: The Last Aborigine," *World's Work* 24 (Jul. 1912): 304–8; Karl Kroeber and Clifton Kroeber, eds., *Ishi in Three Centuries* (Lincoln: University of Nebraska Press, 2003). Though see J. Worden Pope, "The North American Indian: The Disappearance of the Race a Popular Fallacy," *Arena* 16 (Nov. 1896): 945–59. The "weird and waning race" is from Duncan Campbell Scott's poem "The Onondaga Madonna" (1898). Laura Stevens, "Like Snow Against the Sun," in Nancy Isenberg and Andrew Burstein, eds., *Mortal Remains* (Philadelphia: University of Pennsylvania Press, 2003); Patrick Brantlinger, *Dark Vanishings* (Ithaca: Cornell University Press, 2003).

18. Andrew Lang, "Red Indian Imagination," *The Independent*, 18 Jan. 1900, 163–65; Arthur Farwell, "Artistic Possibilities of Indian Myth," *Poet-Lore* 1 (1904): 46–61. Other "Indianists" included Charles Wakefield Cadman and Edward MacDowell; see C. W. Cadman, "Idealization of Indian Music," *Musical Quarterly* 1 (July 1915): 387–96. Native influence on avant-garde music continued into the 1920s with the work of Frederick Jacobi, who drew on Pueblo motifs: Carol J. Oja, *Making Music Modern* (New York: Oxford University Press, 2000).

19. Frances Densmore, *The American Indians and Their Music* (New York: The Woman's Press, 1926); Kenneth Rexroth, "American Indian Songs" (1956), at *http://www.bopsecrets.org/rexroth/Indiansongs.htm*.

20. Natalie Curtis, *The Indians' Book* (New York: Harper, 1907). Charles Fletcher Lummis, *Bullying the Moqui*, eds. Robert Easton and Mackenzie Brown (Prescott, Ariz.: Prescott College Press, 1968); William Thomas Hagan, *Theodore Roosevelt and Six Friends of the Indian* (Norman: University of Oklahoma Press, 1997). For Curtis, see "Natalie Curtis," *Southern Workman* (Mar. 1926): 127–40; Alfred R. Bredenberg, "Natalie Curtis Burlin (1875–1921)," *Connecticut Review* (Spring 1994): 1–15. For her link to the Arts and Crafts movement, see Natalie Curtis, "A Visit to Craftsman Farms," *Craftsman* (Sep. 1910): 638.

21. "Here among us" is from Curtis, *The Indians' Book*, xxxvi; "We who look to Europe" is from Curtis, "Plea for Our Native Art," *Musical Quarterly* 6 (Apr. 1920): 178. "Why it is that America" is from Curtis, "Indians' Part in the Dedication of the New Museum," *Art and Archaeology* 7 (Jan. 1918): 30–32; Curtis, "The Perpetuating of Indian Art," *Outlook*, 22 Oct. 1913, 623.

22. Mary Austin, "Introduction," *The Path on the Rainbow*, ed. George William Cronyn (New York: Liveright, 1934); Maynard Dixon is quoted from *http://www.tfaoi.com/aa/2aa/2aa319.htm*

23. Mary Austin, *Earth Horizon* (Boston: Houghton Mifflin, 1932), 276–83; Mark T. Hoyer, *Dancing Ghosts* (Reno: University of Nevada Press, 1998).

24. Hagan, *Theodore Roosevelt and Six Friends of the Indian.*

25. Frederick E. Hoxie, ed., *Talking Back to Civilization* (New York: Bedford/St. Martin's Press, 2001); Peter Iverson, *Carlos Montezuma and the Changing World of American Indians* (Albuquerque: University of New Mexico Press, 1982).

26. For continuing Native religious resistance, see Lee Irwin, "Freedom, Law, and Prophecy: A Brief History of Native American Religious Resistance," at *http://www.sacredland.org/Irwin.html*. Hoxie, *Talking Back to Civilization*, 32; Simon Pokagon, "An Indian on the Problems of His Race," *Review of Reviews* 12 (Dec. 1895): 694–95; Pokagon, "The Future of The Red Man," *Forum* 23 (1896): 693–708; Pokagon, "Indian Superstitions and Legends," *Forum* 25 (Jul. 1898): 618–29; B. O. Flower, "Interesting

Representative of a Vanishing Race," *Arena* 16 (Jul. 1896): 240–50. Of course, this was not the first generation of Native writers in English. The first major figure was William Apess, who wrote his autobiography, *A Son of the Forest,* in 1829: William Apess, *On Our Own Ground,* ed. Barry O'Connell (Amherst: University of Massachusetts Press, 1992). See also Bernd Peyer, *The Tutor'd Mind* (Amherst: University of Massachusetts Press, 1997); Karen L. Kilcup, ed., *Native American Women's Writing c.1800–1924* (Oxford: Blackwell Publishers, 2000).

27. "A Notable Indian's Good Work; Dr. Charles C. Eastman's Labors in Behalf of His Race," *NYT,* 7 Apr. 1895.

28. Zitkala-Sa, "Why I Am a Pagan," *Atlantic Monthly* 90 (1902): 801–3; Zitkala-Sa, *American Indian Stories, Legends and Other Writings* (New York: Penguin, 2003); Betty Louise Bell, "If This Is Paganism," in *Native American Religious Identity,* ed. Jace Weaver (Maryknoll, N.Y.: Orbis, 1998), 61–68.

29. For Eastman's wife, see Elaine Goodale, "Some Lessons from Barbarism," *Popular Science Monthly* 38 (Nov. 1890): 82–86; " 'The Soul of the Indian'; Revealed by a Cultivated Sioux Whose Wife Is a New England Poet," *NYT,* 23 Apr. 1911. Kay Graber, ed., *Elaine Goodale Eastman, Sister to the Sioux* (Lincoln: University of Nebraska Press, 1985).

30. Eastman is conflating the Delaware Prophet who inspired Pontiac in 1762, with the Shawnee Prophet of the early nineteenth century.

31. Hoxie, *Talking Back,* 15, quoting Charles Eastman, *From the Deep Woods to Civilization* (Boston: Little, Brown, 1916).

32. "Charles Lummis: Indian Rights Crusader," at *http://www.charleslummis.com/Indianrights.htm* . Lummis, *Bullying the Moqui*; Patrick T. Houlihan and Betsy E. Houlihan, *Lummis in the Pueblos* (Flagstaff, Ariz.: Northland Press, 1986).

33. Hamlin Garland, "The Red Man's Present Needs," *North American* 174 (Apr. 1902): 476–88; Hamlin Garland, *Forty Years of Psychic Research* (New York: Macmillan, 1936); Lonnie E. Underhill and Daniel F. Littlefield, Jr., eds., *Hamlin Garland's Observations on the American Indian, 1895–1905* (Tucson: University of Arizona Press, 1976). "The Iron Khiva" was reprinted in Hamlin Garland, *The Book of the American Indian* (New York: Harper, 1923).

34. John M. Oskison, "The Problem of Old Harjo," *Southern Workman* 36 (Apr. 1907): 235–41.

35. Eastman, *Soul of the Indian.*

36. The Episcopal minister was the Rev. Sherman Coolidge. He is quoted in Peter Nabokov, ed., *Native American Testimony,* rev. ed. (New York: Penguin, 1999), 284. Gustav Stickley, "We Also Have a Religion," *Craftsman* 22 (May 1912): 237–38. Owanah Anderson, *400 Years: Anglican Episcopal Mission Among American Indians* (Cincinnati, Ohio: Forward Movement, 1998), 225–29.

37. Mabel Dodge was born Mabel Ganson, but by 1920 she was in her third marriage. In 1923, she married Tony Luhan, and was commonly known thereafter as Mabel Dodge Luhan. Her Taos circle has attracted a vast literature. Mabel Dodge Luhan, *Lorenzo in Taos* (New York: Knopf, 1932); idem, *Winter in Taos* (New York: Harcourt, Brace, 1935); idem, *Intimate Memories: The Autobiography of Mabel Dodge Luhan,* 4 vols. (New York: Harcourt, Brace, 1933–1937); particularly useful is vol. 4: *Edge of Taos Desert.* Charles C. Eldredge, Julie Schimmel, and William H. Truettner, eds., *Art in New Mexico, 1900–1945* (Washington, D.C.: National Museum of American Art, 1986); Lois Palken Rudnick, *Mabel Dodge Luhan: New Woman, New Worlds* (Albuquerque: University of New Mexico Press, 1988); and idem, *Utopian Vistas* (Albuquerque: University of

New Mexico Press, 1996); Chris Wilson, *The Myth of Santa Fe* (Albuquerque: University of New Mexico Press, 1997); Sherry Lynn Smith, *Reimagining Indians* (New York: Oxford University Press, 2000); Lois Palken Rudnick, "Mabel Dodge Luhan and New Mexico's Anglo Arts Community," in *New Mexican Lives,* ed. Richard W. Etulain (Albuquerque: University of New Mexico Press, 2002). For the cultural context, see Adele Heller and Lois Rudnick, eds., *1915, The Cultural Moment* (New Brunswick, N.J.: Rutgers University Press, 1991); Steven Watson, *Strange Bedfellows* (New York: Abbeville Press, 1991); Christine Stansell, *American Moderns* (New York: Metropolitan Books, 2000); Ross Wetzsteon, *Republic of Dreams* (New York: Simon & Schuster, 2002).

38. Alice Corbin Henderson, *The Turquoise Trail* (Boston: Houghton Mifflin, 1928); Henderson, *Brothers of Light* (New York: Harcourt, Brace, 1937); W. Jackson Rushing III, *Native American Art and the New York Avant-Garde* (Austin: University of Texas Press, 1995); John N. Swift and Joseph R. Urgo, eds., *Willa Cather and the American Southwest* (Lincoln: University of Nebraska Press, 2002).

39. Natalie Curtis, "Plea for Our Native Art," *Musical Quarterly* 6 (Apr. 1920): 178. Elsie Clews Parsons, *Pueblo Mothers and Children,* ed. Barbara A. Babcock (Santa Fe, N.M.: Ancient City Press, 1991); Rosemary Levy Zumwalt, *Wealth and Rebellion* (Urbana: University of Illinois Press, 1992); Desley Deacon, *Elsie Clews Parsons: Inventing Modern Life* (Chicago: University of Chicago Press, 1999).

40. Patricia R. Everett, ed., *A History of Having a Great Many Times Not Continued to Be Friends* (Albuquerque: University of New Mexico Press, 1996), 246.

41. Natalie Curtis Burlin, "Indians' Part in the Dedication of the New Museum," *Art and Archaeology* 7 (Jan. 1918): 30–32.

42. Jeffers, "New Mexican Mountain."

43. Marsden Hartley, "Red Man Ceremonials; An American Plea for American Esthetics," *Art and Archaeology* 9 (Mar. 1920): 7–14. Townsend Ludington, *Marsden Hartley* (Boston: Little, Brown and Co., 1992); Marsden Hartley, *Somehow a Past* (Cambridge: MIT Press, 1997). For the sophisticated theatrical quality of ceremonials, compare Oliver La Farge, "Plastic Prayers: Dance of the Southwestern Indians," *Theatre Arts Magazine* 14 (Mar. 1930): 218–24.

44. Quoted in Carter Jones Meyer, "Saving the Pueblos," in Carter Jones Meyer and Diana Royer, eds., *Selling the Indian* (Tucson: University of Arizona Press, 2001), 192. Edgar Lee Hewett, *Ancient Life in the American Southwest* (Indianapolis: Bobbs-Merrill, 1930); idem, *Two Score Years* (Albuquerque: University of New Mexico Press, 1946). Molly H. Mullin, *Culture in the Marketplace* (Durham, N.C.: Duke University Press, 2001).

45. C. G. Jung, *Memories, Dreams, Reflections,* rev. ed. (New York: Vintage, 1965), 252.

46. D. H. Lawrence, *Phoenix: The Posthumous Papers of D. H. Lawrence,* ed. Edward D. McDonald (New York: Viking Press, 1936), 142–47. D. H. Lawrence, "The Hopi Snake Dance," in Lawrence, *Mornings in Mexico, and Etruscan Places* (London: Heineman, 1956), 61–80, and "Dance of the Sprouting Corn," in ibid., 54–61.

47. D. H. Lawrence, *The Plumed Serpent,* ed. L. D. Clark (New York: Cambridge University Press, 1987). Frank Waters, *Of Time and Change* (Denver, Colo.: MacMurray & Beck, 1998), 86.

48. John Collier, *The Indians of the Americas* (New York: W. W. Norton, 1947), 19–20. For the Gulicks, see Philip J. Deloria, *Playing Indian* (New Haven, Conn.: Yale University Press, 1998).

49. John Collier, *From Every Zenith* (Denver, Colo.: Sage Books, 1963), 125–26.

50. Collier, *From Every Zenith*; Jenkins, *Mystics and Messiahs*, 171–72.

51. For the race-soul see Collier, *From Every Zenith*, 11; "Man was sundering himself": ibid., 32.

52. Collier, *Indians of the Americas*, 177. T. J. Jackson Lears, *No Place of Grace* (first published 1981; repr., Chicago: University of Chicago Press, 1994).

53. Collier, *From Every Zenith*, 282–83.

54. Ibid., 115, 119.

55. Collier, *Indians of the Americas*, 15.

56. For the Teutonic racial theory of these years, see Madison Grant, *The Passing of the Great Race* (New York: Scribner, 1916); Lothrop T. Stoddard, *The Rising Tide of Color Against White World Supremacy* (New York: Scribner, 1920).

57. "These 'pagan' religions" is from John Collier, "The Religion of the Pueblos," *NYT*, 16 Nov. 1924. Kenneth R. Philp, *John Collier's Crusade for Indian Reform, 1920–1954* (Tucson: University of Arizona Press, 1977); Lawrence C. Kelly, *The Assault on Assimilation* (Albuquerque: University of New Mexico Press, 1983); E. A. Schwartz, "Red Atlantis Revisited: Community and Culture in the Writings of John Collier," *AIQ* 18 (1994): 507–31.

58. James Wilson, *The Earth Shall Weep* (New York: Atlantic Monthly Press, 1999), 335; John Collier, "Indians Come Alive," *Atlantic Monthly* 170 (Sep. 1942): 76.

59. Robert H. Ruby and John A. Brown, *Dreamer-Prophets of the Columbia Plateau* (Norman: University of Oklahoma Press, 1989). Smohalla is quoted from James Mooney, "The Ghost Dance Religion and the Sioux Outbreak of 1890," Annual Report, Bureau of American Ethnology, xiv 2 (Washington, D.C., 1896), 724–26.

Chapter 5

1. Philip Jenkins, *Moral Panic* (New Haven, Conn.: Yale University Press, 1998); Jenkins, *Mystics and Messiahs* (New York: Oxford University Press, 2001). The Supreme Court case on educational liberty is *Pierce v. Society of Sisters*, 268 U.S. 510 (1925).

2. "Pipe Smokers Who Sought to Appease the Gods," *NYT*, 13 Jan. 1924.

3. Omer Call Stewart, *Peyote Religion* (Norman: University of Oklahoma Press, 1987); Weston La Barre, *The Peyote Cult*, 5th ed. (Norman: University of Oklahoma Press, 1989); Robert C. Fuller, *Stairways to Heaven* (Boulder, Colo: Westview, 2000).

4. Quoted in Omer Stewart, "The Native American Church and the Law," in Deward E. Walker, ed., *The Emergent Native Americans* (Boston: Little, Brown, 1972), 383.

5. Ruth Shonle Cavan, *Peyote, The Giver of Visions* (Washington, D.C.: American Anthropological Association, 1925); Vincenzo Petrullo, *The Diabolic Root* (Philadelphia, 1934); James Sydney Slotkin, *The Peyote Religion* (New York: Octagon Books, 1956); Monroe Tsa To Ke, *The Peyote Ritual*, ed. Leslie Van Ness Denman (San Francisco: Grabhorn Press, 1957); C. Burton Dustin, *Peyotism and New Mexico* (Farmington, N.M.: C. Burton Dustin, 1960); David Friend Aberle, *The Peyote Religion Among the Navaho*, 2nd ed. (Chicago: University of Chicago Press, 1982); L. G. Moses, *The Indian Man* (Urbana: University of Illinois Press, 1984); Edward F. Anderson, *Peyote: The Divine Cactus*, 2nd ed. (Tucson: University of Arizona Press, 1996); Paul B. Steinmetz, *Pipe, Bible, and Peyote Among the Oglala Lakota* (Syracuse, N.Y.: Syracuse University Press, 1998).

6. Jenkins, *Mystics and Messiahs*.

7. Delavan L. Pierson, "American Indian Peyote Worship," *MRW* 38 (Mar. 1915): 201–6; this article uses the term "debauche." G. Seymour, "Peyote Worship; An Indian Cult

and a Powerful Drug," *Survey*, 13 May 1916, 181–84. "The Indian's cocaine" is from G. E. E. Lindquist, *The Red Man in the United States* (New York: G. H. Doran, 1923), xiv; ibid., 69–73, for "the greatest and most insidious evil." "Indian's Dream Diet Revealed in Senate," *NYT*, 6 Jan. 1923; A. J. Cuffee, "Peyote and Piety," *NYT*, 9 Jan. 1923; "Peyote Used as Drug in Indians' 'Cult of Death'; New 'Religious' Movement," *NYT*, 14 Jan. 1923; "Indians Find Substitute for Outlawed Firewater," *NYT*, 27 Sept. 1925. The phrase "peyote séances" is from Martin E. Marty, *Modern American Religion*, vol. 1: *The Irony of It All* (Chicago: University of Chicago Press, 1986), 97.

8. The *Denver Post* story is quoted by Stewart in "The Native American Church and the Law," 387. "Inimical to Christianity" is quoted from Pierson, "American Indian Peyote Worship." "How long will the Christian citizenship" is from "Peyote Used as Drug . . ."

9. Zitkala-Sa, *American Indian Stories, Legends and Other Writings* (New York: Penguin, 2003), 241. For white experiments with peyote, see Huntington Cairns, "Divine Intoxicant," *Atlantic Monthly* (Nov. 1929): 638–45; Norman Taylor, "Come and Expel the Green Pain," *Scientific Monthly* 58 (Mar. 1944): 176–84; John Carter, *Sex and Rockets* (Venice, CA: Feral House, 1999), 123–25.

10. Mabel Dodge Luhan, *Intimate Memories*, vol. 3: *Movers and Shakers* (New York: Harcourt, Brace, 1936), 265–79; Hutchins Hapgood, *A Victorian in the Modern World* (New York: Harcourt, Brace, 1939), 363–68; Stewart, *Peyote Religion*, 233–37.

11. These conflicts are described in Kenneth R. Philp, *John Collier's Crusade for Indian Reform, 1920–1954* (Tucson: University of Arizona Press, 1977); Lawrence C. Kelly, *The Assault on Assimilation* (Albuquerque: University of New Mexico Press, 1983).

12. Lindquist, *The Red Man in the United States*, 68–69; Peter Phillip, "Red Men Still With Us but Not of Us," *NYT*, 24 Jun. 1923.

13. David H. Stratton, *Tempest over Teapot Dome* (Norman: University of Oklahoma Press, 1998). Alvin M. Josephy, *Now that the Buffalo's Gone* (Norman: University of Oklahoma Press, 1985), 114–23; Kenneth Dauber, "Pueblo Pottery and the Politics of Regional Identity," *Journal of the Southwest* 32(4) (1990), at *http://digital.library.arizona.edu/jsw/3204/pueblo.html*.

14. The "Protest of Artists and Writers" is reproduced in Kelly, *The Assault on Assimilation*, 215; Collier's remark on the Catholic Church is from his *From Every Zenith* (Denver, Colo.: Sage Books, 1963), 133. The meeting of the Pueblo council is described in John Collier, *The Indians of the Americas* (New York: W. W. Norton, 1947), 250. Mabel Dodge Luhan is quoted from Mary Hunter Austin, *Literary America, 1903–1934*, ed. T. M. Pearce (Westport, Conn.: Greenwood Press, 1979), 172. James Wilson, *The Earth Shall Weep* (New York: Atlantic Monthly Press, 1999), 337–38.

15. Charles H. Burke, "A Message to All Indians," 24 Feb. 1923. The document is reproduced at *http://www.iwchildren.org/redholocaust/1665message.htm*.

16. Edith Manville Dabb, "Evils of Tribal Dances," *NYT*, 2 Dec. 1923.

17. "According to statements by well informed people" is from Lindquist, *The Red Man in the United States*, 267–68; "characterized by orgies" is from ibid., 272; for "special privileges" see ibid., 287. For "the sexual crimes of the koshare" see Kelly, *The Assault on Assimilation*, 303. Collier describes the leaking of the BIA dossier in *From Every Zenith*, 138.

18. "Rights and Wrongs of American Indians," *MRW* (Apr. 1925): 265–67.

19. "Out of a stone-age condition" is quoted from Philp, *John Collier's Crusade for Indian Reform*, 55. "Children are being deliberately instructed" is from Herbert Welsh, "The Pueblo Indian Rites," *NYT*, 19 Oct. 1924; Frederick W. Hodge, "Rites of the Pueblo Indians," *NYT*, 26 Oct. 1924. William T. Hagan, *The Indian Rights Association* (Tucson: University of Arizona Press, 1985).

20. M. K. Sniffen, "Secret Dances of the Pueblos," *NYT*, 9 Nov. 1924. For the persecution of Christian Pueblo Indians, see Collier, *From Every Zenith*, 141. "Rights and Wrongs of American Indians," *MRW* (Apr. 1925): 266.

21. Helena Huntington Smith, "Red Man Dances," *North American* 228 (Jul. 1929): 78.

22. Alice Corbin Henderson, "On the Need of Scholarships for the Study of Indian Culture," *Poetry* 22 (Sep. 1923): 325–26; Kenneth R. Philp, "John Collier and the Crusade to Protect Indian Religious Freedom 1920–26," *Journal of Ethnic Studies* 1 (1973): 22–38. For the publicity tour see Carter Jones Meyer, "Saving the Pueblos," in Carter Jones Meyer and Diana Royer, eds., *Selling the Indian* (Tucson: University of Arizona Press, 2001), 197.

23. Meyer, "Saving the Pueblos." For Hart, see "Red-Letter Day for Red Americans," *Literary Digest*, 29 Sept. 1923, 36–40; William S. Hart, *My Life East and West* (Boston: Houghton Mifflin, 1929). See also Hart's introduction to Luther Standing Bear, *My People, the Sioux*, ed. E. A. Briminstool (Boston: Houghton Mifflin, 1928).

24. Henderson, "On the Need of Scholarships for the Study of Indian Culture."

25. Adele Heller and Lois Rudnick, eds., *1915, The Cultural Moment* (New Brunswick, N.J.: Rutgers University Press, 1991); W. Jackson Rushing III, *Native American Art and the New York Avant-Garde* (Austin: University of Texas Press, 1995); Sandra Adickes, *To Be Young Was Very Heaven* (New York: St. Martin's Press, 1997).

26. Alida Sims Markus, "Those Doomed Indian Dances," *NYT*, 8 Apr. 1923.

27. Markus, "Those Doomed Indian Dances"; Hodge, "Rites of the Pueblo Indians."

28. Hodge, "Rites of the Pueblo Indians"; Elizabeth Shepley Sergeant, "Death to the Golden Age," *New Republic*, 22 Aug. 1923, 354–57; Helena Huntington Smith, "Red Man Dances," *North American* 228 (Jul. 1929): 79. For Elizabeth Shepley Sergeant and the Southwest, see her *Willa Cather, a Memoir* (Lincoln: University of Nebraska Press, 1953); Molly H. Mullin, *Culture in the Marketplace* (Durham, N.C.: Duke University Press, 2001).

29. H. A. Studdert Kennedy, "The Indian and Religious Freedom," *The Independent*, 6 Mar. 1926, 267.

30. Mary Austin, "American Indian Dance Drama," *Yale Review* 19 (Jun. 1930): 732–45; Lummis is quoted from Cash Asher, "Pueblo Indians Fear for Their Religion," *NYT*, 13 Jul. 1924; Collier is quoted from "A History of American Indians in California: 1905–1933," at *http://www.cr.nps.gov/history/online_books/5views/5views1e.htm* . For the new awareness of genocide, see Peter Balakian, *The Burning Tigris* (New York: HarperCollins, 2003). Harry Emerson Fosdick, "Shall the Fundamentalists Win?" *Christian Work*, 10 Jun. 1922, 716–22.

31. "The Indians' Lament," *NYT*, 19 Aug. 1923; Carl Moon, "Navajo's Plea for His Dances," *NYT*, 18 Nov. 1923; Asher, "Pueblo Indians Fear for Their Religion"; Phillip, "Red Men Still with Us but Not of Us"; Dabb, "Evils of Tribal Dances"; John Collier, "Indian Dances Defended," *NYT*, 16 Dec. 1923; "There is no future" is from Wilson, *The Earth Shall Weep*, 340.

32. For the Mormon analogy, see Asher, "Pueblo Indians Fear for Their Religion." "They feel that they have a right" is from Alanson Skinner, "Not Modern Indians, nor True to the Old Types," *NYT*, 3 Jun. 1914. "Red-Letter Day For Red Americans," *Literary Digest*, 29 Sept. 1923, 36–40.

33. Moon, "Navajo's Plea for His Dances"; "Taking the Indianism Out of the Indian," *Literary Digest*, 28 Apr. 1923, 28–29. The cartoon cited is from Kelly, *The Assault on Assimilation*, 304.

34. Markus, "Those Doomed Indian Dances." Marsden Hartley, "Red Man Ceremonials," *Art and Archaeology* 9 (Mar. 1920): 7–14; C. G. Jung, *Memories, Dreams, Reflections*, rev. ed. (New York: Vintage, 1965), 250.

35. Sergeant, "Death to the Golden Age."
36. "Breaking Faith with the Indian," *New Republic*, 25 Jul. 1928, 240–41.
37. Jaime De Angulo, "Five Thousand Years," *The Independent*, 1 Jul. 1925, 11–12; D. H. Lawrence is quoted from "Taking the Indianism Out of the Indians."
38. "Substantially all of the Indian dance-drama ceremonials" is from Collier, "Indian Dances Defended." For the Sun Dance, see Collier, *The Indians of the Americas*, 234.
39. "Deeply and universally religious" is quoted from "A History of American Indians in California: 1905–1933." The reference to "forcible Christianization" is from John Collier, "The Religion of the Pueblos," *NYT*, 16 Nov. 1924.
40. Henderson, "On the Need of Scholarships for the Study of Indian Culture."
41. Lewis Meriam et al., *The Problem of Indian Administration* (Baltimore, Md.: Johns Hopkins University Press, 1928). Vera L. Connolly, "Cry of a Broken People," *Good Housekeeping* 88 (Feb. 1929): 30–31; Connolly, "We Still Get Robbed," *Good Housekeeping* 88 (Mar. 1929): 34–35. For the continuity of pro-Indian activism during the 1920s, see Randolph C. Downes, "A Crusade for Indian Reform, 1922–1934," *Mississippi Valley Historical Review* 32(3) (1945): 331–54.

Chapter 6

1. George William Cronyn, ed., *The Path on the Rainbow* (New York: Liveright, 1934), foreword.
2. John Collier, *From Every Zenith* (Denver, Colo.: Sage Books, 1963).
3. John Collier, "We Took Away Their Best Lands, Broke Treaties," at *http://historymatters.gmu.edu/d/5058/* . Randolph C. Downes, "A Crusade for Indian Reform, 1922–1934," *Mississippi Valley Historical Review* 32(3) (1945): 331–54; Lawrence C. Kelly, *The Navajo Indians and Federal Indian Policy, 1900–1935* (Tucson: University of Arizona Press, 1968); Kenneth R. Philp, *John Collier's Crusade for Indian Reform, 1920–1954* (Tucson: University of Arizona Press, 1977); Lawrence C. Kelly, *The Assault on Assimilation* (Albuquerque: University of New Mexico Press, 1983).
4. John Collier, "Indians Come Alive," *Atlantic Monthly* 170 (Sept. 1942): 79.
5. For religious liberty debates on the Pueblos, see Philp, *John Collier's Crusade for Indian Reform*, 193–97; Kenneth William Townsend, *World War II and the American Indian* (Albuquerque: University of New Mexico Press, 2000). R. L. Chambers, "Old vs. New at Taos," *Nation*, 25 March 1950, 273.
6. Lewis Meriam et al., *The Problem of Indian Administration* (Baltimore, Md.: Johns Hopkins Press, 1928), 845–47.
7. Martin E. Marty, *Modern American Religion*, vol. 2: *The Noise of Conflict* (Chicago: University of Chicago Press, 1991), 107.
8. L. C. McEwen, "Indians Attack Commissioner," *CC*, 5 Jun. 1935, 767; Elaine Goodale Eastman, "The American Indian and His Religion" *MRW* (Mar. 1937): 128–30. The wendigo reference is from Eastman, "Does Uncle Sam Foster Paganism?" *CC*, 8 Aug. 1934, 1016–20; idem, "Uncle Sam and Paganism," *CC*, 22 Aug. 1934, 1073.
9. C. M. Bogert, "Hopi Snake Dance," *Natural History* 48 (May 1941): 276–283. Compare "Snake Dance Secret Bared," *Scientific American* (Apr. 1937): 237; Mischa Titiev, "Hopi Snake Handling," *Scientific Monthly* 57 (Jul. 1943): 44–51. Also showing that attitudes had not quite perished, we recall the triumphalist story about Alaska from 1927, "Alaska's Rise Told by Veteran Pastor," *NYT*, 28 Nov. 1927.
10. William J. Schaldach, "Want to Collect Indian Relics?" *Natural History* (June 1955): 313–18.

11. Collier, *From Every Zenith*. Peter A. Huff, *Allen Tate and the Catholic Revival* (New York: Paulist Press, 1996).

12. John Chamberlain, "A Sioux Indian Tells His Tragic Story," *NYT*, 6 Mar. 1932; R. L. Duffus, "An Indian's Story of His People," *NYT*, 4 Jun. 1933; Duffus, "Sitting Bull, Who Was a Real Indian and a Real Man; Stanley Vestal's Biography Makes of Him a More Notable Figure Than General Custer," *NYT*, 2 Oct. 1932; "Indianizing the Red Man: Tribal Ways of Life Stressed in Reservation Schools," *Newsweek*, 14 Apr. 1941, 77.

13. Harvey Fergusson, "Cult of the Indian," *Scribner's*, Aug. 1930, 129. Margaret Mead, *Coming of Age in Samoa* (New York: W. Morrow, 1928). Lois W. Banner, *Intertwined Lives* (New York: Knopf, 2003). For the African American analogy, see David Levering Lewis, *When Harlem Was in Vogue* (New York: Penguin, 1997).

14. "The civilization of the White man": Ernest Thompson Seton, *The Gospel of the Red Man* (Garden City, N.Y.: Doubleday, Doran, 1936), 114; for "The culture and civilization of the white man": ibid., 1.

15. George Bird Grinnell, *The Cheyenne Indians* (New Haven, Conn.: Yale University Press, 1923); Dane Coolidge and Mary Roberts Coolidge, *The Navajo Indians* (Boston: Houghton Mifflin, 1930); Coolidge and Coolidge, *The Last of the Seris* (New York: E. P. Dutton, 1939). Mary Roberts Coolidge, *The Rain-Makers* (Boston: Houghton Mifflin, 1929). Also from this period was Franz Boas, *Religion of the Kwakiutl Indians*, 2 vols. (New York: Columbia University Press, 1930).

16. Ruth L. Bunzel, *Introduction to Zuñi Ceremonialism* (Washington, D.C.: Government Printing Office, 1932); Gladys A. Reichard, *Spider Woman* (New York: Macmillan, 1934); Reichard, *Navaho Religion* (New York: Pantheon, 1950); Ruth Benedict, *Patterns of Culture* (Boston: Houghton Mifflin, 1934); and Benedict, *Zuñi Mythology* (New York: Columbia University Press, 1935); Elsie Clews Parsons, *Pueblo Indian Religion* (Chicago: University of Chicago Press, 1939). For the social context of the anthropologists of these years, see Barbara A. Babcock and Nancy J. Parezo, *Daughters of the Desert* (Albuquerque: University of New Mexico Press, 1988); Rosemary Levy Zumwalt, *Wealth and Rebellion* (Urbana: University of Illinois Press, 1992); Nancy J. Parezo, ed., *Hidden Scholars* (Albuquerque: University of New Mexico Press, 1993).

17. John G. Neihardt, *Black Elk Speaks* (Lincoln: University of Nebraska Press, 1961); Chamberlain, "A Sioux Indian Tells His Tragic Story"; Clyde Holler, ed., *The Black Elk Reader* (Syracuse, N.Y.: Syracuse University Press, 2000); Brian R. Holloway, *Interpreting the Legacy* (Boulder: University Press of Colorado, 2003).

18. Oliver La Farge, *Laughing Boy* (New York: Signet Classic, 1971), 191–92; D'Arcy McNickle, *Indian Man* (Bloomington: Indiana University Press, 1971); Robert A. Hecht, *Oliver La Farge and the American Indian* (Metuchen, N.J.: Scarecrow Press, 1991); Dorothy R. Parker, *Singing an Indian Song* (Lincoln: University of Nebraska Press, 1994); Robert Dale Parker, *The Invention of Native American Literature* (Ithaca, N.Y.: Cornell University Press, 2003). Another significant Native novel from these years was John Joseph Mathews, *Sundown* (New York: Longmans, Green, 1934).

19. Paul Radin, ed., *Crashing Thunder* (New York: D. Appleton, 1926); Henry H. Balos, "What a Winnebago Thinks About," *NYT*, 30 Jan. 1927; Walter Dyk, ed., *Son of Old Man Hat* (New York: Harcourt, Brace, 1938); Clellan S. Ford, *Smoke from Their Fires* (Hamden, Conn.: Archon, 1971); Don C. Talayesva, *Sun Chief*, Leo W. Simmons, ed. (New Haven, Conn.: Yale University Press, 1942). Other biographies from these years include Frank B. Linderman, *American: The Life Story of a Great Indian* (New York: John Day, 1930); and Linderman, *Red Mother* (New York: John Day, 1932); Stanley Vestal, *Warpath* (Boston: Houghton Mifflin Company, 1934). One popular Indian

book of these years was James Willard Schultz, *My Life as an Indian:* (New York: Houghton Mifflin 1935).

20. Luther Standing Bear, *Land of the Spotted Eagle* (Boston: Houghton Mifflin, 1933).

21. Duffus, "An Indian's Story of His People."

22. R. L. Duffus, "Life Among the Pueblo Indians of the City of Acoma," *NYT*, 16 Oct. 1932.

23. Mari Sandoz, "What the Sioux Taught Me," *Reader's Digest*, May 1952, 121–24; Malcolm A. Nelson, "These Were Mari Sandoz's Sioux," in *Telling the Stories*, eds. Elizabeth Hoffman Nelson and Malcolm A. Nelson (New York: Peter Lang, 2001).

24. "Indian Tribe Trained by Sympathetic Plan," *NYT*, 19 Dec. 1926.

25. "Alaskan Folklore Is Dying, Says Smithsonian Expert," *NYT*, 23 Oct. 1927.

26. Aldous Huxley, *Brave New World* (Garden City, N.Y.: Garden City Publishers, 1932), ch. 7.

27. Charles Fletcher Lummis, *Some Strange Corners of Our Country* (New York: The Century Co., 1892); Lummis, *Mesa, Cañon and Pueblo* (New York: The Century Co., 1925); William Henry Robinson, *Under Turquoise Skies* (New York: Macmillan, 1928); Leo Crane, *Desert Drums* (Boston: Little, Brown, 1928); Earle R. Forrest, *Missions and Pueblos of the Old Southwest* (Cleveland, Ohio: A. H. Clarke, 1929); Ross Calvin, *Sky Determines* (New York: Macmillan, 1934); Marta Weigle and Barbara A. Babcock, eds., *The Great Southwest of the Fred Harvey Company and the Santa Fe Railway* (Phoenix, Ariz.: Heard Museum/University of Arizona Press, 1996); Mark Thompson, *American Character* (New York: Arcade Publishing, 2001).

28. John Marin, *The Selected Writings of John Marin,* ed. Dorothy Norman (New York: Pellegrini & Cudahy, 1949), 129. For Taos in 1950, see John Gunther, *Inside USA* (New York: Harper, 1951), 982.

29. "New Mexico officials" is from Walter G. Weisbecker and Wyatt Davis, "Southwest Festivals; Next Year's Centennial Stirs Wide Interest in Indian Rites," *NYT*, 7 May 1939; Ruth A. Laughlin, "Indians Vie in Pageants; Ceremonials and Dances Held in New Mexico Attract Tourists," *NYT*, 22 Aug. 1937. For the Snake Dance, see D. Maitland Bushby, "The Dance of the Snake," *Overland* 87 (1929): 167–68; C. M. Bogert, "Hopi Snake Dance," *Natural History* 48 (May 1941): 276–83; D. H. Lawrence, "The Hopi Snake Dance," in Lawrence, *Mornings in Mexico, and Etruscan Places* (London: Heineman, 1956), 61–80; Joseph Morris Richards, *The Hopi Snake Dance* (Winslow, Ariz.: 1949). For the Penitentes as a tourist attraction, see D. Woodward, *The Penitentes of New Mexico* (New Haven, Conn., 1935); Alice Corbin Henderson, *Brothers of Light* (New York: Harcourt, Brace, 1937); Harry Sylvester, *Dayspring* (New York: Appleton-Century, 1945). Jacqueline Hoefer, ed., *A More Abundant Life* (Santa Fe, N.M.: Sunstone Press, 2002).

30. Anna Nolan Clark, "Indians to Gallup," *Reader's Digest*, Aug. 1938, 112.

31. P. Coze, "The Indian's Altar to His God," *Travel* (Jan. 1940): 18. Erna Fergusson, "Ceremonial Dances of the Pueblos," *Travel* (Dec. 1931): 15–19; Fergusson, *Dancing Gods* (Albuquerque: University of New Mexico Press, 1931).

32. Elizabeth S. Bird, ed., *Dressing in Feathers* (Boulder, Colo.: Westview Press, 1996); Patsy West, *The Enduring Seminoles* (Gainesville: University Press of Florida, 1998); for Palm Springs, see Muriel Rukeyser, "Indian Fiesta Huge Success," *Nation*, 29 May 1937, 616–18. Richard V. Humphrey, ed., *The Mystery Hill Source Book* (Salem, N.H.: Teaparty Books, 1979).

33. Douglas Cole, *Captured Heritage* (Norman: University of Oklahoma Press, 1995); Ruth Kirk, *Tradition and Change on the Northwest Coast* (Seattle: University of Washington

Press, 1988); Ira Jacknis, *The Storage Box of Tradition* (Washington, D.C.: Smithsonian Institution Press, 2002). Natalie Curtis, *The Indians' Book* (New York: Harper, 1907), 295–311. Franz Boas, *Kwakiutl Tales* (New York: Columbia University Press, 1910). The Northwest Coast had attracted its share of commentators since the late nineteenth century, but before the 1930s, the number of articles published in the popular media was trivial when compared to the coverage of the Great Plains, not to mention the Southwest. For earlier commentary, see "The Yakutats; How They Served the Times Expedition," *NYT*, 3 Oct. 1886; "The Thlinkets of Alaska," *NYT*, 8 Nov. 1886; Charles De Kay, "Kwakiutls of North America," *NYT*, 13 Aug. 1899; M. W. Leighton, "Haidah Indians," *Overland* 37 (Jun. 1901): 1083–86; "Religious Beliefs of the Northwest Coast Indians," *Scientific American*, 16 Jun. 1917, 379; Charles Harrison, *Ancient Warriors of the North Pacific* (London: H. F. & G. Witherby, 1925). For the traditional cultures of the region, see, for instance, Robert Bringhurst, *A Story as Sharp as a Knife* (Lincoln: University of Nebraska Press, 2000).

34. Alice Henson Ernst, "Northwest Coast Animal Dances," *Theatre Arts Monthly* 23 (Sept. 1939): 665.

35. "The full-voice chorus" is from Ernst, "Northwest Coast Animal Dances," 661. Boas, *Religion of the Kwakiutl Indians*; Alice Henson Ernst, "Masks of the Northwest Coast," *Theatre Arts Monthly* 17 (Aug. 1933): 646–56; and Ernst, *The Wolf Ritual of the Northwest Coast* (Eugene: University of Oregon Press, 1952). Heister Dean Guie, "Nature and the Northwestern Red Man," *Nature Magazine*, Feb. 1939, 71–73; Nowell, *Smoke from Their Fires*; Fred J. Ostler, "Blood on the Totem Pole," *Travel* 89 (Jun. 1947): 27–29+; "Can You Read a Totem Pole?" *Science Illustrated* 3 (Sep. 1948): 8–9; Charlotte Baker Montgomery, "Animal Symbols In Northwest Coast Indian Design," *School Arts* 49 (Sept. 1949): 24–27; Robert Bruce Inverarity, *Art of the Northwest Coast Indians* (Berkeley: University of California Press, 1950); Thomas B. Lesure, "How To Read a Totem Pole," *Travel* (Jun. 1955): 27–29.

36. "Indian Masks: Gods and Demons of the North Pacific Coast," *Travel* 77 (Jun. 1941): 31. John Collier, "More Beautiful than Totem Poles," *Time*, 9 Dec. 1950, 9–10.

37. For the Coolidge inauguration, see Etta J. Oliver, "Mystic Dances of the Painted Desert," *Travel* 47 (Jul. 1926): 27–29; "To preserve the best in native cultures" is from Ida Cherioli, "The Conservation of Indian Arts and Crafts," *School Arts* 35 (Oct. 1935): 120. Contemporary scholars have written at length of the cultural and ethical dilemmas faced by anthropologists and scholars who intervene in traditional societies. See, for example, James Clifford, *The Predicament of Culture* (Cambridge, Mass.: Harvard University Press, 1988).

38. Carter Jones Meyer, "Saving the Pueblos," in *Selling the Indian*, eds. Carter Jones Meyer and Diana Royer (Tucson: University of Arizona Press, 2001), 190–211. For the Museum of Northern Arizona, see Jimmy Miller, *Life of Harold Sellers Colton* (Tsaile, Ariz: Dine College Press, 1991). For the Indian Arts Fund, see Kenneth Dauber, "Pueblo Pottery and the Politics of Regional Identity," *Journal of the Southwest* 32(4) (1990), at *http://digital.library.arizona.edu/jsw/3204/pueblo.html* . J. J. Brody, *Pueblo Indian Painting* (Santa Fe: School of American Research Press, 1997); Shepard Krech and Barbara A. Hail, eds., *Collecting Native America, 1870–1960* (Washington, D.C.: Smithsonian Institution Press, 1999); Molly H. Mullin, *Culture in the Marketplace* (Durham, N.C.: Duke University Press, 2001); Margaret D. Dubin, *Native America Collected* (Albuquerque: University of New Mexico Press, 2001); Leah Dilworth and Mary C. Tuominen, eds., *Acts of Possession* (New Brunswick, NJ: Rutgers University

Press, 2003). Among the books from this era serving the growing collector market, see Gene Meany Hodge, *The Kachinas Are Coming* (Los Angeles: Steller-Millar, 1936). The standard kachina guide would be Harold S. Colton, *Hopi Kachina Dolls* (Albuquerque: University of New Mexico Press, 1979). For the emergence and popularization of a wholly new craft tradition (as recently as the 1960s), see Barbara A. Babcock, *The Pueblo Storyteller* (Tucson: University of Arizona Press, 1987).

39. Franc Johnson Newcomb, *Hosteen Klah, Navaho Medicine Man and Sand Painter* (Norman: University of Oklahoma Press, 1964). Another anthropological text secured with the active assistance of a Native informant was Frank Gouldsmith Speck, *A Study of the Delaware Indian Big House Ceremony: In Native Text Dictated by Witapanoxwe* (Harrisburg, Penn.: Pennsylvania Historical Commission, 1931).

40. Rose V. S. Berry, "The Navajo Shaman and His Sacred Sand-Paintings," *Art and Archaeology* 27 (Jan. 1929): 1, 3–16; Manly P. Hall, "Sand Magic for the Navaho," *Overland* 87 (May 1929): 137; D. Reynolds, "Navajo Sand Paintings," *School Arts Magazine* 36 (Nov. 1936): 153–57; Gladys Amanda Reichard, *Navajo Medicine Man* (New York: J. J. Augustin, 1939); "Good Medicine," *Time*, 23 Feb. 1948, 71; "Sand Paintings," *School Arts*, 49 (Nov. 1949): 87–88. For modern interpretations, see Nancy Parezo, *Navajo Sandpainting* (Albuquerque: University of New Mexico Press, 1991); Trudy Griffin-Pierce, *Earth Is My Mother, Sky Is My Father* (Albuquerque: University of New Mexico Press, 1995).

41. Francis Paul Prucha, ed., *Documents of United States Indian Policy*, 2nd ed. (Lincoln: University of Nebraska Press, 1990), 229; Robert Fay Schrader, *The Indian Arts and Crafts Board* (Albuquerque: University of New Mexico Press, 1983); Susan L. Meyn, *More Than Curiosities* (Lanham, Md.: Lexington Books, 2001). Collier, *From Every Zenith*, 194. For Mexican analogies, see Mary Austin, "American Indian Dance Drama," *Yale Review* 19 (Jun. 1930): 732–45; V. F. Calverton, "Mexico Goes American," *The Living Age*, Feb. 1936, 510; Leonard Wilcox, *V. F. Calverton: Radical in the American Grain* (Philadelphia: Temple University Press, 1992).

42. Marsden Hartley, *Somehow a Past* (Cambridge, Mass.: MIT Press, 1997), 97; John Marin, *The Selected Writings of John Marin*, 132; Chamberlain, "A Sioux Indian Tells His Tragic Story." Edward Alden Jewell, "A Tradition Lives On," *NYT*, 6 Dec. 1931. For the 1931 Exposition, see Frederick Webb Hodge, Herbert J. Spinden, and Oliver La Farge, eds., *Introduction to American Indian Art: To Accompany the First Exhibition of American Indian Art Selected Entirely with Consideration of Esthetic Value* (New York: The Exposition of Indian Tribal Arts, 1931); Molly H. Mullin, "The Patronage of Difference," *Cultural Anthropology* 7(4) (1992): 395–424; Mullin, *Culture in the Marketplace*. Sharyn Rohlfsen Udall, *Modernist Painting in New Mexico, 1913–1935* (Albuquerque: University of New Mexico Press, 1984); Charles C. Eldredge, Julie Schimmel, and William H. Truettner, eds., *Art in New Mexico, 1900–1945* (Washington, D.C.: National Museum of American Art, 1986); Janet Catherine Berlo, ed., *The Early Years of Native American Art History* (Seattle: University of Washington Press, 1992).

43. Clyde Holler, *Black Elk's Religion* (Syracuse, N.Y.: Syracuse University Press, 1995); Holler, *The Black Elk Reader*; Holloway, *Interpreting the Legacy*.

44. "Pueblos Perform Tribal Dance," *NYT*, 15 Dec. 1931.

45. The quotes from Edward Alden Jewell are from his article "The Redman's Culture," *NYT*, 26 Jan. 1941. "In less than a generation": Cole, *Captured Heritage*, 285; "Art of The Indian," *NYT*, 19 Jan. 1941; compare Howard Devree, "Display of Masks Seen in Brooklyn," *NYT*, 25 Oct. 1939. Frederic H. Douglas and Rene d'Harnoncourt, *Indian Art of the United States* (1941; repr., New York: Museum of Modern Art, Publications in reprint, 1975); W. Jackson Rushing III, "Marketing the Affinity of the Primitive and

the Modern,'" in *The Early Years of Native American Art History,* ed., Janet Catherine Berlo (Seattle: University of Washington Press, 1992), 191–236; W. Richard West, ed., *The Changing Presentation of the American Indian* (Seattle: University of Washington Press, 2000).

46. Isabelle Anthony, "Permanent Sand Painting," *School Arts Magazine* (Dec. 1951): 306; Dorothy Reynolds, "Navajo Sand Paintings," *School Arts Magazine* 36 (Nov. 1936): 153–57.

Chapter 7

1. Philip Jenkins, *Mystics and Messiahs* (New York: Oxford University Press, 2000).
2. "Flocking To A Quack Doctor," *NYT,* 12 Jul. 1880; Jason Berry, *The Spirit of Black Hawk* (Jackson: University Press of Mississippi, 1995).
3. Charles Eastman, *The Soul of the Indian* (Boston: Houghton Mifflin, 1911); Ernest Thompson Seton, *The Gospel of the Red Man* (Garden City, N.Y., Doubleday, Doran, 1936), 9–10. For parallels between primitive religion and modern occultism, see, for instance, Andrew Lang, *The Making of Religion* (New York: Longmans, Green, 1898).
4. For Theosophical approaches, see "Sources of Early American Civilization," *Theosophy* 15(12) (1927): 543–49, at *http://www.wisdomworld.org/additional/ancientlandmarks /SourceAmericanCiviliza.html* ; Robert S. Ellwood, "The American Theosophical Synthesis," in *The Occult in America,* eds. Howard Kerr and Charles L. Crow (Urbana: University of Illinois Press, 1983), 111–34; Michael Gomes, *The Dawning of the Theosophical Society* (Wheaton, Ill.: Theosophical Society, 1987); K. Paul Johnson, *The Masters Revealed* (Albany, N.Y.: State University of New York Press, 1994), and Johnson, *Initiates of Theosophical Masters* (Albany, N.Y.: State University of New York Press, 1995); Joscelyn Godwin, *The Theosophical Enlightenment* (Albany: State University of New York Press, 1994); Peter Washington, *Madame Blavatsky's Baboon* (New York: Schocken, 1995); Paul Jordan, *The Atlantis Syndrome* (Stroud, England: Sutton, 2001). For the "new" lost continents, see Rudolf Steiner, *The Submerged Continents of Atlantis and Lemuria* (Chicago: Rajput Press, 1911); James Churchward, *The Lost Continent of Mu* (New York: Ives Washburn, 1931); Lewis Spence, *The Problem of Lemuria* (London: Rider, 1932); Wishar S. Cerve, *Lemuria: The Lost Continent of the Pacific* (San Jose, Calif.: Rosicrucian Press, AMORC College, 1935). For the Serpent Mound, see F. J. Koch, "The Riddle of the American Sphinx," *American Antiquarian* 34(4)(1912): 290–293; A. S. Wilson, "The Naga and the Lingam of India and the Serpent Mounds of Ohio," *Ohio Archaeological and Historical Society Publications* 30(1921): 77–89.
5. Mabel Dodge Luhan, *Intimate Memories,* vol. 4: *Edge of Taos Desert* (New York: Harcourt, Brace, 1937).
6. Manly P. Hall, "Sand Magic for the Navaho," *Overland* 87 (May 1929): 137. "The North American Indian" is from Hall, *Secret Teachings of All Ages* (San Francisco: H. S. Crocker, 1928). For Nazi connections, see Kenneth R. Philp, *John Collier's Crusade for Indian Reform, 1920–1954* (Tucson: University of Arizona Press, 1977). The swastika emblem does appear in Native art, usually as a sun symbol.
7. Frank Waters, *Book of the Hopi* (New York: Viking, 1963). Vine Deloria, Jr., ed., *Frank Waters: Man and Mystic* (Athens, Ohio: Swallow Press, 1993).
8. Marjory Stoneman Douglas, *The Everglades: River of Grass,* 50th anniversary ed. (Sarasota, Fla.: Pineapple Press, 1997); Robert Graves, *The White Goddess* (New York: Vintage, 1948); Aldo Leopold, *A Sand County Almanac* (New York: Oxford University Press, 1949); Joseph Campbell, *The Hero with a Thousand Faces* (New York: Pantheon,

1949). The French original of Mircea Eliade's *Shamanism: Archaic Technique of Ecstasy* appeared in 1951. Another critical book from this era was Howard Thurman's *Jesus and the Disinherited* (New York: Abingdon-Cokesbury Press, 1949), a primary inspiration for Martin Luther King and the Civil Rights movement.

9. "New Mexico's Fiestas," *Travel* (Mar 1947): 31.

10. Paul Radin is quoted from Stan Steiner, *The New Indians* (New York: Dell, 1968), xi. John Collier, *The Indians of the Americas* (New York: W. W. Norton, 1947). Collier followed this with his magnificently illustrated *Patterns and Ceremonials of the Indians of the Southwest* (New York: Dutton, 1949). John Collier, "The Indian Speaks for Himself," *NYT*, 3 Dec. 1950; and Collier, "More Beautiful Than Totem Poles," *Saturday Review of Literature*, 9 Dec. 1950, 9–10. Collier was much in demand as a writer of forewords and introductions to books on Native Americans. See Alexander H. Leighton and Dorothea C. Leighton, *The Navaho Door* (Cambridge, Mass., Harvard University Press, 1944); and Laura Thompson, *Culture in Crisis* (New York: Harper, 1950). Another survey of Indian peoples from this time was D'Arcy McNickle, *They Came Here First* (Philadelphia: J. B. Lippincott, 1949).

11. Laura Thompson and Alice Joseph, *The Hopi Way*, 2nd ed. (Chicago: University of Chicago Press, 1947); Thompson, *Culture in Crisis*. The reviewer quoted was Ward Shepard, from "Our Indigenous Shangri-La," *Scientific Monthly* 62 (Feb. 1946): 158–64; Edmund Wilson, *Red, Black, Blond, and Olive* (New York: Oxford University Press, 1956).

12. Frank Waters, "Navajo *Yei-Bet-Chai*," *Yale Review* 28 (Mar. 1939): 558–71; Waters, *Masked Gods: Navaho and Pueblo Ceremonialism* (Albuquerque: University of New Mexico Press, 1950); Waters, *The Man Who Killed the Deer* (Athens, Ohio: Swallow Press/Ohio University Press, 1989); Waters, *Mexico Mystique: The Coming Sixth World of Consciousness* (Athens, Ohio: Swallow Press/Ohio University Press, 1989); Waters, *Mysticism and Witchcraft* (Fort Collins, Colo.: Colorado State University Press, 1966); Waters, *Of Time and Change* (Denver, Colo.: MacMurray & Beck, 1998); Waters, *Pure Waters: Frank Waters and the Quest for the Cosmic*, ed. Barbara Waters (Athens, Ohio: Swallow Press/Ohio University Press, 2002).

13. Kluckhohn wrote *Navaho Witchcraft* (Boston: Beacon Press, 1944) and *Mirror for Man* (New York: Whittlesey House, 1949). Waters, *Of Time and Change*, 17–21.

14. For Gurdjieff, see, for example, Waters, *Masked Gods*, 182; Waters, *Of Time and Change*, 20–21, 80–82.

15. The passage on the Deer Dance is from John R. Milton, ed., *Conversations with Frank Waters* (Chicago: Swallow Press, 1971), 66. See also Waters, *Masked Gods*, 182–92.

16. For Graves and the Essenes, see Waters, *Masked Gods*, 417–18.

17. Sir John George Woodroffe ("Arthur Avalon"), ed., *The Serpent Power* (New York: Dover, 1974); W. Y. Evans-Wentz, *The Tibetan Book of the Dead*, 4th ed. (Oxford University Press, 1972); idem, *Cuchama and Sacred Mountains*, ed. Frank Waters and Charles L. Adams (Athens: Ohio University Press, 1981). For Jung's use of Buddhist symbolism, see his *Mandala Symbolism* (Princeton, N.J.: Princeton University Press, 1972); C. G. Jung, *The Psychology of Kundalini Yoga*, ed. Sonu Shamdasani (Princeton, N.J.: Princeton University Press, 1996). Kathleen Taylor, *Sir John Woodroffe, Tantra and Bengal* (Richmond: Curzon Press, 2000).

18. "It is only by such a synthesis": Waters, *Masked Gods*, 225; Richard Wilhelm, ed., *The Secret of the Golden Flower* (New York: Harcourt, Brace, 1932).

19. "A submerging yet unverified": Waters, *Masked Gods*, 22; Waters, *Book of the Hopi*, 304, 32.

20. Waters, *Man Who Killed the Deer*, 233–34 (the kiva), 243 (raising the pyramids).

21. Waters, *Masked Gods,* 161 ("by his own space-time concept of reality"), 208 ("it may not be wholly a coincidence"), 418 (Los Alamos and Mesa Verde). "An inseparably interrelated field or continuum" is from Waters, *Book of the Hopi,* xviii.

22. John C. Culver and John Hyde, *American Dreamer* (New York: W. W. Norton, 2000).

23. John Thomas Noonan, *The Lustre of Our Country* (Berkeley: University of California Press, 1998), 170–72; Monroe Tsa To Ke, *The Peyote Ritual* (San Francisco: Grabhorn Press, 1957).

24. Black Elk, *The Sacred Pipe,* ed. Joseph Epes Brown (Norman: University of Oklahoma Press, 1953); Joseph Epes Brown, *The Spiritual Legacy of the American Indian* (New York: Crossroad, 1982). Mark Sedgwick, *Against the Modern World* (New York: Oxford University Press, 2004).

25. Huntington Cairns, "Divine Intoxicant," *Atlantic Monthly* (Nov. 1929): 638–45.

26. D'Arcy McNickle, "Peyote and the Indian," *Scientific Monthly* 57 (Sept. 1943) 220–29; Norman Taylor, "Come and Expel the Green Pain," *Scientific Monthly* 58 (Mar. 1944): 176–84; Alice Marriott, "Opened Door," *New Yorker,* 9 Aug. 1954, 90. For peyote in San Francisco, see Gary Snyder, *Earth House Hold* (New York: New Directions, 1969). Robert C. Fuller, *Stairways to Heaven* (Boulder, Colo.: Westview Press, 2000). For Jack Parsons, see John Carter, *Sex and Rockets* (Venice, CA: Feral House, 1999), 123-25.

27. Bob Callahan, ed., *A Jaime De Angulo Reader* (San Francisco: Turtle Island Foundation, 1979). Jaime De Angulo and L. S. Freeland, "A New Religious Movement in North-Central California," *American Anthropologist,* n.s., 31(2) (1929): 265–70; Jaime De Angulo, *Indian Tales* (New York: A. A. Wyn, 1953); idem, *Coyote Man and Old Doctor Loon* (San Francisco: Turtle Island Foundation, 1973); idem, *Indians in Overalls* (San Francisco: Turtle Island Foundation, 1973); idem, *Coyote's Bones* (San Francisco: Turtle Island Foundation, 1974); idem, *Jaime in Taos* (San Francisco: City Lights, 1999). The remark about "a now legendary departed Spanish shaman" is from Snyder, *Earth House Hold.* For Jung's interest in these areas, see his commentary to Paul Radin, *The Trickster* (New York: Bell Publishing, 1956).

28. John Sheehy, "The Tao of Gary Snyder," *Reed Magazine,* Feb. 1999, at *http://Web.Reed. Edu/Community/Newsandpub/Feb1999/Index.html* ; Gary Snyder, *He Who Hunted Birds in His Father's Village* (Bolinas, Calif: Grey Fox Press, 1979).

29. Ann Charters, *The Portable Beat Reader* (New York: Penguin, 1992), 227 ("peyoteist"); 265–72 (*Peyote Poem*); 275–79 (*Berry Feast*).

30. Aldous Huxley, *The Doors of Perception, and Heaven and Hell* (New York: Harper & Row, 1956).

31. Richard Evans Schultes, "Peyote and the American Indian," *Nature Magazine,* Sept. 1937, 155–57; Victor H. Gaddis, "Cult of the Sacred Cactus," *Travel* 92 (Nov. 1948): 16–17+; E. X. Green, "Peyote Cult," *Hobbies* 55 (Mar. 1950): 142; J. H. Howard, "Omaha Peyotism," *Hobbies* 56 (Sep. 1952): 142; Laura Bergquist, "Peyote: The Strange Church of Cactus Eaters," *Look,* 10 Dec. 1957, 36–41. Cyril Kornbluth, "Two Dooms," in *Hitler Victorious,* eds. Gregory Benford and Martin H. Greenberg (New York: Garland, 1986).

32. R. G. Wasson, "Seeking the Magic Mushroom," *Life,* 13 May 1957, 100–107. Thomas J. Riedlinger et al., eds., *The Sacred Mushroom Seeker* (Rochester, Vt.: Park Street Press, 1997).

33. F. Densmore, "Use of Music in the Treatment of the Sick by American Indians," *Musical Quarterly* 13 (Oct. 1927): 555–65; Morris Edward Opler, *Some Points of Comparison and Contrast between the Treatment of Functional Disorders by Apache Shamans and Modern Psychiatric Practice* (Baltimore, Md.: American Psychiatric Association, 1936);

Alexander H. Leighton and Dorothea C. Leighton, "Elements of Psychotherapy in Navaho Religion," *Psychiatry* 4 (1941): 515–23.

34. Elizabeth A. Ferguson, "Primitive Medicine," *Scientific American* (Sep. 1948): 24–27.

35. "Indians Had Dream Theory," *Science News Letter,* 22 Mar. 1958, 183; "The Case of Mary Grey-Eyes," *Time,* 10 Nov. 1958, 60. Jackson Steward Lincoln, *The Dream in Primitive Cultures* (Baltimore, Md.: Williams & Wilkins, 1935).

36. J. B. Rhine, *New Frontiers of the Mind* (New York: Farrar & Rinehart, 1937); Vincent H. Gaddis, "Cult of the Sacred Cactus," *Travel* 92 (Nov. 1948): 16–17.

37. Philip Jenkins, *Moral Panic* (New Haven, Conn.: Yale University Press, 1998).

38. "Return of the Redskins," *Newsweek,* 27 Aug. 1956, 68. For the emergence of professionalism in the pow-wow tradition during the 1950s, see Tara Browner, *Heartbeat of the People* (Urbana: University of Illinois Press, 2002).

39. Oliver La Farge, "Wakan Tanka and the Seven Rituals of the Sioux," *NYT,* 22 Nov. 1953. Another critical work on Indian religion from this period is Hartley B. Alexander, *The World's Rim* (Lincoln: University of Nebraska Press, 1953).

40. Francis Paul Prucha, ed., *Documents of United States Indian Policy,* 2nd ed. (Lincoln: University of Nebraska Press, 1990), 234–38. Larry W. Burt, *Tribalism in Crisis* (Albuquerque: University of New Mexico Press, 1982); Kenneth R. Philp, *Termination Revisited* (Lincoln: University of Nebraska Press, 2002). For urban Indians, see James B. Lagrand, *Indian Metropolis* (Urbana: University of Illinois Press, 2002); Deborah Davis Jackson, *Our Elders Lived It* (DeKalb: Northern Illinois University Press, 2002). For cultural policy in these years, Joy L. Gritton, *The Institute of American Indian Arts: Modernism and U.S. Indian Policy* (Albuquerque: University of New Mexico Press, 2000).

41. D'Arcy McNickle, "It's Almost Never Too Late," *CC,* 20 Feb. 1957. "Are Indian Rights Again Being Betrayed?" *CC,* 15 Apr. 1953, 437; John Collier, "Back To Dishonor?" *CC,* 12 May 1954, 578–80.

Chapter 8

1. Carey McWilliams, *California: The Great Exception,* 50th anniversary ed. (Berkeley: University of California Press, 1999), 51; "Racism: A Factor in Future of Indians," *CC,* 21 Jan. 1948, 69.

2. William A. Brophy et al., *The Indian: America's Unfinished Business* (Norman: University of Oklahoma Press, 1966).

3. Philip J. Deloria, *Playing Indian* (New Haven, Conn.: Yale University Press, 1998), 132. Robin Richman, "Happy Hippie Hunting Ground," *Life,* 1 Dec. 1967, 66.

4. Deloria, *Playing Indian,* 154–90; Gary Snyder, *Turtle Island* (New York: New Directions, 1974), 105.

5. Dee Brown, *Bury My Heart at Wounded Knee* (New York: Holt, Rinehart & Winston, 1970). Also influential in this era was Peter Farb's 1969 book *Man's Rise to Civilization,* rev. ed. (New York: Dutton, 1978).

6. Stan Steiner, *The New Indians* (New York: Dell, 1968); Vine Deloria, Jr., *Custer Died for Your Sins* (Norman: University of Oklahoma Press, 1988); Paul Chaat Smith and Robert Allen Warrior, *Like a Hurricane* (New York: W. W. Norton, 1996); Troy R. Johnson, Joane Nagel, and Duane Champagne, eds., *American Indian Activism* (Urbana: University of Illinois Press, 1997); Alvin M. Josephy, Joane Nagel, and Troy Johnson, eds., *Red Power* (Lincoln: University of Nebraska Press, 1999); Peter Nabokov, ed., *Native American Testimony,* rev. ed. (New York: Penguin, 1999); Mario Gonzalez and Elizabeth Cook-

Lynn, *The Politics of Hallowed Ground* (Urbana: University of Illinois Press, 1999); James Treat, *Around the Sacred Fire* (New York: Palgrave Macmillan, 2003).

7. Alvin M. Josephy, *Now that the Buffalo's Gone* (Norman: University of Oklahoma Press, 1985).

8. Steven M. Tipton, *Getting Saved from the Sixties* (Berkeley: University of California Press, 1982).

9. Frank Waters, *Book of the Hopi* (New York: Viking, 1963); Waters, *Of Time and Change* (Denver, Colo.: MacMurray & Beck, 1998), 22–25. For the long-standing familiarity between the Hopi and visiting anthropologists, see Don C. Talayesva, *Sun Chief*, ed., Leo W. Simmons (New Haven, Conn.: Yale University Press, 1942).

10. Waters, *Book of the Hopi*, xvi.

11. Ibid., xvii–xix. The vision of WASP America is from ibid., 339

12. Ibid., 33.

13. Waters, *Of Time and Change*, 242–43. Waters's ideas about Atlantis and ancient wisdom are again treated at length in his 1975 book *Mexico Mystique* (repr., Athens, Ohio: Swallow Press/Ohio University Press, 1989).

14. Snyder, *Turtle Island*, 104–5.

15. For the Smohalla quote, see Mircea Eliade, *The Sacred and the Profane* (New York: Harcourt, Brace, 1959), 138–39. Mark Sedgwick, *Against the Modern World* (New York: Oxford University Press, 2004).

16. William A. Brophy et al., *The Indian: America's Unfinished Business*.

17. Lynn White, Jr., "The Historical Roots of Our Ecological Crisis," *Science* 155 (1967): 1203–7.

18. Albert Furtwangler, *Answering Chief Seattle* (Seattle: University of Washington Press, 1997).

19. Eliza McFeely, *Zuñi and the American Imagination* (New York: Hill & Wang, 2001).

20. Black Elk's reputation continues to grow. See Raymond J. Demallie, ed., *The Sixth Generation* (Lincoln: University of Nebraska Press, 1984); Michael F. Steltenkamp, *Black Elk: Holy Man of the Oglala* (Norman: University of Oklahoma Press, 1993); Hilda Neihardt Petri, *Black Elk and Flaming Rainbow* (Lincoln: University of Nebraska Press, 1995); Therese Archambault, *A Retreat with Black Elk* (Cincinnati, Ohio: St. Anthony Messenger Press, 1998); Esther Black Elk Desersa, *Black Elk Lives*, eds. Hilda Neihardt and Lori Utecht (Lincoln: University of Nebraska Press, 2000); Clyde Holler, ed., *The Black Elk Reader* (Syracuse, N.Y.: Syracuse University Press, 2000); Brian Holloway, *Interpreting the Legacy* (Boulder, Colo.: University Press of Colorado, 2003).

21. John Fire/Lame Deer and Richard Erdoes, *Lame Deer, Seeker of Visions* (New York: Simon & Schuster, 1972); David E. Jones, *Sanapia, Comanche Medicine Woman* (New York: Holt, Rinehart & Winston, 1972); Joseph Medicine Crow, *Memories of a White Crow Indian* (Lincoln: University of Nebraska, 1974); Brad Steiger, *Medicine Talk* (Garden City, N.Y.: Doubleday, 1975).

22. Hyemeyohsts Storm, *Seven Arrows* (New York: Harper & Row, 1972); Storm, *Lightningbolt* (New York: Ballantine Books, 1994). *http://www.hyemeyohstsstorm.com/dedpla/wolflewolf.htm* . Vine Deloria, Jr., *God Is Red* (New York: Grosset & Dunlap, 1973), 67.

23. Storm, *Seven Arrows*, 1, 5.

24. E. Z. Vogt, "Acculturation of American Indians," *American Academy of Political and Social Science* 311 (May 1957): 144–46; James H. Howard, "Pan-Indian Culture of Oklahoma," *Scientific Monthly* (Nov. 1955): 215–20; Hazel W. Hertzberg, *The Search for an American Indian Identity* (Syracuse, N.Y.: Syracuse University Press, 1971).

25. Carlos Castaneda, *Teachings of Don Juan* (New York: Pocket Books, 1985); Castaneda, *Tales of Power* (New York: Pocket Books, 1992); Castaneda, *The Wheel of Time* (New York: Washington Square Press, 2001). See also Richard DeMille, *Castaneda's Journey* (Santa Barbara, Calif.: Capra Press, 1976); Daniel C. Noel, *Seeing Castaneda* (New York: Putnam, 1976); Victor Sanchez, *The Teachings of Don Carlos* (Santa Fe, N.M.: Bear, 1995). For the cultural context of the anthropological profession and the initial willingness to accept Castaneda's claims, see Susan R. Trencher, *Mirrored Images* (Westport, Conn.: Bergin & Garvey, 2000).

26. Richard DeMille, ed., *The Don Juan Papers: Further Castaneda Controversies* (Belmont, Calif.: Wadsworth, 1990); Jay Courtney Fikes, *Carlos Castaneda, Academic Opportunism and the Psychedelic Sixties* (Victoria, Can.: Millenia Press, 1993); Simon Romero, "Peyote's Hallucinations Spawn Real-Life Academic Feud," *NYT*, 16 Sept. 2003; Amy Wallace, *Sorcerer's Apprentice: My Life with Carlos Castaneda* (Berkeley, Calif: Frog, 2003).

27. Victor Sanchez, *Toltecs of the New Millennium* (Santa Fe, N.M.: Bear, 1996); Sanchez, *The Toltec Path of Recapitulation* (Rochester, Vt: Inner Traditions International, 2001); Mary Carroll Nelson and Miguel Ruiz, *Beyond Fear: A Toltec Guide to Freedom and Joy* (Tulsa, Ok: Council Oak Books, 1997); Susan Gregg and Don Miguel Ruiz, *The Toltec Way* (Los Angeles, Calif: Renaissance Books, 2000); Frank Díaz, *The Gospel of the Toltecs* (Rochester, Vt.: Bear, 2002); Susan Gregg, *Mastering the Toltec Way* (York Beach, Me.: Red Wheel, 2004).

28. Doug Boyd, *Rolling Thunder* (New York: Dell Publishing, 1974), 91 ("the concepts of agents and spirit power"), 112 ("the earth was a being"), 233 ("Indians were the most natural"). Compare Doug Boyd, *Mad Bear* (New York: Touchstone Books, 1994).

29. Sun Bear, Wabun, and Nimimosha, *The Bear Tribe's Self-Reliance Book* (Spokane, Wash.: Bear Tribe Publishing Co., 1977); Sun Bear and Wabun, *The Medicine Wheel: Earth Astrology* (New York: Prentice-Hall, 1980); Sun Bear, Wabun Wind, and Crysalis Mulligan, *Dancing with the Wheel* (Lithia Springs, Ga: New Leaf Distributors, 1992); Sun Bear, Wabun, and Crysalis Mulligan, *Walk in Balance* (New York: Prentice Hall, 1989); Catherine L. Albanese, *Nature Religion in America* (Chicago: University of Chicago Press, 1991), 155–63.

30. Evelyn Eaton, *The Shaman and the Medicine Wheel* (Wheaton, Ill.: Theosophical Publishing House, 1982), 190–98. The tribe has a website at *http://www.ewebtribe.com/WestWinds/WindDaughter/chantscd.html.*

31. Winona LaDuke, *All Our Relations* (Cambridge, Mass.: South End Press, 1999). For Wabun Wind, see *http://www.voiceofwomen.com/power.html.*

32. "Resolution of the Fifth Annual Meeting of the Tradition Elders Circle," at *http://www.yvwiiusdinvnohii.net/history/elders.html.*

Chapter 9

1. Ruth Beebe Hill, *Hanta Yo: An American Saga* (New York: Warner Books, 1981).

2. Thomas Matchie, "Writing About Native Americans," *Midwest Quarterly* 42(3) (2001): 320–33.

3. For the development of the New Age, see Marilyn Ferguson, *The Aquarian Conspiracy* (Los Angeles: J. P. Tarcher, 1980); James R. Lewis and J. Gordon Melton, eds., *Perspectives on the New Age* (Albany, N.Y.: State University of New York Press, 1992); Michael F. Brown, *The Channeling Zone* (Cambridge, Mass.: Harvard University Press, 1999); Steven Sutcliffe, *Children of the New Age* (New York: Routledge, 2003). Amanda

Porterfield, "American Indian Spirituality as a Countercultural Movement," in *Religion in Native North America,* ed. Christopher Vecsey (Moscow, Idaho: University of Idaho Press, 1990), 152–64.

4. Starhawk, *The Spiral Dance,* 10th anniversary ed. (San Francisco: Harper San Francisco, 1989).

5. Carol P. Christ and Judith Plaskow, eds., *Womanspirit Rising* (San Francisco: Harper & Row, 1979); Margot Adler, *Drawing Down the Moon* (New York: Viking, 1979); Elaine H. Pagels, *The Gnostic Gospels* (New York: Random House, 1979); James R. Lewis, ed., *Magical Religion and Modern Witchcraft* (Albany, N.Y.: State University of New York Press, 1996); Ellen Evert Hopman and Lawrence Bond, *People of the Earth* (Rochester, Vt.: Destiny Books, 1996); Graham Harvey, *Contemporary Paganism* (New York: New York University Press, 1997).

6. Michael J. Harner, *The Way of the Shaman,* 10th anniversary ed. (San Francisco: Harper San Francisco, 1990).

7. Lynn V. Andrews, *Medicine Woman* (San Francisco: Harper & Row, 1981).

8. Hyemeyohsts Storm, *Seven Arrows* (New York: Harper & Row, 1972) 9; Alice B. Kehoe, "Primal Gaia: Primitivists and Plastic Medicine Man," in *The Invented Indian,* ed. James A. Clifton (New Brunswick, N.J.: Transaction, 1990), 203–6, at *http://www.lynnandrews.com/Pages/frameteach.html*

9. The Cree medicine woman is from Andrews, *Medicine Woman,* 21. Authentic medicine women are well-documented: see David E. Jones, *Sanapia, Comanche Medicine Woman* (New York: Holt, Rinehart & Winston, 1972); Frank Linderman, *Pretty-Shield: Medicine Woman of the Crows* (Lincoln: University of Nebraska Press, 1974). Linderman's book was originally published in 1932 as *Red Mother.* For Lynn Andrews's later works, see her *Flight of the Seventh Moon* (San Francisco: Harper & Row, 1984); *Jaguar Woman and the Wisdom of the Butterfly Tree* (San Francisco: Harper & Row, 1985); *Star Woman* (New York: Warner Books, 1986); *Crystal Woman* (New York: Warner Books, 1987); *Windhorse Woman* (New York: Warner Books, 1989); *Teachings Around the Sacred Wheel* (San Francisco: Harper San Francisco, 1989); and *The Woman of Wyrrd* (San Francisco: Harper & Row, 1990). Andrews's website can be found at *http://www.lynnandrews.com/.* For a critique of Andrews, see, for example, "Irene," "New Age Feminists and Native American Spirituality," at *http://users.pandora.be/gohiyuhi/articles/art00070.htm.*

10. Andrews, *Medicine Woman,* 111. For the post-Andrews interest in medicine women, see Brooke Medicine Eagle, *Buffalo Woman Comes Singing* (New York: Ballantine Books, 1991); Paula Gunn Allen, *Grandmothers of the Light* (Boston: Beacon Press, 1991); Cinnamon Moon, *A Medicine Woman Speaks* (London: New Page Books, 2001).

11. Ellen Bass and Laura Davis, *The Courage to Heal* (New York: Harper & Row, 1988); Helen Palmer, *The Enneagram* (San Francisco: Harper & Row, 1988). The recent literature on "Native healing" is vast. See Donald Sandner, *Navaho Symbols of Healing* (New York: Harcourt Brace Jovanovich, 1979); Carl A. Hammerschlag, *The Dancing Healers* (San Francisco: Harper San Francisco, 1989); Hammerschlag, *Healing Ceremonies* (New York: Perigee, 1997); Sandra Ingerman, *Soul Retrieval* (San Francisco: Harper San Francisco, 1991); Mary Dean Atwood, *Spirit Healing* (New York: Sterling, 1991); Teresa Pijoan, *Healers on the Mountain* (Little Rock, Ark.: August House, 1993); Steve Wall, *Shadowcatchers: A Journey in Search of the Teachings of Native American Healers* (New York: HarperCollins, 1994); J. T. Garrett and Michael Tlanusta Garrett, *Medicine of the Cherokee* (Santa Fe, N.M.: Bear, 1996); Wolf Moondance, *Star Medicine* (New York: Sterling, 1997); Gary Null, *Secrets of the Sacred White Buffalo* (New York: Prentice Hall,

1998); Andrew Weil and Lewis Madrona, *Coyote Medicine* (New York: Scribner, 1997); Mary Summer Rain, *Earthway: A Native American Visionary's Path to Total Mind, Body, and Spirit Health* (New York: Pocket Books, 2000); Alberto Villoldo, *Shaman, Healer, Sage* (New York: Harmony Books, 2000); Elena Avila and Joy Parker, *Woman Who Glows in the Dark* (London: Thorsons, 2000); Kenneth Cohen, *Honoring the Medicine* (New York: Ballantine, 2004). For the NIH report, see *Alternative Medicine: Expanding Medical Horizons* (Washington, D.C.: Government Printing Office, 1994), at *http://www.naturalhealthvillage.com/reports/rpt2oam/toc.htm*. For Native healing traditions, see *http://www.naturalhealthvillage.com/reports/ rpt2oam/altsystems.htm*

12. Steven Foster and Meredith Little, *The Roaring of the Sacred River* (New York: Simon & Schuster, 1989), 40. Cynthia MacAdams, Hunbatz Men, and Charles Bensinger, *Mayan Vision Quest* (San Francisco: Harper San Francisco, 1991); Denise Linn, *Quest: A Guide to Creating Your Own Vision Quest* (New York: Ballantine Wellspring, 1999). Compare Lee Irwin, *The Dream Seekers* (Norman: University of Oklahoma Press, 1994).

13. Robert Bly, *Iron John* (Reading, Mass.: Addison-Wesley, 1990); Clarissa Pinkola Estes, *Women Who Run with the Wolves* (New York: Ballantine, 1992).

14. Thomas E. Mails, *Secret Native American Pathways* (Tulsa, Okla.: Council Oak Books, 1988).

15. See, for instance, Robert Boissiere, *The Hopi Way* (Santa Fe, N.M.: Sunstone Press, 1985); Boissiere, *Meditations with the Hopi* (Santa Fe, N.M.: Bear, 1986); Boissiere, *Po Pai Mo: The Search for White Buffalo Woman* (Santa Fe, N.M.: Sunstone Press, 1997); James A. Swan, *Sacred Places: How the Living Earth Seeks Our Friendship* (Santa Fe, N.M.: Bear, 1990); Rudolf Kaiser, *The Voice of the Great Spirit—Prophecies of the Hopi Indians* (Boston: Shambhala, 1989); Amber Wolfe, *In the Shadow of the Shaman* (St. Paul, Minn.: Llewellyn, 1989); Ted Andrews, *Animal-Speak* (St. Paul, Minn.: Llewellyn, 1993). For the different companies mentioned, see *http://www.parkstpress.com/; http://www.shambhala.com/; http://www.sunstonepress.com/; http://www. llewellyn.com/*

16. Andrews, *Teachings Around the Sacred Wheel;* Ed McGaa, *Mother Earth Spirituality* (San Francisco: Harper San Francisco, 1990); and McGaa, *Rainbow Tribe* (San Francisco: Harper San Francisco, 1992); Joan Halifax, *The Fruitful Darkness* (San Francisco: Harper San Francisco, 1994); MacAdams, Men, and Bensinger, *Mayan Vision Quest.*

17. Jamie Sams, *Sacred Path Cards: The Discovery of Self through Native Teachings* (San Francisco: Harper San Francisco, 1990); idem, *Other Council Fires Were Here Before Ours* (San Francisco: Harper San Francisco, 1991); idem, *Earth Medicine* (San Francisco: Harper San Francisco, 1994); idem, *The Thirteen Original Clan Mothers* (San Francisco: Harper San Francisco, 1994); idem, *Dancing the Dream* (New York: HarperCollins, 1999); *http://www.jamiesams.com;* David Carson, *Making Medicine* (New York: St. Martin's Press, 2002).

18. *http://www.shamanicvisions.com*

19. Indicating the dominance of Lakota/Sioux imagery in modern Indian stereotypes, *Dances with Wolves* shifted the action from a Comanche community, as in the original novel, to the Lakota of the film version.

20. *http://www.lelandra.com/comptarot/tarotIndian.htm. Shaman Wisdom Cards* (United States Games Systems, 1999).

21. For the remark about "just the right shamanic intensity," see *http://www.emeraldgreensound.com/chacocanyon.html*. For "the spirituality of the Adena," see *http://www.emeraldgreensound.com/serpentmound.html*

22. For Sedona, see Adrian J. Ivakhiv, *Claiming Sacred Ground* (Bloomington: Indiana University Press, 2001). For medicine bags, see, for instance, *http://www.sacredspiral-*

gallery.com/Indian-medicine-bags.cfm; *http://www.folkart-etc.com/maryisrael/*; *http:// www.nativecircle.com/MEDICINEBAGS.htm* ; *http://www.sunshineoriginals.com/ medbagshields.html*; *http://www.paralumun.com/ shampouch.htm* . The quote about the mandella is from *http://www.nativecircle.com/MANDELLAS.htm* . Reuben Ellis, ed., *Stories and Stone: An Anasazi Reader* (Boulder, Colo: Pruett Publishing Co., 1996), 11. Dennis Slifer and James Duffield, *Kokopelli* (Santa Fe, N.M.: Ancient City Press, 1994); Dave Walker, *Cuckoo for Kokopelli* (Flagstaff, Ariz: Northland, 1998).

23. McGaa, *Mother Earth Spirituality,* 41. Raymond Bucko, *The Lakota Ritual of the Sweat Lodge* (Lincoln: University of Nebraska Press, 1998).

24. Wolf Moondance, *Rainbow Medicine* (New York: Sterling, 1994); Moondance, *Spirit Medicine* (New York: Sterling, 1995); Moondance, *Star Medicine* (New York: Sterling, 1997); Moondance, *Bone Medicine* (New York: Sterling, 1999); Moondance, *Rainbow Spirit Journeys* (New York: Sterling, 2000). The "shaman's necklace" is from *Bone Medicine,* 162.

25. Moondance, *Spirit Medicine,* 33–37; "I see the dark eyes of the raven": 47. Alan Richardson, *The Magical Life of Dion Fortune* (London: Aquarian, 1991).

26. Brooke Medicine Eagle, *Buffalo Woman Comes Singing,* 110 ("the nine most powerful sacred objects"), 426 (the earth medicine contract), 387 ("support hoop").

27. Stephen C. Simms, *A Wheel-Shaped Stone Monument in Wyoming* (Chicago: Field Museum, 1903); *The Medicine Wheel: Prehistoric Mystery of the Big Horns,* 5th ed. (Lovell, Wyo.: Lovell Chamber of Commerce, 1958); "A Mountain Mystery," *NYT,* 31 May 1959; "What strange fate overcame them" is from Christopher Dane, *The American Indian and the Occult* (New York: Popular Library, 1973), 21. Sun Bear and Wabun, *The Medicine Wheel: Earth Astrology* (New York: Prentice-Hall, 1980); Kehoe, "Primal Gaia: Primitivists and Plastic Medicine Men." For the wheels of the Sun Dance, see George A. Dorsey, *The Arapaho Sun Dance,* Field Columbian Museum, pub. 75, Anthropological series, vol. 4 (Chicago: Field Columbian Museum, 1903).

28. Evelyn Eaton, *The Shaman and the Medicine Wheel* (Wheaton, Ill.: Theosophical Publishing House, 1982), 11. *http://www.lynnandrews.com/* ; Andrews, *Jaguar Woman,* 119.

29. Eaton, *The Shaman and the Medicine Wheel,* 49. From a great many recent books on the Medicine Wheel, see Sun Bear, Wabun Wind, and Crysalis Mulligan, *Dancing with the Wheel* (Lithia Springs, Ga: New Leaf Distributors, 1992); Richard Dannelley, *Sedona Power Spot, Vortex and Medicine Wheel Guide* (Sedona, Ariz.: Vortex Society, 1992); Alberto Villoldo and Erik Jendresen, *Island of the Sun* (Rochester, Vt: Inner Traditions International, 1994); Vicki May and Cindy V. Rodberg, *Medicine Wheel Ceremonies* (Happy Camp, Calif.: Naturegraph, 1996); Kenneth Meadows, *Earth Medicine,* rev. ed. (Rockport, Mass.: Element, 1996); Marie Herbert, *Healing Quest* (York Beach, Me.: Red Wheel/Weiser, 1997); Wa-Na-Nee-Che and Eliana Harvey White Eagle, *Medicine Wheel* (New York: St. Martin's Press, 1997); Roy I. Wilson, *Medicine Wheels: Ancient Teachings for Modern Times* (New York: Crossroad/Herder & Herder, 2001); E. Barrie Kavasch, *The Medicine Wheel Garden* (New York: Bantam, 2002); Marie-Lu Lörler, *Shamanic Healing within the Medicine Wheel* (Las Vegas, Nev.: Brotherhood of Life Books, 2003). For Seton's older symbol, see Ernest Thompson Seton, *The Birch Bark Roll of Woodcraft,* 20th ed. (New York: Brieger, 1925), frontispiece.

30. Kenneth Meadows, *Little Earth Medicine Library: Beaver* (London: Dorling Kindersley, 1998), 14.

31. These comments are taken from Kenneth Meadows, *Little Earth Medicine Library: Salmon* (London: Dorling Kindersley, 1998); Meadows, *Little Earth Medicine Library: Beaver.*

32. Hyemeyohsts Storm, *Seven Arrows* (New York: Harper & Row, 1972), 6. *http://Open-Mind.Org/Wheel.htm*

33. Brooke Medicine Eagle, *Buffalo Woman Comes Singing*, 285–87.

34. Sams, *Dancing the Dream*, 91–126.

35. Sams, *Thirteen Original Clan Mothers*.

36. Brooke Medicine Eagle, *Buffalo Woman Comes Singing*, 281–91.

37. *http://www.jamiesams.com/heyokah.html*

38. *http://www.pathwaystohealth.com/programs/shamanworkshop.htm*

39. The Deer Tribe website has a home page at *http://www.dtmms.org/*. For individual lodges, see *http://www.dtmms.org/locations.htm* . Thunder Strikes and Jan Orsi, *Song of the Deer* (Malibu, Cal: Jaguar Books, 1999).

40. "We are a Metis Sweet Medicine Sundance lodge" is from *http://www.spiritualsexuality.com/sweat_history1.html* . "Earth Sky (sweat) Lodge" is from *http://www.spiritofnature.org/lodge.htm*. For Ozark Avalon, see *http://www.ozarkavalon.org/shamans_journey_aug_03.shtml*

41. *http://www.thewildrose.net/direction.htm*. For Maine's Standing Bear Center see *http://www.thestandingbear.com/eventsandcontact.htm* . The Florida program is from *http://www.thecrystalgarden.com/Newsletter/OCALA/ocala2002.htm*

42. Marjory Stoneman Douglas, *The Everglades*, 50th anniversary ed. (Sarasota, Fla.: Pineapple Press, 1997).

43. For Mount Shasta, see *http://www.newagetravel.com/robert/northam.htm* . The "psycho-spiritual, meta-historical expression" is from *http://www.psyearth.com/chaco.html* . Yashah Oswanta, *The Harmonic Convergence: Seven Days at Mount Shasta* (Salmon Arm, B.C., Canada: Alahoy Publications, 1987). For Ballard and Mount Shasta, see Philip Jenkins, *Mystics and Messiahs* (New York: Oxford University Press, 2000). For New Age pilgrims to Chaco, see Brendan Doherty, "Barefoot in the Park," at *http://weeklywire.com/ww/08-10-98/alibi_feat1.html*

44. Alan Klevit, *Three Days in Sedona: A Personal Harmonic Convergence* (Sedona: Stardust, 1990); Ivakhiv, *Claiming Sacred Ground*.

45. Ivakhiv, *Claiming Sacred Ground*, 179. The tour description is from publicity for the firm Earth Wisdom Jeep Tours. "You'll also receive a blessing" is from a flyer for the Arizona firm Native American Journeys.

46. *http://www.luminati.net/new_mexico_September%205-12-2003.htm*; *http://www. sedonasouladventures.com/pages/vortex.html*

Chapter 10

1. Loren Cruden, *Coyote's Council Fire* (Rochester, Vt.: Inner Traditions International, 1995); Cruden, *Compass of the Heart* (Rochester, Vt.: Destiny, 1996); Bobby Lake-Thom and Medicine Grizzly Bear, *Native Healer* (Wheaton, Ill.: Quest, 1991); Bobby Lake-Thom and Medicine Grizzly Bear, *Spirits of the Earth* (New York: Plume, 1997); Bobby Lake-Thom, *Call of the Great Spirit* (Rochester, Vt.: Bear, 2001).

2. The word is properly spelled métis, but the accent is commonly omitted in U.S. usage. Brooke Medicine Eagle, *Buffalo Woman Comes Singing* (New York: Ballantine, 1991), 237. *http://www.americanmetis.org/*

3. "Native American Indians" is from Ed McGaa, *Mother Earth Spirituality* (San Francisco: Harper San Francisco, 1990), xiv. For "blending with the land": see Thomas E. Mails, *The Hopi Survival Kit* (New York: Penguin, 1997), 1.

4. Gerald Hausman, ed., *Meditations with Animals* (Santa Fe, N.M.: Bear, 1986): Berry is quoted from the Introduction, 5, 7. "We must learn" is from ibid., 14. For Esalen, see *http://www.esalen.org/air/essays/esselenhands.shtml* . Jerry Mander, *In the Absence of the Sacred: The Failure of Technology and the Survival of the Indian Nations* (San Francisco: Sierra Club Books, 1991).

5. "Places where the veils are thin": Evelyn Eaton, *The Shaman and the Medicine Wheel* (Wheaton, Ill.: Theosophical Publishing House, 1982), 31. "The native people of North America": *http://www.newagetravel.com/robert/northam.htm* . James W. Mavor and By-ron E. Dix, *Manitou: The Sacred Landscape of New England's Native Civilization* (Rochester, Vt.: Destiny, 1989); James A. Swan, *Sacred Places* (Santa Fe, N.M.: Bear, 1990); Swan, ed., *The Power of Place* (Wheaton, Ill.: Quest, 1991); Arthur Versluis, *Sacred Earth* (Rochester, Vt.: Inner Traditions International, 1992); Bron Taylor, "Re-sacralizing Earth: Pagan Environmentalism and the Restoration of Turtle Island," in *American Sacred Space,* eds. David Chidester and Edward T. Linenthal (Bloomington: Indiana University Press, 1995).

6. Mails, *Hopi Survival Kit,* 1–2; for the Hopi Jesus, see 138.

7. McGaa, *Mother Earth Spirituality,* 17. Martha F. Lee, *Earth First!* (Syracuse, N.Y.: Syracuse University Press, 1995); Bron Taylor, "Earthen Spirituality or Cultural Genocide?" *Religion* 27 (1997): 183–215.

8. John Smith, *A Map of Virginia. With a Description of the Countrey, the Commodities, People, Government and Religion,* at *http://etext.lib.virginia.edu/etcbin/jamestown-browse?id=J1008.*

9. William Bright, *A Coyote Reader* (Berkeley: University of California Press, 1993); Howard L. Harrod, *The Animals Came Dancing* (Tucson: University of Arizona Press, 2000).

10. Timothy Roderick, *The Once Unknown Familiar* (St. Paul, Minn.: Llewellyn, 1994); Deanna J. Conway, *Animal Magick* (St. Paul, Minn.: Llewellyn, 1995); Brad Steiger, *Totems: The Transformative Power of Your Animal Totem* (San Francisco: Harper San Francisco, 1997); Nicki Scully, *Power Animal Meditations* (Rochester, Vt: Bear, 2001). Kenneth Meadows, *The Medicine Way* (Rockport, Mass: Element, 1991), 45.

11. *http://www.powerattunements.com/s.html;* The same passage is also found at *http://www.kundalinireiki.com/sha.html* . The contemporary New Age literature on shamanism is immense. Some recent titles include Joan Halifax, *Shamanic Voices* (New York: Penguin, 1992); Wolf Moondance, *Rainbow Medicine* (New York: Sterling, 1994); John M. Perkins, *The World Is as You Dream It* (Rochester, Vt.: Inner Traditions Inter-national, 1994); Perkins, *Shapeshifting* (Rochester, Vt.: Inner Traditions International, 1997); Caitlin Matthews, *Singing the Soul Back Home* (Rockport, Mass.: Element, 1995); Luis Espinoza, *Chamalu: The Shamanic Way of the Heart* (Rochester, Vt.: Inner Traditions International, 1995); Thomas Dale Cowan, *Shamanism as a Spiritual Practice for Daily Life* (Freedom, Calif: Crossing Press, 1996); Douglas Gillette, *The Shaman's Secret* (New York: Bantam, 1997); Stephen Larsen and Joan Halifax, *The Shaman's Doorway* (Rochester, Vt.: Inner Traditions International, 1998); Sarangerel, *Chosen by the Spirits* (Rochester, Vt.: Inner Traditions International, 2001); Kenneth Meadows, *Shamanic Experience,* 2nd ed. (Rochester, Vt.: Inner Traditions International, 2003); Dagmar Wernitznig, *Going Native or Going Naïve? White Shamanism and the Neo-Noble Savage* (Lanham, Md.: University Press of America, 2003).

12. Meadows, *Medicine Way,* 136–38.

13. Wolf Moondance, *Rainbow Medicine,* 13; Jamie Sams, *Dancing the Dream* (New York: HarperCollins, 1999), 28.

14. Brooke Medicine Eagle, *Buffalo Woman Comes Singing*, 237.

15. A sizable recent literature explores the spiritual experience of Native American women: Steve Wall and Harvey Arden, *Wisdom's Daughters* (New York: HarperCollins, 1993); Mary Brave Bird, Mary Crow Dog and Richard Erdoes, *Lakota Woman* (New York: HarperPerennial Library, 1994); Susan Hazen-Hammond, *Spider Woman's Web* (Perigee, 1999).

16. Sam D. Gill, "Mother Earth: An American Myth," in James A. Clifton, ed., *The Invented Indian* (New Brunswick, N.J.: Transaction Publishers, 1990), 129–43; Clifton, *Mother Earth: An American Story* (Chicago: University of Chicago Press, 1987). The traditional idea is reasserted by Vine Deloria, Jr., in *Natives and Academics*, ed. Devon A. Mihesuah (Lincoln: University of Nebraska Press, 1998), 75–79. Robert H. Ruby and John A. Brown, *Dreamer-Prophets of the Columbia Plateau* (Norman: University of Oklahoma Press, 1989).

17. Paula Gunn Allen, *The Sacred Hoop* (Boston: Beacon Press, 1992), 11, 13; Allen, *Grandmothers of the Light* (Boston: Beacon Press, 1991); Allen, *Pocahontas* (San Francisco: Harper San Francisco, 2003); Mary Summer Rain, *Tao of Nature* (New York: Fireside, 2002), 1–2.

18. Wallace Black Elk is quoted from *http://www.Indianreader.com/blackelk.html* . Wallace H. Black Elk and William S. Lyon, *Black Elk: The Sacred Ways of a Lakota* (San Francisco: Harper San Francisco, 1990); McGaa, *Mother Earth Spirituality*, 19. Judith Todd, "On Common Ground," in *Politics of Women's Spirituality*, ed. Charlene Spretnak (New York: Doubleday, 1986).

19. Jamie Sams, *The Thirteen Original Clan Mothers* (San Francisco: Harper San Francisco 1994): "the traditions": 1; "to continue weaving": 281.

20. A. L. Kroeber, *The Religion of the Indians of California* (Berkeley, Calif.: The University Press, 1907).

21. "Traditionally, the Moontime" is from "Women's Moon Lodge," at *http://www.moonsurfing.com/moonlodge.html* ; Brooke Medicine Eagle, *Buffalo Woman Comes Singing*. "We gather to talk" is from *http://www.thegreenwoman.com/moonlodge.html* ; "the offering of menstrual blood to the Earth" is from *http://www.healthynewage.com/howto.html*

22. Will Roscoe, ed., *Living the Spirit: A Gay American Indian Anthology* (New York: St. Martin's Press, 1988). Will Roscoe, *The Zuñi Man-Woman* (Albuquerque: University of New Mexico Press, 1992); and idem, *Changing Ones: Third and Fourth Genders in Native North America* (New York: St. Martin's Press, 2000); Walter L. Williams, *Spirit and the Flesh* (Boston: Beacon Press, 1992). Richard C. Trexler, "Making the American Berdache," *Journal of Social History*, 35(3)(2002).

23. Warren is quoted from *http://www.sacredhoop.demon.co.uk/HOOP-35/Two-Spirits.html* ; Sue-Ellen Jacobs, Wesley Thomas, and Sabine Lang, eds., *Two-Spirit People* (Urbana: University of Illinois Press, 1997).

24. Alexander Thom, *Megalithic Sites in Britain* (Oxford: Clarendon Press, 1967). Ray A. Williamson, *Living the Sky* (Norman: University of Oklahoma Press, 1984), 2–3; Trudy Griffin-Pierce, *Earth Is My Mother, Sky Is My Father* (Albuquerque: University of New Mexico Press, 1995); Marsha C. Bol, ed., *Stars Above, Earth Below* (Niwot, Colo.: Roberts Rinehart Publishers, 1998); E. C. Krupp, *Skywatchers, Shamans and Kings* (New York: John Wiley & Sons, 1999); William F. Romain, *Mysteries of the Hopewell* (Akron, Ohio: University of Akron Press, 2000).

25. Gary Snyder, *Turtle Island* (New York: New Directions, 1974).

26. Kendrick Frazier, *People of Chaco*, rev. ed. (New York: W. W. Norton, 1999); David Grant Noble, ed., *New Light on Chaco Canyon* (Santa Fe, N.M.: School of American Research Press, 2001). For an ambitious theory about the extent of Chacoan power, see Stephen H. Lekson, *The Chaco Meridian* (Walnut Creek, Calif: Altamira Press, 1999). For ley lines, see Alfred Watkins, *The Old Straight Track* (London: Methuen, 1925); *http://www.mind.net/aware/irley.htm*. For Ohio, Roger G. Kennedy, *Hidden Cities* (New York: Free Press, 1994). The quote about Serpent Mound is from http:// www.crystalinks.com/pyrnorthamerica.html ; compare Ross Hamilton, *The Mystery of The Serpent Mound* (Berkeley, Calif.: Frog, 2001).

27. Erich Von Däniken, *Chariots of the Gods* (New York: Putnam, 1968); Von Däniken, *Gods from Outer Space* (New York: Putnam, 1970); Von Däniken, *The Gold of the Gods* (New York: Putnam, 1973); James R. Lewis, ed., *The Gods Have Landed* (Albany: State University of New York Press, 1995); C. D. B. Bryan, *Close Encounters of the Fourth Kind* (New York: Knopf, 1995). John F. Michell, *The View Over Atlantis* (London: Garnstone Press, 1972. The book was first published in Great Britain in 1969); idem, *City of Revelation* (New York: D. McKay Co., 1972); idem, *Secrets of the Stones* (New York: Penguin Books, 1977).

28. Vine Deloria, Jr., *God Is Red* (Grosset & Dunlap, 1973), 154–56.

29. Vine Deloria, Jr., *Red Earth, White Lies* (Golden, Colo.: Fulcrum, 1997).

30. John M. Jenkins, *Maya Cosmogenesis 2012* (Santa Fe, N.M.: Bear, 1998).

31. Sidney D. Kirkpatrick, *Edgar Cayce: An American Prophet* (New York: Riverhead, 2000); Nancy Red Star, *Star Ancestors* (Rochester, Vt.: Destiny, 2000); Nancy Red Star, ed., *Legends of the Star Ancestors* (Rochester, Vt.: Inner Traditions International, 2002), 3. Mary Summer Rain, *Phoenix Rising: No-Eyes' Vision of the Changes to Come* (Norfolk, Va: Hampton Roads Publishing, 1993).

32. Mails, *The Hopi Survival Kit*: "knew immediately": 7–8; "a new age will appear": 218; "shelter for mankind": 197; "incredibly accurate predictions": 172. Compare Brad Steiger, *American Indian Magic* (New Brunswick, N.J.: Inner Light, 1986); Rudolf Kaiser, *The Voice of the Great Spirit* (Boston: Shambhala, 1989); Elisabeth Dietz and Shirley Jonas, *Now Is the Hour* (Nevada City, Calif: Blue Dolphin, 1998); Scott Peterson, *Native American Prophecies,* 2nd ed. (St. Paul, Minn.: Paragon House, 1999); Maria Yraceburu, *Legends and Prophecies of the Quero Apache* (Rochester, Vt.: Inner Traditions International, 2002).

33. Armin W. Geertz, *The Invention of Prophecy* (Berkeley: University of California Press, 1994); Geertz, "Contemporary Problems in the Study of Native North American Religions with Special Reference to the Hopis," *AIQ* 20(3–4) (1996): 393–414. Mails is attacked at length by Hopi authorities in "Cultural Theft and Misrepresentation," at *http://users.telenet.be/gohiyuhi/articles/art00075.htm* . For the continuing function of prophecy in Native societies, see Tom Mould, *Choctaw Prophecy* (Tuscaloosa: University of Alabama Press, 2003).

34. "In the northwestern corner of New Mexico": *http://www.psyearth. com/chaco.html* ; "the Anasazi had been lifted off in space ships" is from *http://www.bestfriends. org/gc/ac/handprints.htm*

35. The three episodes were "Anasazi," "Blessing Way," and "Paper Clip."

36. Jamie Sams, *Midnight Song* (Santa Fe, N.M.: Bear, 1988): "There was a terrible war": 25; "I have traveled through time": xiii; the Bermuda Triangle: 105.

37. *http://www.insight-books.com/catalog/0939680386.htm*

38. *Dancing the Dream*, 27. Sun Bear, Wabun, and Nimimosha, *The Bear Tribe's Self-Reliance Book* (Spokane, Wash.: Bear Tribe Publishing Co., 1977), 54.

39. Kenneth Meadows, *Earth Medicine,* rev. ed. (Edison, N.J.: Castle Books, 2002), 11. Thunder Strikes and Jan Orsi, *Song of the Deer* (Malibu, Calif: Jaguar Books, 1999); Susy Buchanan, "Sacred Orgasm," *Phoenix New Times,* 13 Jun. 2002, at *http://www.mail-archive.com/native_american@topica.com/msg01503.html*

40. Richard M. Garvin, *The Crystal Skull* (Garden City, N.Y.: Doubleday, 1973); Alice Bryant and Phyllis Galde, *The Message of the Crystal Skull* (St. Paul, Minn.: Llewellyn, 1988); Chris Morton and Ceri Louise Thomas, *The Mystery of the Crystal Skulls,* 2nd ed. (Rochester, Vt.: Inner Traditions International, 2002); *http://www.crystalskullsociety.org/* . The skulls mythology has also joined forces with Edgar Cayce lore: John Van Auken and Lora Little, *The Lost Hall of Records* (Memphis, Tenn: Eagle Wing Books, 2000).

41. Sams, *The Thirteen Original Clan Mothers,* 303–4. For "the stone people": Sams, *Dancing the Dream,* 231–32.

42. Many recent books freely integrate Asian and Native American traditions: Klaus Holitzka, *Native American Mandalas* (New York: Sterling, 2000).

43. Steven A. Leblanc, *Prehistoric Warfare in the American Southwest* (Salt Lake City: University of Utah Press, 1999); Christy G. Turner and Jacqueline A. Turner, *Man Corn* (Salt Lake City: University of Utah Press, 1999); Glen E. Rice and Steven A. LeBlanc, eds, *Deadly Landscapes* (Salt Lake City: University of Utah Press, 2001); Steven LeBlanc and Katherine E. Register, *Constant Battles* (New York: St. Martin's Press, 2003); Alan Gallay, *The Indian Slave Trade* (New Haven, Conn.: Yale University Press, 2003).

44. For Native American witchcraft see Clyde Kluckhohn, *Navaho Witchcraft* (Boston: Beacon Press, 1944); Keith H. Basso, *Western Apache Witchcraft* (Tucson: University of Arizona Press, 1969); Marc Simmons, *Witchcraft in the Southwest* (Lincoln: University of Nebraska Press, 1980); Deward E. Walker, ed., *Witchcraft and Sorcery of the American Native Peoples* (Moscow, Id: University of Idaho Press, 1990); Alan Kilpatrick, *The Night Has a Naked Soul* (Syracuse, N.Y.: Syracuse University Press, 1998).

45. Shepard Krech, *The Ecological Indian* (New York: W. W. Norton, 2000); Roger Sandall, *The Culture Cult* (Boulder, Colo.: Westview, 2000).

46. Lawrence Osborne, "The Numbers Game," *Lingua Franca* (Sept. 1998): 49–58; David P. Henige, *Numbers from Nowhere* (Norman: University of Oklahoma Press, 1998). For the genocide interpretation, see Ward Churchill, *A Little Matter of Genocide* (San Francisco: City Lights, 1998).

Chapter 11

1. R. C. Gordon-McCutchan, *The Taos Indians and the Battle for Blue Lake* (Santa Fe, N.M.: Red Crane Books 1995); George Pierre Castile, *To Show Heart* (Tucson: University of Arizona Press, 1998); Eva M. Garroutte, *Real Indians* (Berkeley: University of California Press, 2003).

2. Fergus M. Bordewich, *Killing the White Man's Indian* (New York: Doubleday, 1996), 83 . For ongoing struggles about land rights, see E. Richard Hart, ed., *Zuñi and the Courts* (Lawrence: University Press of Kansas, 1995); Clifford M. Lytle and Vine Deloria, Jr., *The Nations Within,* reissue ed. (Austin: University of Texas Press, 1998).

3. Ianthe Jeanne Dugan, "New Tribal Tradition: Counting Its Millions," *Wall Street Journal,* 14 Jun. 2003.

4. Angela Mullis and David Kamper, eds., *Indian Gaming: Who Wins?* (Los Angeles: UCLA American Indian Studies Center, 2000); Donald L. Barlett and James B. Steele, "Dirty Dealing," *Time,* 8 Dec. 2002.

5. Census figures refer to those claiming Native descent alone, as opposed to Native and one other race. If this latter category is included, then the number of Americans reporting Native stock as of 2000 rises to over four million. Nancy Shoemaker, *American Indian Population Recovery in the Twentieth Century* (Albuquerque: University of New Mexico Press, 1999); Jeff Benedict, *Without Reservation* (New York: HarperCollins, 2000); Kim Isaac Eisler, *Revenge of the Pequots* (New York: Simon & Schuster, 2001). For changing legal attitudes, see George Roth, "Federal Tribal Recognition in the South," in *Anthropologists and Indians in the New South*, eds. Rachel A. Bonney and J. Anthony Paredes (Tuscaloosa: University of Alabama Press, 2001), 49–70.

The new casinos stressed their Native cultural roots: Connecticut's Mohegan Sun casi-no claims that its "circular design and Native American themes are directly influenced by the Tribe's beliefs and culture. The Casino of the Earth is separated into four quadrants, each featuring its own seasonal theme—Winter, Spring, Summer and Autumn—highlighting the importance of seasonal changes to Mohegan life. The walls of rock marking entry to Mohegan Sun, curvilinear signs, Mohegan Sun logo and symbols such as the sacred turtle also hold great significance, as do the giant entry skins and scenes." *http://www.mohegansun.com/about/the_tribe.jsp*

6. Garroutte, *Real Indians*. For Canadian developments, see Boyce Richardson, *People of Terra Nullius* (Vancouver, Can.: Douglas & McIntyre, 1994); Wayne Warry, *Unfinished Dreams* (Toronto, Can.: University of Toronto Press, 1998); David A. Long and Olive P. Dickason, eds., *Visions of the Heart* (Harcourt, Brace, 2000); Alan Cairns, *Citizens Plus* (Vancouver, Can.: University of British Columbia Press, 2000); Tom Flanagan, *First Nations, Second Thoughts* (Montreal, Can.: McGill-Queens University Press, 2000); R. Cole Harris, *Making Native Space* (Vancouver, Can.: University of British Columbia Press, 2002); John Borrows, *Recovering Canada* (Toronto, Can.: University of Toronto Press, 2002).

7. Ward Churchill, *Indians Are Us?* (Monroe, Me.: Common Courage Press, 1994); idem, *From a Native Son* (Boston: South End Press, 1996); idem, *A Little Matter of Genocide* (San Francisco: City Lights, 1998); idem, *Fantasies of the Master Race* (San Francisco: City Lights, 1998); idem, *Struggle for the Land* (San Francisco: City Lights, 2002); idem, *Acts of Rebellion* (New York: Routledge, 2003).

8. Jake Page, *In the Hands of the Great Spirit* (New York: Free Press, 2003).

9. For *Akwesasne Notes*, see Margot Adler, *Drawing Down the Moon* (New York: Viking Press, 1979), 376. For the cultural and spiritual revival, see *A Basic Call to Consciousness* (Rooseveltown, NY: *Akwesasne Notes*, 1978); Alvin M. Josephy, *Now that the Buffalo's Gone* (Norman: University of Oklahoma Press, 1985), 77–123; Robert Allen Warrior, *Tribal Secrets* (Minneapolis: University of Minnesota Press, 1994); Ralph T. Coe, "Art and Indian Culture at the Crossroads of a New Century," in Mary Louise Krumrine and Susan Clare Scott, *Art and the Native American* (University Park, Penn.: Penn State Press, 2001), 268–301; Margaret Connell-Szasz, "The Cultural Renaissance in Native American and Celtic Worlds, 1940–2000," in *The American West in 2000*, eds. Richard W. Etulain and Ferenc Morton Szasz (Albuquerque: University of New Mexico Press, 2003); James Treat, *Around the Sacred Fire* (New York: Palgrave Macmillan, 2003).

10. Francis Paul Prucha, ed., *Documents of United States Indian Policy*, 2nd ed., (Lincoln: University of Nebraska Press, 1990), 258–60, 288–89 ("abridgement of religious freedom"). Lee Irwin, "Freedom, Law, and Prophecy: A Brief History of Native American Religious Resistance," at *http://www.sacredland.org/Irwin.html* . Richard A. Grounds, George E. Tinker, and David E. Wilkins, eds., *Native Voices* (Lawrence: University Press of Kansas, 2003).

11. N. Scott Momaday, *House Made of Dawn* (New York: Harper & Row, 1968), 58.

12. Gerald Vizenor, *Bearheart: The Heirship Chronicles* (Minneapolis: University of Minnesota Press, 1990) (the book was originally published as *Darkness in Saint Louis: Bearheart*).

13. Leslie Marmon Silko, *Almanac of the Dead* (New York: Simon & Schuster, 1991), 735.

14. "A Public Declaration to the Tribal Councils and Traditional Spiritual Leaders of the Indian and Eskimo Peoples of the Pacific Northwest," at *http://www.Thewac.Org/Apology%201987.htm* . Diana Eck, *A New Religious America* (San Francisco: Harper San Francisco, 2001); Mark Oppenheimer, *Knocking on Heaven's Door* (New Haven, Conn.: Yale University Press, 2003).

15. Matthew Fox, *Confessions* (San Francisco: Harper San Francisco, 1996), 139, 185–92.

16. Michael Rose, *Goodbye Good Men* (Chicago: Regnery, 2002), 125.

17. George E. Tinker, *Missionary Conquest* (Minneapolis, Minn.: Fortress Press, 1993); James Treat, ed., *Native and Christian* (New York: Routledge, 1996); Owanah Anderson, *400 Years: Anglican Episcopal Mission Among American Indians* (Cincinnati, Ohio: Forward Movement, 1998); Michael D. McNally, "The Practice of Native American Christianity," *Church History* 69(4) (2000): 834–59; Kirk Dombrowski, *Against Culture* (Lincoln: University of Nebraska Press, 2001); Grounds, Tinker, and Wilkins, eds., *Native Voices*. These issues arise in several of the essays in Jace Weaver, ed., *Native American Religious Identity* (Maryknoll, N.Y.: Orbis, 1998), especially in George Tinker, "Jesus, Corn Mother and Conquest," 134–54.

18. *Church of Lukumi Babalu Aye v. Hialeah*, 508 U.S. 520 (1993). Christopher Vecsey, ed., *Handbook of American Indian Religious Freedom* (New York: Crossroad, 1991); John Thomas Noonan and Edward McGlynn Gaffney, Jr., *Religious Freedom* (New York: Foundation Press, 2001).

19. Robert Sullivan, *A Whale Hunt* (New York: Scribner, 2002).

20. Little Rock Reed, ed., *The American Indian in the White Man's Prisons* (Taos, N.M.: Uncompromising Books, 1993).

21. James Waldram, *The Way of the Pipe* (Orchard Park, NY: Broadview Press, 1997).

22. Pemina Yellow Bird and Kathryn Milun, "Interrupted Journeys: The Cultural Politics of Indian Reburial," in *Displacements,* ed. Angelika Bammer (Durham, N.C.: Duke University Press, 1994); Devon A. Mihesuah, ed. *Repatriation Reader* (Lincoln, Neb: Bison Books, 2000); Andrew Gulliford, *Sacred Objects and Sacred Places* (Boulder: University Press of Colorado, 2000); Tamara Bray, ed., *The Future of the Past* (New York: Garland, 2001); Kathleen S. Fine-Dare, *Grave Injustice* (Lincoln: University of Nebraska Press, 2002).

23. David Hurst Thomas, *Skull Wars* (New York: Basic Books, 2000); Roger Downey, *The Riddle of the Bones* (New York: Copernicus Books, 2000); James C. Chatters, *Ancient Encounters* (New York: Simon & Schuster, 2001); Elaine Dewar, *Bones* (New York: Carroll & Graf, 2002); Jeff Benedict, *No Bone Unturned* (New York: HarperCollins, 2003).

24. Chris Kortright, "Spirit Cave Mummy and NAGPRA," at *http://www. geocities.com/anthropologyresistance/spirit.html* . For the "immemorial" claim, see the tribal website at *http://www.umatilla.nsn.us/*

25. The law is 25 U.S.C. §3002.

26. Vine Deloria, Jr., *Red Earth, White Lies* (Golden, Colo.: Fulcrum, 1997), 198–206; Deloria, *Evolution, Creationism, and Other Modern Myths* (Golden, Colo.: Fulcrum, 2002). Recent studies have validated Native traditions of dramatic natural events that occurred a few centuries ago, such as a great tsunami that affected the Northern Pacific

region in 1700: Tom Paulson, "When Thunderbird Battled Whale, the Earth Shook," *Seattle Post-intelligencer*, 2 Mar. 2001; Paulson, "Tale of a Whale in the River and the Tide that Never Left," Ibid., 19 Jun. 2002. For the view that academics need to pay much greater respect to Native traditions, see the essays in Nancy Shoemaker, ed., *Clearing a Path* (New York: Routledge, 2002).

27. Mindy Sink, "Climbers, Native Americans Clash Over Use of Wyoming Monument," *NYT*, 1 Jul. 1996; Lloyd Burton, *Worship and Wilderness* (Madison: University of Wisconsin Press, 2002); Michael F. Brown, *Who Owns Native Culture?* (Cambridge, Mass.: Harvard University Press, 2003). For the long-running feud over the Black Hills, see Donald Worster, *Under Western Skies* (New York: Oxford University Press, 1992), 106–53.

28. 485 US 439 (1988). This decision was protested in a dissent by the court's liberal wing. Compare *Sequoyah v. Tennessee Valley Authority*, 620 F.2d 1159, 1980.

29. Sara Hebel, "On a Mountaintop, a Fight between Science and Religion," *Chronicle of Higher Education*, 28 Jun. 2002; Bordewich, *Killing the White Man's Indian*, 204–39.

30. *http://www.sacredland.org/woodruff_butte.html* . Woodruff Butte was one of several holy sites highlighted in the 2001 documentary film *In the Light of Reverence;* see the links at *http://www.sacredland.org/*

31. *Employment Division, Department of Human Resources of Oregon v. Smith*, 484 US 872 (1990). Huston Smith et al., eds., *One Nation Under God* (Santa Fe, N.M.: Clear Light Publishers, 1996). Carolyn N. Long, *Religious Freedom and Indian Rights* (Lawrence: University Press of Kansas, 2000); Garrett Epps, *To an Unknown God* (New York: St. Martin's Press, 2001).

32. Christopher Parker, "A Constitutional Examination of the Federal Exemptions for Native American Religious Peyote Use," *BYU Journal of Public Law* 16(1) (2001): *http://www.law2.byu.edu/jpl/volumes/vol16_no1/PARK-PUB2.pdf*

33. Brown, *Who Owns Native Culture?* For "Cherokees Against Twinkies," see *http://catlodge.tripod.com/* ; "How to Recognize an Exploiter" at *http://shameons.bravepages.com/checklist.html* ; compare "Plastic Medicine Men and Shamans," at *http://www.comanchelodge.com/plastic-shamans.html* . Susan Mumm, "Aspirational Indians," in *Belief Beyond Boundaries,* ed. Joanne Pearson (Burlington, Vt.: Ashgate, 2002), 103–31. Myke Johnson, "Wanting to Be Indian," in *Belief Beyond Boundaries,* 277–93.

34. *http://shameons.bravepages.com/* ; Alice B. Kehoe, "Primal Gaia: Primitivists and Plastic Medicine Man," in *The Invented Indian,* ed. James A. Clifton (New Brunswick, N.J.: Transaction Publishers, 1990), 193–209; Wendy Rose, "The Great Pretenders," in *The State of Native America,* ed. Annette Jaimes (Boston: South End Press, 1992), 403–21; Terry Macy and Daniel Hart, *White Shamans and Plastic Medicine Men* (documentary video) (Bozeman, Mont.: Native Voices Public Television, 1995). For Wallace Black Elk, see Avis Little Eagle, "Sacred Pipe Keeper Fears Feds Will Step In," at *http://users.telenet.be/gohiyuhi/articles/art00086.htm*

35. The declaration can be found in several places online, including *http://www.aics.org/war.html*

36. Brooke Medicine Eagle, *Buffalo Woman Comes Singing* (New York: Ballantine, 1991), 291; idem, *The Last Ghost Dance* (New York: Wellspring/Ballantine, 2000).

37. Lisa Aldred, "Plastic Shamans and Astroturf Sun Dances," *AIQ* 24(3) (2000): 329–52. For one of several sites attacking Harley Swift Deer Reagan, see *http://users.telenet.be/gohiyuhi/brochures/broc0001.pdf* . See also Susy Buchanan, "Sacred Orgasm," *Phoenix New Times,* 13 Jun. 2002, at *http://www.mail-archive.com/native_american@topica.com/msg01503.html*

38. Andy Smith, "For All Those Who Were Indian in a Former Life," *Cultural Survival Quarterly* (Winter 1994): at *http://users.telenet.be/gohiyuhi/articles/art00018.htm* ; "Ceremonies are crossing" is from Avis Little Eagle, "Sacred Pipe Keeper Fears Feds Will Step In"; the Onondaga quote is from Ward Churchill, "The Rise of the Plastic Medicine Men," at *http://www.hartford-hwp.com/archives/41/398.html*

39. The shamanic handbill is reproduced in Susan Mumm, "Aspirational Indians," in *Belief Beyond Boundaries*, ed. Joanne Pearson (Burlington, Vt.: Ashgate, 2002), 122.

40. Christopher Ronwanien: Te Jocks, "Spirituality for Sale," *AIQ* 20(3–4) (1996): 415–31; Churchill, "Spiritual Hucksterism," in *From A Native Son*; Laurie Anne Whitt, "Cultural Imperialism and the Marketing of Native North America," in *Natives and Academics,* ed. Devon A. Mihesuah (Lincoln: University of Nebraska Press, 1998), 139–71; Laura E Donaldson, "On Medicine Women and White Shame-Ans," *Signs* 24(3) (1999): 677–96. A collection of texts attacking cultural exploitation and New Age Indianism can be found at *http://www.lelandra.com/comptarot/tarotIndian.htm* ("Pseudo Native American Tarot Decks"). See also "Readings on Cultural Respect," at *http://www.alphacdc.com/treaty/r-explt.html* ; and "Resolutions and Warnings Against Cultural Theft by Native Americans," at *http://users.telenet.be/gohiyuhi/articles/*

41. Smith, "For All Those Who Were Indian in a Former Life"; "These people don't realize" is from "The Ripoff of Native American Spirituality," at *http://www.geocities.com/CapitolHill/Congress/9134/spirit.html* . Russell Means is quoted from Richard Smoley, "A Non-Indian's Guide to Native American Spirituality," *Yoga Journal,* Jan.–Feb. 1992, 84.

Conclusion

1. Philip K. Dick, *The Man in the High Castle* (New York: Vintage, 1992).

2. *Red Road Collective Newsletter,* at *http://www.geocities.com/redroadcollective/Newsletter-Fall2001.html*

3. Aidan Kelly, *Crafting the Art of Magic* (St. Paul, Minn.: Llewellyn, 1991).

4. *United States v. Ballard*, 322 U.S. 78 (1944).

5. Philip Jenkins, *Hidden Gospels* (New York: Oxford University Press, 2001), 110. "Catholic Archdiocese Files Suit, Calling Church Network a Fraud," *NYT,* 20 Sept. 2003.

6. Snyder is quoted in Laurie Anne Whitt, "Cultural Imperialism and the Marketing of Native North America," in *Natives and Academics,* ed. Devon A. Mihesuah (Lincoln: University of Nebraska Press, 1998), 145.

7. Frederick J. Dockstader, *The Kachina and the White Man,* rev. ed. (Albuquerque: University of New Mexico Press, 1985); E. Charles Adams, *The Origin and Development of the Pueblo Katsina Cult* (Tucson: University of Arizona Press, 1991); Polly Schaafsma, ed., *Kachinas in the Pueblo World* (Salt Lake City: University of Utah Press, 2000).

8. Michael F. Brown, *Who Owns Native Culture?* (Cambridge, Mass.: Harvard University Press, 2003).

Index